Welcome to *Computerized Accounting with QuickBooks Online*!

order to use this textbook, you'll need access to:

QuickBooks Online

The Excel set up files for the homework company assigned by your instructor available at https://cambridgepub.com/book/qbo2018#supplements

Instructions for activating your QuickBooks Online subscription:

ease refer to page 2-7 of your textbook for complete instructions.

Go to https://quickbooks.intuit.com/start/retail_sui.

You will need the following license and product numbers to complete the registration.

Product Number: 860-708

License Number: 6317-0123-0631-489

Check the box to agree to Agree to the Terms of Service once you're comfortable.

Click on the orange "Set Up Account" button.

See page 2-9 in your textbook for the remaining details for completing your registration and importing the set up files for your homework company.

my BusinessCourse

FREE WITH NEW COPIES OF THIS TEXTBOOK*

Start using BusinessCourse Today: **www.mybusinesscourse.com**

myBusinessCourse is a web-based learning and assessment program intended to complement your textbook and faculty instruction.

Student Benefits

eLectures: These videos review the key concepts of each Learning Objective in each chapter.

Guided examples: These videos provide step-by-step solutions for select problems in each chapter.

Auto-graded assignments: Provide students with immediate feedback on select assignments. (**with Instructor-Led course ONLY**).

Quiz and Exam preparation: myBusinessCourse provides students with additional practice and exam preparation materials to help students achieve better grades and content mastery.

You can access myBusinessCourse 24/7 from any web-enabled device, including iPads, smartphones, laptops, and tablets.

Interactive content that runs on any device.

Built for PCs, iPads, Laptops, Tablets, Smartphones

Computerized Accounting with QuickBooks® Online
2018 Update

GAYLE WILLIAMS
Sacramento City College

JENNIFER JOHNSON
The University of Texas at Dallas

Cambridge
BUSINESS PUBLISHERS

To my son, Marcus Williams, who has inspired me and encouraged me and remains my biggest fan.
—Gayle Williams

To my husband, Brad, who helps me stay balanced.
—Jennifer Johnson

Editor-in-Chief: George Werthman
Vice President, Brand Management: Marnee Fieldman
Digital Marketing Manager: Dana Vinyard
Managing Editor: Katie Jones-Aiello
Development Editor: Jocelyn Mousel
Product Developer: Jill Sternard
Compositor: T&D Graphics
Designer: Michael Warrell, Design Solutions

COMPUTERIZED ACCOUNTING WITH QUICKBOOKS ONLINE 2018 Update, by Gayle Williams and Jennifer Johnson

ISBN 978-1-61853-293-0

Bookstores & Faculty: to order this book, contact the company via email **customerservice@cambridgepub.com** or call 800-619-6473.

Students: to order this book, please visit the book's Website and order directly online.

About the Authors

Gayle Williams is an Adjunct Professor of Accounting at Sacramento City College, where she teaches computerized accounting, auditing, and cost accounting. She received a BA in Comparative Literature and an MBA with a concentration in Accounting from the University of Washington. Professor Williams is licensed as a CPA in Washington and California and has worked in public accounting, with Voldal Wartelle & Co, P.S and Moss Adams LLP, and in private industry.

Jennifer Johnson is a Senior Lecturer at the University of Texas at Dallas where she teaches accounting information systems courses and related software courses, cost accounting, and seminars in Excel. She is a CPA licensed in the state of Texas. In 2017 she was named as an Outstanding Accounting Educator by the Texas Society of CPAs. Prior to joining UT Dallas in 2009, Professor Johnson spent time in both public accounting and industry as an auditor with PwC, an Assistant Controller at a regional financial services firm, and a Finance Manager at Dr Pepper Snapple Group. Professor Johnson holds both a BBA and MS in Accounting from Texas A&M University. Jennifer is a Certified QuickBooks User and is on the Board of Directors for the Dallas CPA Society and the Texas Society of CPAs. Professor Johnson has a passion for using systems and accounting to communicate the language of business.

Preface

Welcome to *Computerized Accounting with QuickBooks Online*. We wrote this book to give students an introduction to QuickBooks Online that focuses not only on the software mechanics, but also on the basic accounting concepts that underlie all accounting systems.

This book is not meant to be a user manual. It is our intention that students will come away from this book with an understanding that it is their knowledge of the principles of accounting, not their data-entry skills, that is needed to be successful in business.

TARGET AUDIENCE

This book is primarily intended for use in undergraduate accounting programs, although it could be used in business or computer information programs as well. It is expected that students taking this course have already successfully completed a course in financial accounting and have a firm understanding of the basic principles of accounting.

ACCESS TO QUICKBOOKS ONLINE PLUS

Each new copy of this book includes a full year of access to QuickBooks Online Plus. Students should refer to the insert at the front of the book, which contains the license number and product code and instructions on accessing the complimentary cloud-based software. With QuickBooks Online, students use their Internet browser to use the software—no installation required—and it can be used on any device with Internet access. (A high-speed Internet connection is recommended, such as DSL or cable modem. For more information go to https://community.intuit.com/quickbooks-online and type in System Requirements in the search field.)

NEW TO THIS EDITION

- New co-author Jennifer Johnson joins this edition.
- A second homework company option has been added to the end of chapter assignments (Salish Software Solutions).
- The first chapter has been updated to provide an overview of QBO only, and setting up company files has been moved to a separate chapter.
- Homework in the payroll chapter has been rewritten to provide opportunity to assess students' understanding of QBO's full payroll system. (Homework is completed in the QBO payroll Test Drive company file.)
- Added a new appendix, Understanding the Reconciliation Report, to the End-of-Period Activity (Service Company) chapter.

- A Midterm and a Final Exam are available for instructors (using QBO's Test Drive company).
- Additional eLecture videos have been developed demonstrating common sales, purchase, and payroll transactions.

OUTSTANDING FEATURES OF THIS BOOK

Structure

The book is designed in such a way that the accounting concepts, as well as the software mechanics, get more complex with each section. Other books focus primarily on software data entry. This book allows the students to see why events are recorded the way they are in a computerized accounting system while refreshing students' knowledge of accounting concepts and reinforcing the accounting and journal entries behind transactions.

- *Section One—Introduction*
  - The first chapter introduces students to the basic structure of QuickBooks Online Plus (QBO).
    - Moving around in QBO
    - QBO organization
    - Reporting using QBO
  - In the second chapter, the process of creating new company files is covered.
    - Customizing settings
    - Importing data into QBO
- *Section Two—Service Companies*
  - The next three chapters (Chapters 3, 4, and 5) cover the sales, purchase, and end-of-month cycles in a service company.
  - Students are introduced to accounting for basic transactions in a computerized environment.
    - Sales on account and cash sales
    - Purchases on account and cash purchases
    - Customer collections and vendor payments
    - Bank reconciliations
    - Standard end-of-month adjusting entries
    - Financial statement reporting
- *Section Three—Merchandising Companies*
  - The section introduction includes a description of internal controls in QBO.
  - Chapters 6, 7, and 8 cover the sales, purchase, and end-of-month cycles in a merchandising company.
  - Students are introduced to accounting for more complex transactions in a computerized environment.
    - Purchase and sale of inventory
    - Sales tax
    - Sales and purchase discounts
    - Inventory tracking, adjustment, and valuation
    - Bad debts and bounced checks

- *Section Four—Paying Employees, Project Costing, and Billing for Time*
    - Chapter 9 covers basic payroll functions that would be used in all types of companies (service, merchandising, and manufacturing).
        - Setting up payroll policies
        - Managing employees
        - Processing payroll
    - Chapter 10 covers billing for time and expenses.
        - Tracking projects
        - Billing for time and expenses
        - Tracking and reporting profitability by project
- *Section Five—Beyond the Basics*
    - Chapter 11 covers budgeting and segment reporting.
        - Creating budgets and budget variance reports
        - Using location and class tracking to report on business segments
    - Chapter 12 covers a number of special tools in QBO.
        - Saving customized reports
        - Customizing forms
        - Managing attachments
        - Exporting reports to Excel
        - Creating recurring transactions
        - Creating reversing entries

Clear Writing

The book is written clearly to aid student understanding of difficult concepts. Clear explanations of why certain procedures are used in QBO are supported by relevant examples and relatable end-of-chapter assignments, serving to bridge the gap between computerized accounting concepts and real-world application.

Real-World Scenarios

Most computerized accounting textbooks on the market approach the teaching of Quick-Books in a prescriptive manner, going through the procedures of the software while overlooking how an accountant would actually utilize the software in the real world. The book takes a practical approach and shows the student how the software is used in a business environment. In addition to the standard financial reports, students are exposed to job, segment, and variance reports.

Unique Pedagogy

The book's four-color format facilitates student understanding and draws attention to the key concepts and pedagogy. Ample screenshots provide students realistic snapshots of what they will see when working in the software. A host of pedagogical elements serve as helpful illustrations, providing additional context and further concept reinforcement.

HINT Boxes

HINT boxes appear throughout to provide helpful quick tips and tricks for working more efficiently in QBO.

 HINT: All of your transactions and settings will be deleted/cleared each time you log out or time out of QBO's test drive company. You would need to clear the automation functions each time you start a new work session.

WARNING Boxes

WARNING boxes highlight common technical pitfalls to avoid.

! **WARNING:** Do not click the **Finish Now** button if you haven't finished the reconciliation (the **difference** isn't zero). QBO will give you a warning if you try but if you persist, it will allow you to "reconcile" without actually reconciling. That would leave what my former accounting professors would call a "dangling" credit or debit. Of course QBO won't actually allow you to create an unbalanced transaction so it will either debit (or credit) an account called **Reconciliation Discrepancies** for the **Difference** amount. You'd then have to fix that later.

BEHIND THE SCENES Boxes

BEHIND THE SCENES boxes provide additional context in support of the accounting that is going on inside the computer.

 **BEHIND THE SCENES** In QBO, deleted transactions don't appear on reports. Voided transactions do appear but with zero dollar amounts. (Keeping a record of voided transactions is a good internal control policy.)

QuickChecks

When students are learning accounting application software, it's natural for them to focus on the software mechanics and forget that they're taking an accounting course. To help put some of their focus back on accounting, students are periodically asked a question related to material covered in the chapter. The questions are intended to remind them, either directly or indirectly, of underlying accounting concepts. The answers are included at the end of each chapter.

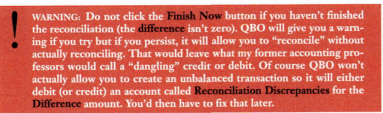 Why aren't purchase orders and estimates accounting transactions? (Answer at end of chapter.) **Quick**Check **1-2**

Key Terms

Appearing in red, bold font in the first instance, key terms are defined for the student in the margins of the text for a quick refresher. A comprehensive glossary is included in the back of the book.

These are some of the things that QBO automatically knows:

- It knows that behind every transaction is a **journal entry** and that each journal entry must balance. You will not be allowed to enter an unbalanced journal entry.

- It knows that accounts identified as assets, liabilities, or equity appear on the **balance sheet** and accounts identified as income or expense accounts appear on the profit and loss statement (QBO's name for the **income statement**).

These are some of the things that QBO **doesn't** automatically know (so make sure you DO know):

- It doesn't know whether the account you just set up as an asset really does represent a resource owned or controlled by the company that is expected to provide future benefit.

- It doesn't know whether the amounts on the invoice you just created represent income the company has already earned or income that will be earned in the future.

- It doesn't know whether there are salaries that employees have earned but haven't been paid for.

- Etc., etc.

Journal entry An entry of accounting information into a journal (a tabular record in which business transactions are analyzed in debit and credit terms and recorded in chronological order).

Balance sheet A financial statement showing a business's assets, liabilities, and stockholders' equity as of a specific date.

Income statement A financial statement reporting a business's sales revenue and expenses for a given

Practice Exercises

Practice Exercises are included at the end of every section in the first ten chapters. The exercises provide students an immediate opportunity to practice the material they just learned and prepare them for completing the chapter assignments. The exercises use the QBO test drive company, a fictional company called Craig's Landscaping and Design set up by Intuit.

The Practice Exercises can be done in class, with the instructor, or can be done by the students, on their own, as part of the lab component of a face-to-face course or in online courses. Check figures are included with the exercises to reassure students that they are recording the transactions accurately.

PRACTICE EXERCISE

Set up a new credit term for Craig's Design and Landscaping.
(Craig's is considering offering an early payment discount to some of his customers.)

1. Click the **gear** icon on the icon bar.

2. Click **All Lists** in the **Lists** column.

3. Click **Terms**.

4. Click **New**.

5. Enter "2% 10, net 30" as the **Name**.

6. Click **due in fixed number of days** and enter "30" in the **days** field.

7. Check **Apply discount if paid early**.

8. Enter "2" in the **%** field.

9. Enter "10" in the **days** field.

10. Click **Save**.

End-of-Chapter Material

End-of-chapter review material includes:

- Chapter shortcuts.

- Chapter review with **matching of terms** to definitions and **multiple choice questions** that are a combination of accounting concepts and QuickBooks application questions.

- A choice of two end-of-chapter assignments featuring fictional companies that move from selling services exclusively in the early chapters to selling both services and products in the later chapters.

  The assignments include check numbers for students. This allows them to focus on the process and reduces student frustration.

Appendices

There are a number of additional topics that are helpful to students as they master QBO, and these have been included as end-of-chapter and end-of-book appendices. Instructors may wish to cover these topics in class or have students go over them on their own time. End-of-chapter appendices on special topics include:

Appendix	Title	Description
Appendix 2A	Setting Up a Google Gmail Account	Instructions for opening a separate Gmail account used in registering the student's company file
Appendix 3A	Using Sub-service and Sub-product Items	Covers sub-items used in place of categories in the academic trial version of QBO
Appendix 4A	Reporting 1099 Activity	Covers 1099 setup and reporting tools available in QBO
Appendix 5A	Getting It Right	Suggestions to help students find errors in the month-end financial statements, mirroring what accountants in industry might look at before publishing financial statements
Appendix 5B	Understanding the Reconciliation Report	Provides a review of temporary and permanent differences and covers the sections in QBO's reconciliation report.
Appendix 8A	Banking Activity	Covers QBO features allowing the download of banking and credit card activity
Appendix 10A	Tracking Projects using Sub-Customers	Instructions for using sub-customers instead of projects if the student's company file does not include the project tracking feature.
Appendix 10B	Working With Estimates	Covers creating and managing customer estimates

Students often have a difficult time seeing any similarities between computerized accounting systems and the more manual systems they saw in their introductory financial accounting classes (the journal entries, T-accounts, and general ledgers). To help students connect the two, **Appendix A (Is Computerized Accounting Really the Same as Manual Accounting?)** is an accounting refresher that compares manual and computerized accounting and provides examples of how journal entries, journals, T-accounts, and trial balances show up in QBO. It also covers cash versus accrual accounting.

Appendix	Title	Description
Appendix A	**Is Computerized Accounting Really the Same as Manual Accounting?**	Comparison of manual and computerized accounting
Appendix B	**Account and Transaction "Types"**	A summary of account types and transaction types in QuickBooks Online
Appendix C	**Common Options Available on *Form* Toolbars**	Common options available on various toolbars in QuickBooks Online

Certiport-Mapped

The book has been mapped to the 10 domains that comprise the exam objectives for the QuickBooks Certified User Exam.

What Is the QuickBooks Certified User Exam?

The Intuit® QuickBooks Certification exam is an online exam that is proctored at Certiport Authorized Testing Centers. The certification program validates QuickBooks accounting skills while providing students with credentials that demonstrate real-world abilities to prospective employers. Once passed, test takers receive an official digital certificate representing their skills in QuickBooks.

A map correlating the chapter content to the Certiport domains will be available to students so they can streamline their exam preparation.

Supplement Package

For Instructors

- **Solutions Manual** files prepared by the authors contain solutions to all the assignment material.

- **PowerPoint** presentations illustrate chapter concepts and outline key elements with corresponding screenshots for each chapter.

- **Test Bank** questions written by the authors include true/false and multiple-choice questions for each chapter.

- **Extra credit** project suggestions including solutions

- A **Midterm** and **Final Exam** are provided with solution files. The exams are designed to test students' understanding of the fundamentals of accounting and the mechanics of QBO. The exams can be completed in a two-hour class session using the Test Drive company available in QBO.

- ^my^BusinessCourse: A web-based learning and assessment program intended to complement your textbook and classroom instruction. This easy-to-use course management system includes question banks comprised of practice exercises, test bank questions, and assignment questions related to the end of chapter content that can be graded automatically. eLecture videos created and narrated by the authors are also available (see below for list). myBusiness Course provides students with additional help when you are not available. In addition, detailed diagnostic tools assess class and individual performance. myBusinessCourse is ideal for online courses or traditional face-to-face courses for which you want to offer students more resources to succeed.

- **Website:** All instructor materials are accessible via the book's website (password protected) along with other useful links and marketing information. www.cambridgepub.com.

For Students

- Access to QuickBooks Online software with purchase of each new copy of the book.
- **my BusinessCourse**: A web-based learning and assessment program intended to complement your textbook and faculty instruction. This easy-to-use program grades assignments automatically and provides you with additional help when your instructor is not available. Access is free with new copies of this textbook (look for the page containing the access code towards the front of the book).
- **eLecture Presentations** created and narrated by the authors and available in myBusinessCourse cover essential topics and procedures in QuickBooks Online:
  - Moving around in QBO
  - Setting up accounts
  - Setting up customers
  - Recording sales transactions
  - Setting up vendors
  - Recording purchase transactions
  - Setting up and managing payroll
  - Tracking and billing for time in QBO
  - Setting up *items* (one for service, one for product)
  - Reconciling bank and credit card accounts
  - Customizing reports
  - Setting up budgets
  - Creating custom forms
  - Hints for finding errors
- **Check Figures** are included for assignments, allowing students to focus on the process and reduce frustration.
- **Website:** Additional useful links are available to students on the book's website.

ACKNOWLEDGMENTS

We would like to thank the following people for their assistance and support. In particular, Qianchang Liang. We can't thank Qianchang enough. Without her, this book would not exist.

Thank you also to the following computer accounting faculty from across the country who provided review feedback on the book:

Dave Alldredge, *Salt Lake Community College*
Rick Andrews, *Sinclair Community College*
Ulises Arcos-Castrejon, *North Shore Community College*
Felicia Baldwin, *Richard J. Daley College*
Patricia Ball, *Massasoit Community College*
Sara Barritt, *Northeast Community College*
Bryan Bouchard, *Southern New Hampshire University*
Lisa Briggs, *Columbus State Community College*
Marilyn Brooks-Lewis, *Warren County Community College*
Regina Butts, *Fort Valley State University*
Karlencia Calvin, *Baton Rouge Community College*
Amy Chataginer, *Mississippi Gulf Coast Community College*
Russell Ciokiewicz, *Brenau University*
Dana Cummings, *Lower Columbia College*

Patricia Davis, *Keystone College*
Susan Davis, *Green River College*
Suryakant Desai, *Cedar Valley College*
Anne Diamond, *Sierra College*
Doris Donovan, *Dodge City Community College*
Carol Dutchover, *Eastern New Mexico University, Roswell*
Pennie Eddy, *Lanier Technical College*
Jen Emerson, *Cincinnati State*
Keith Engler, *Richland College*
Rena Galloway, *State Fair Community College*
Patricia Goedl, *University of Cincinnati*
James Halstead, *Neosho County Community College*
Becky Hancock, *El Paso Community College*

Pat Hartley, *Chaffey College*

Merrily Hoffman, *San Jacinto College*

Janet Hosmer, *Blue Ridge Community College*

Bill Jefferson, *Metropolitan Community College*

Angela Kirkendall, *South Puget Sound Community College*

Becky Knickel, *Brookhaven College*

Christopher Kwak, *De Anza College*

Amber Lamadrid, *Mt. Hood Community College*

Miriam Lefkowitz, *Brooklyn College*

John Long, *Jackson College*

Heather Lynch, *Northeast Iowa Community College*

Kristy McAuliffe, *San Jacinto College*

Molly McFadden-May, *Tulsa Community College*

Paul McLester, *Florida State College at Jacksonville*

Allen Montgomery, *Bridge Valley Community & Technical College*

Sheila Muller, *Northern Essex Community College*

Carolyn Nelson, *Coffeyville Community College*

Brian Newman, *Macomb Community College*

Jeffrey Niccum, *Spokane Falls Community College*

Lisa Novak, *Mott Community College*

Joanne Orabone, *Community College of Rhode Island*

Margaret Pond, *Front Range Community College*

Mark Quinlan, *Madison College*

Kristen Quinn, *Northern Essex Community College*

Michelle Randall, *Schoolcraft College*

Robin Reilly, *American River College*

Cecile Roberti, *Community College of Rhode Island*

Joanne Salas, *Olympic College*

Perry Sellers, *Lone Star College*

Chrysta Singleton, *Sacramento City College*

Sherrie Slom, *Hillsborough Community College*

Stephanie Swaim, *North Lake College*

Christine VanNamee, *Mohawk Valley Community College*

Vasseliki Vervilos, *American River College*

Lori Yecoshenko, *Lake Superior College*

Melissa Youngman, *National Technical Institute for the Deaf*

Additionally, we would like to thank the following students who provided feedback on the texts:

Qianchang Liang, *Sacramento City College*

Mei Ern Cheng, *University of California–Davis*

Bethany Harman, *Sacramento City College*

Chrysta Singleton, *Sacramento City College*

We would also like to thank George Werthman, Katie Jones-Aiello, Jocelyn Mousel, Marnee Fieldman, Jill Sternard, Dana Vinyard, Lorraine Gleeson, Debbie McQuade, Terry McQuade, and everyone at Cambridge Business Publishers for their encouragement, guidance, and dedication to this book.

Finally, thank you to the instructors and students using this book.

Gayle Williams & Jennifer Johnson
April 2018

Brief Table of Contents

Contents

Section Two

Service Companies *3-1*

③ Sales Activity (Service Company) *3-5*

Section Four

Paying Employees, Project Costing, and Billing for Time *9-1*

9 Payroll Activity *9-3*

Appendix A
Is Computerized Accounting Really the Same as Manual Accounting?   *A-1*

Appendix B
Account Category Types and Common Transaction Types used in QBO   *B-1*

Appendix C
Common Options Available on Various Forms   *C-1*

Glossary   *G-1*

Index   *I-1*

QuickBooks

SECTION ONE

Introduction

Before we go any further, let's be clear about two facts.

First, "computerized accounting" uses the same accounting principles and processes you're learning in your financial accounting courses.

- **Assets** = **Liabilities** + **Equity**.

- **Debits** are on the left; **credits** are on the right.

- Transactions are recorded through journal entries.

- Assets, liabilities, and equity accounts are reported on the balance sheet; revenue and expense accounts are reported on the income statement.

The advantage of using accounting software is that certain processes are automated, which makes the job of the accountant a little easier. For example, in QuickBooks Online (the software that you'll be using in this class), when you prepare an invoice for a customer:

- A journal entry will automatically be created,

- the entry will automatically be posted to the general ledger,

- and the balance sheet and income statement will automatically be adjusted to reflect the new account balances.

The second fact you should be clear about is this: a computer application only knows as much accounting as has been programmed into it. For example:

- QuickBooks Online (QBO) is programmed to know that an account that's been identified by the user as an asset should appear on the balance sheet but it doesn't know whether or not the account you just set up and named "prepaid insurance" SHOULD have been identified as an asset or a liability or an expense, etc.

Assets The economic resources of a business that can be expressed in money terms.

Liabilities The obligations or debts that a business must pay in money or services at some time in the future as a consequence of past transactions or events.

Equity The residual interest in the assets of a business after all liabilities have been paid off; it is equal to a firm's net assets, or total assets less total liabilities.

Debit An entry on the left side (or in the debit column) of an account.

Credit An entry on the right side (or in the credit column) of an account.

- QuickBooks Online (QBO) is also programmed to know that a journal entry must balance (the sum of the debits must equal the sum of the credits) and it will not allow you to create an unbalanced entry. However, it doesn't know whether the specific accounts you just debited and credited in an adjusting journal entry are the appropriate accounts.

It's important that you remember these two facts as you're going through this book. The software is not an accountant; you are. You are the one who ultimately controls the accuracy of the financial data. You are the one who is ultimately responsible for providing meaningful information to users of the financial reports.

SECTION OVERVIEW

Chapter 1 covers:

- Getting in and out of QuickBooks Online (QBO)

- The general organization of QBO

- Customizing and navigating QBO

- Reporting using QBO

Introduction to QuickBooks Online (QBO)

Objectives

After completing Chapter 1, you should be able to:

1. Recognize the various versions of Intuit's QuickBooks series.

2. Log into the test-drive version of QuickBooks Online.

3. Use the various access tools in QuickBooks Online.

4. Open common transactions forms.

5. Use the Search function.

6. Demonstrate an understanding of the various lists in QuickBooks Online.

7. Recognize various account category and detail types used in QuickBooks Online.

8. Create, edit, and delete accounts in the chart of accounts.

9. Create and modify reports.

A LITTLE BACKGROUND

There are many, many different accounting software applications available for purchase. They range in price from a few hundred dollars to a few million dollars. In this book, we're going to look at QuickBooks Online Plus, an application developed and marketed by Intuit.

Intuit Inc. creates accounting software solutions for consumers and professionals. Quicken (a personal finance management software program) was created by Intuit in 1983. Shortly after that, Intuit came out with accounting software for small businesses—QuickBooks. Intuit offers four primary desktop versions of QuickBooks.

QuickBooks Pro	Basic version used by many small businesses. Users can: ✓ Record and track receivables, payables, banking transactions, inventory, and payroll. ✓ Create budgets and track operations by class.
QuickBooks Premier	Includes all the basics PLUS users can: ✓ Create and manage sales orders. ✓ Track assembled inventory (light manufacturing). Premier can accommodate up to 5 users working simultaneously in the same QuickBooks file.
QuickBooks Enterprise	Includes all features in Premier PLUS users can: ✓ Manage inventory in multiple warehouses. ✓ Adopt FIFO costing. Enterprise can accommodate up to 30 users working simultaneously in the same QuickBooks file.
QuickBooks Mac Desktop	Similar in functionality to QuickBooks Pro. Can accommodate up to 3 users working simultaneously in the same QuickBooks file. (Intuit has announced that QuickBooks for Mac 2016 is the final Mac version. Support for the 2016 version will end in May, 2019.)

The software for desktop versions is loaded on to your computer (either downloaded from Intuit's website or loaded using a disk). QuickBooks desktop company files can be networked but each user must have the software loaded on his or her computer.

Intuit introduced QuickBooks Online in 2000. The software was completely rebuilt in 2013. There are currently three primary versions of QuickBooks Online.

Version	Basic Features	Number of Users Allowed
Simple Start	Users can: ✓ Create estimates and bill customers. ✓ Track income and expenses. ✓ Download banking and credit card transactions.	1
Essentials	Includes all the features of Simple Start plus users can: ✓ Enter vendor bills for payment later. ✓ Set up recurring customer invoices. ✓ Limit access by user.	3
Plus	Includes all the features of Essentials plus users can: ✓ Create purchase orders. ✓ Track inventory. ✓ Track employee hours. ✓ Create budgets. ✓ Categorize income and expenses by class and/or location.	5

Payroll is an add-on feature available to users of Simple Start, Essentials, and Plus. There is also a QuickBooks Online Accountant version that includes additional features for those users who are working with multiple clients.

QuickBooks Online is a cloud-based system. This means that the software and the accounting data of all customers is stored (hosted) on a web server by Intuit. Users can access the software from any computer with Internet access. Although Intuit does back up company data, backups are not currently accessible to users.

There are a variety of apps developed by other companies that work with QuickBooks Online. Although we will not be using any apps in this course, those of you who are interested can check them out at https://apps.intuit.com. (There will also be a link to apps on the navigation bar of your company file. The link does not appear in the navigation bar of the test drive company.)

QuickBooks Online is a subscription service. Users pay a monthly fee based on the version of QuickBooks Online being used. Access codes for a free one-year subscription to QuickBooks Online Plus are included in the front section of your textbook. You will be using that subscription to set up and complete your homework assignments. Directions for setting up that service are included in Chapter 2.

In this textbook, the terms QuickBooks Online and QBO are used interchangeably to refer to the QuickBooks Online Plus version you will be using.

QUICKBOOKS ONLINE

QBO is a **powerful** tool for small businesses.

- It is flexible (can be used by most small businesses).

- It is intuitive (easy to understand).

- It is accessible from any desktop computer with an Internet connection.
  - Supported browsers for QBO include Google Chrome, Internet Explorer, Mozilla Firefox, and Safari.

- It is accessible (through the QBO mobile app) from most smartphones and tablets.

- It is updated and improved regularly and automatically.

These are some of the things that QBO automatically knows:

- It knows that behind every transaction is a **journal entry** and that each journal entry must balance. You will not be allowed to enter an unbalanced journal entry.

- It knows that accounts identified as assets, liabilities, or equity appear on the **balance sheet** and accounts identified as income or expense accounts appear on the profit and loss statement (QBO's name for the **income statement**).

These are some of the things that QBO **doesn't** automatically know (so make sure you DO know):

- It doesn't know whether the account you just set up as an asset really does represent a resource owned or controlled by the company that is expected to provide future benefit.

- It doesn't know whether the amounts on the invoice you just created represent income the company has already earned or income that will be earned in the future.

- It doesn't know whether there are salaries that employees have earned but haven't been paid for.

- Etc., etc.

Journal entry An entry of accounting information into a journal (a tabular record in which business transactions are analyzed in debit and credit terms and recorded in chronological order).

Balance sheet A financial statement showing a business's assets, liabilities, and stockholders' equity as of a specific date.

Income statement A financial statement reporting a business's sales revenue and expenses for a given period of time.

BEFORE WE GO ANY FURTHER

Writing about QBO is a little like trying to throw a dart at a moving target. By the time the book gets written, the software has changed! So, fair warning: The information and screenshots in this chapter are based on QuickBooks Online Plus as it existed at the beginning of 2018.

Of course, continuous updating is one of the benefits of QBO. Corrections can be made and new features can be added without users needing to download and install a new release. Given the popularity of cloud computing, Intuit is choosing to put a great deal of energy into developing its online accounting software products and that benefits all users.

Although QBO is a very intuitive program, there are a lot of "places to go and things to see" and that can be intimidating. It's easy to forget what was covered in a previous chapter. Most of the time, you'll be able to find the answer by using the index for this book. If you can't, here are some options:

- Use the Help feature in QBO. It's really pretty good.
  - Help is accessed by clicking

- You can ask for help from your instructor, from a student assistant (if there is one), or from your fellow students (if they're willing and you're not taking a test!).

- As an additional resource, abbreviated step-by-step instructions for the various transactions and procedures are included at the end of each chapter under **Chapter Shortcuts**.

PRACTICE

Throughout this textbook, you will practice the steps necessary to record transactions and use the various tools available in QBO using an imaginary company set up by Intuit to allow users to test drive the software. The test drive company, Craig's Design and Landscaping, provides landscaping services for individuals and small businesses.

Your homework will be done in a different company. The homework company will be introduced in Chapter 2.

Practice Exercises using Craig's Design and Landscaping will be located at the end of each section. Read through each section **before** you attempt the exercises. The explanations and screenshots provided in each section are meant to help you complete the Practice Exercises and your assignments.

Some Practice Exercises will include an instruction to **make a note** of certain information. Your instructor may ask you questions about the Practice Exercises so it's a good idea to have a notebook handy where you can write down this information.

To access the practice company file, you'll need to enter https://qbo.intuit.com/redir/testdrive as the URL in your browser. In the first screen, you'll be asked to check **I'm not a robot**.

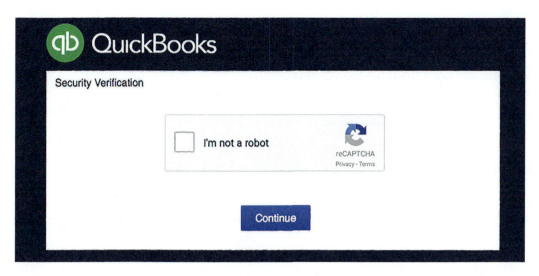

You may be denied access when you enter the listed code. Don't worry. A new code will automatically appear. Simply retry with the new code provided. You may need to do this more than once.

Occasionally, QBO will ask you to identify pictures containing specific content (mountains, trains, etc.) after you've checked the **I'm not a robot** box. These are security measures so try to be patient.

You may get a message denying access because of privacy settings related to cookies. The message looks something like this:

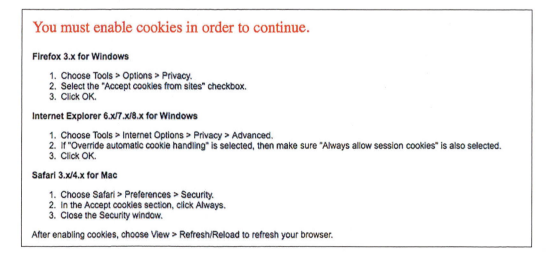

Most of the time, refreshing the browser, reentering the URL for the test-drive company, and checking the **I'm not a robot** box will allow you to access the program. If you continue to get the message, you will need to adjust your browser's security settings before you can move forward.

The screen (the **Dashboard** screen) will look something like this when your identity as a human and not a robot has been confirmed!

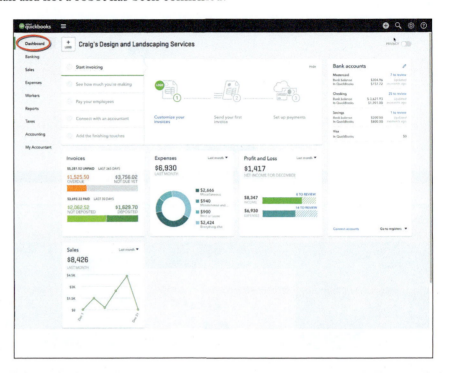

WARNING: Whenever you close out of the test drive website (or whenever you're automatically logged out for lack of activity), <u>nothing you previously entered will be saved</u>. The next time you access the site, the Intuit-developed transactions will likely stay the same in name and amount, but the dates will most likely differ. The Practice Exercises have been developed with that in mind.

To save yourself time and minimize frustration, complete each Practice Exercise in one study session. If you log off in the middle of a Practice Exercise, you will need to start the exercise over from the beginning when you return.

MOVING AROUND IN QUICKBOOKS ONLINE

Accessing Tools

You can access lists, forms, reports, and anything else you might need from a variety of locations in QBO.

Icon Bar

The icon bar is located at the top of the **Dashboard** screen. The far right edge of the icon bar looks something like this:

Each icon on the icon bar has a purpose:

⊕ Opens to a **Create** menu where transaction forms are accessed.

🔍 Opens to a search tool.

⚙ Opens to a menu where company preferences can be set and other general operational tools can be accessed.

⑦ Opens a Help screen.

The two icons you'll be accessing most often are the **plus** icon and the **gear** icon.

The **Create** menu accessed through the **plus** icon looks like this:

As you can see, the options here are related to recording activity (transactions).

The menu accessed through the **gear** icon looks like this:

Craig's Design and Landscaping Services			
Your Company	**Lists**	**Tools**	**Profile**
Account and Settings	All Lists	Import Data	User Profile
Manage Users	Products and Services	Export Data	Feedback
Custom Form Styles	Recurring Transactions	Reconcile	Privacy
Chart of Accounts	Attachments	Budgeting	
QuickBooks Labs		Audit Log	🔒 Sign Out
		Order Checks ↗	

This menu is sometimes called the **Company** menu. The options here primarily relate to setting up and managing the overall structure of the company file.

Navigation Bar

The navigation bar is located at the far left of the screen. The navigation bar looks something like this:

> ! **WARNING: At the time this book was written, Intuit was considering changing Workers to Employees in the navigation bar. This is a name change only.**

Clicking **Banking** on the navigation bar opens a screen listing cash transactions. Users who download banking transactions directly into QBO verify and accept the transactions through this screen. Banking activities are covered in more detail in Appendix 8A.

Clicking **Sales** on the navigation bar opens a screen with four tabs.

The **All Sales** tab includes a list of all sales related transactions. New sales transactions can be initiated in this tab. The **Invoices** tab includes a list of recent invoices and their payment status. The **Customers** tab includes a list of all current customers. Customers can be added or edited in the tab. The **Products and Services** tab includes a list of all products held for sale and all services performed by the company. Products and services can be added and edited in the tab.

Clicking **Expenses** on the navigation bar opens a screen with two tabs. In the **Expenses** tab, all purchase related transactions are listed. New purchase transactions can be initiated in this tab. The Vendors tab includes a list of all current vendors. **Vendors** can be added or edited in the tab.

Clicking **Workers** (or **Employees**) on the navigation bar also opens a screen with two tabs. Adding and editing employees is done on the **Employees** tab. Adding and editing independent contractors is done on the **Contractors** tab.

Clicking **Reports** on the navigation bar opens a screen with three tabs. The **All** tab includes various reports developed by Intuit, by category. The screenshot below shows a partial list of the canned reports.

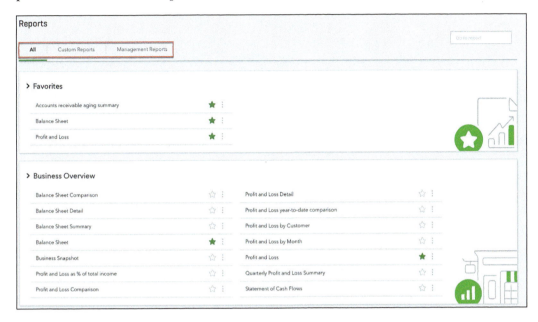

Reports that have been customized by users are included on the **Custom Reports** tab. More sophisticated report packages developed by Intuit are included on the **Management Reports** tab. **Management reports** are covered in Chapter 12.

Clicking **Taxes** on the navigation bar opens a screen listing taxes due by taxing authority. Within the screen, users can record tax payments, add or edit tax rates or taxing authorities, and view tax reports.

Clicking **Accounting** on the navigation bar opens a Chart of Accounts screen. Accounts can be added or edited in the screen. Users can also access all transactions recorded in a specific account.

Users can give their outside accountant access to their company file by clicking **My Accountant** on the navigation bar. Your instructor may ask you to give them access to your homework company file. If so, all you need to do is click this link and enter your instructor's email address.

The navigation bar can be closed by clicking the triple lines at the far left edge of the icon bar, right above the navigation bar. Re-clicking the triple lines will reopen the navigation bar.

Display Area of the Dashboard

The display area of the **Dashboard** page includes various sections related to company operations.

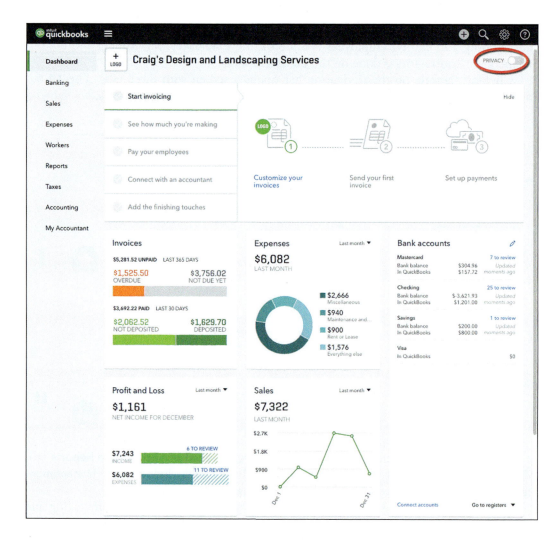

The data is generally displayed graphically (charts and graphs). Clicking some, but not all, of the amounts allows you to drill down to more detail.

Users who don't want any financial information detail displayed on the **Dashboard** screen can toggle the **Privacy** button in the top right of the display area.

As discussed earlier, Intuit is constantly improving QBO in response to user needs and requests. The **Dashboard** page is one area that tends to change fairly frequently so if your screen doesn't look exactly like the screenshots above, don't be alarmed.

Open Windows

A "window," in QBO, is an open form, list, tool or report. For example, the form used to create a check would be a window.

To open the **check** form using the icon bar, click the **plus sign** ➕ on the bar.

The **Create** menu will appear.

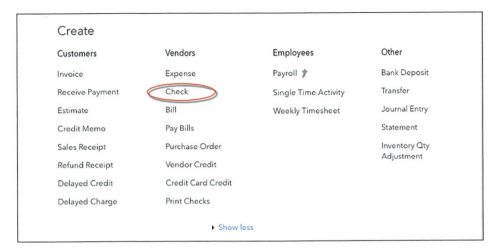

Click **Check.** You are now in a new window.

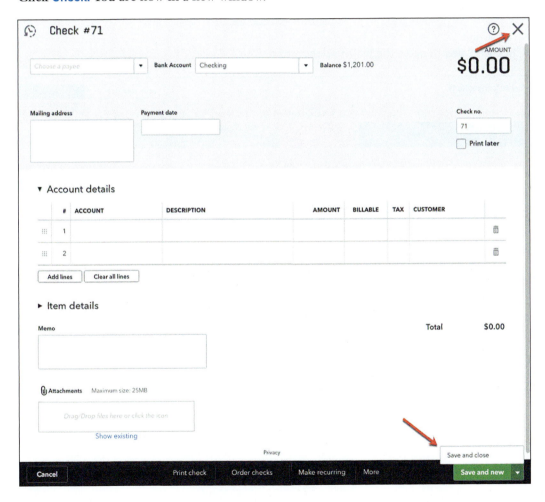

Most of the time, a window will have a **Save and close** or **Save and new** button that is used to save a transaction and automatically exit the window. (The dropdown menu has been clicked so that both options are displayed.) If you want to close the form without saving, simply click the **X** at the top right of the window.

Remember, you can also access forms from the navigation bar. To open a customer invoice, click **Sales** on the navigation bar.

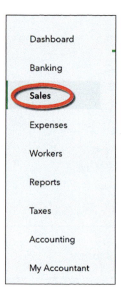

Click **All Sales** to open the list of sales transactions.

Click **New Transaction** and select **Invoice**. The window will look something like this:

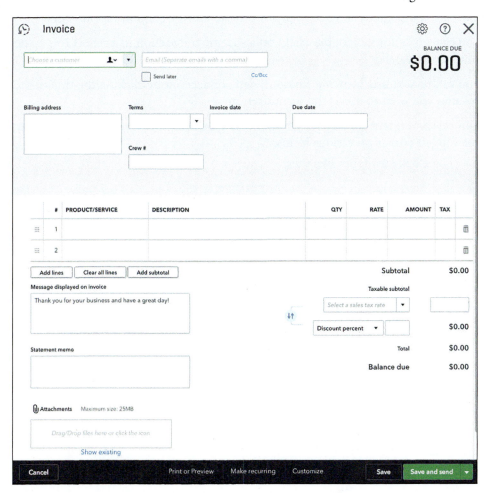

Most of the time, a user will only need one window open at a time. Sometimes, though, it's convenient to have multiple windows open. It's possible to do this by opening windows in different tabs in your browser.

If you wanted to have a form open in a new tab, simply right-click the new form in the **Create** menu and select **Open Link in New Tab**.

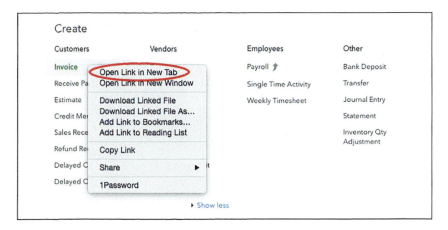

You can also right-click links in the navigation bar to have those windows open in a new window.

Finding Transactions

You can find transactions and details about transactions in QBO in various ways:

- You can "drill down" (double-click) on a specific transaction in a report to see the transaction details.

- You can re-sort lists by name, amount, date, or account by clicking the title of the column you want to use as the sort criterion.

- You can find recent transactions of a certain type using the **clock** icon that appears in the top left corner on various forms.

    - The **clock** icon looks like this:

- You can use the **Search** feature to look for transactions using one or more filters.

The **Search** tool has the most flexibility.

The **Search** tool is accessed by clicking the **magnifying glass** in the icon bar.

The screen will look something like this:

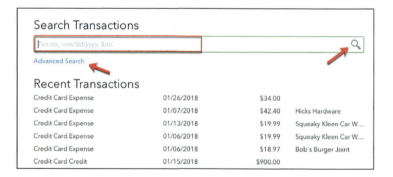

On this screen, you can enter a single detail about a transaction. Clicking the **magnifying glass** will open the form that matches your search.

Clicking **Advanced Search** under the search field opens a new window:

The first dropdown menu allows you to narrow the search by selecting a certain transaction type. A partial list of options is shown here:

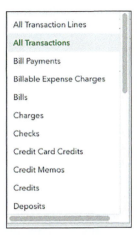

The next dropdown menu will change depending on what you filtered initially. If **Bills** was selected, the set of filtering options would show as:

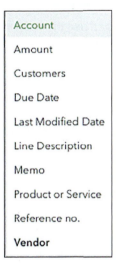

If **Vendor** was selected, you would be able to enter details about your search in the next two fields.

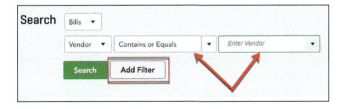

Clicking **Add Filter** allows users to add a date filter to their search.

Clicking **Apply** completes the search.

If a search for **Bills** received from Cal Telephone during the period 1/1/17–12/31/18 was selected, the screen would look something like this:

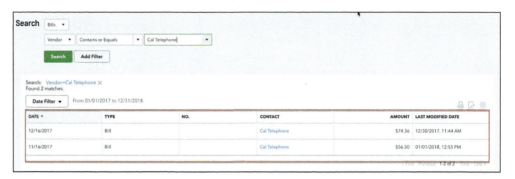

> ✳ **HINT:** Remember, your QBO file will have different dates than the screen-shots that appear in this book.

PRACTICE
EXERCISE

Access forms using the icon bar and use the Search tool in Craig's Design and Landscaping to locate specific transactions.

1. To access a form using the icon bar:

   a. Click on the icon bar.

   b. Click **Receive Payment**.

   c. Close the **Receive Payment** window by clicking the **X** (upper right corner of the window).

2. To search using the **Search** feature:

   a. Click the **magnifying glass** on the icon bar.

   b. Click **Advanced Search**.

   c. Open the first (top) dropdown menu and select **Bills** as the filter.

   d. In the next set of fields, select **Vendor**, **Contains or Equals**, and **Norton Lumber and Building Materials**.

   e. Click **Search**.

   f. Click on the bill for $205.00 to open the vendor bill.

   g. **Make a note** of the descriptions for the two items purchased from Norton Lumber.

      i. Remember, **make a note** instructions may be used by your instructor to make sure you completed the exercises. It would be a good idea to keep a notebook handy.

   h. Close the window by clicking the **X** in the upper right corner of the window.

ORGANIZATION OF QUICKBOOKS ONLINE

The Importance of "Lists"

QBO uses lists as part of the organizational structure of the software so it's important that you have a good understanding of the types and uses of the various lists.

Chart of Accounts

The primary list in QBO is the **chart of accounts**. A **category type** and a **detail type** must be selected for each **account** used by an organization.

The **category and detail type** chosen will determine:

- the financial statement on which an account will appear.
- where on that statement the account will be displayed.
- which QBO features are available for that account.

QBO prepares **classified balance sheets** and **multi-step income statements**. There are lots of groupings and subtotals in those statements (as you might remember from your previous classes). To provide the necessary flexibility, QBO uses an expanded list of account **category types**. Here's a list of financial statement account classifications and the corresponding **category types** used by QBO:

Financial Accounting Classifications				
Assets	**Liabilities**	**Equity**	**Revenues**	**Expenses**
QuickBooks Online Account Category Types				
Bank	Accounts payable (A/P)	Equity	Income	Cost of Goods Sold
Accounts receivable (A/R)	Credit card		Other income	Expenses
Other Current Assets	Other Current Liabilities			Other expense
Fixed Assets	Long Term Liabilities			
Other Assets				

You can have many different accounts with the same **category** type in your chart of accounts.

Here are some examples of the way **account type** determines placement in a financial statement: Let's say you are going to set up an account called Petty Cash. You would want to set the account up as type **Bank** so that it shows up at the top of the balance sheet along with any checking or savings accounts the company has. (Checking and savings accounts would also be set up with the account type **Bank**.) A Salaries Payable account would be set up as type **Other Current Liabilities**. That way it shows up on the balance sheet as a current liability along with accounts like Interest Payable and Payroll Taxes Payable.

Here are some examples of the way **account type** is associated with various features in QBO: If an account were set up as an **Accounts Receivable (A/R)** type, you would be able to use that account when preparing customer invoices. You would also be able to pull an accounts receivable aging report for that account. You would not be able to do either of those things with an account set up as an **Other Current Asset** type. You will learn more about these features as you go through the textbook. For now, just be aware that selecting the appropriate account type is important for a variety of reasons.

Detail types are subsets of each **category type**. Both **category** and **detail types** are defined by QBO and cannot be modified. Although it should be easy for you to determine the correct **category type**, it's sometimes difficult to find an appropriate **detail type**. If you don't find an exact match, select the available **detail type** that most closely matches the account you're setting up.

Adding, Editing, or Deleting Accounts

To add, edit, or delete accounts, click the **gear** on the icon bar.

Sidebar notes:

Account A record of the additions, deductions, and balances of individual assets, liabilities, stockholders' equity, dividends, revenues, and expenses.

Classified balance sheet A balance sheet in which items are classified into subgroups to facilitate financial analysis and management decision making.

Multi-step income statement An income statement in which one or more intermediate performance measures, such as gross profit on sales, are derived before the continuing income is reported.

The screen will look something like this:

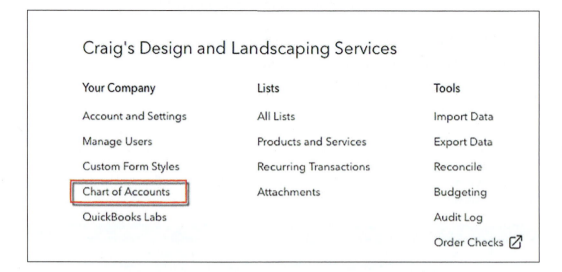

Click **Chart of Accounts** to open the list.

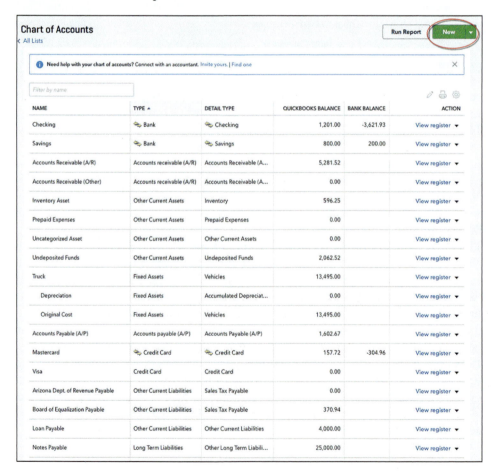

Adding an Account

Click **New** in the account list window to open the **Account** window.

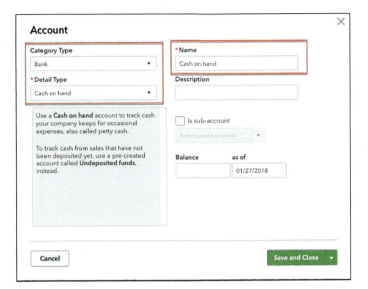

The appropriate **category type** is selected first.

The available **Detail Types** will appear after the **Category Type** is selected. Most categories will have a number of available **Detail Types** to choose from.

You can then enter a **Name** for the account. You should enter a name that accurately describes the account. The **Name** is what will appear on the financial statements.

The **Description** field can be used when users want to include additional detail about the account.

To group similar accounts together for presentation purposes, you can create a **parent account** and then identify other accounts as **sub-accounts** of the parent. In the chart of accounts list, sub-accounts appear as follows: Parent account name:Sub-account name. Sub-accounts must have the same **category type** as the parent account.

The window for a new Repair & Maintenance account might look something like this if it's set up as a sub-account of Automobile:

You can use account numbers in QBO. To include an account number, you need to elect that as a preference. Setting that preference will be covered in Chapter 2. You will be using account numbers in your homework assignments.

Editing an Account

To edit an account in the chart of accounts list, open the dropdown menu next to the account you wish to edit.

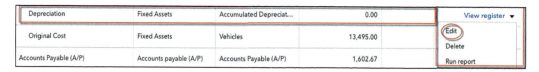

Click **Edit** to open the **Account** window.

You can change the account's name, number (if applicable), **category type**, or **detail type**. You can also make it a **sub-account**.

Deleting an Account

To delete an account, you would follow the procedures listed above for editing an account but instead of clicking **Edit**, you would click **Delete**.

You should only delete accounts that have never been used in a transaction. If you do delete an account with activity, QBO will make the account inactive. An inactive account would not be available in new transactions but the account would appear in any financial statements covering the period the account was used. Reactivating accounts is covered in Chapter 8.

Also in Chapter 8, we will cover how to manage accounts that are no longer useful but can't be deleted.

QuickCheck
1-1

True or False? QBO will allow you to create an account with the name Salaries Payable with an Expenses category type. (Answer at end of chapter.)

Work with Craig's Design and Landscaping's chart of accounts.

(Craig needs an account to track airfare to conferences and wants to change some existing accounts.)

PRACTICE

EXERCISE

1. Click the **gear** in the icon bar.

2. Click **Chart of Accounts**.

   a. You may get a screen that says "**Take a peek under the hood**." If you do, click **See your Chart of Accounts**.

3. To add a new account:

   a. Click **New**.

   b. Select **Expenses** as the **category type**.

   c. Select **Travel** as the **detail type**.

   d. Type in "Airfare" as the **name**.

   e. Check **Is sub-account** and select Travel.

   f. Click **Save and Close**.

4. To edit an account:

   a. Select **Edit** in the dropdown menu for the **Travel Meals** account.

   b. Change the **detail type** to **Travel.**

   c. Change the **name** to "Hotel and meals."

   d. Click **Is sub-account** and select Travel.

   e. Click **Yes** if asked about changing the detail type.

   f. Click **Save and Close**.

5. To delete an account:

   a. Select **Delete** in the dropdown menu for **Other Portfolio Income** account.

   b. Answer Yes when prompted.

6. **Make a note** of the number of sub-accounts under **Legal & Professional Fees**.

7. Click **Dashboard**.

Other Lists in QuickBooks Online

There are a number of other lists used in QBO.

The **Products and Services** list contains sales and purchase (if applicable) information about every product sold or service provided by the organization. Individual products and services are identified as **items** in QBO. **Items** are used when billing customers and when purchasing inventory in QBO. There are various **item** types available in QBO. The various types will be covered in Chapter 3 and Chapter 6.

Some lists represent options that might be used. For example, there is a list of payment terms that can be used for setting due dates for customer invoices or payments to vendors.

There are also lists related to payroll. Payroll will be covered in Chapter 9.

These (and other) lists will be covered in more detail in later chapters but, just for practice, we'll look at editing **items** here.

Editing an Item

Click the **gear** on the icon bar.

The screen will look something like this:

Click **Products and Services** to open the **item** list.

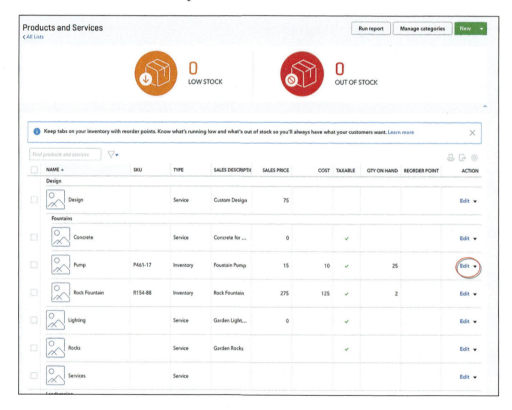

Click **Edit** next to Pump. The Edit screen looks like this:

Because pumps are products purchased for resale, the screen includes sales, purchase, and inventory tracking information. Any of this information can be changed using the Edit feature. Service **items** require less detail.

PRACTICE

EXERCISE

Work with Craig's Design and Landscaping items.
(Craig wants to change the price charged for Supervision services.)

1. Click the **gear** in the icon bar.

2. Click **Products and Services**.

3. To edit an **item**:
   a. Select **Edit** in the far right column for **Design**.
   b. Change the **Name** to "Custom Design."
   c. Change the **Sales price/rate** to "$80."
   d. Click **Save and close**.

4. **Make a note** of the cost listed for **Rock Fountains** in the **Products and Services** list.

5. Make a note of the sales price listed for **Pest Control** in the **Product and Services** list.

6. Click **Dashboard**.

Behind the Scenes with "Transaction Types"

In a manual accounting system, the mechanics of accounting work something like this:

✓ Documentation (for transactions) is received from outside sources or prepared internally.

✓ Details from the documents are recorded in **journals**.

Journal A tabular record in which business transactions are analyzed in debit and credit terms and recorded in chronological order.

General ledger An accounting record with enough flexibility so that any type of business transaction may be recorded in it; a diary of a business's accounting transactions.

✓ Journal entries are posted (transferred) to the **general ledger** and, as appropriate, to **subsidiary ledgers**.

✓ A **trial balance** is prepared.

✓ Financial statements are prepared from the trial balance and subsidiary ledger reports are prepared from the subsidiary ledgers.

In QBO, the mechanics work like this:

Subsidiary ledger A ledger that provides detailed information about an account balance.

✓ Certain documents are prepared directly in QBO (invoices and checks, for example) using specific "forms."

✓ Documents received from outside sources (vendor invoices for example) are entered into QBO using other "forms."

✓ That's all the user has to do (other than making those pesky adjusting journal entries!).

> **BEHIND THE SCENES** The journal entries related to transactions are automatically created by QBO and posted to the general ledger when the "form" is completed (saved). Subsidiary ledgers, trial balances, and financial statements are also automatically updated every time a transaction is entered.

Trial balance A list of the account titles in the general ledger, their respective debit or credit balances, and the totals of the debit and credit balances.

There is a journal entry behind every completed form in QBO EXCEPT (there are always exceptions, right?):

● Purchase orders (not **accounting transactions**)

● Estimates (not accounting transactions)

● Timesheets

● Delayed charges and delayed credits

    ■ These transactions are unique to QBO and are covered in Chapter 6.

> **BEHIND THE SCENES** Timesheets are, strictly speaking, accounting transactions. (A liability is created as soon as employees work.) Wages are only recorded in QBO, however, when payroll checks are created or when general journal entries are made by the user to recognize earned but unpaid salaries.

QuickCheck
1-2

> Why aren't purchase orders and estimates accounting transactions? (Answer at end of chapter.)

Accounting transaction An economic event that requires accounting recognition; an event that effects any of the elements of the accounting equation—assets, liabilities, or stockholders' equity.

Each form is identified as a specific **transaction type** in QBO. Knowing the various types allows you to easily find transactions or modify reports.

There are many **transaction types**. Here are a **few** of them (see Appendix B for a list of all transaction types):

● **Sales receipt** (cash sales)

● **Invoice** (sales on account)

● **Payment** (collections from customer for sales on account)

- **Check** (payments by check NOT including payments on account or payroll checks)

- **Bill** (purchases from vendors on account)

- **Bill payment** (Check) (payments by check to vendors for purchases on account)

- **Journal entry** (adjusting entries)

Transaction type names in QBO are **very** specific.

In business, we might "bill" a customer OR we might receive a "bill" from a vendor. In QBO, we **invoice** customers and we record **bills** from vendors that we will be paying at a later date. You cannot enter a sale to a customer, on account, using a **bill**.

In business, we write "checks" to pay for something on the spot. We write "checks" to pay the phone bill we recorded in the general ledger last month. We also write checks to pay our employees. In QBO there are three different **transaction types** for those activities. **Check** is the **transaction type** used when we pay for something on the spot. Checks written to vendors to pay account balances are **bill payment transaction types**. **Paycheck** is the **transaction type** for employee payroll checks.

REPORTING

There are lots of reports already set up in QBO. You'll be using many of those reports during the class term.

Reports are accessed by clicking **Reports** on the navigation bar. The screen will look something like this:

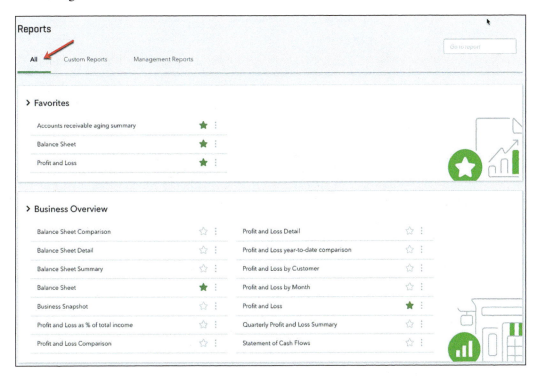

The **All** tab includes the reports already set up in QBO. The screenshot above gives you a partial view of the **All** tab on the **Reports** window.

Reports on this tab are grouped by category. Some reports are included in multiple categories. The categories are:

Favorites—the most popular reports from all the categories. Reports can be added or deleted from this list by clicking the star next to the report name. Reports added to **Favorites** will still be listed in the original category.

Business Overview—the typical accounting reports created at the end of each accounting period

Who Owes You—reports related to accounts receivable

Sales and Customers—reports related to sales and customer activity

What You Owe—reports related to accounts payable

Expenses and Vendors—reports related to purchase and vendor activity

Sales Tax—reports related to state and local sales taxes

For My Accountant—common accounting reports created at the end of each accounting period plus fairly detailed reports of financial activity. Journal reports are included in this category.

Payroll—reports related to employees

The **Management Reports** tab includes three report packages developed by Intuit.

Management Reports are covered in Chapter 12.

Reports customized and saved by users are included on the **Custom Reports** tab.

Customizing Reports

Most reports in QBO can be customized and you'll likely need to be able to customize reports to complete your homework assignments.

There are many ways you can customize reports:

- You can add or delete the types of information that appear on the report and/or the order in which the information is presented.

- You can specify which transactions are included in the report.

- You can modify the appearance of the reports (fonts, titles, etc.).

Simple Report Modification

Certain report modifications can easily be made on the face of most report screens.

For an example, click **Reports** on the navigation bar. On the **All** tab, click **Journal** report in the **For My Accountant** section.

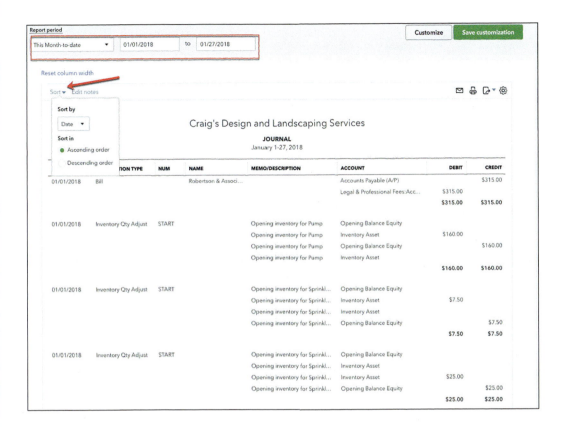

On the **Journal** report shown in the screenshot above, simple modifications include:

- Changing the date range of the report.

- Changing how the data in the report is sorted (under **Sort**).

- Changing the column widths (done by clicking the separator bar just to the right of the column name and dragging left to decrease the width and dragging right to increase the width).

Other reports, the Profit and Loss statement for example, have many more modifications that can easily be made on the face of the report screen.

Reports can be created with differing levels of detail for different users. For example, a creditor might need less detail on an income statement than an owner. If there are sub-accounts set up for income or expense accounts, the income statement can easily be modified to:

- Show all sub-accounts with subtotals by parent account.

- Show only parent accounts.

QBO calls changing this level of detail *expanding* or *collapsing* a report. This option, when available, is included on the face of the report screen.

When a report is initially opened, the report will show all detail. A **profit and loss** report, for example, would appear something like this:

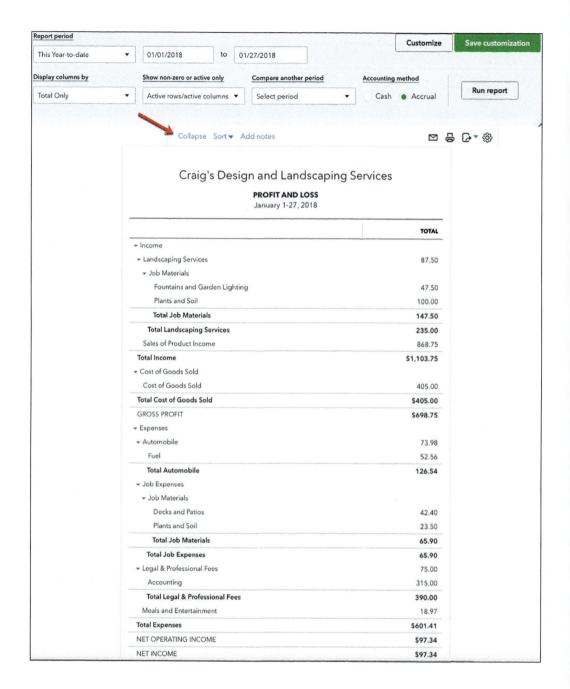

Click the **Collapse** button to include only parent accounts. The report would look something like this when **collapsed**:

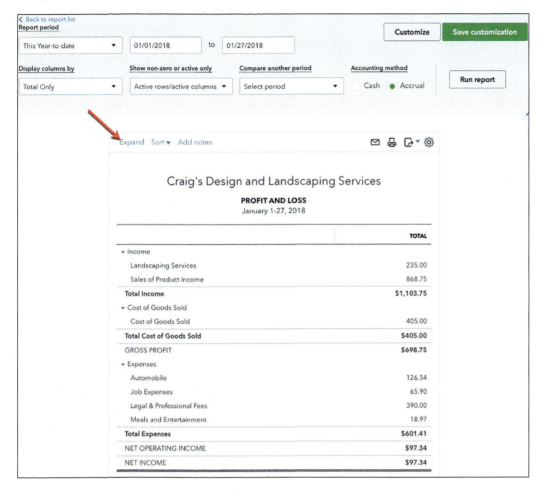

To return to the more detailed report, you would just need to click the **Expand** button.

Advanced Report Modification

Sometimes a company might want to limit the type of information included in a report or do more extensive modifications to the appearance of the report. For example, a company might want to limit a sales report to include only sales to certain customers. Or a company might want to show reports in whole dollars.

Modifying the type of information that is included in a report is done through a filtering process. Modifying the appearance of a report is done through a selection process. Both are done through a customization window.

To more extensively modify a **Journal** report, click **Customize** in the top right of the report screen.

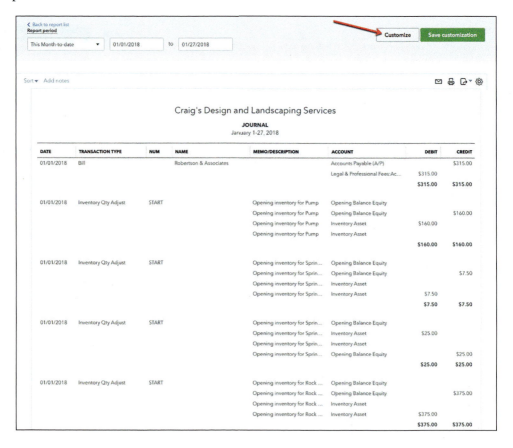

You'll see a window that looks something like this (different reports have different customization options so the screens will differ):

I have opened all the modification categories to show the type of options available. As you can see, you can filter this report by **transaction type**, account, name, etc. You can change the general appearance as well.

Clicking **Change columns** gives additional options.

You can select the columns you want to include in the report. You can also reorder the columns by clicking the **keypad icon** just to the left of the column name and dragging it up or down.

Printing Reports

Reports can be printed, emailed, or exported to Excel or PDF.

All of the options are accessible from the toolbar at the top of each report. The toolbar looks like this:

The first two links take you first to a new window where page orientation (portrait or landscape) is selected. Final links for printing or emailing appear in the new window.

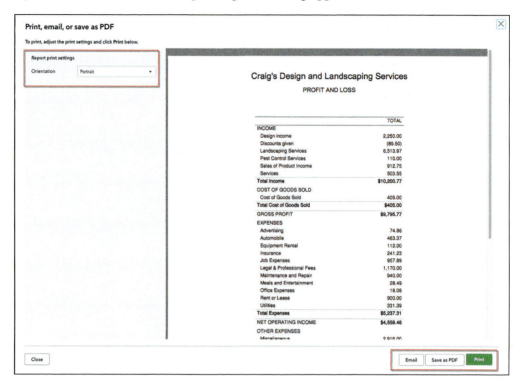

The **Export** dropdown menu allows you to select **Export to Excel** or **Export to PDF**. Page orientation can be selected for an export to PDF but not for an export to Excel.

The options available by clicking the **gear** icon at the far right of the tool bar vary depending on the report. For some reports, columns can be changed or reordered in the **gear** window. In other reports, the only option included is to change the display density to compact.

    k. **Make a note** of the number of sub-accounts associated with **Maintenance and Repair**.

    l. Click the export link and select **Export to PDF**.

    m. Select **Portrait** as the orientation.

    n. Click **Save as PDF**.

    o. Save to your desktop, laptop, or USB drive.

        i. Close out of Adobe Acrobat if needed.

    p. Click **Close** (bottom left corner of the report) to exit out of the report window.

    q. Click **Back to report list** (top left corner of the window).

2. Modify a Journal report.

    a. Click **Journal** in the **For My Accountant** section of **Reports**.

    b. Click **Customize**.

    c. In the **General** section, change **Report period** to **All Dates**.

    d. Click **Rows/Columns**

        i. Click **Change Columns**.

        ii. Remove the checkmarks next to **Num, Memo/Description**.

    e. Click **Filters** tab.

        i. Check the **Transaction Type** field.

        ii. In the dropdown menu, click **Bill**.

    f. Click **Header/Footer**.

        i. Change the **Report Title** to "Vendor Bills."

    g. Click **Run report**.

    h. Select **Date** in the **Sort** dropdown menu.

    i. **Make a note** of the total (dollars) in the **Debit** column.

3. Click **Dashboard** to exit out of **Reports**.

Yes. The user creates the account name and chooses the account type. Be careful that the account type you select is correct.

ANSWER TO
QuickCheck
1-1

Purchase orders and estimates are not considered accounting transactions because the **accounting equation** does not change as a result of those transactions.

ANSWER TO
QuickCheck
1-2

Accounting equation An expression of the equivalency of the economic resources and the claims upon those resources of a business, often stated as Assets = Liabilities + Stockholders' Equity.

CHAPTER SHORTCUTS

Open the test drive company

1. Open your browser
2. Enter https://qbo.intuit.com/redir/testdrive as the URL
3. Enter the access code that appears on the screen

Change the company name

1. Click Company/Company Information

Change settings

1. Click the gear on the icon bar
2. Click Accounts and Settings

Add an account

1. Click the gear on the icon bar
2. Click Chart of Accounts
3. Click New

Edit an account

1. Click the gear on the icon bar
2. Click Chart of Accounts
3. In the far right column of the account you want to edit, select Edit from the dropdown menu

Delete an account

1. Click the gear on the icon bar
2. Click Chart of Accounts
3. In the far right column of the account you want to edit, select Delete from the dropdown menu

CHAPTER REVIEW (Answers available on the publisher's website.)

Matching

Match the term or phrase (as used in QuickBooks Online) to its definition.

1. item
2. transaction type
3. expand or collapse
4. account detail type
5. icon bar
6. privacy
7. account category type
8. navigation bar

_____ name given to a specific form

_____ toggle button used to remove all financial data from the display area of the Dashboard

_____ subset of account types

_____ specific type of customer or inventory charge

_____ modifying the level of detail included on a report

_____ set of links to the left of the display area of the Dashboard

_____ type associated with each account to identify where it should appear in the financial statements

_____ set of links on the bar above the display area of the Dashboard

Multiple Choice

1. QuickBooks Online can be accessed through _____.
   a. Safari
   b. Internet Explorer
   c. Google Chrome
   d. Any of the above

2. Which QBO **account category** should be selected when setting up the general ledger account "Buildings"? (Assume the buildings are used as the corporate headquarters.)

    a. Other asset

    b. Property, plant & equipment

    c. Asset

    d. Fixed Asset

3. Sales forms can be accessed _____.

    a. only through links on the icon bar

    b. only through links on the navigation bar

    c. through links on either the icon bar or the navigation bar

4. Which of the following statements is false?

    a. General ledger accounts can be added to QBO by users.

    b. You can have more than one account set up as an "Accounts receivable (A/R)" **category type** in QuickBooks Online.

    c. You cannot make an account of **category type** "Expenses" a sub-account of an account of **category type** "Cost of Goods Sold."

    d. The chart of accounts is considered a "list" in QBO.

5. In QBO, the **transaction type** for recording a sale on account is _____.

    a. **Sale**

    b. **Sales receipt**

    c. **Bill**

    d. **Invoice**

ASSIGNMENT

In this assignment you will be working in the test drive company, Craig's Design and Landscaping Services.

Assignment 1

1. Open the **Expenses** screen from the navigation bar.

    a. On the **Expenses** tab, determine the **Total** amount for

        i.   Check No. 75, Hicks Hardware payee

        ii. Bill Payment (check) 6, PG&E payee

    b. On the **Vendors** tab,

        i.   determine the total amount due to Brosnahan Insurance Agency

        ii. determine the email address for Computers by Jenni

Assignments with the MBC are available in myBusinessCourse.

2. Click the **Plus** icon on the icon bar, click **Receive Payment**. Determine what must be selected in the first dropdown menu (top left):

    a. Date

    b. Customer name

    c. Vendor name

    d. Account name

3. Identify the appropriate financial statement classifications for the following QBO account **category types**.
   a. Accounts Receivable
   b. Other Current Liabilities
   c. Cost of Goods Sold
   d. Bank
   e. Fixed Assets

4. Identify the appropriate QBO account **category type** for the following general ledger accounts in a law firm.
   a. Prepaid expenses
   b. Interest payable
   c. Gain on sale of office equipment
   d. Office furniture
   e. Accumulated depreciation
   f. Inventory

5. What are the steps for opening multiple QBO windows in your browser?

6. Using the **Search** function, determine how many transactions have occurred between Books by Bessie (a vendor) and Craig's Design and Landscaping Services.

7. Create a **Journal** report. Set the **report period** as **All Dates**. Filter the report to only include **journal entry transaction types**. What is the total in the debit column?

8. Would you be able to find the following on the navigation bar, the icon bar, or both?
   a. Balance sheet report?
   b. Form for recording a cash sale?
   c. Past transactions with employees?
   d. List of Products and Services?

9. Create a **Profit and Loss** report for **All Dates**. Collapse the report and export the report to PDF.

10. Open the **Create** menu. How many different types of vendor transactions (financial transactions) can be created in QBO?

Setting Up Company Files

After completing Chapter 2, you should be able to:

1. Set up a new company in QuickBooks Online.

2. Convert an existing company not currently using an Intuit product to QuickBooks Online.

3. Customize settings in company files.

4. Import Excel data into QuickBooks Online.

INTRODUCTION

New company files can be created in QBO for:

- Newly formed companies.

- Existing companies that are converting from a manual system (or other accounting software system) to QBO.

- Existing companies that are converting from QuickBooks Desktop software to QBO. (Desktop conversions will not be covered in this textbook.)

In any case, obtaining a clear understanding of business operations and the organization's informational needs is the best place to start. Some questions you might ask your client or yourself (if you're the owner or the accountant) include:

- Does the company currently sell or anticipate selling products, services, or both?
  - If products are currently being sold:
    - Does the company manufacture the products?
    - Is a product inventory maintained, or are products purchased to order?
    - Are products sold to consumers, to distributors, or to both?
  - Is the company responsible for collecting sales taxes from customers?

- Are there significant business segments within the company currently or expected in the future?

- Does the company have employees?

- Does the company have specific reporting needs (internal or external) currently, or does it expect to have such needs in the future?

There is a reason that "anticipated" operations are part of some of the questions. If you understand the direction of the company, you can design a system that will accommodate expected changes. For example, let's say you're opening a barbershop. You have some great ideas and expect that you will be able to open several more shops within the next year. When you have multiple shops, you're going to want to track operations by shop. QBO has features that can handle multiple locations.

If this is an existing company, management will need to decide the conversion date (start date). Although you can start recording transactions at any point in time, it is important to understand the implications of selecting various dates. For example, all payroll reporting is based on calendar quarters or calendar years, so companies often convert data as of the first day of a calendar quarter or calendar year.

As of early 2018, the fee for the QBO plan we will be using in this course (QBO Plus) was $60 per month. This fee covers all the basic recordkeeping functions other than payroll. Users can sign up for a 30-day free trial at https://quickbooks.intuit.com/pricing/.

You have been provided with a one-year, no fee license as part of your textbook purchase. Students can also obtain a one-year, free license through Intuit's Education website. The URL for that site is http://www.intuiteducationprogram.com/students/.

In this chapter, we're going to go over the basics of setting up company files in QBO. We will also practice setting up a company file for an existing company. This is the company file you'll be using for your homework assignments. We'll use data imported from Excel files to create your homework company.

SETTING UP COMPANY FILES IN QBO

Setting Up Brand New Companies in QBO

The initial set up of a new company in QBO is very straightforward. To start, a user only needs an email address and some general information about the company and about which QBO features the user expects to use.

WARNING: This section gives you a basic overview of a new company set up in QBO. The steps for setting up your homework company file are covered in **SETTING UP YOUR HOMEWORK COMPANY** section later in this chapter. Make sure you follow those steps carefully.

The initial registration can be done through the Intuit website once you select the QBO product of your choice. The website is: https://search2.quickbooksonline.com/qb-online/

The initial screen looks like this:

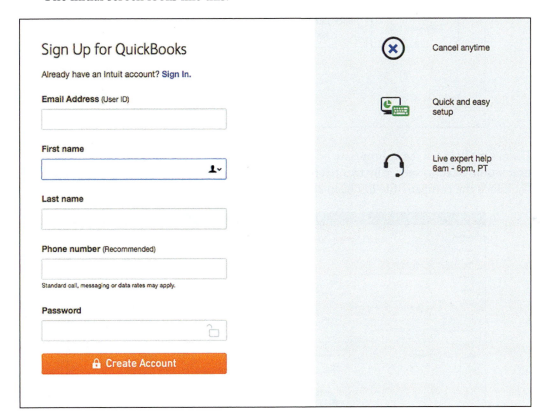

In the next screen, users are asked to enter the company name and indicate that this is a brand-new company.

In the next screen, the user is asked about the features needed in the business. The screen looks like this:

Users simply check the appropriate boxes and click **All set**. If **Pay employees** is checked, the user would need to subscribe to a payroll service.

Once the company file has been created, the new company's **Dashboard** will appear.

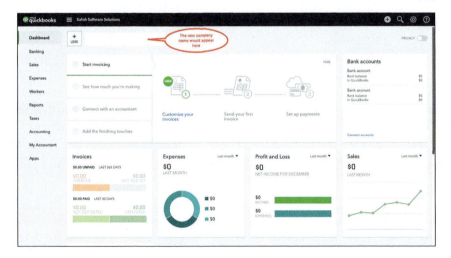

QBO automatically sets up a basic chart of accounts and various **items** based on the features selected as part of the setup.

In addition to setting up accounts and **items**, QBO also makes other selections. For example, QBO will assume the user uses accrual, not cash, as their basis of accounting. Certain other features in QBO will also be turned on or off automatically as part of the setup.

If a company has just started business, the software is now ready for use. All users need to do is review and modify, if necessary, the settings, the chart of accounts, and the **items** created to match the needs of the company. Modifying settings is covered in the

Customizing QuickBooks Online section of this chapter. Modifying accounts and **items** was covered in Chapter 1.

Converting Existing Companies to QBO

The initial set up outlined in the **Setting up brand new companies in QBO** section of this chapter is also required for converting existing companies to QBO.

- Users register with an email address.
- Users enter the company name and identify the length of time the business has been operating.
- Users select the basic features needed.
- A company file is created.
- Users can then modify settings as needed.

Of course, if an existing company is converting to QBO, additional steps are necessary. The products and services, customers, vendors, and employees must be set up. To make it easier, all of these lists can be imported into QBO.

In addition, account balances as of the conversion date must be entered. For some accounts, the balances can easily be entered using a journal entry. For other accounts, new users must decide how much detail to bring into QBO. For example, a user can enter outstanding customer invoices individually or they can simply enter the full customer balance. The same is true for vendor balances. If the company sells products, the quantity and value of items on hand must be entered.

You will be practicing the steps for converting an existing company into QBO as you set up your homework company in the **Setting Up Your Company File** section of this chapter.

CUSTOMIZING QUICKBOOKS ONLINE

One of the reasons QBO is so popular is that it can be used in different types of organizations and in many different industries. That flexibility, however, presents some challenges. The tools needed by a retail store (the ability to track inventory held for sale, for example) are not the same as the tools needed by a law firm (the ability to bill clients from timesheets, for example). If all the tools needed in all the different industries were visible all the time, users might justifiably complain that the menu options are a little TOO extensive.

QBO solves this by allowing companies to customize the program. Users can select or deselect features (known as **settings**). If you don't need to track inventory, you don't turn that feature on. If you don't use purchase orders, you don't turn that feature on. Not all features can be turned on or off but many can and that makes the program more streamlined and user friendly.

You can customize the features available in QBO in a variety of ways:

- As part of the initial company setup.
  - Edit settings as part of the initial setup will be covered in the "Setting Up Your Company File" section of this chapter.
- By changing the **settings** in an existing company.

Editing Settings In a Company File

To change settings, click the **gear** in the icon bar.

The screen will look something like this:

Click **Account and Settings** under the **Your Company** column.

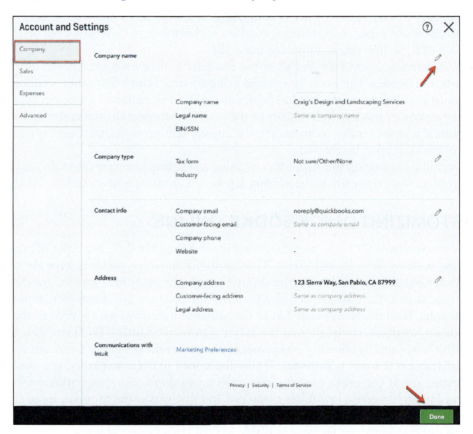

There are four tabs on the left side of the page. On each tab, various settings can be changed. On the **Company** tab, basic information about the company is entered (name, address, etc.). Changes are made on all tabs by clicking the **pencil** icon in the top right corner of the appropriate section. Clicking **Save** in the modified section saves the changes. Click **Done** to exit the window.

On the **Sales** tab, preferred invoice terms can be selected and default messages can be set up to appear automatically on sales forms.

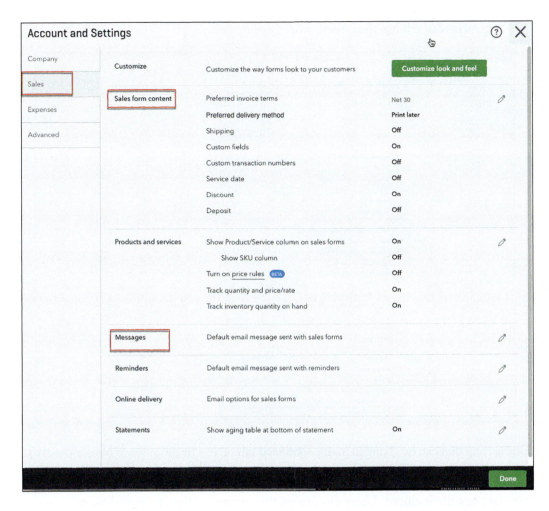

On the **Expenses** tab, features such as purchase orders and expense tracking by customer can be turned on and off.

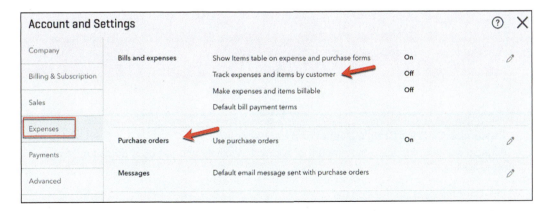

The **Advanced** tab has the largest number of options.

One setting that can be changed in the **Advanced** tab relates to the amount of user inactivity (in hours) that the software will allow before automatically signing off. This is especially important for you to change in the test drive company because all work is lost whenever the company file is closed. Users can extend the amount of time to three hours.

Settings will be discussed in more detail in the "Setting Up Your Company File" section of this chapter and in future chapters.

> **!** **WARNING:** When you make changes in **settings**, the appearance of various forms will often change.

PRACTICE EXERCISE

Customize QBO for Craig's Design and Landscaping.
(Craig's wants to increase the amount of allowed inactivity and set up a default message for sales forms.)

1. Click the **gear** on the icon bar.

2. Click **Account and Settings**.

3. Click **Advanced** to change the amount of time of inactivity allowed.

    a. In the **Other preferences** section, click **Sign me out if inactive for**.

    b. Select **3 hours** on the dropdown menu.

    c. Click **Save**.

(continued)

4. Click **Sales** to set up the default message for sales forms.

    a. Click **Default message sent on sales forms**.

    b. Under **Default message shown on sales form** (bottom of the screen **Messages** section), select **Invoices and other sales forms** from the dropdown menu.

    c. Change the message to "We appreciate your business."

    d. Click **Save**.

5. **Make a note of** the following:

    a. the Company address on the **Company** tab.

    b. the **Preferred invoice terms** on the **Sales** tab.

    c. whether the **Purchase order** feature is activated on the **Expenses** tab.

    d. the **First month of fiscal year** on the **Advanced** tab

    e. the **Accounting method** selected on the **Advanced** tab.

6. Click **Done** (bottom right corner of screen) to exit the **Account and Settings** window.

SETTING UP YOUR COMPANY FILE

Your homework assignments will be done in a company file set up using the access codes (license number and product code) included with your textbook. General information about the company assigned by your instructor is given to you at the end of this chapter (under Chapter Two Assignments). In this section, we'll go through the steps necessary to get your homework company file set up.

STEP 1—Decide on the email account you want to use.

Before you can start setting up a company, you need to have an email account. The email address (and the related password) will be used each time you log in to QBO.

You can use your own personal email address or you can set up an email address specifically for this course.

 HINT: Your instructor may ask you for your email address and password in order to check your work. If so, you should create a separate email address for this course. To make it easier for your instructor, you might want to put your name and the course number in the address. Your instructor might have other requirements so make sure you check before you go any further.

Intuit accepts passwords that have the following characteristics:

1. It must be at least 8 characters long.

2. It must include both lowercase and uppercase letters.

3. It must include a number.

4. It must include a symbol.

If you're using your personal email address, you may be required to change your password if it doesn't meet the requirements listed above.

Instructions for setting up a Gmail account are provided in the Appendix to this chapter if you don't want to use your personal email.

STEP 2—Read the background information for the homework company assigned by your instructor included at the end of the chapter.

Having a good understanding of the company you're setting up should help as you move through the process.

STEP 3—Activate your subscription.

Open your browser and enter http://quickbooks.intuit.com/start/retail_sui as the URL. The first screen will look something like this:

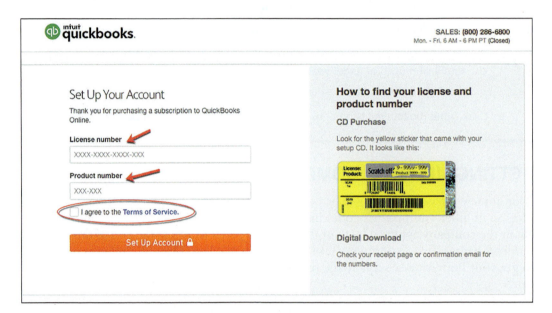

Enter your license number and product number in the appropriate fields. Your license and product numbers are listed at the front of the book.

> **BEHIND THE SCENES** The product number is a code used to identify the version of QBO being accessed (QBO Plus in this class). The license number is used to identify a specific QBO user. Intuit matches the license number to the user's email address.

Check the **I agree to the Terms of Service** box once you're comfortable.
　　Click **Set Up Account**.

Complete the **Sign Up for QuickBooks** form.

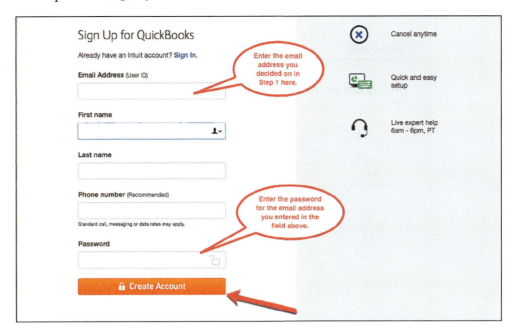

Click **Create Account**.

STEP 4—Answer the informational questions that appear in the next set of screens.

General information needs to be entered in the screens showing in QBO. The screenshots may differ from those shown below. (Remember, Intuit is updating QBO regularly.) For your company, enter the following information:

- Company Name—Enter as *Your Name Company Name*. (Use your real name. For example, if my instructor assigned Math Revealed! for homework I would enter Gayle Williams Math Revealed! as the company name.)

- Business Age—1-2 years

The screen would look something like this if the instructor assigned Math Revealed!:

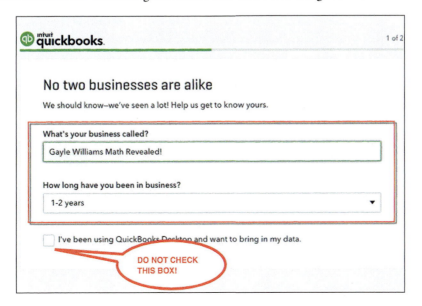

Click **Next**.

The screen should look something like this:

QBO is asking about services needed so that needed features can be activated in QBO. Additional features can be added later if appropriate.

● Check all the boxes except **Pay Employees**.

Click **All Set**.

QBO will take a few minutes to set up your company. When the process is complete, the screen should look something like this:

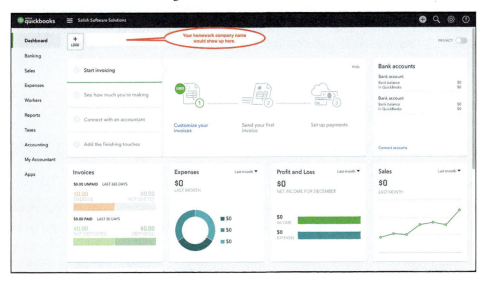

STEP 5—Change the Settings.

Now that you have a company file, it's time to change some of the settings. Click the **gear** on the icon bar and select **Account and Settings**.

On the **Company** tab, click the **pencil** icon in the **Address** section and enter "3835 Freeport Blvd. Sacramento, CA 95822." Make sure the **Company name** includes your name and the name of the homework company. Edit the field if necessary.

Click **Save**.

Click the **Sales** tab. Check the box next to **Custom transactions numbers** to turn the feature **On**. Click **Save**.

Many of the sales settings were automatically changed when you selected the services needed. For example, when you checked **Manage your inventory** in the initial set up of your company file (Step 4), QBO automatically made changes to the **Products and services** section. Your screen should look something like this:

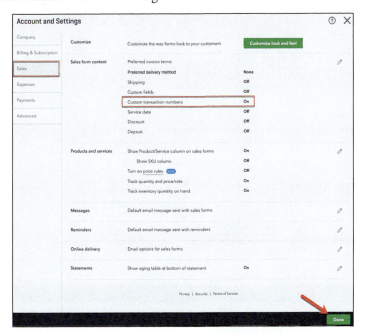

Click **Done**.

No changes need to be made on the **Expenses** tab.

Since this is a real company file, not the test drive file, two additional tabs are included in **Account and Settings**. The **Billing & Subscription** tab gives information about your subscription. The **Payments** tab provides links to additional services. There are no settings to change on these tabs.

Click the **Advanced** tab and make the following changes:

- **Company Type**—Click **Tax form** and select **Corporation, one or more shareholders (Form 1120)** in the dropdown menu. Click **Save**.

- **Chart of accounts**—Click **Enable account numbers** and check the box to turn the feature on. Check the box next to **Show account numbers** and click **Save**.

- **Automation**—Click **Pre-fill forms with previously entered content** and uncheck the box to turn the feature to **Off**.

- **Other preferences**—Click **Warn if duplicate bill number is used** and check the box in the appropriate field. Click **Save**.

    - You may also want to extend the amount of time QBO remains open when you're not actively working on your assignments. If so, make the change in the dropdown menu next to **Sign me out if inactive for**.

The screen should look something like this when you've made the changes:

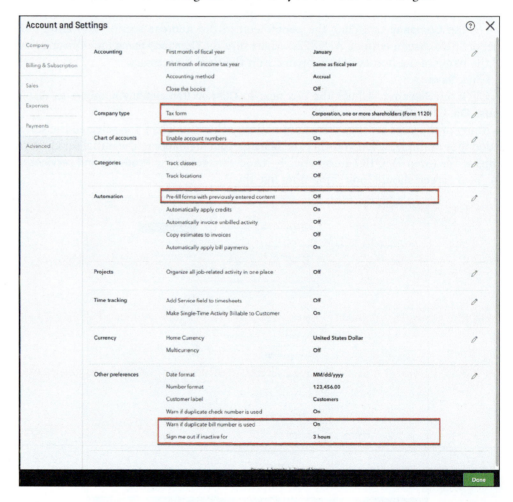

Click **Done** to exit **Account and Settings**.

STEP 6—Purge the chart of accounts.

QBO automatically created quite a few accounts for you when you set up your company in Step 4. Unfortunately, many of the accounts that were set up are not needed in your homework company and many of the accounts you will need were not created by QBO.

To see the chart of accounts set up by QBO, click the **gear** on the icon bar and click **Chart of accounts.** There are probably more than 50 accounts set up.

Instead of adding and deleting these accounts (which is quite a tedious process), you will be purging the chart of accounts QBO set up and importing your own accounts into the company file.

With QBO open, type https://qbo.intuit.com/app/purgecompany in the URL. The screen will look something like this (you may have a different number of accounts):

Enter **YES** and click **OK**. The screen will look something like this:

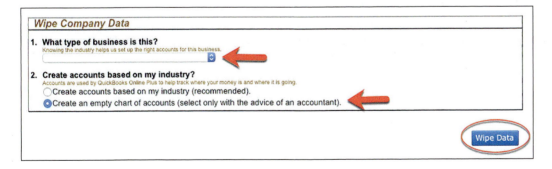

If your instructor assigned Math Revealed!, select "Teachers, Tutors, Coaches" in the drop-down menu for the first question. If your instructor assigned Salish Software Solutions, select "Other Consulting, Professional, and Technical Services."

Select "Create an empty chart of accounts" to answer the second question.

Click **Wipe Data**. The chart of accounts has now been purged. Click the **gear** on the icon bar and click **Chart of Accounts** in the **Your Company** column to see the new chart of accounts. The screen should look something like this:

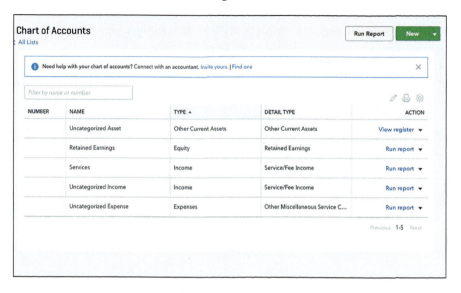

The accounts remaining in the chart of accounts are default accounts that can't be deleted.

BEHIND THE SCENES The chart of accounts and all transactions are deleted when a company file is purged. All of the settings remain intact. Purging a company and importing data into a company can be done multiple times (unlimited) within the first 60 days of a new subscription.

You are now ready to start importing data.

STEP 7—Import a new chart of accounts.

Go to https://cambridgepub.com/book/qbo2018#supplements. Download the Excel file **Chart of Accounts for Importing** (for the homework company you've been assigned) to your desktop, your hard drive, or to a USB drive.

In QBO, click the **gear** on the icon bar.

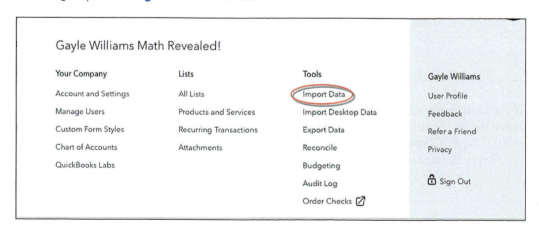

Click **Import Data**. The screen should look something like this:

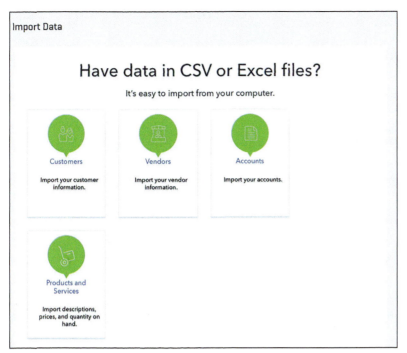

Click **Accounts**.

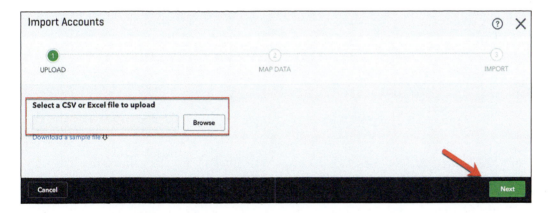

Upload your **Chart of Accounts for Importing** file. The account selected may be barely visible in the field. As long as you can see it, you're fine.

   Click **Next**.

BEHIND THE SCENES QBO automatically maps the fields on the Excel worksheet to the fields in the chart of accounts in QBO. Only certain data can be uploaded. Any fields that can't be imported, like account balances, will need to be entered manually.

The screen should look like this:

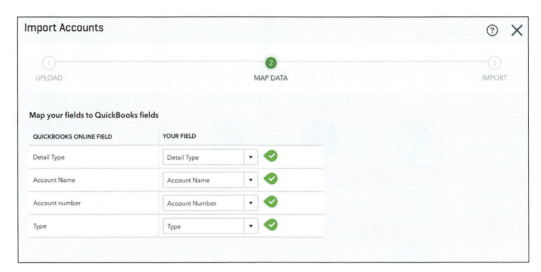

Click **Next**.

 HINT: Depending on which homework company your instructor has assigned, your window may show a different number of accounts ready to be imported.

Scroll down through the next screen. Any problems will be highlighted in red.

> **WARNING: If the Import light is not bright green, there is a problem with the data. Click Back to see if you uploaded the correct file. QBO is very sensitive to issues in import files. If changes have inadvertently been made to the Excel file, you will not be able to import the accounts.**

Click **Import**.

You may receive a message that some of the accounts can't be imported because they are duplicates. If so, simply remove them (uncheck the box next to those accounts) and proceed. You can make corrections later.

Click the **gear** on the icon bar. Click **Chart of Accounts** to see the new chart of accounts. It should include all of the accounts listed on the Excel spreadsheet.

There's still some work to do in the chart of accounts but first you need to import customers, vendors, and products and services. You will complete the work on the chart of accounts in your homework assignment for Chapter 2.

STEP 8—Import the item list. (This process will be similar to the import of the chart of accounts.)

Download the Excel file **Products and Services List for Importing** (for the homework company you've been assigned) to your desktop, your hard drive, or to a USB drive.

In QBO, click the **gear** on the icon bar. Click **Import Data**.

Click **Products and Services**.

Upload the **Products and Services List for Importing** file and click **Next**.

The screen should look like this:

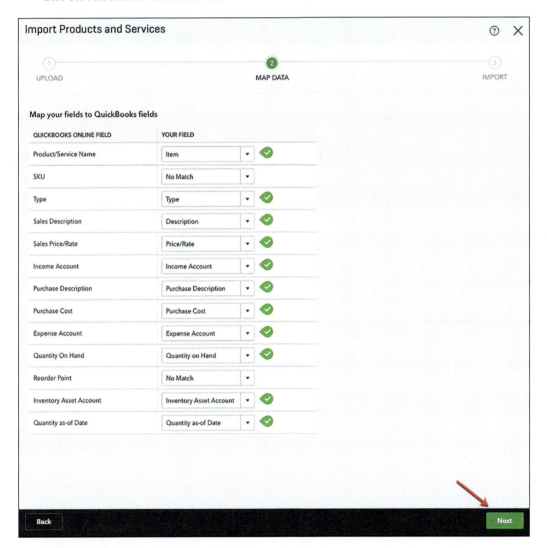

BEHIND THE SCENES QBO automatically maps the fields on the Excel worksheet to the fields in the **Products and Services** in QBO. Not all data fields need to be completed with an upload.

Click **Next**.

The screen, without data included, would look something like this:

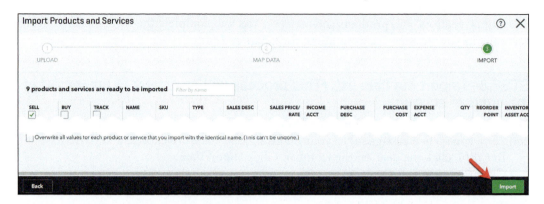

 HINT: Depending on which homework company your instructor has assigned, your window may show a different number of products and services ready to be imported.

All of the data from the Excel spreadsheet should show on your screen.

WARNING: If the Import light is not bright green or there are fields highlighted in red, there is a problem with the data. Click Back to see if you uploaded the correct file. QBO is very sensitive to issues in import files. If changes have inadvertently been made to the Excel file, you will not be able to import the accounts.

Click **Import**.

Click the **gear** on the icon bar and click **Account and Settings**. Click **Products and Services** to see the new **item list**. It should include all of the products and services listed on the Excel spreadsheet.

You may see the following message when you open the **Products and Services** list:

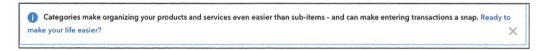

The ability to group **items** by type, called **Categories** in QBO, is a relatively new feature. If you see the message, click **Ready to make your life easier?**

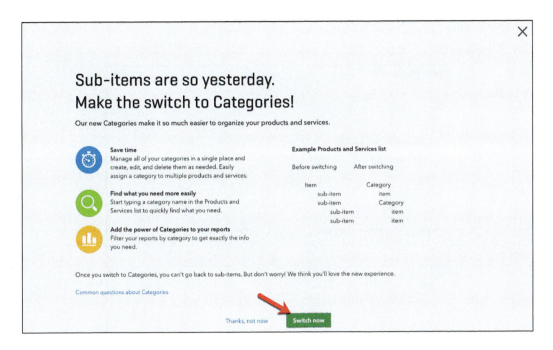

Click **Switch Now**. This will activate the feature in your company file. **Categories** will be covered in more detail in Chapter 3.

STEP 9—Import customers. (This process will be similar to the import of products and services.)

Download the Excel file **Customer List for Importing** (for the homework company you've been assigned) to your desktop, your hard drive, or to a USB drive.

In QBO, click the **gear** on the icon bar. Click **Import Data**.

Click **Customers**.

Upload the **Customer List for Importing** file and click **Next**. The screen should look like this:

BEHIND THE SCENES QBO automatically maps the fields on the Excel worksheet to the fields in the **Customer List** in QBO. Not all fields need to be uploaded.

Click **Next**.

The screen, without data included, would look something like this:

  HINT: Depending on which homework company your instructor has assigned, your window may show a different number of customers ready to be imported.

> **!** **WARNING:** If the **Import** light is not bright green or if any of the fields are red, there is a problem with the data. Click **Back** to see if you uploaded the correct file. QBO is very sensitive to issues in import files. If changes have inadvertently been made to the Excel file, you will not be able to import the accounts.

Click **Import**.

Click **Sales** on the navigation bar and select the **Customers** tab. The customer list should include all of the customers and balances included on the Excel spreadsheet.

STEP 10—Import vendors. (This process will be similar to the import of customers.)

Download the Excel file **Vendor List for Importing** (for the homework company you've been assigned) to your desktop, your hard drive, or to a USB drive.

In QBO, click the **gear** on the icon bar. Click **Import Data**.

Click **Vendors**.

Upload the **Vendor List for Importing** file and click **Next**. The screen should look like this:

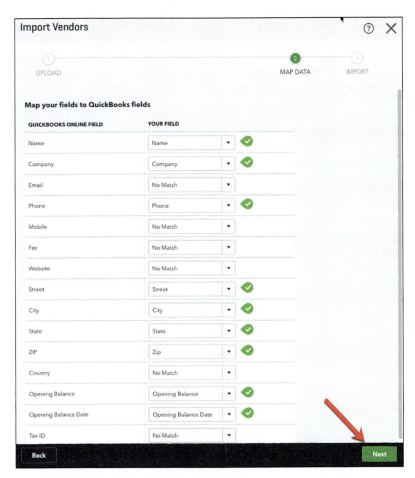

> **BEHIND THE SCENES** QBO automatically maps the fields on the Excel worksheet to the fields in the **Vendor List** in QBO. Not all fields need to be uploaded.

Click **Next**.

The screen, not including data, should look like this:

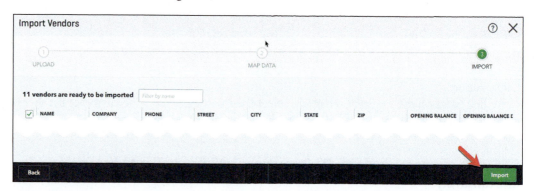

> ✳ **HINT:** Depending on which homework company your instructor has assigned, your window may show a different number of vendors ready to be imported.

> ❗ **WARNING:** If the **Import** light is not bright green or if any of the fields are red, there is a problem with the data. Click **Back** to see if you up-loaded the correct file. QBO is very sensitive to issues in import files. If changes have inadvertently been made to the Excel file, you will not be able to import the accounts.

Click **Import**.

Click **Expenses** on the navigation bar and select the **Vendors** tab. The vendor list should include all of the vendors and balances included on the Excel spreadsheet.

STEP 11—Check your balances.

This is still accounting so all the importing you just did should have resulted in a number of balanced journal entries, right?

To make sure you've got a good start, click **Reports** on the navigation bar.

Click **Balance Sheet** in the **Favorites** section. Change the date to 12/31/18.

Your balance sheet should look like one of the following (depending on the homework company assigned by your instructor). If it doesn't, go back to Step 6 and start the import process over.

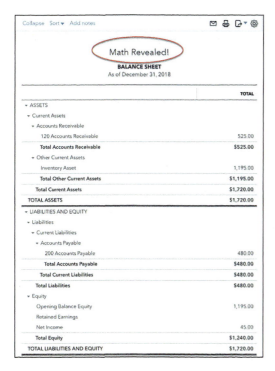

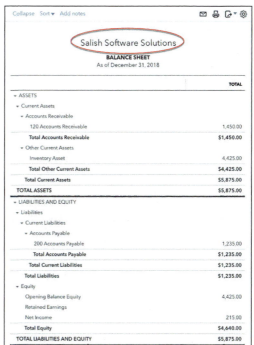

Yes. The user creates the account name and chooses the account type. Be careful that the account type you select is correct.

Purchase orders and estimates are not considered accounting transactions because the **accounting equation** does not change as a result of those transactions.

Accounting equation An expression of the equivalency of the economic resources and the claims upon those resources of a business, often stated as Assets = Liabilities + Stockholders' Equity.

CHAPTER SHORTCUTS

Activate your subscription

1. Open your browser
2. Enter http://quickbooks.intuit.com/start/retail_sui as the URL
3. Enter the license number and product number included on the first page of the textbook in the appropriate fields

Change settings

1. Click the gear on the icon bar
2. Click Account and Settings

Purge the chart of accounts

1. Open your company file.
2. Enter http://qbo.intuit.com/app/purge-company as the URL
3. Type YES in the "If you agree" field

4. Click OK
5. Choose a business similar to your homework company in the "What type of business is this?" dropdown menu
6. Select "Create an empty chart of accounts"
7. Click Wipe Data

Import data

1. Click the gear on the icon bar
2. Click Import Data
3. Select the type of list to be imported
4. Upload the appropriate Excel file

Make a journal entry

1. Click the plus on the icon bar
2. Click Journal Entry

CHAPTER REVIEW (Answers available on the publisher's website.)

Matching

Match the term or phrase (as used in QuickBooks Online) to its definition.

1. Setting
2. Importing
3. Product number
4. License number
5. Purge
6. Opening balance equity

_____   the act of bringing external data into a company file

_____   default account used by QBO as part of the import process

_____   number used to identify a specific user of QBO

_____   removal of all data from a company file

_____   customizable features

_____   number used to identify specific versions of QBO

Multiple Choice

1. Which of the following cannot be imported into QBO?
    a. Cash balances
    b. Inventory balances
    c. Accounts receivable balances
    d. Accounts payable balances

2. Which of the following is not deleted when a company file is purged?
    a. Transactions
    b. Most general ledger accounts
    c. Company settings
    d. None of the listed answers are correct. Transactions, accounts, and settings are all deleted.

3. A company file _____.
    a. can be purged an unlimited number of times as long as the user's subscription is active
    b. can be purged an unlimited number of times within the first 60 days of a new subscription
    c. can be purged up to 60 times
    d. cannot be purged

4. Which account might be debited when a customer list is imported? (Refer to the FINAL CONVERSION section of the assignment for help answering this question.)
    a. Sales revenue
    b. Inventory
    c. Accounts receivable
    d. Opening balance equity

5. Which account might be credited when a Product and Services list is imported?(Refer to the FINAL CONVERSION section of the assignment for help answering this question.)

    a. Inventory

    b. Cost of goods sold

    c. Accounts payable

    d. Opening balance equity

ASSIGNMENTS

Background information: Martin Smith, a college student and good friend of yours, has always wanted to be an entrepreneur. He is very good in math, so, to test his entrepreneurship skills, he has decided to set up a small math tutoring company serving local high school students who struggle in their math courses. He set up the company, Math Revealed!, as a corporation in 2018. Martin is the only owner. He has not taken any distributions from the company since it opened.

The business has been successful so far. In fact, it's been so successful he has decided to work in his business full time now that he's graduated from college with a degree in mathematics.

He has decided to start using QuickBooks Online to keep track of his business transactions. He likes the convenience of being able to access his information over the Internet. You have agreed to act as his accountant while you're finishing your own academic program.

He currently has a number of regular customers that he tutors in Pre-Algebra, Algebra, and Geometry. His customers pay his fees by cash or check after each tutoring session but he does give terms of Net 15 to some of his customers. He has developed the following fee schedule:

Name	Description	Rate
Refresher	One-hour session	$40 per hour
Persistence program	Two one-hour sessions per week	$75 per week
Crisis program	Five one-hour sessions per week	$150 per week

The tutoring sessions usually take place at his students' homes but he recently signed a two-year lease on a small office above a local coffee shop. The rent is only $200 per month starting in January 2019. A security deposit of $400 was paid in December 2018.

The following equipment is owned by the company:

Description	Date placed in service	Cost	Life	Salvage Value
Computer	7/1/18	$3,000	36 months	$300
Printer	7/1/18	$240	24 months	$0
Graphing Calculators (2)	7/1/18	$294	36 months	$60

All equipment is depreciated using the straight-line method.

As of 12/31/18, he owed $2,000 to his parents who initially helped him get started. They are charging him interest at a 6% annual rate. He has been paying interest only on a monthly basis. His last payment was 12/31/18.

Over the next month or so, he plans to expand his business by selling a few products he believes will help his students. He has already purchased a few items:

Assignment 2A

Math Revealed!

Assignments with the MBC are available in myBusinessCourse.

Category	Description	Vendor	Quantity On Hand	Cost per unit	Sales Price
Books and Tools					
	Geometry in Sports	Books Galore	20	12	16
	Solving Puzzles: Fun with Algebra	Books Galore	20	14	18
	Getting Ready for Calculus	Books Galore	20	15	20
	Protractor/Compass Set	Math Shack	10	10	14
	Handheld Dry-Erase Boards	Math Shack	25	5	9
	Notebooks (pack of 3)	Paper Bag Depot	10	15	20

You already started setting up your company file using the instructions in the "Setting Up Your Company File" section of the chapter. In this assignment, you will be finishing the conversion of Math Revealed! and doing some additional organizing.

FINAL CONVERSION WORK

The basic structure for Math Revealed! was set up in QBO as part of your work on pages 2-7 to 2-22 in this chapter. Now it's time to update all the account balances.

The values for Accounts Receivable, Accounts Payable, and Inventory were brought in when the customer, vendor, and item lists were imported. For example, QBO debited A/R for the balances due from customers included in the customer list. Of course, QBO had to credit some account(s) for the amount, right? The first step will be to determine what those offsetting accounts were and make any necessary corrections.

Click **Reports** on the navigation bar, click **Balance Sheet** in the **Favorites** section, and change the dates to 12/31/18 to 12/31/18.

Click **Run Report**. The report should look something like this:

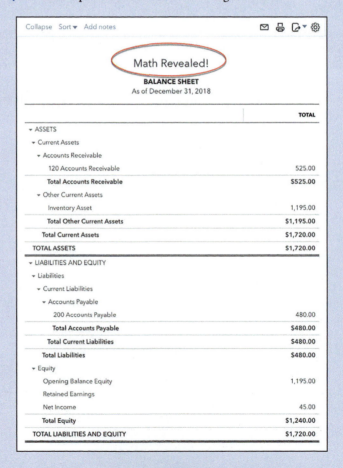

The balances are correct for Accounts Receivable, Accounts Payable, and Inventory but notice the amounts for **Opening Balance Equity** ($1,195) and **Net Income** ($45). **Opening Balance Equity** is a default account credited by QBO when inventory is imported into the system. There is no business account called "opening balance equity."

Click the $1,195 balance to see the underlying transactions. The report should look something like this:

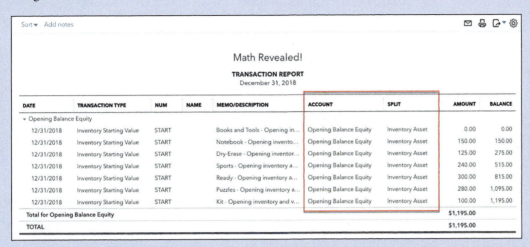

You can see that as part of the import of **items** on hand, the Opening Balance Equity was credited when **Inventory Asset** was debited. You could click each line item to correct the entry. Instead, the entire balance will be adjusted as part of a journal entry created later in this section.

Click **Dashboard** to close the window.

Click **Reports** on the navigation bar and click **Profit and Loss** in the **Favorites** section. Change the dates to 12/31/18 to 12/31/18. (All of the data was imported with an effective date of 12/31.)

Click **Run Report**. The report should look something like this:

Collapse Sort ▾ Add notes

Math Revealed!

PROFIT AND LOSS
December 31, 2018

	TOTAL
▾ Income	
Services	525.00
Total Income	**$525.00**
GROSS PROFIT	**$525.00**
Expenses	
Total Expenses	
NET OPERATING INCOME	**$525.00**
▾ Other Expenses	
700 Interest Expense	480.00
Total Other Expenses	**$480.00**
NET OTHER INCOME	**$ -480.00**
NET INCOME	**$45.00**

QBO has credited an account named **Services** for the $525 balance imported for accounts receivable. **Interest Expense** was debited for the $480 balance imported for accounts payable.

Click the $525 amount in the **Services** row. The report will look something like this:

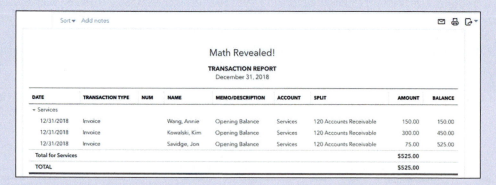

Click the $150.00 amount in the **AMOUNT** column to open the transaction form. The window should look something like this:

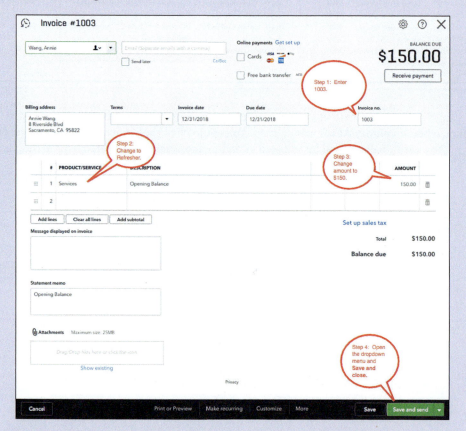

Enter 1003 in the **Invoice no.** field

Since we want to use the Math Revealed! **items** we just set up, we'll need to make a change. Open the dropdown menu in the **PRODUCT/SERVICE** column and select **Refresher**.

When you change the **item** to **Refresher**, QBO will automatically change the **AMOUNT** to 40. That's because the rate for **Refresher** in the imported **item** list was set at $40. The amount due from this customer is $150, though, so you'll need to change the **AMOUNT** column back to $150.

BEHIND THE SCENES QBO allows you to change the sales price for an **item** when a sales form is created. This type of change will not permanently update the price in the **Products and Services** list.

Click **Save and close** to return to the transaction report.

You will need to correct the remaining invoices included on the **Transaction Report** as follows:

- Click Jon Savidge
  - Enter 1002 as the **Invoice No.**
  - Change **PRODUCT/SERVICE** to **Refresher**.
  - Enter 75 in the **AMOUNT** column.
  - Click **Save and close**.

- Click Kim Kowalski
  - Enter 1001 as the **Invoice No.**
  - Change **PRODUCT/SERVICE** to **Refresher**.
  - Enter 300 in the **AMOUNT** column.
  - Click **Save and close**.

Click **Back to report summary** (top left corner of report window) to return to the **Profit and Loss** report.

Click the $480 amount listed for **Interest Expense**. The report looks like this:

As you can see, QBO debited **Interest Expense** to offset the credit to Accounts Payable recorded as part of the import of vendors. Since you will only be recording Math Revealed! activity starting January 1st, we won't take the time to correct these entries. Interest Expense will be closed to Retained Earnings as part of the final journal entry.

The final step is to bring in the remaining **permanent account** balances as of December 31. There's more than one way to do this. The easiest way is to create a journal entry.

Click the ➕ sign on the icon bar. The screen will look something like this:

Permanent account
An account used to prepare the balance sheet—that is, an asset, liability, or stockholders' equity account. Any balance in a permanent account at the end of an accounting period is carried forward to the following accounting period.

Click **Journal Entry**. The screen should look something like this:

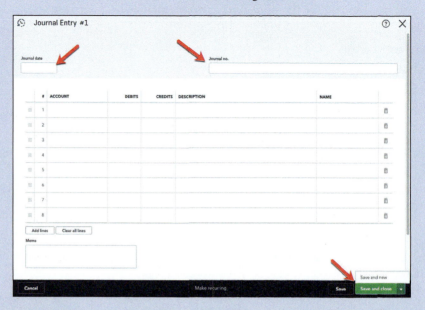

You'll be learning more about journal entries in Chapter 5. For now, the basics are all you need. Change the **Journal date** to 12/31/18 and enter "Opening Entry" as the **Journal no.** Enter the journal entry exactly as it appears below:

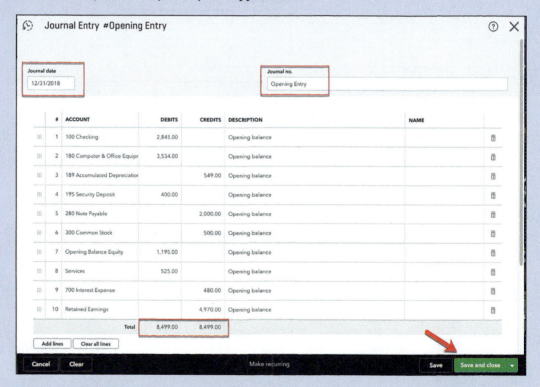

 HINT: You can directly enter the accounts (using account names or numbers) or you can use the dropdown menu. QBO will constantly try to "help" you by populating the debit or credit field with an amount that will balance the entry. Don't get distracted. Continue to enter the amounts as shown in the screenshot above.

Click **Save and close**.

Click **Reports**. Click **Balance Sheet**. Change the dates to 12/31/18 to 12/31/18.

Click **Run report**. The report should look like this:

Math Revealed!

BALANCE SHEET
As of December 31, 2018

	TOTAL
▼ ASSETS	
▼ Current Assets	
▼ Bank Accounts	
100 Checking	2,845.00
Total Bank Accounts	**$2,845.00**
▼ Accounts Receivable	
120 Accounts Receivable	525.00
Total Accounts Receivable	**$525.00**
▼ Other Current Assets	
Inventory Asset	1,195.00
Total Other Current Assets	**$1,195.00**
Total Current Assets	**$4,565.00**
▼ Fixed Assets	
180 Computer & Office Equipment	3,534.00
189 Accumulated Depreciation	-549.00
Total Fixed Assets	**$2,985.00**
▼ Other Assets	
195 Security Deposit	400.00
Total Other Assets	**$400.00**
TOTAL ASSETS	**$7,950.00**
▼ LIABILITIES AND EQUITY	
▼ Liabilities	
▼ Current Liabilities	
▼ Accounts Payable	
200 Accounts Payable	480.00
Total Accounts Payable	**$480.00**
Total Current Liabilities	**$480.00**
▼ Long-Term Liabilities	
280 Note Payable	2,000.00
Total Long-Term Liabilities	**$2,000.00**
Total Liabilities	**$2,480.00**
▼ Equity	
300 Common Stock	500.00
Opening Balance Equity	0.00
Retained Earnings	4,970.00
Net Income	0.00
Total Equity	**$5,470.00**
TOTAL LIABILITIES AND EQUITY	**$7,950.00**

If it does, you're ready to start making some changes in the chart of accounts. If not, go back through the section and see where you went wrong. Although QBO is a fairly easy system to use for day-to-day operations, it can be tough to get everything set up.

CHART OF ACCOUNTS WORK

1/1/19

✓ It's your first day helping out Martin. You take a look at the chart of accounts and notice a few accounts that can be deleted. (Some accounts are QBO default accounts that can't be deleted.) You delete the following accounts:

- Billable Expense Income
- Purchases

NOTE: Although it says "delete," you're actually making the accounts inactive. Inactive accounts can be re-activated, if needed later.

✓ You decide to change the name of the **Services** account to Tutoring. You use 400 as the account number.

✓ You also that several accounts don't have account numbers. You edit the following accounts:

Account Name	New Account Number
Inventory Asset	130
Retained Earnings	350
Sales of Product Income	420
Cost of Goods Sold	500

✓ Although QBO did a great job of importing the chart of accounts (which saved you a LOT of time), sub-account status is not included in the import process. You decide to edit the expense accounts so that you will be able to group the accounts as you'd planned (see the table below). **TIP:** You only need to edit the sub-accounts. The parent accounts are listed so that you know how the accounts should be grouped.

ACCOUNT #	ACCOUNT NAME	
600	Labor costs	Parent
601	Salaries & wages expense	Sub-account
602	Payroll tax expense	Sub-account
610	Vehicle costs	Parent
611	Gasoline expense	Sub-account
615	Vehicles repair & maintenance	Sub-account
620	Facility costs	Parent
621	Rent expense	Sub-account
625	Utilities expense	Sub-account
630	Marketing costs	Parent
631	Advertising expense	Sub-account
635	Client relations expense	Sub-account
640	Office costs	Parent
641	Office supplies expense	Sub-account
649	Office equipment depreciation expense	Sub-account
650	Taxes, insurance, and professional fees	Parent
651	Professional fees	Sub-account
653	Insurance expense	Sub-account
655	Business taxes	Sub-account
690	Other costs	Parent
691	Bank service charges	Sub-account
699	Miscellaneous expense	Sub-account

Reports to create and save for Chapter 2 assignment

All reports can be found by clicking **Reports** on the navigation bar. All reports should be in portrait orientation.

- Balance Sheet (in the **Favorites** section)
  - Report date should be December 31, 2018.
  - Customize the report as follows:
    - In the **General** section, select **(100)** in the **Negative Numbers** dropdown menu. This is a normal accounting convention for displaying negative numbers.
    - In the **Rows/Columns** section, select **Non-zero** for both rows and columns in the **Show non-zero or activity only** dropdown menu.
  - Save as a PDF (export to PDF).

- Account List (in the **For My Accountant** section)
  - Customize the report so just the Account #, Account, and Type columns appear.
  - Save as PDF (export to PDF).

- Product/Service List (in the **Sales and Customers** section)
  - Customize the report so that the following columns appear (in this order):
    - Product/Service
    - Type
    - Description
    - Qty On Hand
    - Price
    - Income Account
    - Cost
    - Expense Account
  - In the **Sort** dropdown menu on report toolbar (left edge), select **TYPE** and click **ascending order**.
  - Save as a PDF (export to PDF).

Background information: Sally Hanson, a good friend of yours, double majored in Computer Science and Accounting in college. She worked for several years for a software company in Silicon Valley but the long hours started to take a toll on her personal life.

Last year she decided to open up her own company, Salish Software Solutions. Sally currently advises clients looking for new accounting software and assists them with software installation. She also provides training to client employees and occasionally troubleshoots software issues.

She has decided to start using QuickBooks Online to keep track of her business transactions. She likes the convenience of being able to access financial information over the Internet. You have agreed to act as her accountant while you're working on your accounting degree.

Sally has a number of clients that she is currently working with. She gives 15-day payment terms to her corporate clients but she asks for cash at time of service if she does work for individuals. She has developed the following fee schedule:

Assignment 2B

Salish Software Solutions

Name	Description	Rate
Select	Software selection	$500 flat fee
Set Up	Software installation	$ 50 per hour
Train	Software training	$ 40 per hour
Fix	File repair	$ 60 per hour

Sally rents office space from Alki Property Management for $800 per month.

The following furniture and equipment is owned by Salish:

Description	Date placed in service	Cost	Life	Salvage Value
Office furniture	6/1/18	$1,400	60 months	$200
Computer	7/1/18	$4,620	36 months	$300
Printer.	5/1/18	$ 900	36 months	$ 0

All equipment is depreciated using the straight-line method.

As of 12/31/18, she owed $3,500 to Dell Finance. The monthly payment on that loan is $150 including interest at 5%. Sally's last payment to Dell was 12/1/18.

Over the next month or so, Sally plans to expand her business by selling some of her favorite accounting and personal software products directly to her clients. She has already purchased the following items.

Item Name	Description	Vendor	Quantity On Hand	Cost per unit	Sales Price
Easy1	Easy Does it	Abacus Shop	15	$100	$175
Retailer.	Simply Retail	Simply Accounting	2	$400	$700
Contractor.	Simply Construction	Simply Accounting	2	$500	$800
Organizer	Organizer	Personal Solutions	25	$ 25	$ 50
Tracker	Investment Tracker	Personal Solutions	25	$ 20	$ 40

Final Conversion Work

Now that the basic structure has been set up in QBO as part of your work on pages 2-7 to 2-22 in this chapter, it's time to update the account balances.

The values for Accounts Receivable, Accounts Payable, and Inventory were brought in when the customer, vendor, and item lists were imported. For example, QBO debited A/R for the balances due from customers included in the customer list. Of course, QBO had to credit some account(s) for the amount, right? The first step will be to determine what those offsetting accounts were and make any necessary corrections.

Click **Reports** on the navigation bar, click **Balance Sheet** in the **Favorites** section, and change the dates to 12/31/18 to 12/31/18.

Click **Run Report**. The report should look something like this:

Collapse Sort ▾ Add notes		✉ 🖨 ⤴▾ ⚙

Salish Software Solutions

BALANCE SHEET
As of December 31, 2018

	TOTAL
▾ ASSETS	
▾ Current Assets	
▾ Accounts Receivable	
120 Accounts Receivable	1,450.00
Total Accounts Receivable	**$1,450.00**
▾ Other Current Assets	
Inventory Asset	4,425.00
Total Other Current Assets	**$4,425.00**
Total Current Assets	**$5,875.00**
TOTAL ASSETS	**$5,875.00**
▾ LIABILITIES AND EQUITY	
▾ Liabilities	
▾ Current Liabilities	
▾ Accounts Payable	
200 Accounts Payable	1,235.00
Total Accounts Payable	**$1,235.00**
Total Current Liabilities	**$1,235.00**
Total Liabilities	**$1,235.00**
▾ Equity	
Opening Balance Equity	4,425.00
Retained Earnings	
Net Income	215.00
Total Equity	**$4,640.00**
TOTAL LIABILITIES AND EQUITY	**$5,875.00**

The balances are correct for Accounts Receivable, Accounts Payable, and Inventory but notice the amounts for **Opening Balance Equity** ($4,425) and **Net Income** ($215). **Opening Balance Equity** is a default account credited by QBO when inventory is imported into the system. There is no business account called "opening balance equity."

Click the $4,425 balance to see the underlying transactions. The report should look something like this:

You can see that as part of the import of **items** on hand, the Opening Balance Equity was credited when Inventory Asset was debited. You could click on each line item to correct the entry. Instead, the entire balance will be adjusted as part of a journal entry created later in this section.

Click **Dashboard** to close the window.

Click **Reports** on the navigation bar and click **Profit and Loss** in the **Favorites** section. Change the dates to 12/31/18 to 12/31/18. (All of the data was imported with an effective date of 12/31.)

Click **Run Report**. The report should look something like this:

Collapse   Sort ▼   Add notes

Salish Software Solutions

PROFIT AND LOSS
December 31, 2018

	TOTAL
▼ Income	
Services	1,450.00
Total Income	**$1,450.00**
GROSS PROFIT	$1,450.00
Expenses	
Total Expenses	
NET OPERATING INCOME	$1,450.00
▼ Other Expenses	
700 Interest expense	1,235.00
Total Other Expenses	**$1,235.00**
NET OTHER INCOME	$ -1,235.00
NET INCOME	$215.00

QBO has credited an account named **Services** for the $1,450 balance imported for accounts receivable. **Interest expense** was debited for the $1,235 balance imported for accounts payable.

Click the $1,450 amount in the **Services** row. The report will look something like this:

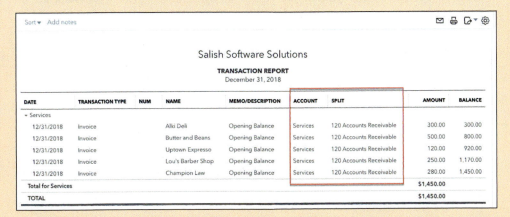

Click the $300.00 amount in the **Amount** column to open the transaction form for Alki Deli. The window should look something like this:

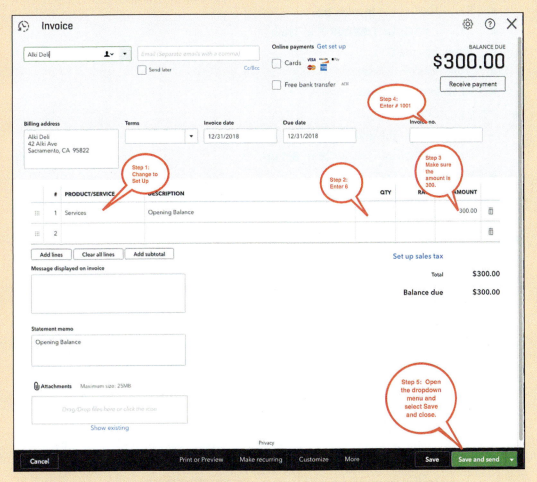

Enter 1001 in the **Invoice no.** field.

Since we want to use the Salish Software Solutions **items** we just set up, we'll need to make a change. Open the dropdown menu in the **PRODUCT/SERVICE** column and select **Set Up**.

When you change the **item** to **Set Up**, QBO will automatically change the **AMOUNT** to 50. That's because the rate for **Set Up** in the imported **item** list was set at $50. The amount due from this customer is $300, though, so you'll need to change the **QTY** to 6.

> **BEHIND THE SCENES** QBO allows you to change the sales price for an **item** when a sales form is created. This type of change will not permanently update the price in the **Products and Services** list.

Click **Save and close** to return to the transaction report.

You will need to correct the remaining invoices included on the **Transaction Report** as follows:

- Click Butter and Beans
    - Enter 1002 as the **Invoice No.**
    - Change **PRODUCT/SERVICE** to **Select**.
    - Enter 1 as the **QTY**.
    - Make sure total is $500.
    - Click **Save and close**.

- Click Champion Law
    - Enter 1003 as the **Invoice No.**
    - Change **PRODUCT/SERVICE** to **Train**.
    - Enter 7 as the **QTY**.
    - Make sure total is $280.
    - Click **Save and close**.

- Click Lou's Barber Shop
    - Enter 1004 as the **Invoice No.**
    - Change **PRODUCT/SERVICE** to **Set Up**.
    - Enter 5 as the **QTY**.
    - Make sure total is $250.
    - Click **Save and close**.

- Click Uptown Espresso
    - Enter 1005 as the **Invoice No.**
    - Change **PRODUCT/SERVICE** to **Fix**.
    - Enter 2 as the **QTY**.
    - Make sure total is $120.
    - Click **Save and close**.

Click **Back to report summary** (top left corner of **Transaction Report** window) to return to the **Profit and Loss** report.

Click the $1,235 amount listed for **Interest expense**. The report looks like this:

DATE	TRANSACTION TYPE	NUM	NAME	MEMO/DESCRIPTION	ACCOUNT	SPLIT	AMOUNT	BALANCE
▾ 700 Interest expense								
12/31/2018	Bill		Abacus Shop		700 Interest expense	200 Accounts Payable	200.00	200.00
12/31/2018	Bill		Simply Accounting		700 Interest expense	200 Accounts Payable	900.00	1,100.00
12/31/2018	Bill		Personal Software		700 Interest expense	200 Accounts Payable	135.00	1,235.00
Total for 700 Interest expense							$1,235.00	
TOTAL							$1,235.00	

Salish Software Solutions
TRANSACTION REPORT
December 31, 2018

As you can see, QBO debited **Interest expense** to offset the credit to Accounts Payable recorded as part of the import of vendors. Since you will only be recording Salish Solutions activity starting January 1st, we won't take the time to correct these entries. Interest expense will be closed to Retained Earnings as part of the final journal entry.

The final step is to bring in the remaining **permanent account** balances as of December 31. There's more than one way to do this. The easiest way is to create a journal entry.

Click the ⊕ sign on the icon bar. The screen will look something like this:

Permanent account An account used to prepare the balance sheet—that is, an asset, liability, or stockholders' equity account. Any balance in a permanent account at the end of an accounting period is carried forward to the following accounting period.

Click **Journal Entry**. The screen should look something like this:

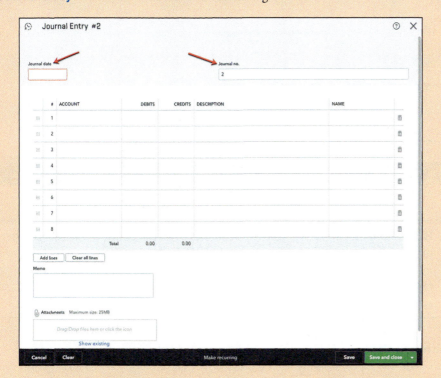

You'll be learning more about journal entries in Chapter 5. For now, the basics are all you need.

Change the **Journal date** to 12/31/18 and enter "Opening Entry" as the **Journal no.**

Enter the journal entry exactly as it appears below:

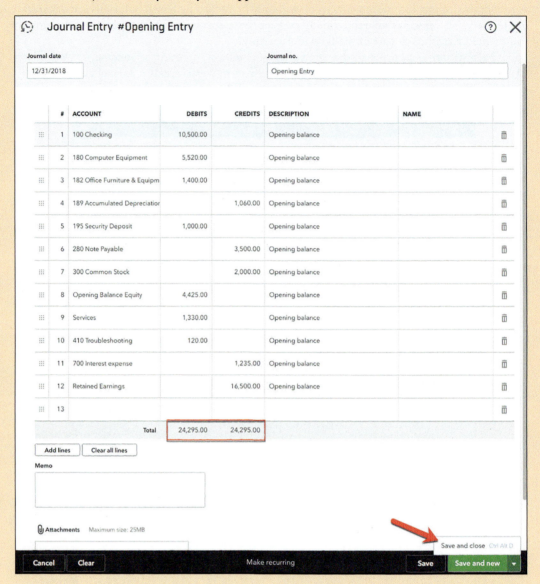

#	ACCOUNT	DEBITS	CREDITS	DESCRIPTION	NAME	
1	100 Checking	10,500.00		Opening balance		
2	180 Computer Equipment	5,520.00		Opening balance		
3	182 Office Furniture & Equipm	1,400.00		Opening balance		
4	189 Accumulated Depreciation		1,060.00	Opening balance		
5	195 Security Deposit	1,000.00		Opening balance		
6	280 Note Payable		3,500.00	Opening balance		
7	300 Common Stock		2,000.00	Opening balance		
8	Opening Balance Equity	4,425.00		Opening balance		
9	Services	1,330.00		Opening balance		
10	410 Troubleshooting	120.00		Opening balance		
11	700 Interest expense		1,235.00	Opening balance		
12	Retained Earnings		16,500.00	Opening balance		
13						
	Total	24,295.00	24,295.00			

HINT: You can directly enter the accounts (using account names or numbers) or you can use the dropdown menu. QBO will constantly try to "help" you by populating the debit or credit field with an amount that will balance the entry. Don't get distracted. Continue to enter the amounts as shown in the screenshot above.

Click **Save and close**.
   Click **Reports**. Click **Balance Sheet**. Change the dates to 12/31/18 to 12/31/18.

Click **Run report**. The report should look like this:

Salish Software Solutions

BALANCE SHEET

As of December 31, 2018

	TOTAL
▾ ASSETS	
▾ Current Assets	
▾ Bank Accounts	
100 Checking	10,500.00
Total Bank Accounts	**$10,500.00**
▾ Accounts Receivable	
120 Accounts Receivable	1,450.00
Total Accounts Receivable	**$1,450.00**
▾ Other Current Assets	
Inventory Asset	4,425.00
Total Other Current Assets	**$4,425.00**
Total Current Assets	**$16,375.00**
▾ Fixed Assets	
180 Computer Equipment	5,520.00
182 Office Furniture & Equipment	1,400.00
189 Accumulated Depreciation	-1,060.00
Total Fixed Assets	**$5,860.00**
▾ Other Assets	
195 Security Deposit	1,000.00
Total Other Assets	**$1,000.00**
TOTAL ASSETS	**$23,235.00**
▾ LIABILITIES AND EQUITY	
▾ Liabilities	
▾ Current Liabilities	
▾ Accounts Payable	
200 Accounts Payable	1,235.00
Total Accounts Payable	**$1,235.00**
Total Current Liabilities	**$1,235.00**
▾ Long-Term Liabilities	
280 Note Payable	3,500.00
Total Long-Term Liabilities	**$3,500.00**
Total Liabilities	**$4,735.00**
▾ Equity	
300 Common Stock	2,000.00
Opening Balance Equity	0.00
Retained Earnings	16,500.00
Net Income	0.00
Total Equity	**$18,500.00**
TOTAL LIABILITIES AND EQUITY	**$23,235.00**

If it does, you're ready to start making some changes in the chart of accounts. If not, go back through the section and see where you went wrong. Although QBO is a fairly easy system to use for day-to-day operations, it can be tough to get everything set up.

Chart of Accounts Work

1/1/19

✓ It's your first day working with Sally. You take a look at the chart of accounts and notice one account that can be deleted. (Some accounts are QBO default accounts that can't be deleted.) You delete the following account:

• Purchases

TIP: Although it says "delete", you're actually making the accounts inactive. Inactive accounts can be re-activated, if needed later.

✓ You change the name of the **Services** account to Software Selection and Installation. You use 400 as the account number.

✓ You also notice that several accounts you'll be using don't have account numbers. You edit the accounts as follows:

Account Name	New Account Number
Inventory Asset	130
Retained Earnings	350
Sales of Product Income	420
Cost of Goods Sold	500

✓ Although QBO did a great job of importing the chart of accounts (which saved you a LOT of time), sub-account status is not included in the import process. You decide to edit the expense accounts so that you will be able to group the accounts as you'd planned (see the table below).. **TIP:** You only need to edit the sub-accounts. The parent accounts are listed so that you know how the accounts should be grouped.

ACCOUNT #	ACCOUNT NAME	
600	Labor Costs	Parent
601	Salaries & wages expense	Sub-account
602	Payroll tax expense	Sub-account
610	Professional Development	Parent
611	Technical reading materials	Sub-account
615	Software seminars	Sub-account
620	Facility Costs	Parent
621	Rent expense	Sub-account
622	Telephone expense	Sub-account
625	Utilities expense	Sub-account
630	Marketing Costs	Parent
631	Advertising expense	Sub-account t
635	Client relations expense	Sub-account
640	Office Costs	Parent
641	Office supplies expense	Sub-account
649	Depreciation expense	Sub-account
650	Taxes, Insurance, and Professional Fees	Parent
651	Professional fees	Sub-account
653	Insurance expense	Sub-account
655	Business tax expense	Sub-account
690	Other Costs	Parent
691	Bank service charges	Sub-account
699	Miscellaneous expense	Sub-account

Reports to create and save for Chapter 2 assignment

All reports can be found by clicking Reports on the navigation bar. All reports should be in portrait orientation.

- Balance Sheet (in the Favorites section)
  - Report date should be December 31, 2018.
  - Customize the report as follows:
    - In the General section, select (100) in the Negative Numbers dropdown menu. This is a normal accounting convention for displaying negative numbers.
    - In the Rows/Columns section, select Non-zero for both rows and columns in the Show non-zero or activity only dropdown menu.
  - Save as a PDF (export to PDF).
- Account List (in the For My Accountant section)
  - Customize the report so just the Account #, Account, and Type columns appear.
  - Save as a PDF (export to PDF).
- Product/Service List (in the Sales and Customers section)
  - Customize the report so that only the following columns appear (in this order):
    - Product/Service
    - Type
    - Description
    - Qty On Hand
    - Price
    - Income Account
    - Cost
    - Expense Account
  - Sort the list by **Type** in ascending order.
  - Save as a PDF (export to PDF).

APPENDIX 2A SETTING UP YOUR GOOGLE GMAIL ACCOUNT

If this is Your First Gmail Account

Open your Internet browser and enter www.google.com as the URL. You should see the following screen.

Click **Sign In**. The next screen should look something like this:

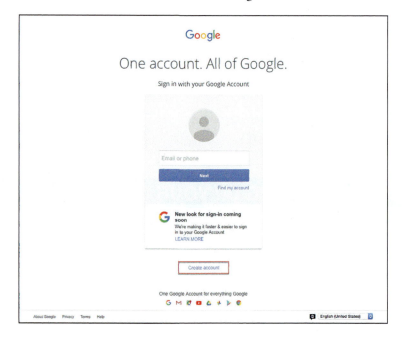

Click **Create Account** to set up your new Gmail address and enter other information requested by Google.

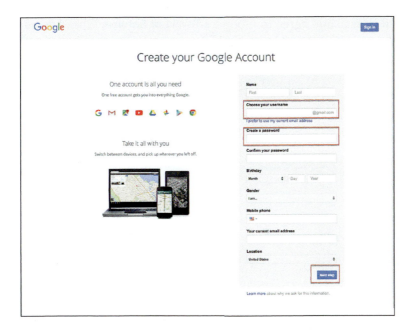

You may want to use your own name followed by your homework company name or your accounting course number as your Gmail address. For example, my Gmail address might be GayleWilliamsACCT341@gmail.com is automatically added by Google.

The password you create next should be unique. You should not use a password that you use for other purposes.

Answer the rest of the questions on the screen and click **Next step**.

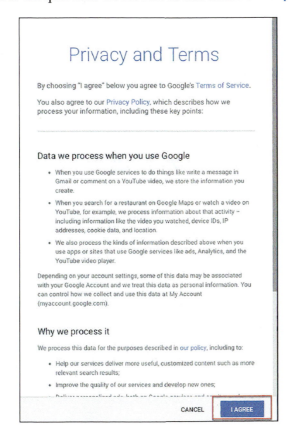

You will need to read and agree to Google's **Terms of Service**. Click **I agree** when you've completed your review.

The **Welcome** screen will include your new Gmail address.

If You Already Have a Gmail Account

It's probably best to set up a new Gmail account for use with your homework assignments. That way you won't get personal email in with school email if your instructor uses the Gmail account associated with your company file.

To set up a new Gmail account, open your Internet browser and enter www.google.com as the URL.

Click **Sign In**. Sign in using your existing Gmail account.

Click your account icon at the top right corner of the page. The screen should look something like this:

Click **Add account** to progress to the next screen.

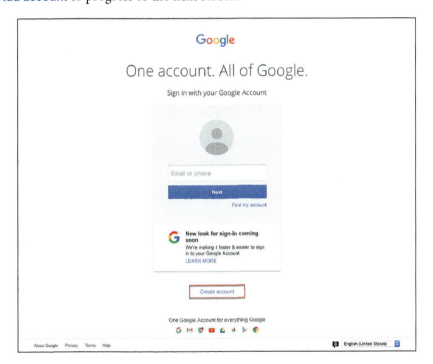

Click **Create account** to set up your new Gmail address and enter other information requested by Google.

If you see a **Choose an account** screen instead of the one shown above, click **Use another account**, click **More options**, then click **Create account**.

You may want to use your own name followed by your homework company name or your accounting course number as your Gmail address. For example, my Gmail address might be GayleWilliamsACCT341@gmail.com is automatically added by Google.

The password you create next should be unique. You should not use a password that you use for other purposes.

Answer the rest of the questions on the screen and click **Next step**.

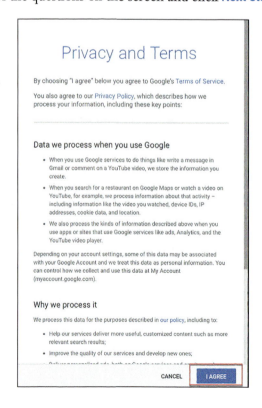

You will need to read and agree to Google's **Terms of Service**. Click **I agree** when you've completed your review.

The **Welcome** screen will include your new Gmail address.

QuickBooks

Service Companies

Businesses are frequently classified by primary source of revenue.

- Service companies earn revenue by charging a fee for services they perform.

- Merchandising companies earn revenue by buying products from one company and selling those products to consumers (or to distributors).

- Manufacturing companies earn revenue by making products and selling them to consumers (or to merchandisers).

In this textbook, we'll be looking at how QuickBooks Online can be used by service and merchandising companies. Currently, the features needed for managing inventory in a manufacturing company are not available in QBO. There are, however, a few apps (add-on products) that can be purchased by manufacturing companies interested in using QBO.

We'll look at service companies first because the accounting for service companies is, in general, the least complex.

WHEN YOU MAKE MISTAKES

QBO is very forgiving. You can change, void, or delete most transactions pretty much at will.

Just remember, in a regular company transactions are not generally changed or deleted if the transaction has been completed. (For example, the invoice has been sent out or a deposit has been brought to the bank.) Why? Because the transaction has already occurred. (The customer has the invoice. The bank has recorded the deposit.) Instead, errors are corrected by creating a new transaction. (A credit memo is issued. An additional deposit is recorded.) In some cases, transactions can be voided. For example, a check was written but not mailed. The check physically exists but it can be voided and not sent out.

That being said, we're not in a real business so you will probably want to edit or delete transactions that you enter incorrectly in your homework assignments.

There is one thing you need to know before you start changing or deleting transactions in QuickBooks Online. Oftentimes, transactions are related. For example, you record a customer invoice. You record the customer payment of that invoice. You record the deposit of the customer payment. Those are three related transactions that are linked in QBO. If you attempt to change a linked transaction, QBO will give you a warning.

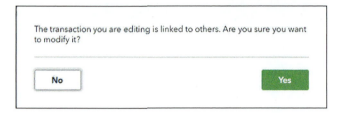

Although QBO will allow you to make the change, related transactions will likely be automatically changed by QBO as well. Make sure you consider the full impact of your changes.

> **BEHIND THE SCENES** In QBO, deleted transactions don't appear on reports. Voided transactions do appear but with zero dollar amounts. (Keeping a record of voided transactions is a good internal control policy.)

Suggestions for Finding Mistakes

You will be given check figures to help you as you complete your homework assignments. If all your numbers agree to the check figures, you have a reasonably good chance of having completed the assignment correctly. (Agreeing to check figures is not a **guarantee** that all the entries are recorded correctly but it's certainly a comfort!)

What if you don't agree? Where do you start looking? Here are some suggestions.

- **CHECK DATES.** Entering an incorrect date is the single most common cause of student errors (and student headaches!). QBO enters default dates when you first open a form. It defaults to the current date when you start entering transactions during a work session. If you change the date on the first invoice, it will default to that new date when you enter the second invoice. If you open a new form, however, it will default back to the current date. Accounting is date driven, so your financial statements won't match the check figures if you enter a transaction in the wrong month. First thing to do? Pull a report of transactions dated BEFORE the first transaction date in the assignment and then one of transactions dated AFTER the last transaction date of the assignment.

Double-entry accounting A method of accounting that results in the recording of equal amounts of debits and credits.

Debit An entry on the left side (or in the debit column) of an account.

Credit An entry on the right side (or in the credit column) of an account.

- **There are always two sides to every story.** This is **double-entry accounting** so if one account is wrong, then at least one other account is also wrong. It's hard to find errors in cash, accounts receivable, and accounts payable due to the sheer volume of transactions that affect these accounts. So, if your numbers don't match the check figures, see if you can find the other account(s) that is (are) also off. If you can find the error(s), you can fix all the affected accounts.

- **Debits on the left, credits on the right.** QBO gets the debit and credit part down really well when it comes to standard transactions (invoices, checks, etc.). However, when it comes to journal entries, QBO relies completely on you. It will debit (credit) whatever you tell it to debit (credit). We're all human. Sometimes we get our journal entries reversed. You can often fairly quickly spot those errors by looking at the balance sheet. Does Accumulated Depreciation show a debit balance? That's a problem. Look at supplies accounts, prepaid accounts, and accrued expense accounts and see if the balances look reasonable. Adjusting journal entries are frequently made to those accounts.

- **Math hints.** Errors can also be found, sometimes, by checking the difference between the check figure and your total. Is the number divisible by nine? You may have a transposition error (for example, you entered 18 instead of 81). All differences due to transposition errors are divisible by nine. Is the difference equal to the amount of a transaction? Maybe you forgot to enter it (or entered it on the wrong date). Is the difference equal to twice one of your transactions? You may have entered in a journal entry backwards (watch those debits and credits!).

SECTION OVERVIEW

Chapter 2 will cover the sales cycle in a service company.
Chapter 3 will cover the purchase cycle in a service company.
Chapter 4 will cover end-of-period accounting in a service company.

3

Sales Activity
(Service Company)

Objectives

After completing Chapter 3, you should be able to:

1. Set up standard sales settings.

2. Add and edit customers.

3. Add and edit **service items**.

4. Set up credit terms.

5. Record sales on account and cash sales.

6. Record and apply credit memos.

7. Record customer refunds.

8. Record customer payments on account.

9. Record deposits to bank.

10. Create and modify sales and receivables reports.

WHAT IS THE SALES CYCLE IN A SERVICE COMPANY?

The sales cycle in a service company normally follows these steps:

- Get the job (client).

- Provide the service.

- Bill for the service.

- Collect the fee.

Getting the job (or the client) is outside the accounting function, but the accounting system does need to maintain records related to the transactions with every customer.

At the very least, the following information must be maintained for each customer:

- Contact information

- Terms of payment

- Record of past transactions

- Record of any unpaid invoices

SETTING UP STANDARD SALES SETTINGS

Companies may have standard policies applicable to all customers. For example, a company might have standard credit (payment) terms. Some companies send out bills in batches. Invoices might be created when work is performed but instead of printing the invoice immediately, it is batched with other invoices and printed later.

Settings in QBO can be changed to reflect those policies.

Click the **gear** icon in the navigation bar. Click **Account and Settings**.

Click **Sales**. Click **Sales form content** (or the **pencil** icon) in the top right corner, to open the section for editing. The window should look like this:

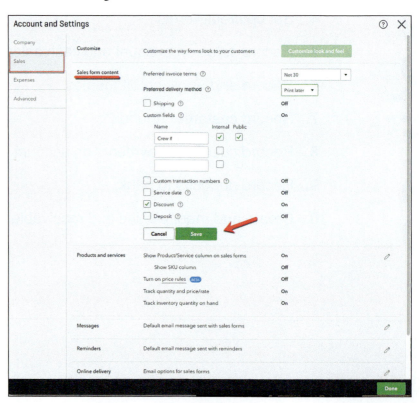

Settings are changed by checking or unchecking the boxes to turn features on or off. Features with multiple options use dropdown menus.

Clicking **Save** updates the features.

The **Sales** tab would look like this for a company that:

- had standard payment terms of Net 10

- did not do batch processing

- gave discounts to customers on occasion

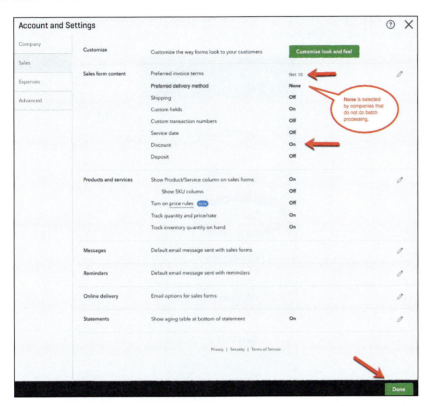

Clicking **Done** exits **Account and Settings**.

> **BEHIND THE SCENES** The settings selected are defaults. Many defaults can be changed when specific transactions are entered.

Make some changes to the sales settings for Craig's Design and Landscaping.

1. Change settings.

   a. Click the **gear** on the icon bar.

   b. Click **Account and Settings**.

   c. Click **Sales**.

   d. Click **Preferred invoice terms**.

   e. **Make a note** of the various terms available in QBO.

PRACTICE EXERCISE

(continued)

> *f.* Select **Net 15** as the preferred terms.
>
> *g.* Click **Save**.
>
> *h.* Click **Done** to close the **settings** window.

MANAGING CUSTOMERS

Customers are managed in the Customer Center. The Customer Center is accessed through the **Sales** link on the navigation bar.

Select the **Customers** tab.

The Customer Center screen looks something like this:

At the top right side of the screen are three small icons.

The **printer** icon (far left) allows users to print a list of all vendors. The list includes all customer information included on the screen.

Clicking the **export** icon (the middle icon) automatically downloads the list as an Excel file.

Clicking the third icon (the **gear**) allows users to customize the fields displayed in the Customer Center.

In the Customer Center, you can:

- access the new customer setup window.

- access forms necessary to record activity with existing customers.

- access existing customer data for editing.

Modifying the Customer Center Display

The columns displayed in the Customer Center can be modified by clicking the **gear** icon.

> **BEHIND THE SCENES** Having the phone number and/or the email address displayed can be time-saving for accountants working directly with customers on a regular basis.

Adding a Customer

To add a new customer, open the Customer Center by clicking **Sales** in the navigation bar and selecting the **Customer** tab.

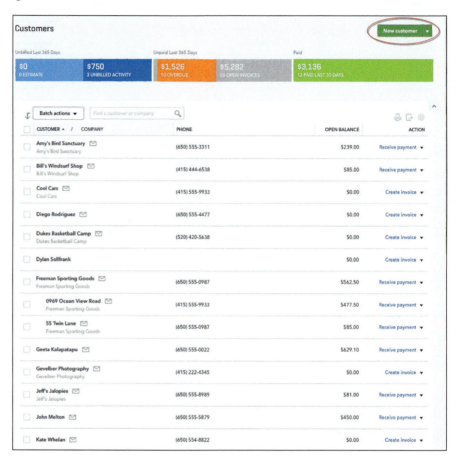

Click **New customer** to open the **Customer Information** window. It should look something like this:

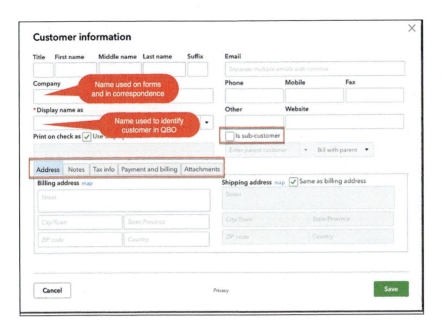

The name entered in the **Company** field is the name used in any correspondence with the customer (on invoices for example).

The **Display Name** is used as a customer identifier. It could be a number or a shortened version of the name. This is the primary name used to organize the customer list. It's also the name used in any search functions. The **Display Name** is used for internal purposes only and would not appear on customer correspondence. In this class, we'll use the **Company** name as the **Display Name**.

Phone and other contact information is entered in the top section of the **Customer Information** window. If the company were tracking various projects for a customer or a customer was a branch location, the project or branch should be set up as a sub-customer. (Project tracking will be covered in Chapter 10.)

As you can see in the screenshot above, there are five tabs in the lower left section of the window. Billing and shipping addresses are included on the **Address** tab.

The **Payment and billing** tab looks something like this:

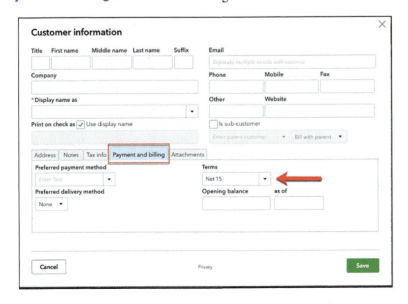

Default credit terms for the customer are noted on the **Payment and billing** tab. This is an important field. Payment terms need to be communicated to customers and payment status needs to be tracked by companies. Users can also indicate information about the customer's preferred payment method (check, cash, credit card, etc.). If the user normally prints or emails invoices in batches, that would be noted in the **Preferred delivery method** field. If batch processing is not appropriate, **None** would be selected in the field. Remember: these are all defaults. Terms and payment methods can be changed when a specific sales transaction is entered.

A new sales tax feature was added to QBO in 2017. All customers are now identified as taxable unless the user provides exemption details in the **Tax Info** tab of the customer record.

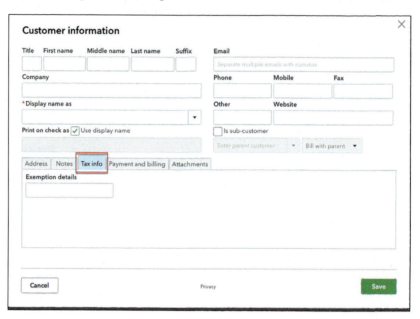

WARNING: At the time this textbook was printed, the new sales tax feature was not included in the test drive company. If it's still not included, the Tax Info tab in the test drive company will not match the screenshot above.

Sales taxes will be covered in Chapter 6.

The **Notes** tab can be used for adding unique information about the customer. There are no fields in the **Notes** tab.

If companies have other documents that apply specifically to the customer, they can be uploaded to the **Attachments** tab. **Attachments** will be discussed in Chapter 12.

Viewing Customer Information

To view information about a specific customer, click the customer's name in the Customer Center. The new window that opens should look something like this:

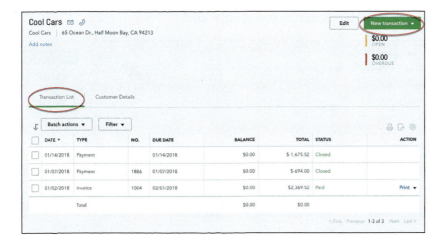

On the **Transaction List** tab, prior transactions are listed. Double clicking any of the trans-actions listed will open the appropriate form. You can also add new transactions through this screen by clicking **New transaction**.

Basic information about the customer is included on the **Customer Details** tab.

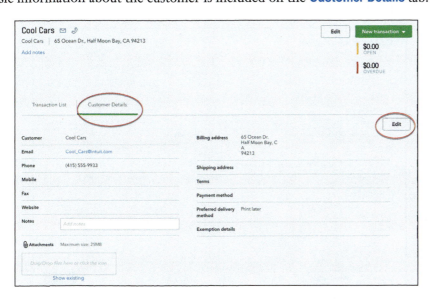

Clicking the **Edit** link allows users to change customer details. Customer information can also be changed using the procedure outlined in the "Changing Customer Information" section below.

Changing Customer Information

Customer information can be changed at any time. To edit an existing customer, open the Customer Center by clicking **Customers** in the navigation bar.

Click the name of the company you wish to edit.

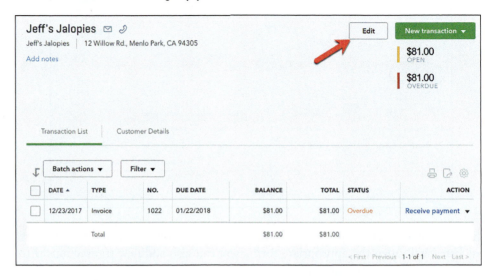

Click **Edit** to open the **Customer Information** window.

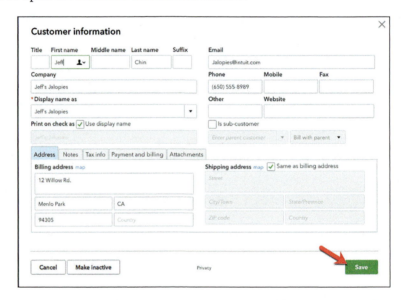

Make the desired changes and click **Save** to close the window.

Inactivating a Customer

Although customers with activity (current or past) cannot be deleted, customers can be identified as inactive.

To inactivate a customer, open the Customer Center by clicking **Customers** in the navigation bar.

On the dropdown menu in the far-right column of the customer name, select **Make inactive**. This option wouldn't be available on the dropdown menus for customers with open balances.

Inactive customers can't be used in transactions and aren't visible in the Customer Center unless the user elects to show inactive customers, although they will show up on appropriate reports.

To reactivate a customer, all inactive customers must be visible in the Customer Center. Click the **gear** icon right above the **ACTION** column in the Customer Center to make inactive customers visible.

An option to reactivate the customer will now appear in the **Action** column next to the customer name.

© 2019 Cambridge Business Publishers

PRACTICE
EXERCISE

Add and edit customers for Craig's Design and Landscaping.
(Craig's gets a new client and receives an address change for an existing client.)

1. Click **Sales** (navigation bar).

2. Click the **Customers** tab.

3. Click **New Customer** and set up Barrio Café as a new customer:
   a. Enter "Barrio Cafe" in the **Company** field.
   b. Tab to the **Phone** field and enter "415-199-2222."
   c. Leave the checkmark next to **Use display name**.
   d. In the **Billing Address** section:
      i. Enter "1515 Oceanspray Drive; Sausalito, CA 94965"
   e. Click the **Payment and billing** tab.
      i. Select **Net 15** in the **Terms** dropdown menu.
      ii. Click **Save**.

4. Click **Sales** (navigation bar).

5. Click the **Customers** tab.

6. Edit a customer. (Change the billing address for Jeff's Jalopies.)
   a. Click the name **Jeff's Jalopies** in the Customer Center.

(continued)

<blockquote>
b.   Click **Edit**.

c.   Change street address to "4848 Dragrace Road."

d.   Open the **Payment and billing** tab and select **Net 15** as the **Terms**.

e.   **Make a note of** Jeff's last name.

f.   Click **Save**.

g.   Click **Dashboard**.
</blockquote>

MANAGING SERVICE ITEMS

As you might recall from Chapter 1, there are various types of **items**. In this chapter, we are concerned only with **service items**. **Service items** represent charges for the various services performed by a company as part of its regular operations and are used when entering sales transactions and when reporting sales activity.

The following information is included in the setup of a **service item**:

- The standard rate (price) to be charged to the client.

- The description that should appear on a client invoice.

- The income account that should be credited when the client is charged.

Each **item** can be associated with only one general ledger account but one general ledger account can be associated with many **items**. This allows the company to keep considerable detail in subsidiary ledgers but keep the general ledger (and the financial statements) relatively simple.

Items are set up through the **Products and Services Center**.

To access the center, click the **gear** on the icon bar and select **Products and Services** under **Lists**. The screen should look something like this:

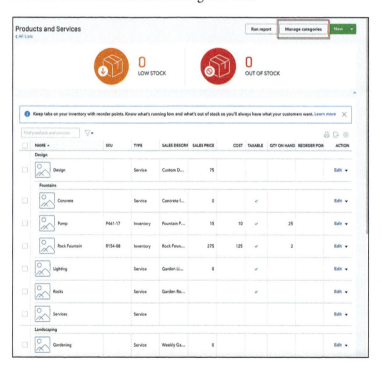

Organizing Items

Items can be grouped into **categories** in QBO. Grouping **items** makes it easier for users to access (find) specific **items** when entering specific transactions. Grouping also makes it easier to create effective reports about company operations.

> **BEHIND THE SCENES** **Categories** are only used for organizing **items**. Assigning an **item** to a **category** does not determine the general ledger account debited or credited when the **item** is used in a transaction. See the **Adding a Service Item** section in this chapter for information about assigning general ledger accounts to **items**.

To set up **categories**, click the **gear** on the icon bar and select **Products and Services** under **Lists**.

 HINT: You should have activated the **categories** feature as part of homework company file. If you missed that step, click **Sales** on the navigation bar and open the **Products and Services** tab. You should see a message with instructions for activating **categories**.
> **TIP:** **Categories** is a relatively new feature in QBO. If your homework company file does not have the feature, you will be able to use **sub-items** as a substitute. Working with **sub-items** is covered in Appendix 2A.

Click **Manage categories**. The screen should look something like this:

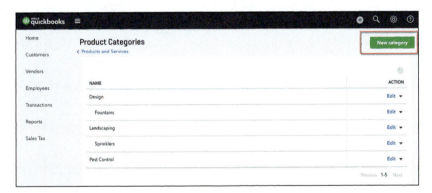

To add a new **category**, click **New category.** A sidebar will open:

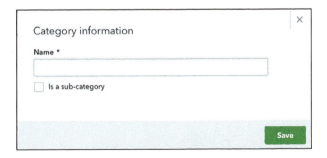

Enter a category name.

Users can group categories together by identifying sub-categories. Up to three **sub-categories** can be created for each primary **category**.

BEHIND THE SCENES On reports, the entire name (including the category and all sub-categories) will appear. This can be quite confusing to viewers of the report. In a small company, having only one level of sub-categories is probably the best practice.

Categories can be changed or deleted. Open the **Products and Services** list.

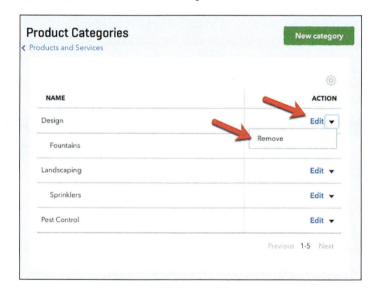

Select **Manage categories** on the **More** dropdown menu.

Click **Edit** to change the name or **Remove** to delete the **category**. If you delete a **category**, any related **sub-categories** will be moved up one level.

To return to the **Products and Services** list, click the **back arrow** under **Product Categories**.

Adding a Service Item

To add a new **service item**, click the **gear** on the icon bar and select **Products and Services** under **Lists**.

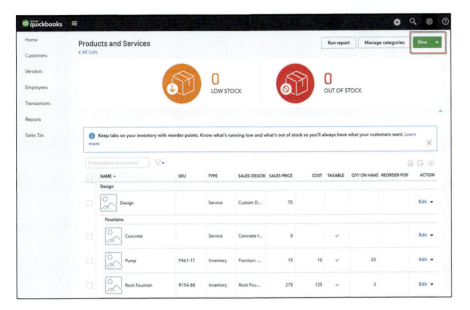

Click **New**. A sidebar will appear that looks like this:

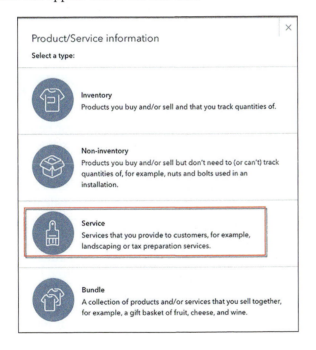

Click **Service** to open the **service item** setup window:

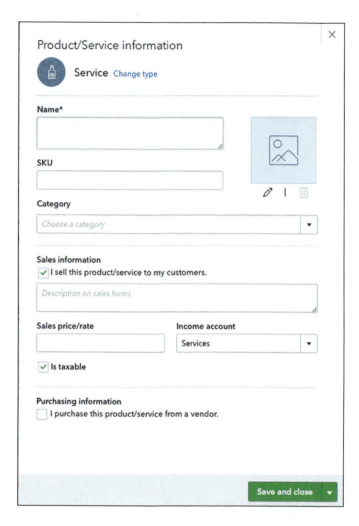

An **item** name must be entered and an **Income account** must be identified. The general ledger account identified here is the account that will be credited (debited) when a sale (credit) transaction is recorded.

The following fields are also available:

- **SKU**—a SKU (stock keeping unit) is a product or service identification code assigned by the company.
  - A SKU is similar to the UPCs (Universal Product Codes) used by most retailers. Both are codes used for tracking purposes. The difference is that a SKU is unique to a particular company. UPCs are standardized for all businesses.

- **Category**—group assigned for tracking purposes

- **Sales information**—the default description that will appear on all sales forms

- **Sales price/rate**—the default selling price

Because most services are not taxable in most states, you would deselect (uncheck) **Is taxable** when creating a service item.

If a service may be performed by an outside vendor (an independent contractor for example), **I purchase this product/service from a vendor** should be checked. If the box is checked, the sidebar will expand to show the following:

Default descriptions and costs (rates) can be entered. The defaults appear when a transaction with the vendor is entered. The general ledger account to be debited when the purchase of the service is recorded is identified in the **Expense account** field.

Editing Items

To edit **items**, click the **gear** on the icon bar and select **Products and Services**.

Click **Edit** in the **ACTION** column of the appropriate item. You can edit the **item** name or description, the default rate, the general ledger account associated with the **item**, and any other fields. If you edit the general ledger account associated with the **item**, you will be asked if you want to update existing transactions (called historical transactions in QBO) in addition to changing the account for future transactions:

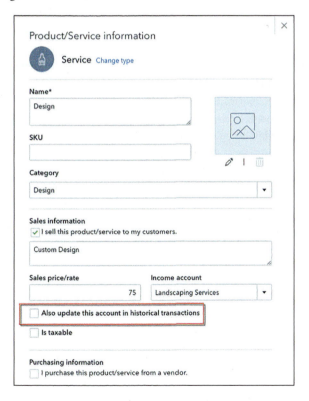

Items can also be duplicated.

A user might choose to duplicate an item instead of creating a new item from scratch to save time. Only the name would need to be changed if all other selections (rates, categories, etc.) were the same.

> **BEHIND THE SCENES** If the duplicated item name isn't changed by the user, QBO will save the new item using the original name and adding—copy at the end. For example, if the Deck Design item was duplicated and the name wasn't changed, the new item would be saved with the name Deck Design—copy.

Items can be made inactive but cannot be deleted.

PRACTICE EXERCISE

Add and edit items for Craig's Design and Landscaping.

(Craig's Design and Landscaping has decided to offer deck design and construction. It will start by working only on residential projects but the company may later decide to expand its deck business so it sets up a new category (Decks) with two sub-categories (Commercial and Residential). Because it will be designing and constructing decks, it sets up two service items (Deck Design and Deck Construction). All deck income is to be tracked in the Other Income general ledger account. It also needs to adjust the default rate for landscaping hours.)

1. Set up categories.
   a. Click the **gear** icon and select **Products and Services** in the **Lists** column.
   b. Click **Manage categories** in the **More** dropdown menu in the top right corner.
      i. Click **New category**.
      ii. Enter "Decks" as the name.
      iii. Click **Save**.
   c. Add another **category**.
      i. Click **New category**.
      ii. Enter "Commercial" as the name.
      iii. Check **Is a sub-category**.
      iv. Select **Decks** in the dropdown menu.

(continued)

     v. Click **Save**.

d. Add another **category**.

     i. Click **New category**.

     ii. Enter "Residential" as the name.

     iii. Check **Is a sub-category**.

     iv. Select **Decks** in the dropdown menu.

     v. Click **Save**.

e. **Make a note** of the number of primary **categories** there are in the category list. (This would include the primary category you just set up.)

f. **Make a note** of the name of the **sub-category** under **Landscaping**.

g. Click the **back arrow** under **Product Categories** to return to **Products and Services**.

     i. You should now be in the **Products and Services** list window.

h. Click **New**.

     i. Select **Service**.

     ii. Enter "Deck Design" as the **Name**.

     iii. Select **Decks:Residential** as the **Category**.

     iv. Enter "Deck design work" as the description.

     v. Enter "75" as the **Sales price/rate**.

     vi. Select **Design Income** as the **Income account**.

     vii. Remove the check next to **Is taxable**.

     viii. Click **Save and close**

i. Click **New**.

     i. Select **Service**.

     ii. Enter "Deck Construction" as the **Name**.

     iii. Select **Decks:Residential** as the **Category**.

     iv. Enter "Deck construction work" as the description.

     v. Enter "40" as the **Sales price/rate**.

     vi. Select **Services** as the **Income account**.

     vii. Remove the check next to **Is taxable**.

     viii. Check **I purchase this product/service from a vendor**.

     ix. Enter "Deck Construction Work" as the **description**.

     x. Enter "35" as the **Cost** and **Cost of Labor** as the **Expense account**.

     xi. Click **Save and close**.

j. Click **Edit** next to **Hours** under **Landscaping**.

     i. Enter "50" as the **Sales price/rate**.

     ii. Click **Save and close**.

k. **Make a note** of the default sales price set for **Installation** (a sub-category of **Landscaping**).

l. Click **Dashboard** to exit the **Products and Services** list.

SETTING UP CREDIT TERMS

Companies that sell on account set up payment terms for their customers to let them know when payment is due and whether there's a discount if they pay early. A company can, of course, have different terms for different customers.

Required payment dates are usually based on the vendor invoice date. Payment would be due a certain number of days after the date of the invoice. Payment terms of 10, 15, and 30 days are common choices.

Some companies set a particular day of the month as the payment due date. A common date is the last day of the month. An invoice dated January 3rd would be due on January 31st. An invoice dated January 23rd would also be due on the 31st. Companies that use a date driven payment term will usually give an extra month for invoices dated close to the payment date. For example, if the payment date were the last day of the month, an invoice dated January 29th would be due at the end of February instead of the end of January.

A new credit term can be set up within a bill (or invoice) form by selecting **Add new** at the top of the **Terms** dropdown menu.

New credit terms can also be created by clicking the **gear** icon on the icon bar.

Click **All Lists.**

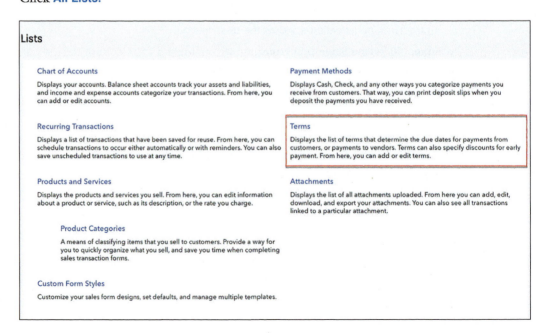

Click **Terms.**

A **Name** for the new term must be entered. Users can either create a new term that is based on the invoice date (**Due in fixed number of days**) or a term that is based on a particular day (**Due by certain day of the month**). The window would look something like this if a user created a new term called EOM that required payment by the last day of the month unless the bill was issued during the last five days of the month.

A credit term that included a discount if payment was made within a certain period can also be entered in QBO. The window would look like this if a user created a new term that offered a 2% discount if payment was made within 10 days of the invoice date and full payment is due no later than 30 days after the invoice date.

At the time this book was written, QBO was not able to automatically keep track of early payment discounts so discounts must be manually entered when the bill is paid. This feature will likely be available in future versions of QBO.

RECORDING SALES REVENUE

In a manual accounting system:

- An invoice is created.

- The invoice is recorded in the sales journal if sales are made on account and in the cash receipts journal for cash sales.

- The journals are posted, in total, to the general ledger.

- Each transaction in the sales journal is posted to the appropriate customer's subsidiary ledger.

In QBO:

- A form is completed for each sale.
  - Each **transaction type** has its own form.

- When the form is saved, QBO automatically records the transaction in the sales journal and automatically posts the transaction to the general ledger and to the appropriate subsidiary ledger.

Because everything is done automatically the form must include all the relevant information needed.

- Who is the customer? (Customer name is needed for posting to the subsidiary ledger.)

- What are we charging them for? (What general ledger account should QBO credit?)

- Have they paid already or will they pay later? (What general ledger account should QBO debit?)

We've already got the customers and the **items** set up so QBO knows which subsidiary ledger should be updated and which income accounts should be credited when the sales form is completed. But how does QBO know which account to debit in a sale? Should it be Cash or Accounts Receivable? QBO solves that problem by setting up two different forms (two separate transaction types).

> **BEHIND THE SCENES** For processing purposes, QBO assigns certain default accounts for common transactions. For example, the default debit account for recording a sale on account is Accounts Receivable. The default credit account for recording a bill from a vendor is Accounts Payable. These accounts are automatically set up (categorized with the proper account type) by QBO. The user can change the name of the account but not the type.

Recording Sales on Account

The form (**transaction type**) used to record **sales on account** is the **Invoice**. The default debit account for **invoices** is Accounts Receivable (A/R).

> **WARNING: Although multiple accounts can be set up in QB Online using account type Accounts Receivable (A/R), only one A/R account can be associated with sales transactions in the current version of QBO. If a company wanted to track accounts receivable in multiple accounts, it would need to be done through journal entries.**

The credit account(s) in the journal entry underlying an invoice transaction will depend, of course, on the **items** included on the invoice. As explained earlier in this chapter, the general ledger account associated with a specific **item** is set up through the **Products and Services** list.

The **invoice** form can be accessed:

- by clicking the ➕ icon on the icon bar and selecting **Invoice** in the **Customers** column.

- by clicking **Sales** on the navigation bar and selecting **Invoice** in the **New transaction** dropdown menu on the **All Sales** tab.

- by clicking **Sales** on the navigation bar and selecting **New invoice** on the **Invoices** tab.

- by clicking **Sales** on the navigation bar, clicking the **Customer** tab, and selecting **Create invoice** in the **Action** column dropdown menu for the customer.

The **Invoice** form looks something like this:

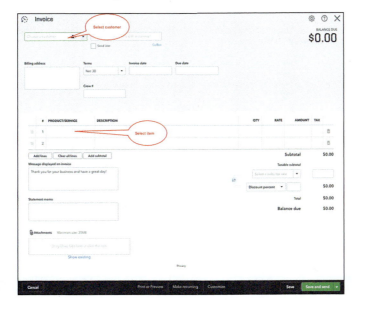

Although invoice numbers do not appear on the screen when an invoice is first created if QBO default settings are active, an invoice (transaction) number is automatically assigned by QBO when the invoice is saved.

> **BEHIND THE SCENES** Companies that want more control over invoice numbers can elect to create custom transaction numbers. To make that election, click the **gear** icon (top right corner of the **invoice**). Check **Custom transaction numbers**. A new field (**Invoice no.**) will automatically appear on sales forms. The election can also be made in the **Sales form content** section of the **Sales** tab in **Account and Settings**. **Custom transaction numbers** were activated in your homework company file as part of the setup process.

To complete an **invoice**, you must enter the customer name, the invoice date, the credit terms, and the **items** to be charged to the customer.

Common credit terms are automatically set up in QBO. They are accessible through the dropdown menu in the **Terms** field.

Setting up new credit terms was covered in the "Setting Up Credit Terms" section of this chapter.

The default customer message set up in the **Sales** tab of **Account and Settings** appears at the bottom of the **invoice**. The message can be modified or deleted for a specific invoice.

For this class, the **Send later** box (under the email address field at the top of the form) and the **Print later** box (in the **Print or Preview** dropdown menu at the bottom of the form) should not be checked.

These options allow you to create batches to be processed later. Once you turn them off for one transaction, they will remain off for other transactions of the same type. If you're using the test drive company, you'll need to turn them off each time you log back in.

To record an **invoice** click **Save and close** (or **Save and new** if you are recording multiple invoices) in the bottom right corner of the form.

> **BEHIND THE SCENES** Remember: As soon as you save a transaction, a journal entry is created and posted to the general ledger and the subsidiary ledgers and financial statements are updated.

Recording Cash Sales

The **transaction type** (form) used to record cash sales is the **Sales Receipt**. The debit default account for **sales receipts** is an asset account called Undeposited Funds although you can elect to record the debit directly to a **Bank** account. (Find out more about the Undeposited Funds account later in this chapter under the section "Making Deposits.") The credit accounts for **sales receipts** depend on the **items** included in the sale.

The **Sales Receipt** form can be accessed in three ways:

- by clicking the ➕ icon on the icon bar and selecting **Sales Receipt** in the **Customers** column.

- by clicking **Sales** on the navigation bar and selecting **Sales Receipt** in the **New transaction** dropdown menu on the **All Sales** tab.

- by clicking **Sales** on the navigation bar, clicking the **Customer** tab, and selecting **Create Sales Receipt** in the **Action** column dropdown menu for the customer.

The form will look something like this:

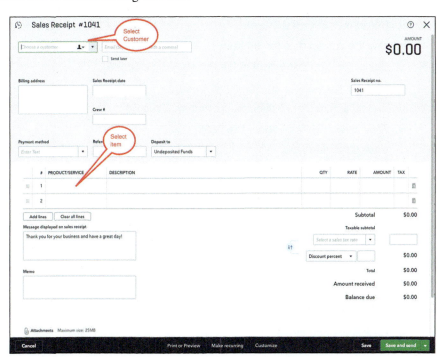

To complete a **sales receipt**, you must enter the customer name, the receipt date, and the items to be charged. You also select the **Payment method**.

If the customer is paying with a check, the customer's check number can be entered in the **Reference no.** field. For security reasons, full credit card numbers would normally not be included in the **Reference no.**

> **HINT:** If a company has a lot of walk-in customers and it doesn't want to track each cash customer's name, it can set up a "Cash Customer" or "Walk-in" customer. Click **Add new** in the **add a customer** dropdown menu, enter the name, and click **save**. The name will appear in the customer list but no additional detail will need to be added to the customer record unless sales at the location are subject to sales tax. In that case, the physical address of the business would need to be added.

You can also add a customer message at the bottom of sales receipts.

Clicking **Save and close** (or **Save and new**) records the transaction.

PRACTICE
EXERCISE

Record cash and credit sales for Craig's Design and Landscaping.

(Craig's Design and Landscaping prepares invoices for some work it did for Kookies by Kathy and Video Games by Dan. It also records the cash collected at time of service for some repair work it did for Red Rock Diner.)

1. Create invoices.

   a. Click **Sales** on the navigation bar.

   b. Select **Invoice** on the **New Transaction** dropdown menu of the **All Sales** tab.

   c. Invoice Kookies by Kathy for 3 hours of Design work.

      i.   Select **Kookies by Kathy** in the **Choose a customer** field.

      ii. Remove the checkmark next to **Send later**.

      iii. Select **Net 30** for the **Terms**.

      iv. Use the current date for the **Invoice Date**.

      v.   Select **Design** as the **Item** in the **Product/Service** field.

      vi. Enter "3" as the **QTY** (hours in this case).

      vii. The default rate of 75 should appear in the next field.

      viii. Total invoice balance should be $225.

      ix. Click **Save and new**.

   d. Invoice Video Games by Dan for some gardening and pest control work.

      i.   Select **Video Games by Dan** in the **Choose a customer** field.

      ii. Select **Net 30** as the **Terms**.

      iii. Use the current date for the **Invoice date**.

      iv. Select **Gardening** as the first **Item** with a **QTY** of "5" and a **Rate** of "$30."

      v.   On the second line select **Pest Control** as the second **Item**. Enter "2" as the **QTY**. Leave the **RATE** at $35.

      vi. Total invoice balance should be $220.

      vii. Click **Save and close**.

(continued)

2. Record a cash sale. (Red Rock Diner paid $180 (by check #6789) for some maintenance work.)

    a.   Click ➕ on the icon bar.

    b.   Select **Sales Receipt** in the **Customers** column.

    c.   Select **Red Rock Diner** in the **Choose a customer** field.

    d.   Enter the current date for the **Sales Receipt date**.

    e.   Select **Check** as the **Payment method**.

    f.   Enter "6789" as the **Reference no**.

    g.   Leave **Undeposited Funds** in the **Deposit to** field.

    h.   Select **Maintenance & Repair** in the **PRODUCT/SERVICE** field.

    i.   Enter a **QTY** of "3" and a **Rate** of "60."

    j.   The total should be $180.

    k.   Click **Save and close**.

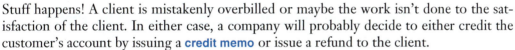

What's the underlying journal entry for Invoice 1038 to Kookies by Kathy? (Answer at end of chapter.)

QuickCheck
3-1

RECORDING CUSTOMER CREDITS AND REFUNDS

Stuff happens! A client is mistakenly overbilled or maybe the work isn't done to the satisfaction of the client. In either case, a company will probably decide to either credit the customer's account by issuing a **credit memo** or issue a refund to the client.

If the client has unpaid invoices, the company will normally decide to credit the client's account using the **transaction type Credit Memo**. The credit account underlying a **credit memo** is Accounts Receivable (A/R). The debit account(s) underlying the transaction depend on the **items** selected in the form.

Depending on the **settings** in the company file, **credit memos** are either:

- automatically applied by QBO or

- manually applied by the user.

Automatic application of **credit memos** is a **setting**. To change the **setting**, click the **gear** icon on the icon bar. Click **Account and Settings** in the **Your Company** column.

On the **Advanced** tab, click **Automatically apply credits** in the **Automation** section.

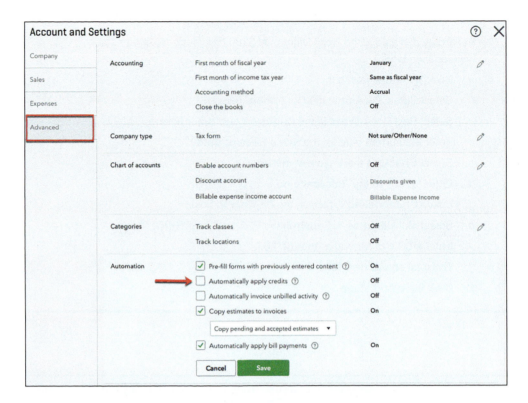

A checkmark in the box next to **Automatically apply credits** turns the feature on. Removing the checkmark allows the user to manually select the specific **invoice** to be credited. Automatic application saves time; manual selection gives the user better control.

Creating Credit Memos with Automatic Application Set as the Preference

Click the ➕ icon on the icon bar.

Click **Credit Memo**. The window will look something like this:

The customer account to be credited must be selected. The credit memo date and number (if custom transaction numbers are being used) must be entered.

The **item** selected in the **PRODUCT/SERVICE** column represents the service for which the credit memo is being issued. For example, if the client is being issued a credit for two hours of gardening services, then the **item** associated with gardening would be selected.

QBO automatically credits specific invoices in this order:

- Oldest open invoice first.

- If the credit is greater than the oldest invoice, the balance is credited to the second oldest.

  - QBO will continue to apply any balances (in reverse chronological order) until the credit is fully applied.

- If the client has no open invoices, the credit will be automatically applied to the **next invoice** recorded.

A completed **credit memo** might look something like this after it was saved.

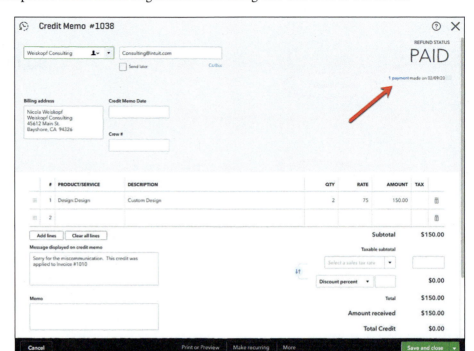

QBO applied the credit by issuing a customer **payment** transaction. The **payment** transaction can be viewed by clicking the link to the payment that appears directly under **PAID** in the top right corner of the form. The **payment** screen would look something like this:

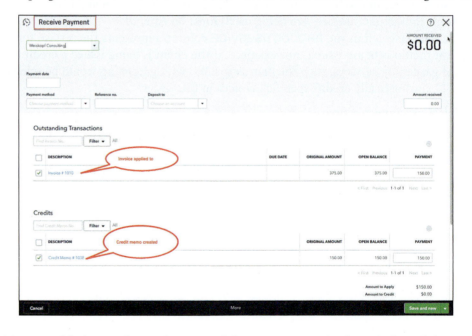

Users could change the application of the **credit memo** in this window if there were other open **invoices** available.

Creating Credit Memos with Manual Application (Automatic Application Preference Turned Off)

The **credit memo** form is accessed by clicking the ➕ icon on the icon bar and clicking **Credit Memo**.

The **credit memo** is completed as described in the above section, "Creating Credit Memos with Automatic Application Set as the Preference."

Once saved, the **credit memo** will show with an **Unapplied** status in the Customer Center. The screen would look something like this:

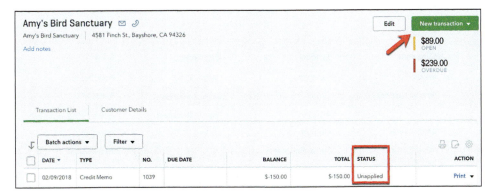

To apply the credit, click **New Transaction** and select **Payment.**

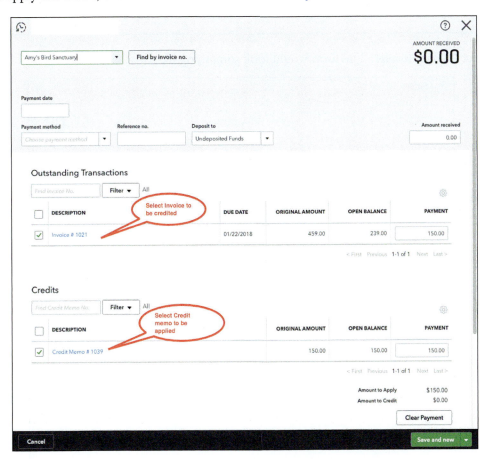

Place checkmarks in the box(es) next to the **credit memo(s)** to be applied and in the box(es) next to the **invoices** to be credited.

Issuing Refunds to Customers

Instead of issuing a credit memo, companies may choose to issue a refund directly to the client. This would most likely occur when the company wants to give a credit to a client with no open (unpaid) invoices.

Refunds to clients are entered as **Refund Receipts**. The underlying credit in the transaction is the **Bank** account. The underlying debit(s) depend on the **item(s)** selected in the form.

To access the form, click on the ➕ icon on the icon bar.

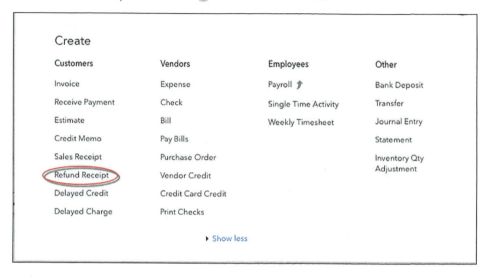

Select **Refund Receipt**. The form would look something like this:

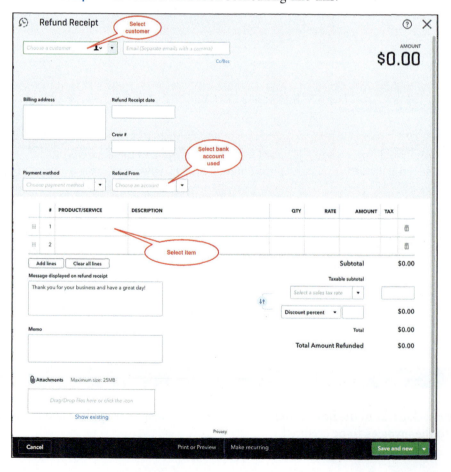

The form must include the customer name, the date of the refund, and **items** to be debited. The **Payment method** used (usually cash or check) and the bank account to be credited must be selected. If the refund is being made using a check, the **Check No.** field must be completed.

A completed **refund receipt** might look something like this if a check was issued for the refund:

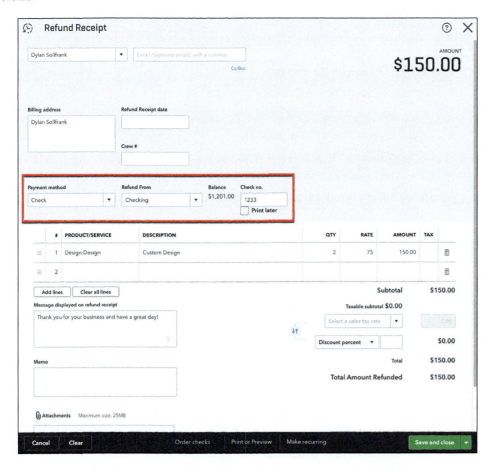

Record a credit memo and a refund for Craig's Design and Landscaping.
(Amy's Bird Sanctuary complained about the amount of its November bill. Craig's Design and Landscaping decides to give Amy's Bird Sanctuary a $150 credit toward that invoice. Dylan Sollfrank paid $337.50 for a custom landscape design. Dylan was happy with the design but has decided to postpone the project. To maintain good client relations, Craig decides to issue Dylan a $75 refund.)

PRACTICE EXERCISE

1. Change settings to allow for manual application of credit memos and custom transaction numbers.

    a. Click the **gear** icon in the icon bar.

    b. Click **Account and Settings**.

    c. Click **Advanced**.

    d. Click the **pencil** icon in the **Automation** section.

    e. Remove the checkmark next to **Automatically apply credits**.

    f. Click **Save**.

(continued)

    g.   Click the **Sales** tab.

    h.   Click the **pencil** icon in the **Sales form content** section.

    i.   Put a check in the **Custom transaction numbers** box, if necessary.

    j.   Click **Save**.

    k.   Click **Done**.

2. Create a credit memo.

    a.   Click the ➕ icon on the icon bar.

    b.   Click **Credit Memo** in the **Customers** column.

    c.   Select **Amy's Bird Sanctuary** as the customer.

    d.   Enter the current date as the date.

    e.   Enter CM1011 as the **Credit Memo no.**

    f.   Select **Design:Design** as the **PRODUCT/SERVICE** and enter "2" as the **QTY**.

    g.   The total credit amount should be $150.00.

    h.   Click **Save and close**.

3. Apply the credit.

    a.   Click **Sales** in the navigation bar and select the **Customer** tab.

    b.   Click **Amy's Bird Sanctuary**.

    c.   Click **New transaction** and select **Payment**.

    d.   Place checkmarks in the boxes next to Credit Memo #CM1011 and Invoice #1021.

    e.   Click **Save and close**.

4. Record a refund.

    a.   Click the ➕ icon on the icon bar.

    b.   Click **Refund Receipt** in the **Customers** column.

    c.   Select **Dylan Sollfrank** as the customer.

    d.   Enter the current date as the date.

    e.   Enter "1045" as the **Refund Receipt no.**

    f.   Select **Check** as the **Payment method**.

    g.   Select **Checking** in the **Refund From** field and enter "1002" as the **Check no.**

    h.   Select **Design:Design** as the **PRODUCT/SERVICE** and enter "1" as the **QTY**.

    i.   The **Total Amount Refunded** should be $75.00.

    j.   Click **Save and close**.

    k.   Click **OK**.

    l.   Click **Dashboard**.

RECORDING PAYMENTS FROM CUSTOMERS

Companies generally give customers or clients a number of payment options.

- Customers can pay with check, cash, or credit card at the time of service.
  - Recorded as **sales receipts** (covered earlier in this chapter).
- Customers can buy on account and pay later.
  - Recorded as **payments**.

Most companies that sell to individuals would generally only accept cash/check or major credit cards. An exception would be retail outlets that have their own credit cards. (Macy's and Nordstrom are two examples.)

Most companies that sell to other companies would sell primarily on account. It would simply be impractical for most companies to pay cash or have checks or credit cards ready whenever goods or services are delivered.

In a manual accounting system, customer payments are recorded through the Cash Receipts Journal. The journal is posted, in total, to the general ledger and each transaction is posted to the appropriate customer's subsidiary ledger (if paying on account). In QBO, all of the steps are done when the form recording the payment transaction is saved.

Payments on Account

Customer payments on account balances are recorded using the **Receive Payment** form (**Payment transaction type**).

To access the form, click on the ✚ icon on the icon bar. The window should look something like this:

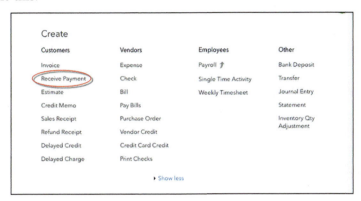

Select **Receive Payment**. The form would look something like this:

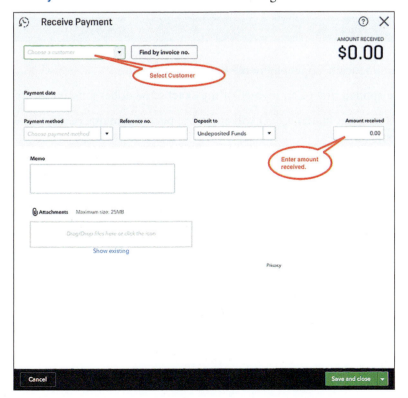

To enter a customer payment, you need to know the customer name, the payment amount, the date received, and the payment method. If payment is made by check, the check number would normally be entered in the **Reference no**. field.

Once the customer is selected, all outstanding invoices from that customer will be displayed. The screen would look something like this:

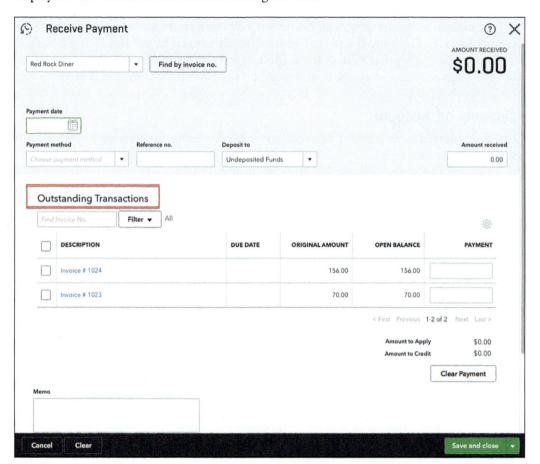

QBO will automatically apply payments for you in this order:

- It will be applied first to an invoice of the **exact** same dollar amount as the payment.

- If there's no exact match, QBO will apply the payment in due date order (oldest invoice first).

You can change how payments were applied if needed.

Full or partial payments can be entered. If a partial payment is received, you should make sure that the amount(s) entered in the **Payment** field(s) agree(s) to the payment amount that should be applied to the specific invoice.

If a partial payment is entered, QBO will leave the unpaid balance for the invoice in Accounts Receivable.

If there are unapplied credits available to the customer, they will appear when the **Receive Payment** form is opened. The user has the option of applying the credit or leaving it as an open credit that would be available at a later date.

For example, the form to record a payment of $375 from a customer with an open credit memo would look something like this if the credit was applied.

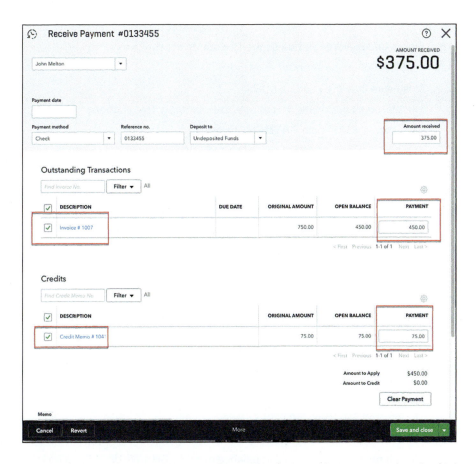

Note that the **Amount to Apply** shows as $450 (the $375 cash payment plus the $75 credit memo).

The default journal entry underlying a **payment** transaction includes a debit to **Undeposited Funds** and a credit to Accounts Receivable. The **Undeposited Funds** account will be discussed in the "Making Deposits" section below.

> **BEHIND THE SCENES** The above process is the QBO default procedure. Users can select another account (normally a **Bank account type**) in the **Deposit to** field if direct entry into the cash account is preferred.

PRACTICE
EXERCISE

Record customer payments on account for Craig's Design and Landscaping.
(Craig's Design and Landscaping received payments from two of its customers.)

1. Record customer payment in full. (Check #5865 for $160 received from Sushi by Katsuyuki in payment of invoices 1018 and 1019)

   a. Click the ➕ icon on the icon bar.

   b. Click **Receive Payment** in the **Customers** column.

   c. Select **Sushi by Katsuyuki** as the customer.

   d. Enter the current date as the **Payment date**.

   e. Select **Check** as the **Payment method**.

   f. Enter "5865" as the **Reference no.**

(continued)

   g. Leave **Undeposited Funds** as the **Deposit to** account.

   h. Enter "$160" as the **Amount** received.

   i. Make sure that QBO automatically:

     i. placed a checkmark next to both **Outstanding Transactions**.

     ii. entered $80 in both **PAYMENT** fields.

   j. The total **Amount to Apply** should be $160.00.

   k. Click **Save and new**.

 2. Record customer partial payment. (Check #6899 for $40 received from Bill's Windsurf Shop in partial payment of invoice 1027)

   a. Select **Bill's Windsurf Shop** as the customer.

   b. Enter the current date as the **Payment date**.

   c. Select **Check** as the **Payment method**.

   d. Enter "6899" as the **Reference no.**

   e. Leave **Undeposited Funds** as the **Deposit to** account.

   f. Enter "$40" as the **Amount** received.

   g. Make sure that QBO automatically:

     i. placed a checkmark next to Invoice #1027 under **Outstanding Transactions**.

     ii. entered $40 in the **PAYMENT** field.

   h. The total **Amount to Apply** should be $40.00.

   i. **Make a note** of the outstanding balance owed by Bill's Windsurf Shop on Invoice 1027 after check #6899 was posted.

   j. Click **Save and close**.

MAKING DEPOSITS

Before you learn how to record bank deposits, you need to understand how QBO handles cash receipts. As you know, there's a journal entry behind every sales receipt (cash sale) and every customer payment on account. Based on your knowledge of accounting, you would probably expect that the debit account for each of the transactions would be Cash, right? (Debit Cash, Credit Revenue for the cash sales and Debit Cash, Credit Accounts Receivable for the customer payments on account.)

  Since QBO updates the general ledger automatically and immediately for every transaction, that would mean there would be a debit entry to the cash account for every check and cash payment received. Why is that a problem? Well, it's not if you're depositing every payment separately. But most companies group checks when they're making deposits. On the bank statement, the actual deposit amount is shown (not each check that makes up the deposit). It would be difficult (not impossible, but difficult) to reconcile the bank account every month if QBO didn't group the payments together to correspond to the actual deposit amount.

  So, here's what QBO does. Instead of debiting Cash for every customer payment, an account called "Undeposited Funds" is debited. **Undeposited Funds** is an **Other Current Asset** account type (not a **Bank** account type). You can think of it as a temporary holding account.

  When the deposit is later recorded, QBO credits **Undeposited Funds** and debits the **bank** (Checking) account for the total of the funds deposited. Now the entries in the Checking account agree (hopefully!) to the entries on the bank statement.

Deposits are recorded using the **Bank Deposit** form (the **transaction type** is **Deposit**). This form is accessed by clicking the ➕ icon on the icon bar.

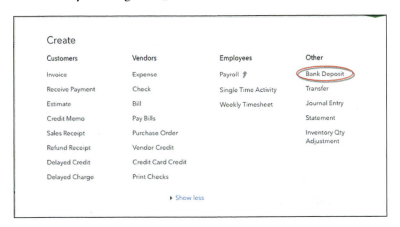

Click **Bank Deposit** in the **Other** column. The window will look something like this:

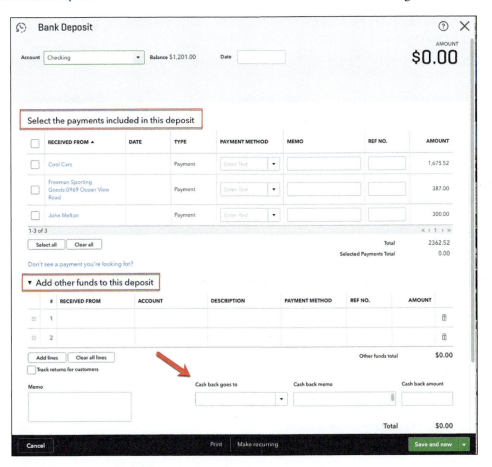

> **!** **WARNING: If you logged out of QBO after the last Practice Exercise was completed (or if you were automatically logged out by QBO), the customer payment transactions you entered in the last Practice Exercise will not appear in the Deposit window shown above. This will not be a problem in completing the Practice Exercises at the end of this section.**

The first step is to select the appropriate bank account in the top left field and enter the deposit date.

Customer payments (receipts) that are being included in the day's bank deposit are selected by placing a checkmark next to the payor's name in the **Select the payments included in this deposit** section (the names are in the **RECEIVED FROM** column). You can select all the payments or just some of them.

You can also add additional cash receipts directly into this form. For example, if a company received a tax refund, the amount would be entered in the **Add other funds to this deposit** section. Cash received from lenders (loan processed) and owner contributions would also be entered in the **Add New Deposits** section.

 HINT: When a customer is paying an account balance, the best practice is to enter it through the **Receive Payment** form. Although QBO does allow direct entry of customer payments on account into the **Deposit** form, the payment would then have to be linked to the appropriate invoice at a later date. This adds another step to the process.

The **cash back** fields at the bottom right corner of the window are used to record cash withdrawals taken directly from a deposit amount.

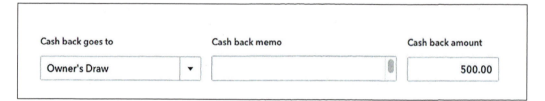

This would rarely be done in a business organization.

Save and close records the transaction.

 HINT: If there are **no** undeposited receipts in the Undeposited Funds account, only the **Add New Deposits** section will appear when you open the **Deposit** form.

PRACTICE EXERCISE

Make a deposit for Craig's Design and Landscaping.
(Craig's Design and Landscaping deposits checks received from customers.)

1. Click the ➕ icon on the icon bar.

2. Click **Bank Deposit** in the **Other** column.

3. Select **Checking** as the account.

4. Enter the current date as the **Date**.

5. Check the boxes next to Cool Cars and Freeman Sporting Goods.

6. **Make a note** of the amount received from Cool Cars.

7. The **Total** should be $2,062.52.

8. Click **Save and close**.

SALES AND CUSTOMER REPORTS

Sales and customer reports can be accessed through **Reports** on the navigation bar.

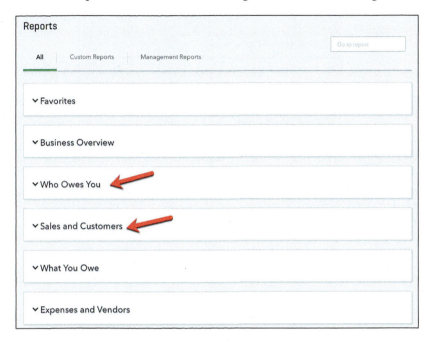

Most of the sales and customer reports are included in the **Who Owes You** and **Sales and Customers** sections. Some of the most commonly used sales reports in service companies are highlighted below:

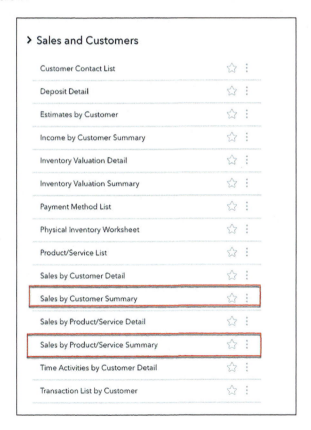

The **Who Owes You** group includes aging reports as seen below:

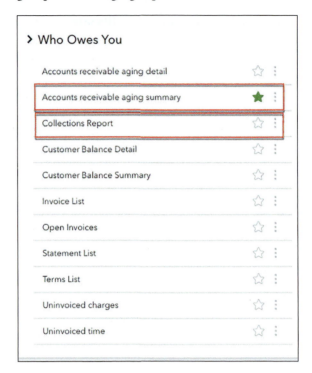

As discussed in Chapter 1, reports can be modified as needed. (Refer to the "Reports" section of Chapter 1 for a refresher on report modification.)

For example, the **AR Aging Summary** default report looks something like this:

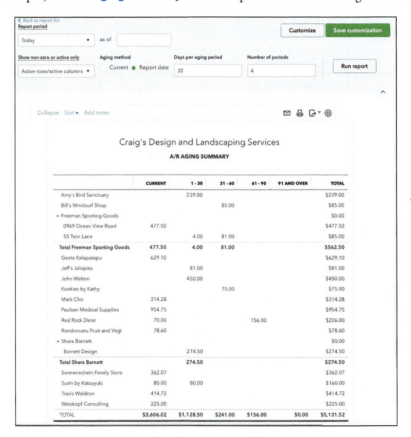

The same report modified to show eight 15-day aging periods would look something like this:

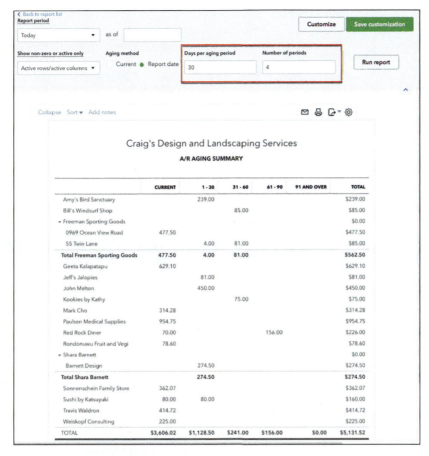

Prepare sales and receivable reports.

(Craig's Design and Landscaping needs an A/R aging and a revenue by type of service report.)

1. Prepare an accounts receivable aging report.

   a. Click **Reports**.

   b. Click **Accounts receivable aging summary** in the **Who Owes You** section.

   c. Drill down (click) on the **TOTAL** column for Sonnenschein.

      i. **Make a note** of the number on the unpaid invoice to Sonnenschein Family Store.

   d. Click **Dashboard**.

2. Prepare a sales report by service **item**.

   a. Click **Reports**.

   b. Click **Sales by Product/Service Detail** in the **Sales and Customers** section.

   c. Change **report period** to **All Dates**.

   d. Click **Customize**.

   e. Open the **Filter** dropdown section.

   f. Check **Product/Service** and select **Design:Design** and **Design:Lighting**.

   g. Open the **Rows/Columns** section.

(continued)

PRACTICE
EXERCISE

> *h.* Click **Change columns**.
>
> *i.* Check **Product Service**.
>
> *j.* Uncheck **Balance**.
>
> *k.* Click **Run Report**.
>
> *l.* **Make a note** of the amount included in the report for **Design:Lighting**.
>
> *m.* Click **Dashboard**.

ANSWER TO
QuickCheck
3-1

Accounts receivable (A/R)	$225	
Design Income		$225

CHAPTER SHORTCUTS

Add a customer
1. Click **Sales** on the navigation bar
2. Click the **Customers** tab to open the Customer Center
3. Click **New Customer**

Edit a customer
1. Open Customer Center
2. Click customer name
3. Click **Edit**

Inactivate a customer
1. Open Customer Center
2. Open the dropdown menu in the **Action** column for the customer to be inactivated
3. Select **Make inactive**

Edit item
1. Click the **gear** in the icon bar
2. Click **Products and Services**
3. Click **Edit** in the **Action** column for the item to be edited

Inactivate an item
1. Click the **gear** icon
2. Click **Products and Services**
3. Open the dropdown menu in the Action column for the item to be inactivated
4. Select **Make inactive**

Record cash sale
1. Click the ➕ icon on the icon bar
2. Click **Sales Receipt** in the **Customers** column

Record sale on account
1. Click the ➕ icon on the icon bar
2. Click **Invoice** in the **Customers** column

Record credit memo
1. Click the ➕ icon on the icon bar
2. Click **Credit Memo** in the **Customers** column

Record customer payments on account balances
1. Click the ➕ icon on the icon bar
2. Click **Record Payment** in the **Customers** column

Record deposits
1. Click the ➕ icon on the icon bar
2. Click **Bank Deposit** in the **Other** column

CHAPTER REVIEW (Answers available on the publisher's website.)

Matching

Match the term or phrase (as used in QuickBooks Online) to its definition.

1. customer name
2. display name
3. sales receipt
4. invoice

5. deposit
6. credit memo
7. undeposited funds
8. payment

_____   transaction type used for recording cash sales

_____   specific customer identifier

_____   transaction type used to record bank deposit

_____   default general ledger account used to initially record cash received

_____   transaction type used for recording customer payments on account

_____   transaction type used to record sales on account

_____   transaction type used to record credit given to customer

_____   customer name appearing on invoices, sales receipts, or credit memos

Multiple Choice

1. A **service item** in QBO
   a. can be linked to more than one general ledger account.
   b. must be linked to one, and only one, general ledger account.
   c. can only be linked to an accounts receivable type account.
   d. can be, but doesn't need to be, linked to an account.

2. The general ledger account Undeposited Funds in QBO represents _____.
   a. all cash sales
   b. the balance in accounts receivable
   c. amount of cash, checks, or credit card payments received and recorded but not yet deposited
   d. None of the above

3. The account that is credited when a credit memo is completed in QBO must have the **account type** _____.
   a. Bank
   b. Accounts receivable
   c. Accounts payable
   d. Other current asset
   e. Other current liability

4. The default account Undeposited Funds has the **account type** _____.
   a. Bank
   b. Other current asset

  c. Other asset

  d. Other current liability

  e. Accounts receivable

5. There is an underlying journal entry behind every completed form listed below **except** _____.

  a. Invoice

  b. Credit memo

  c. Make deposit

  d. Sales receipt

  e. None of the above answers is correct.

ASSIGNMENTS

Assignment 3A

Assignments with the MBC are available in myBusinessCourse.

Background information: Martin Smith, a college student and good friend of yours, has always wanted to be an entrepreneur. He is very good in math so, to test his entrepreneurship skills, he decided to set up a small math tutoring company serving local high school students who struggle in their math courses. He set up the company, Math Revealed!, as a corporation in 2018. Martin is the only owner. He has not taken any distributions from the company since it opened.

  The business has been successful so far. In fact, it's been so successful he has decided to work in his business full time now that he's graduated from college with a degree in mathematics.

  He has decided to start using QuickBooks Online to keep track of his business transactions. He likes the convenience of being able to access his information over the Internet. You have agreed to act as his accountant while you're finishing your own academic program.

  He currently has a number of regular customers that he tutors in Pre-Algebra, Algebra, and Geometry. His customers pay his fees by cash or check after each tutoring session but he does give terms of Net 15 to some of his customers. He has developed the following fee schedule:

Name	Description	Rate
Refresher	One-hour session	$40 per hour
Persistence program	Two one-hour sessions per week	$75 per week
Crisis program	Five one-hour sessions per week	$150 per week

The tutoring sessions usually take place at his students' homes but he recently signed a two-year lease on a small office above a local coffee shop. The rent is only $200 per month starting in January 2019. A security deposit of $400 was paid in December 2018.

  The following equipment is owned by the company:

Description	Date placed in service	Cost	Life	Salvage Value
Computer	7/1/18	$3,000	36 months	$300
Printer	7/1/18	$ 240	24 months	$ 0
Graphing Calculators (2)	7/1/18	$ 294	36 months	$ 60

All equipment is depreciated using the straight-line method.

  As of 12/31/18, he owed $2,000 to his parents who initially helped him get started. They are charging him interest at a 6% annual rate. He has been paying interest only on a monthly basis. His last payment was 12/31/18.

  Over the next month or so, he plans to expand his business by selling a few products he believes will help his students. He has already purchased a few items:

Category	Description	Vendor	Quantity On Hand	Cost per unit	Sales Price
Books and Tools					
	Geometry in Sports	Books Galore	20	12	16
	Solving Puzzles: Fun with Algebra	Books Galore	20	14	18
	Getting Ready for Calculus	Books Galore	20	15	20
	Protractor/Compass Set	Math Shack	10	10	14
	Handheld Dry-Erase Boards	Math Shack	25	5	9
	Notebooks (pack of 3)	Paper Bag Depot	10	15	20

> **!** **WARNING:** You will need to make an adjustment to the assignment if your company file doesn't have the **products and services categories** feature. To verify whether you have the feature, click the **gear icon** on the navigation bar. Click **All Lists.** If you see **Product Categories** listed in the window, you have that feature. If you don't see **Categories**, see Appendix 2A.

1/2/19

✓ You're ready to start recording some transactions for Martin but you know you have some setup work to do first.

✓ You organize the **products/services** list into **categories**.

- You click the **gear** icon and select **Products and Services**.
- You select **Manage categories** on the **More** dropdown menu and you create three categories: Books and Tools, Tutoring, and Other.
- **TIP:** If you don't have **categories** in your homework company file, refer to Appendix 3A.
- You edit the **inventory items** (**Dry Erase**, **Sports**, **Puzzles**, **Ready**, **Kit**, and **Notebooks**) to link them to the **Books and Tools category**. You edit the **service items** (**Refresher**, **Persistence**, **Crisis**, **Hours**, and **Services**) to link them to the **Tutoring category**.
- You edit the default **items** created by QBO (**Hours** and **Services**) to include them in the **Other category**.

✓ You also set some credit terms for Math Revealed!

- You click the **gear** icon and select **All Lists**.
- You set up two new terms in the **Terms** list.
  - You name one term "Net 15." This will be the default terms for most customers. Customers will be expected to pay within 15 days of the invoice date if they don't pay at time of service.
  - You create a second term—"Net 30." You think Martin might decide to give some of his long-time customers a bit more time to pay.

✓ You also decide to set some preferences in the **Sales** tab of **Account and Settings** that you think will be helpful.

- In the **Sales form content** section:
  - You select **Net 15** as the **Preferred invoice terms**.
  - You choose **None** as the **Preferred delivery method** since you intend to print out invoices or receipts to customers when the services are completed.
  - **TIP: Custom transaction numbers** should have been turned **On** as part of the homework in Chapter 2. If you missed that, make sure you turn it on now.
- You want to control how credits are applied so you turn **Automatically apply credits** off in the **Automation** section of the **Advanced** tab in **Account and Settings**.

✓ Martin has let you know that he will be giving payment terms of Net 15 to all existing customers. You edit all existing customers to add the Net 15 payment terms.

   TIP: Terms are added on the **Payment and billing** tab of the customer record.

1/7/19

✓ Martin gives you a check from a new customer for $80 for two **Refresher** tutoring sessions. The check, #56772, is dated 1/7.

   • You set up the new customer.

      ○ The customer is Alonso Luna. You use Luna, Alonso as the **display name**.
        TIP: Enter the **display name** first. Then enter the first and last names.

        4755 Hastings Road, Sacramento, CA 95822

        916-118-8111

   You set the payment terms at Net 15.

   • You create a sales receipt (#101) for the two tutoring sessions.

      ○ You make sure to use 150 Undeposited Funds as the **Deposit to** account. You'll be depositing checks in batches.

✓ Martin also gives you a list of all sessions held this past week. He did not collect payment for any of these sessions so you prepare invoices dated 1/7, with credit terms of Net 15, for the following customers:

   • Debbie Han—**Crisis** $150, #1004

   • Marcus Reymundo—**Refresher** $40, #1005

   • Eliot Williams—**Persistence** $75, #1006

✓ Several customers have also set up tutoring sessions for the next few weeks. Now that Martin has decided to offer payment terms to his customers, you will be invoicing them in advance. All customers have Net 15 terms.

   • Jon Savidge—Three weeks of the **Persistence** program, starting 1/7. $225 (Invoice #1007)

   • Paul Richard—Two weeks of the **Crisis** program, starting 1/14. $300 (Invoice #1008)

      ○ Paul is totally focused on an upcoming Algebra exam. He intends to get an A.

1/9/19

✓ Martin is always looking for ways to expand his services. He decides to offer a walk-in tutoring clinic on January 19th. It will be open to all high school students. He's going to charge each student $20 for the afternoon. A couple of his college friends have agreed to help out.

   • You set up a new **service item**. Martin is calling the clinic "Mathmagic" so that's what you decide to name the **item**. You add the new **item** to the **Tutoring category**. You select Tutoring as the **Income account**. You use "Mathmagic Clinic" as the description. The clinic fees are non-taxable.

1/11/19

✓ You receive two checks in the mail. **TIP:** Make sure you use 150 Undeposited Funds for the **Deposit to** account for both.

   • Check # 189 from Kim Kowalski, dated 1/11, for $200 on Invoice #1001.

      ○ You give Kim a call and remind her that the total amount due was $300. She apologizes and promises to pay the balance before the end of the month.

   • Check #2840 from Annie Wang, dated 1/11, for $150 in full payment of invoice #1003.

✓ You deposit the checks received today with the check received on Monday. The total deposit is $430.

1/14/19

✓ Annie Wang's mother calls. She is so happy with the progress Annie is making in her Advanced Algebra course that she sets up appointments for the next four weeks under the **Persistence** package. You invoice Annie $300, net 15. (Invoice # 1009).

● You realize that some of the revenue just invoiced to Annie will not be earned until February. (The four weeks will be up on February 13th.) You decide to wait until the end of the month to make any necessary adjustments to the income statement. (**TIP:** You'll do this as part of the homework for Chapter 5 so don't worry about it now.)

1/18/19

✓ Martin gives you a list of the sessions for the past two weeks. (He's gotten a little behind on his paperwork and you remind him that his business needs cash to grow!)

● Some of the students paid for the sessions. You use 1/18 as the check date on the **sales receipts**.

○ Marley Roberts paid $150 for two weeks of **Persistence** with check # 1701. (Sales receipt #102)

○ Alonso Luna paid $80 for two **Refresher** sessions with check #56792. (Sales receipt #103)

● Jon Savidge came in with four of his friends. All of them chose the **Crisis** package. Jon's father agreed to pay for all five of them. You bill Jon for $750. (Invoice # 1010, net 30)

1/19/19

✓ Twenty-five high school students show up for the Mathmagic Clinic. All of them pay cash ($500 in total). You decide to create one **sales receipt** (#104) to record all the payments instead of creating a receipt for each student.

● You enter "Drop-In" as the customer in the **sales receipt** name field. You click **Add** and **Details** to open the customer record window. You use 3835 Freeport Blvd, Sacramento, CA 95822 as the address.

✓ One of the students, Navi Patel, decides to also sign up for two **Refresher** sessions. She pays the $80 in cash. Martin schedules the service for 1/22 and 1/28.

● Since she may be an ongoing customer, you decide to set her up as a customer and prepare a separate receipt for the future tutoring sessions (#105).

● Navi's address is 2525 Fractal Drive, Sacramento, CA 95822. Her phone number is 916-121-8282. Credit terms (for future invoices) are Net 15. You use Patel, Navi as the **display name**.

1/22/19

✓ You receive the following checks in the morning mail all dated 1/22:

● $300 from Jon Savidge, check #3334, in payment of Invoice #1002 and #1007.

● $75 from Eliot Williams, check #8114 in payment of Invoice #1006.

● $150 from Debbie Han, check #4499 in payment of Invoice #1004.

✓ You deposit all checks and cash received since 1/11. The total deposit is $1,335.

✓ Martin lets you know that he closed the office on January 21st for Martin Luther King Day. As a result, Paul Richard missed one his **Crisis** sessions. You create a **credit memo** (#CM1008) for $30, dated 1/22. You use **Crisis** as the **PRODUCT/SERVICE** and change the **AMOUNT** to 30. Since Paul has an outstanding invoice, you'll apply the credit when he pays the balance due.

✓ The father of one of Martin's Mathmagic students storms into the office right before closing. Gus Ranting is very upset that Math Revealed! did not get his consent before tutoring his son. Martin talks to the father and explains that the tutoring clinic was voluntary and that there was no pressure on any of the students to sign up for more sessions. Nonetheless, Martin agrees to refund the $20 and that seems to calm Gus down.

- You add Gus Ranting when you create **refund receipt** #RR100. You save the name without adding any additional details to the customer record.
  - You issue the refund from the Checking account. The Math Revealed! check number is 1100.
  - You use Mathmagic as the **PRODUCT/SERVICE**.
  - You add "Sorry for the misunderstanding" in the **Message displayed on refund receipt** box.
  - You go back to Gus Ranting's customer record and change the **display name** to Ranting, Gus and add his first and last names to the name fields.

1/25/19

✓ Martin gets a call from Teacher's College. Mr. Learn, the college president, has heard that Martin has developed some innovative techniques for helping students develop strong math skills. Mr. Learn asks Martin whether he's ever considered training other educators in his techniques. Martin is always up for new challenges and agrees to develop a workshop for the college for $1,500. Mr. Learn expects that there will be at least 50 math teachers from around the area in attendance. The workshop will be held February 15–16.

- You decide to set up a new income account called Workshops to track this new source of revenue. You name the **income** account "Workshops," using **Service/Fee Income** as the **detail type**. You assign 405 as the account number.
- Martin thinks there may be opportunities for other types of workshops in the future so you decide to set up a new **category** named "Workshops."
- You also create a **service item** called "Educator Workshop."
  - You use "Tips for Teaching Math Workshop" as the **item** description and link the item to the Workshops **category**.
  - Workshop fees are non-taxable. You enter a rate of "$1,500" as the default **sales price/rate** and select account 405 Workshops as the **Income account**.
- You also set up Teacher's College as a customer.
  - 21 Academy Avenue, Sacramento, CA 95822.
  - 916-443-3334.
  - Terms are Net 30.

✓ Teacher's College asks you to prepare an **invoice** for them now so that they can start processing the paperwork. You prepare Invoice 1011, dated 1/25, for the $1,500.
  - (**TIP:** You will make an adjustment for unearned income as part of the homework for Chapter 5 so don't worry about it now.)

1/28/19

✓ Martin gives a list of tutoring sessions held this past week.

- You prepare an invoice for:
  - Marley Roberts, one **Persistence** package $75, Invoice 1012, Net 15
- One student paid by check so you created a sales receipt for:
  - Eliot Williams, one **Persistence** package $75 (Check # 8144, Sales receipt #106)

✓ Martin lets you know that he won't be setting up any additional sessions for January 29–31. He's going to use that time to prepare the workshop for Teacher's College.

1/30/19

✓ You receive two checks from customers.

- Check #7788090, dated 1/30, from Teacher's College for $1,500, in payment of Invoice #1011.

- Check # 45678, dated 1/30 from Paul Richard for $270 in payment of invoice #1008.

  ○ You apply CM1008 to the balance when you enter the payment.

✓ You deposit both checks in the bank along with the checks received on 1/22.

- The deposit should total $1,845.

Check numbers 1/31

Checking account balance:. $6,435
January Sales Revenue:. $4,330

Reports to create for Chapter 3:

All reports should be in portrait orientation.

- Journal—1/01 through 1/31 transactions only

- Sales by Product/Service Summary (January sales only)

- A/R Aging Summary dated 1/31

Background information: Sally Hanson, a good friend of yours, double majored in Computer Science and Accounting in college. She worked for several years for a software company in Silicon Valley but the long hours started to take a toll on her personal life.

Last year she decided to open up her own company, Salish Software Solutions (a corporation). Sally currently advises clients looking for new accounting software and assists them with software installation. She also provides training to client employees and occasionally troubleshoots software issues.

She has decided to start using QuickBooks Online to keep track of her business transactions. She likes the convenience of being able to access financial information over the Internet. You have agreed to act as her accountant while you're working on your accounting degree.

Sally has a number of clients that she is currently working with. She gives 15-day payment terms to her corporate clients but she asks for cash at time of service if she does work for individuals. She has developed the following fee schedule:

Name	Description	Rate
Select	Software selections	$500 flat fee
Set Up	Software installation	$ 50 per hour
Train	Software training	$ 40 per hour
Fix	File repair	$ 60 per hour

Sally rents office space from Alki Property Management for $800 per month.
   The following furniture and equipment is owned by Salish:

Description	Date placed in service	Cost	Life	Salvage Value
Office furniture	6/1/18	$1,400	60 months	$200
Computer	7/1/18	$4,620	36 months	$300
Printer.	5/1/18	$ 900	36 months	$ 0

All equipment is depreciated using the straight-line method.
   As of 12/31/18, she owed $3,500 to Dell Finance. The monthly payment on that loan is $150 including interest at 5%. Sally's last payment to Dell was 12/31/18.

Assignment 3B

Salish Software Solutions

Over the next month or so, Sally plans to expand her business by selling some of her favorite accounting and personal software products directly to her clients. She has already purchased the following items.

Item Name	Description	Vendor	Quantity On Hand	Cost per unit	Sales Price
Easy1	Easy Does it	Abacus Shop	15	$100	$175
Retailer	Simply Retail	Simply Accounting	2	$400	$700
Contractor	Simply Construction	Simply Accounting	2	$500	$800
Organizer	Organizer	Personal Solutions	25	$ 25	$ 50
Tracker	Investment Tracker	Personal Solutions	25	$ 20	$ 40

1/2/19

✓ You're excited for the chance to use your accounting knowledge in a real business and you want to get started with an organized QBO file.

✓ You take a look at the product/services list and decide to group items into categories.

- You click the gear icon and choose Products and Services.
- You select Manage categories on the More dropdown menu and you create three categories (Consulting and Installation, Products, and Other).
- You edit the inventory items, (Easy1, Retailer, Contractor, Organizer, and Tracker) to include them in the Products category.
- You edit service items (Select, Set Up, Train, and Fix) to include them in the Consulting and Installation category.
- You edit the default items created by QBO (Hours and Services) to include them in the Other category.

✓ You also set up some credit terms for Salish Software

- You click the gear icon and select All Lists.
- You set up two new terms in the Terms list.
- You name one term Net 15. This will be the default terms for most customers.
- You create a second term—Net 30. You think Sally might decide to give some of her larger customers a bit more time to pay.

✓ You ask Sally about the payment terms on her current customers. She says they all are expected to pay within 15 days. You edit the customer record for all existing customers to add the Net 15 payment terms.

✓ You also decide to set some preferences in the Sales tab of Account and Settings that you think will be helpful.

- In the Sales form content section:
  ○ You select Net 15 as the Preferred invoice terms.
  ○ You choose None as the Preferred delivery method since you intend to print out invoices or receipts for customers when the services are completed.
  ○ Custom transaction numbers should have been turned On as part of the homework in Chapter 2. If you missed that, make sure you turn it on now.
- Since you want to control how credits are applied in QBO, you turn Automatically apply credits to Off in the Automation section of the Advanced tab in Account and Settings.

1/7/19

✓ Sally gives you a check from Dew Drop Inn for $180 for some work she did for the company today. There were some software issues. Sally spent three hours fixing the file. The check (#8134) is dated 1/7.

- You create a sales receipt (#101) for the three hours of file repair (**Fix**).
  - ○ You make sure to use Undeposited Funds as the **Deposit to** account. You'll be depositing checks in batches.

✓ Sally also gives you a list of all of her hours from last week. She did not collect payment from any of these customers so you prepare invoices dated 1/7, with credit terms of Net 15, as follows:

- Lou's Barber Shop—**Set Up**—12 hours ($600, Invoice #1006)
- Alki Deli—**Set Up**—10 hours ($500, #1007)
- Uptown Espresso—**Train** 5 hours ($200, #1008)

1/8/19

✓ Sally is always looking for ways to grow her business. She decides to offer a Software Workshop on January 18th. She will be offering tips on software selection and will be demonstrating some of the software products she expects to start selling in February. She's going to charge participants $75 for the afternoon. A couple of her college friends have agreed to help out with what she hopes is a large crowd.

- You decide to track the revenue from the workshop in a new **income** account (Workshop Fees). You set the account up using 415 as the account number.
  - ○ **TIP:** You can use **Service/Fee Income** as the **Detail Type**.
- You set up a new **category** called **Workshops and Seminars**.
  - ○ **TIP:** If you don't have **categories** in your homework company file, refer to Appendix 3A.
- You also set up a new **service item**. Sally is calling the workshop "Picking the Right Software" so you decide to name the item **Picks**. You set it up in the **Workshops and Seminars category**.
  - ○ You enter "Picking the Right Software Workshop" as the description and 75 as the **sales price/rate**.
  - ○ You select Workshop Fees 415 as the **income account**.

1/10/19

✓ You receive two checks in the mail. **TIP:** Make sure you use 150 Undeposited Funds as the **Deposit** to account for both.

- Check #1998 from Champion Law, dated 1/10, for $200 on Invoice #1001.
  - ○ You call Lawrence (the accountant at the law firm) and remind him that the total amount due was $280. He apologizes and promises to pay the balance before the end of the month.
- Check #3751 from Lou's Barber Shop, dated 1/10, for $250 full payment of invoice #1004.

✓ You deposit the checks received today with the check received last Friday. The total deposit is $630.

1/14/19

✓ The Operations Manager at Butter and Beans calls. The software Sally helped to select is ready for installation. The company would prefer to be billed for the entire cost in one invoice. Sally estimates that the **Set up** work will take 40 hours. (It's a complicated system to set up.) You invoice Butter and Beans for the $2,000 and give them 30-day terms as agreed to by Sally. (Invoice # 1009).

- You realize that some of the revenue just invoiced to Butter and Beans may not be earned until February. You decide to wait until the end of the month to make any necessary adjustments to the income statement. (**TIP:** You'll do this as part of the homework for Chapter 5 so don't worry about it now.)

1/17/19

✓ Sally gives you a breakdown for her hours since 1/8. (She's gotten a little behind on her paperwork and you remind her that her business needs cash to grow!)

- Two of her customers paid her when she completed the work. (You'll send them a copy of the **sales receipts** for their records.):
  - ○ Dew Drop Inn paid for 4 more hours of file repair (**Fix**) work with check #3608. ($240, #102)
  - ○ Lou's Barber Shop paid for 6 more hours of training (**Train**) with check #29765, ($240 #103)
- Sally also did software research work for a new client (Fabulous Fifties). You invoice them the $500 **Select** fee on invoice #1010. Terms are Net 15.
  - ○ The company contact information is:
    - ❑ 834 Fashion Boulevard
      Sacramento, CA 95822
      916-555-5555

1/18/19

✓ Twenty-five people showed up for the "Picking the Right Software" workshop. All of them paid with cash ($1,875 in total), which was convenient but very surprising. You decide to create one sales receipt (#104) to record all the payments instead of creating a receipt for each participant.

- You enter Cash Customer as the customer in the **sales receipt** name field. You click **Add** and **Details** to open the customer record window. You use 3835 Freeport Blvd, Sacramento, CA 95822 as the address.

✓ One of the participants, Leah Rasual, asks Sally to come to her home to do some troubleshooting on her personal computer. She's using QuickBooks to track the fees she gets from her singing engagements and she's having some issues. Since Sally hasn't worked with Leah before she asks for payment in advance for the first two hours. She pays the $120 by check (#241). Sally schedules the appointment with Leah for Wednesday 1/23.

- Since Leah may be an ongoing customer, you decide to set her up as a customer and prepare a separate **sales receipt** for the **Fix** work. (**Sales Receipt** #105).
- Leah's address is 3131 Tyson Avenue, Sacramento, CA 95822. Her phone number is 916-281-2086. Credit terms (for future invoices) are Net 15.

✓ With all that cash, you head straight to the bank and make a deposit. The total (including the checks received earlier in the week) is $2475.

1/22/19

✓ Sally lets you know that she made an error on the **Set Up** hours for Lou's Barber Shop included on Invoice #1006. She actually worked 10 hours not the 12 hours Lou's was billed for. You create a **credit memo** (#CM1006) for $100, dated 1/22. Since Lou's has an outstanding invoice, you'll apply the credit when he pays the balance due.

- You enter "Sorry for the overbilling." in the **Message displayed on credit memo** box.

✓ You receive the following checks in the morning mail:

- $800 from Alki Deli, check #3334, in payment of Invoice #1001 and #1007.
- $80 from Champion Law, check #4228 for the remaining balance due on Invoice #1003.
- $500 from Butter and Beans, check 9191 in payment of Invoice #1002.

✓ One of the participants at Saturday's workshop (Marie Elle) stops by the office. She explains that she was only able to stay for the first 30 minutes of the workshop and would like to request a refund. She had to leave right after she got a call from her office letting her know that the pipes had burst in the warehouse basement. Sally agrees to refund the $75 **Picks** fee and promises to let her know about any future workshops.

- You add Marie Elle when you create **refund receipt** #RR100. You save the name without adding any additional details to the customer record. The Salish Software check number is 1100.

1/23/19

✓ Sally gets a call from Albus Software. Mr. Deposit, the CEO, has heard from several people that Sally does an exceptional job troubleshooting software problems. Mr. Deposit asks Sally whether she would be willing to share some tips and techniques with Albus' technical support staff. Sally thinks this might be an interesting project and agrees to develop a workshop for the company for $2,500. Mr. Deposit expects that there will be around 20 Albus employees in attendance. The workshop will be held February 14–15.

- You set up a new **service item** called **Tips**. You include it in the **Workshops and Seminars category**.
  - You enter Effective Troubleshooting as the description and select 415 Workshop Fees as the **Income Account**.
- You also set up Albus Software as a customer.
  - 11 Potter Road, Sacramento, CA 95822.
  - 916-443-3334.
  - Terms are Net 30.

✓ The accountant for Albus Software asks you to send an **invoice** for the workshop now so that they can start processing the paperwork. You prepare Invoice 1011, dated 1/23, for the $2,500.

- (**TIP:** You will make an adjustment for unearned income as part of the homework for Chapter 5 so don't worry about it now.)

1/25/19

✓ Dew Drop Inn decided they need to install a new accounting software system after paying Sally for multiple hours spent trying to repair their current system. They asked Sally to help them select an appropriate program. She reviewed the company's needs this week and put together a proposal for them that spelled out her recommendation. You prepare the invoice for that service. (**Select**, $500, Invoice 1012, Net 15).

✓ Sally lets you know that she won't be doing much consulting during the last few days of January. She's going to use that time to prepare training materials for the Tips and Techniques workshop at Albus Software.

1/30/19

✓ You receive two checks from customers. Both checks are dated 1/30.

- Check #5333 from Uptown Espresso ($320) in payment of invoices 1005 and 1008.
- Check #4568 from Lou's Barber Shop ($500) in full payment of invoice #1006.
  - You apply CM1006 to the balance when you enter the payment.

✓ You deposit both checks in the bank along with the checks received on 1/22. The deposit should total $2,200.

- You apologize to Sally for being so late getting the 1/22 checks in to the bank.

Check numbers 1/31

Checking account balance:. . . .$15,730
January Sales Revenue:. . . . . . .$ 9,280

Reports to create for Chapter 3:

- Journal—1/01 through 1/31
- A/R Aging Summary dated 1/31
- Sales by Product/Service Summary (January sales only)

APPENDIX 3A USING SUB-SERVICE AND SUB-PRODUCT ITEMS IF CATEGORIES AREN'T AVAILABLE

Most companies sell more than one item or provide more than one service to customers. Many companies have an extensive list of items they sell or services they provide. Grouping items makes it easier for users to find the specific product or service they need to complete the transaction.

Using **Categories** to group **items** in company files is a relatively new feature in QBO. The academic version of the software that's provided to you for use in class may not yet be updated to include that option.

If **categories** aren't available, you can still group items using **sub-services** and **sub-products**. **Sub-items** work much like **sub-accounts** do in the **chart of accounts list**. **Sub-item** fields will not be visible if the **categories** feature has been activated.

Let's say a law firm did trial work and employment law work. There might be typical types of services conducted in each area. In trial work, there might be trial prep and jury selection. In employment law cases, there might be employer interviews and meetings. If there were no groups set up in QBO, the **products and services** list would be displayed in alphabetic order like this:

✓ Employer interviews

✓ Jury selection

✓ Meetings

✓ Trial prep

If there were many types of work and many types of services, the alphabetic list might be difficult to use. Grouping services by type of work would be a practical solution.

The first step would be to create a **service item** for Trial services and a **service item** for Employment law services. These items are created to act as parent **items** (as headers) and would normally not be used in transactions.

 HINT: **Items** are set up by clicking the **gear** icon on the icon bar, selecting **Products and Services**, and clicking **New**.

The next step would be to set up the **sub-service items** (in our example they would include trial prep and employer meetings) and link each one to the appropriate parent **item**.

The setup screen for trial prep would look something like this:

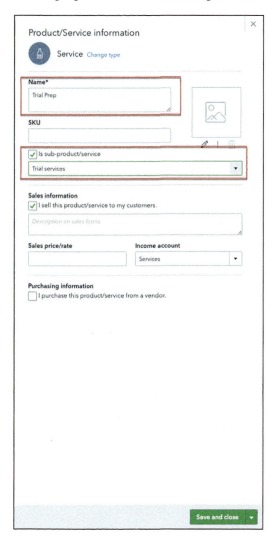

The final **product and services** list would now look like this:

✓ Employment law services
   ○ Employer interviews
   ○ Meetings

✓ Trial services
   ○ Jury selection
   ○ Trial prep

Purchasing Activity
(Service Company)

After completing Chapter 4, you should be able to:

1. Add and edit vendors (including 1099 vendors).

2. Record purchases by cash, check, or credit card.

3. Record purchases on account.

4. Record payments of vendor balances.

5. Create and modify purchase and payables reports.

WHAT IS THE PURCHASE CYCLE IN A SERVICE COMPANY?

The purchase cycle in a service company, like the sales cycle, is fairly straightforward. A company

- Incurs the cost.

- Receives a bill from the vendor.

- Pays the vendor.

Service companies can:

- Pay at the time of purchase of goods or services.

- Pay later (buy "on account" or "on credit").

Before any purchases can be recorded in QuickBooks Online, a vendor must be set up.

MANAGING VENDORS

Vendors are managed in the Vendor Center.

 HINT: A vendor, in business, is an individual or company from whom a company purchases products or services. The phone company, the landlord, the local newspaper are all vendors. In QBO, a **vendor** is set up for any individual (other than an employee) or company that the user expects to pay. Vendors might include owners, lenders, and tax authorities.

The Vendor Center is accessed through the **Expenses** link on the navigation bar.

Select the **Vendors** tab.

The Vendor Center screen looks something like this:

At the top right side of the screen are three small icons.

The **printer** icon (far left) allows the user to print a list of all vendors. The list includes all vendor information currently displayed on the screen (including **OPEN BALANCE**).

Clicking the **export** icon (the middle icon) automatically downloads the list as an Excel file.

Clicking the third icon (the **gear**) allows users to customize the fields displayed in the Vendor Center.

In the Vendor Center, you can:

- access the new vendor setup window.

- access forms necessary to record activity with existing customers.

- access existing customer data for editing.

Adding a Vendor

To add a new vendor, open the Vendor Center by clicking **Expenses** in the navigation bar and clicking the **Vendors** tab.

Click **New Vendor** to open the **Vendor Information** window. It should look something like this:

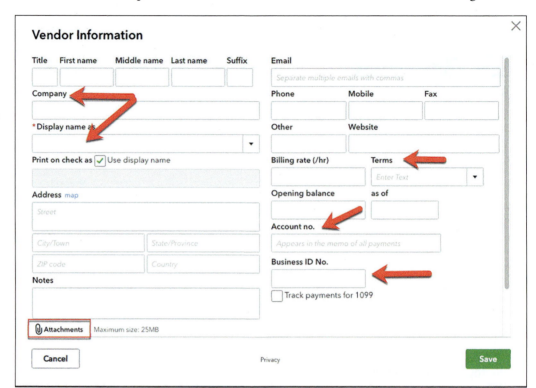

The name entered in the **Company** field is the name used in any correspondence with the vendor. This would normally be the business name used by the vendor.

The **Display Name** is used as a vendor identifier. It could be a number or a shortened version of the vendor name. This is the primary name used to organize the customer list. It's also the name used in any search functions. The **Display Name** is used for internal purposes only. In this class, we'll use the **Company** name as the **Display Name**.

Contact information is entered in the majority of the fields in the **Vendor Information** window.

Other important fields include **Terms** (used to enter the vendor's payment terms) and **Account no.** (used to enter the account number assigned to the company by the vendor).

Documents can be attached to the vendor record for easy access by clicking **Attachments** in the bottom left corner of the screen. **Attachments** will be discussed further in Chapter 12.

Companies are required to report payments to certain types of vendors to the Internal Revenue Service on Form 1099-MISC. 1099-MISC vendors include independent contractors, attorneys, and landlords.

Required tax information for 1099 vendors (including their federal tax identification number) is entered in the fields in the bottom right corner of the window. (Reporting payments to 1099 vendors is covered in the Appendix to this chapter.)

BEHIND THE SCENES QBO has recently added a new feature related to 1099 vendors. Users can now obtain 1099 information directly from vendors through email. The setup is done by clicking the **Workers** tab on the navigation bar and selecting **Add a contractor** on the **Contractors** tab. Any vendor set up through **Workers** will appear in the Vendor Center.

Viewing Vendor Information

To view information about a specific vendor, click the vendor's name in the Vendor Center. The screen should look something like this:

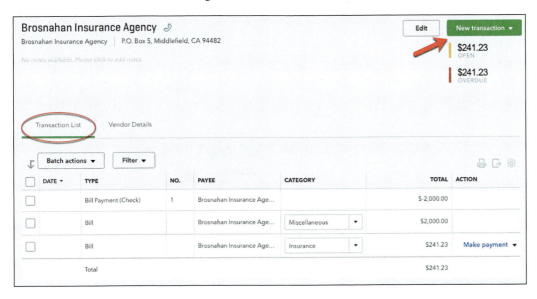

Prior transactions are listed on the **Transaction List** tab. Clicking any of the transactions listed will open the original form to see the transaction details. Once in the form, details can be edited (dates, amounts, distribution accounts, etc.).

New transactions can be entered through this screen by opening the **New transaction** dropdown menu in the top right corner of the screen.

The **Vendor Details** tab screen would look something like this:

Basic contact information is displayed in the **Vendor Details** tab. Clicking **Edit** takes the user to the **Vendor Information** window where changes can be made to the vendor record.

Editing Vendor Information

Vendor information can be changed at any time. To edit an existing vendor, open the Vendor Center by clicking **Expenses** on the navigation bar and selecting the **Vendors** tab.

Click the name of the vendor you wish to edit. A screen similar to this will appear:

Click **Edit** to open the **Vendor Information** window. Make the desired changes and click **Save** to close the window.

Inactivating a Vendor

Vendors with any activity (current or past) cannot be deleted in QBO.

Vendors with zero balances can, however, be inactivated. Most companies would choose to inactivate vendors they don't expect to use in the future to minimize the size of the vendor list.

To inactivate a vendor, open the Vendor Center.

On the dropdown menu in the far right column of the vendor name, select **Make inactive**. This option wouldn't be available on the dropdown menus for vendors with open balances.

Inactive vendors can't be used in transactions and aren't visible in the Vendor Center unless the user elects to show inactive vendors.

To reactivate a vendor, inactive vendors must be visible in the Vendor Center. Click the **gear** icon in the Vendor Center to make inactive customers visible.

An option to reactivate a vendor will automatically appear in the **Action** column next to the vendor name.

☐ Bob's Burger Joint (deleted)	$0.00	Make active

> **BEHIND THE SCENES** Although the vendor shows as "deleted" in the screenshot above, the vendor had been inactivated.

PRACTICE EXERCISE

Set up and edit vendors for Craig's Design and Landscaping.

(Craig's Design adds two new vendors and edits an existing vendor's record.)

1. Enter a new vendor: Office Supplies Shop.

    a. Click **Expenses** in the navigation bar.

    b. Click the **Vendors** tab.

    c. Click **New Vendor** (top right of screen).

    d. Enter the following information on the left side of the **Vendor Information** window:

        i. "Office Supplies Shop" (**Company** and **Display Name** fields)

        "2121 Capital Avenue

        West Sacramento, CA 95691"

    e. Select **Net 30** in the **Terms** dropdown menu on the right side of the window.

    f. Click **Save**.

2. Enter a new 1099 vendor: Beverly Okimoto (accountant who may be hired as contract labor to assist with consulting work).

    a. Click **New Vendor** in the Vendor Center (top right of screen).

    b. Enter the following contact information:

        i. "Beverly" in the **First name** field and "Okimoto" in the **Last name** field

        ii. Use Beverly Okimoto as the **Display name**.

        iii. Enter address information:

        "2525 Paradise Road

        Suite 2502

        Sacramento, CA 95822"

    c. Select **Net 15** in the **Terms** dropdown menu.

    d. Check **Track payments for 1099** and enter "444-22-9898" in the **Business ID No.** field.

    e. Click **Save**.

3. Edit a vendor.

    a. Click **Computers by Jenni** in the Vendor Center.

    b. Click **Edit**.

    c. Change the **Mobile** number to "916-375-5511."

    d. Enter **Business ID No.** as "91-1112222."

    e. Check the box next to **Track payments for 1099**.

    f. **Make a note** of Jenni's last name.

    g. Click **Save**.

RECORDING PURCHASES

In a service company, most purchases are made "on account." It's just an easier, more efficient way to do business. There are times, however, when payment is made at the time of purchase (by cash/check or by credit card). As you can probably guess by now, QBO has a separate form for each alternative. The **transaction types** are:

- **Bill**—used for purchases on account.

- **Check**—used when payment is made with a check or with cash
    - at the time of purchase
    - or when the bill wasn't entered into QBO before payment was made.

- **Expense**—generally used when payment is made at the time of purchase with a credit card. Payments by check can also be entered in the **Expense** form but a check number field is not available in the form.

> **BEHIND THE SCENES** QBO gives users many options for accomplishing the same task. As you continue to work with the software, you'll find yourself developing personal preferences.

Automation in QBO

QBO allows users to automate a number of processes. This is a great tool for many small businesses. While you're learning QBO, however, it can create some confusion. This is especially true in the purchasing cycle. To turn off that automation, click the **gear** icon on the icon bar.

Craig's Design and Landscaping Services

Your Company	Lists	Tools
Account and Settings	All Lists	Import Data
Manage Users	Products and Services	Export Data
Custom Form Styles	Recurring Transactions	Reconcile
Chart of Accounts	Attachments	Budgeting
QuickBooks Labs		Audit Log
		Order Checks ↗

Click **Account and Settings**.

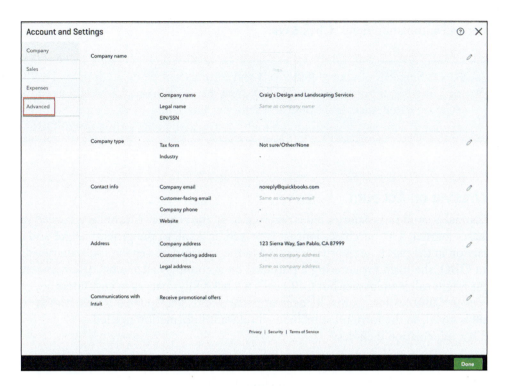

Click **Advanced**.

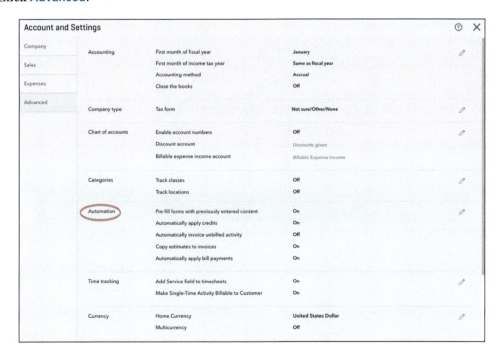

Click **Automation**.

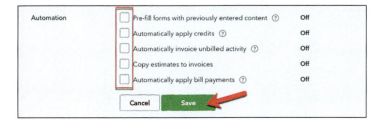

Uncheck all automation fields. Click **Save**.

> **HINT:** Since all of your transactions and settings will be deleted/cleared each time you log out or time out of QBO's test drive company, you would need to clear the automation functions each time you start a new work session. Settings in your assignment file will not change when you log out or time out of QBO.

Purchasing on Account

In a manual accounting system, a bill is received from the vendor. The bill is recorded in the purchases journal. The purchases journal is posted, in total, to the general ledger and each transaction in the purchases journal is posted to the appropriate vendor's subsidiary ledger.

In QBO, the form for entering a purchase on account is called a **bill**. (Remember, the vendor might call it an invoice but QBO calls it a **bill**. Only charges to customers are called invoices in QBO.) All accounts, ledgers, and statements are updated automatically when the **bill** is saved, so the form must include all relevant information needed.

That information includes:

- Who's the vendor? (This is needed for posting to the subsidiary ledger.)

- What are we buying? (What account should QBO debit?)

- When do we have to pay for it? (What are the vendor's credit terms?)

> **WARNING:** Although users can set up multiple accounts payable accounts in the chart of accounts, QBO is not currently designed to work with multiple A/P accounts. **Bills** are automatically credited to the default Accounts Payable (A/P) account set up by Intuit. If a user wanted to maintain more than one accounts payable account, journal entries could be used.

To open the **Bill** form, click the ✚ in the icon bar.

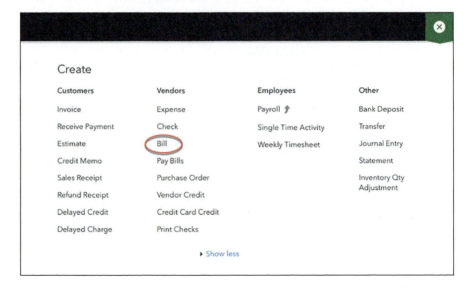

Select **Bill** in the **Vendors** column. The screen looks like this:

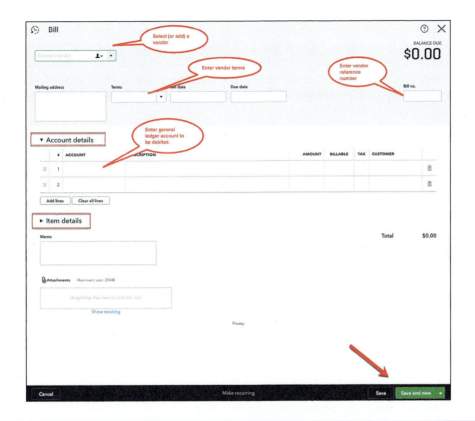

To complete a **bill**, you must **choose a vendor**, enter the **Bill date**, and the **Bill no.** (vendor's reference number) in the top section of the form.

If the vendor hasn't been previously entered, you can click **Add new** at the top of the **Choose a vendor** dropdown menu. After entering the vendor name, click **Save** to enter the new vendor without adding all the vendor detail. Click **Details** to open the **Vendor Information** window and add contact information.

You also need to enter the vendor's credit terms. If you've already set up the credit terms for the vendor, these will show up automatically in the **Terms** field. If you haven't, you will need to enter the terms on the form. QBO uses the terms to keep track of any available early payment discounts so it's important to make sure the date and the terms are entered correctly.

Amounts and the accounts to be debited are entered in the lower section of the form. As you can see in the screenshot above, there are two sections on the bottom half of the form (**Account details** and **Item details**). Clicking the triangle just to the left of the name opens the section.

Both sections are used to specify the account(s) to be debited.

- **Account details**
    - Used to record all purchases other than inventory. Most likely you would be debiting an asset or expense account in this section but you could debit any type of account.

- **Item details**
    - Used to record purchases of inventory items. Inventory purchases will be covered in Chapter 7.

You can enter multiple accounts in the account distribution section of the form. You can even enter negative amounts, which would, of course appear as credits in the underlying journal entry. A negative amount would be entered if, for example, the vendor gives you a discount and you decide to track discounts in a separate account. The sum of all the distributions must equal the total amount of the bill. (This is, after all, still accounting! The underlying journal entry must balance.)

QuickCheck
4-1

> What's the default credit account for a bill? (Answer at end of chapter.)

You can enter additional information about the nature of each charge in the **Description** field. You can also enter general information about the bill in the **Memo** field at the bottom left of the form. The bill itself or other documents related to the charge can be uploaded to QBO by clicking **Attachments** in the bottom left corner of the **bill**. Documents related to the vendor (price lists, contracts, etc.) that are not unique to the bill would normally be uploaded on the **Vendor Information** page. **Attachments** will be covered in greater depth in Chapter 12.

**PRACTICE
EXERCISE**

Enter bills for Craig's Design and Landscaping.
(Craig's Design enters several bills received in the mail.)

1. Click the ➕ icon on the icon bar.

2. Click **Bill** in the **Vendors** column.

3. Enter the telephone bill for the current month. (The total bill was $285. $35 for the phone and a $250 charge for a repair.)

   a. Select **Cal Telephone** as the **Vendor**.

   b. Select **Net 30** for **Terms**.

   c. Enter the current date as the **Bill date**.

   d. Enter "118-1119" as the **Bill No.**

   e. In the **Account details** section, select **Telephone** as the **ACCOUNT** and enter "35" as the **AMOUNT**.

      i. **Make a note** of the parent account for **Telephone**.

   f. On the second line, select **Equipment repairs** as the **ACCOUNT** and enter "250" as the **AMOUNT**.

   g. Click **Save and new**.

4. Enter a $450 bill for an ad placed in the Business Weekly.

   a. Select **Add new** in the **Choose a vendor** dropdown menu.

      i. Enter the name as "Business Weekly."

      ii. Click **Save**.

   b. Select **Net 15** as the **Terms**.

   c. Enter the current date as the **Date**.

   d. Enter "121517" as the **Bill no.**

(continued)

e.   In the **Account details** section, select **Advertising** as the **ACCOUNT**.

f.   Enter "Ad in the Weekly" in the **Memo** field.

g.   Enter "450" as the **AMOUNT.**

h.   Click **Save and new**.

5. Enter a $720 bill from Tania's Nursery for the purchase of a new lawn mower ($650) and 10 boxes of trash bags ($70). The trash bags are expected to be used in the current month.

a.   Select **Tania's Nursery** as the **Vendor**.

b.   Select **Net 15** for the **Terms**.

c.   Enter the current date as the **Bill date**.

d.   Enter "67-1313" as the **Bill no.**

e.   In the **Account details** section, select **Add new** in the **ACCOUNT** dropdown menu to set up a new account.

    i.   **Account Type—Fixed Assets**

    ii. **Detail Type—Machinery & Equipment**

    iii. **Name**—Mowing equipment

        • Check **Track depreciation of this asset**. **TIP:** QBO automatically creates two sub-accounts when this box is checked. One called "Original cost" and one called "Depreciation." Both sub-accounts have the **fixed assets account type**.

    iv. Click **Save and Close**.

f.   Distribute the purchase of the lawn mower to the new **Mowing equipment** account ($650) and the purchase of the trash bags to the **Supplies** expense account ($70).

    i.   The lawn mower represents equipment that will be used for more than one year so it's debited to a **Fixed Asset account type**. The trash bags are expected to be used in the current month so the cost is debited to an **Expense account type**.

g.   Click **Save and close**.

6. Review the accounts set up for the lawn mower.

a.   Click the **gear** icon on the icon bar.

b.   Click **Chart of Accounts**.

c.   **Make a note** of the number of total number of **Fixed Assets** accounts.

d.   Click **Dashboard** to close the window.

Purchasing with Cash or Check

In a manual system, cash payments are recorded in the cash disbursements journal. The journal is recorded, in total, to the general ledger.

In QBO, cash payments made at the time of purchase (or to record a payment to a vendor when the bill wasn't previously entered) are entered through the form (**transaction type**) **Check**.

You can easily access the form by clicking the ➕ icon on the icon bar and clicking **Check** in the **Vendor** column.

The screen will look something like this:

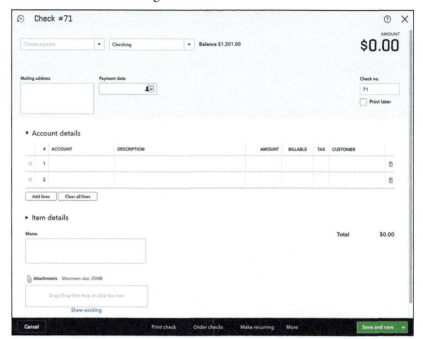

You need to **Choose a payee** and enter the **Payment date**. The **Check no.** will be automatically updated by QBO but you can change the number if necessary.

The **Bank** account you want to be credited for the check amount also needs to be selected. Users can track multiple bank accounts in QBO.

You'll notice the form has the same two distribution sections as the **Bill** form (**Account details** and **Item details**). Both sections are used for entering the general ledger accounts to be debited (or credited if a negative is entered) and the amounts.

PRACTICE
EXERCISE

Enter checks for Craig's Design and Landscaping.
(Craig's Design pays its rent, makes a loan payment, and pays a retainer fee to a consultant.)

1. Record $750 for the current month rent payment.
   a. Click the ➕ icon on the icon bar.
   b. Click **Check**.
   c. Select **Hall Properties** as the vendor.
   d. **Make a note** of the contact name for Hall Properties. (included in the **Mailing address** box.)
   e. Leave **Checking** as the bank account.
   f. Enter the current date as the **Payment date**.
   g. Use "71" as the **Check no.**
   h. In the **Account details** section, select **Rent or Lease** as the **ACCOUNT**.
   i. Enter "1,200" as the **AMOUNT**.
   j. Click **Save and new**.

2. Record a $50 check for the loan payment.
   a. Select **Fidelity** as the vendor.
   b. Leave **Checking** as the bank account.

(continued)

c. Enter the current date as the **Payment date**.

d. Use "72" as the **Check no.**

e. There are two distributions in the **Account details** section.

  i. On the first line select **Notes Payable** as the **ACCOUNT** and enter "45" as the **AMOUNT** (principal).

  ii. On the second line, select **Add new** in the **ACCOUNT** field, choose **Other Current Liabilities** as the **account type**, **Other Current Liabilities** as the **detail type**, and enter "Interest Payable" as the **Name**. Click **Save and close**.

  iii. Enter "5" as the **AMOUNT**.

f. Click **Save and new**.

3. Record check to Computers by Jenni for a retainer fee. (You're giving her an advance for future computer work.)

a. Select **Computers by Jenni** as the vendor.

b. Leave **Checking** as the bank account.

c. Enter the current date as the **Payment date**.

d. Use "73" as the **Check no.**

e. In the **Account details** section, select **Prepaid Expenses** as the **ACCOUNT**.

f. Enter "400" as the **AMOUNT**.

g. Click **Save and close**.

Voiding Checks

If a check is printed but contains an error and won't be distributed, it should be voided (not deleted) in QBO. This ensures that all check numbers are properly accounted for.

The **check** form must be open before it can be voided. There are many ways to find a transaction in QBO. The **Search** feature is a good option.

Click the **magnifying glass** option on the icon bar.

The screen will look something like this:

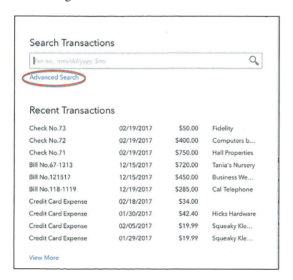

Click **Advanced Search**.

The first dropdown menu is primarily used to narrow the search to a specific transaction type although other options are available. The second dropdown menu is used to further narrow the search by specifying a date, amount, payee, etc. A search can be further narrowed to a range of dates by clicking **Add Filter**. Searching for all checks written to a specific vendor would return something like the following:

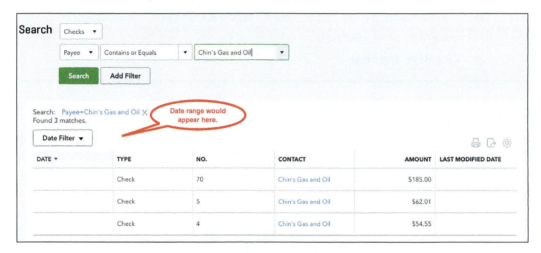

Click the check to be voided to open the form.

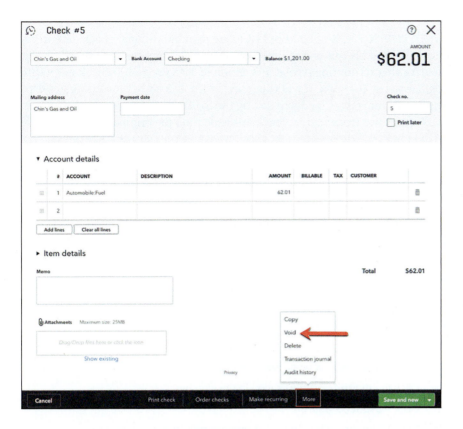

Click **More** on the bottom bar of the **check** form and select **Void**.

You will have an opportunity to cancel the transaction before QBO completes the voiding process.

Voided checks do appear on journal reports (0.00 dollar amounts) and are accessible using the **Search** feature. A voided check would look something like this:

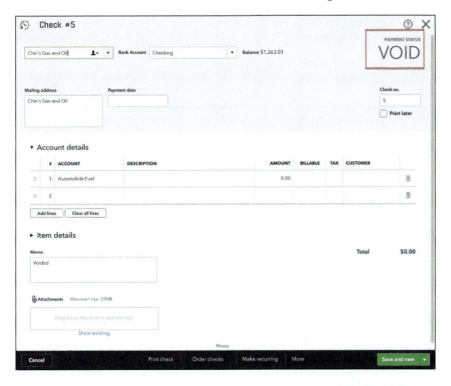

BEHIND THE SCENES QuickBooks Online uses the original check date to record a voided check. This can create problems if financial reports have already been distributed for that accounting period. For example, let's say a $100 check was written in December to pay for some travel expenses. In the December income statement, net income would, of course, be decreased by the $100 travel expense. Now let's say that the $100 check was lost so a new check was issued and the original check was voided in QBO in February. The replacement check would have a February date but the original check would be voided by QBO as of the original December check date. If you then prepared a new December income statement, net income would automatically be $100 higher than it was before due to the voided check. On the other hand, February's net income would be reduced by the $100 December travel expense. The expense is now reported in the wrong accounting period. If the amounts are significant or if tax reports have already been filed, journal entries should be made to correct the balances.

PRACTICE EXERCISE

Void a check for Craig's Design and Landscaping.

(Craig's Design voids a check prepared in error.)

1. Void the check to Books by Bessie. Craig used the company account instead of his own personal checkbook when he bought some books.

   a. Click the **magnifying glass** icon in the icon bar.

   b. Click **Advanced Search**.

   c. Select **Checks** on the first (**All Transactions**) dropdown menu.

   d. Select **Books by Bessie** in the **Enter Payee** dropdown menu.

   e. Click **Search**.

   f. Click check #12. The original check form should appear.

   g. **Make a note** of the amount of the check being voided.

   h. Click **More** at the bottom of the screen.

   i. Click **Void**.

   j. Click **Yes** when asked about voiding the check.

   k. Click **OK**.

Purchasing with a Credit Card

Some companies obtain corporate credit cards. Owners or employees who need to be able to purchase items when they're traveling are the typical users of these cards.

Although the seller might see a payment by credit card as the same as cash, the purchaser is really buying on credit. The company that issued the card is the creditor.

In QBO, credit cards are set up as a separate liability **account type (Credit Card)**. When individual credit card charges are entered, the amounts are credited to the credit card account and debited to the appropriate expense or asset account. This allows the user to track the details of all purchases.

When the credit card statement is received, the user reconciles the amounts recorded in QBO to the statement and processes the credit card bill for payment. (Credit card reconciliations are covered in Chapter 5.)

Before you can enter credit card charges, the general ledger account must be set up. This is done through the Chart of Accounts list. Remember, the account must be set up as a **Credit Card account type**.

To enter a credit card charge, click the ⊕ icon on the icon bar

Click **Expense**.

The screen will look something like this:

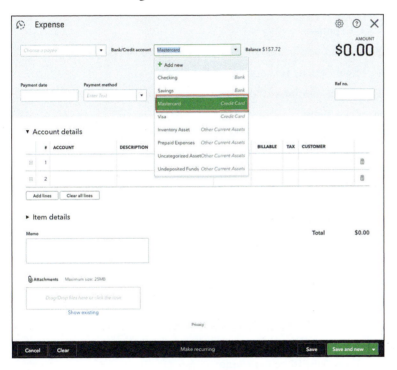

To enter a credit card charge, you need to enter the name of the business where the credit card was used, the credit card used, the date of the charge, and the account(s) you want QBO to debit. Many companies will add the vendor name for credit card transactions but will not add much vendor detail (address, etc.).

> **BEHIND THE SCENES** Remember, you will be paying the entity that issued the card not the business where you used the card. The business name is entered for informational purposes only.

The **Expense** form is similar to the Bill and Check forms. The account credited will be the liability account set up as a **credit card account type**. If multiple credit card accounts are set up, the user will need to identify the appropriate account using the dropdown menu at the top center of the window. The accounts debited will be identified in the **Account details** section, the **Item details** section, or both.

PRACTICE
EXERCISE

Set up and use a credit card in Craig's Design and Landscaping.
(Craig's Design uses its corporate credit card to make several purchases.)

1. Set up a credit card account.

    a. Click the **gear** icon on the icon bar.

    b. Click **Chart of Accounts**.

    c. Click **See your Chart of Accounts**.

    d. Click **New**.

    e. Select **Credit Card** as the **Account Type**.

    f. Select **Credit Card** as the **Detail Type**.

    g. Enter "Global Credit Card" in the **Name** field.

    h. Click **Save and close**.

2. To record a client lunch (paid with credit card):

    a. Click the ➕ icon on the icon bar.

    b. Click **Expense**.

    c. Select **Add new** in the **Choose a payee** dropdown menu.

        i.   Enter "Fancy Restaurant" as the **Name**.

        ii. Select **Vendor** as the **Type**.

        iii. Click **Save**.

    d. Select **Global Credit Card** as the account to be credited.

    e. Enter the current date as **Payment date**.

    f. Select **MasterCard** as the **Payment method**.

    g. Leave **Ref. No.** blank.

    h. In the **Account details** section, select **Meals and Entertainment** as the **ACCOUNT**.

    i. Enter "Lunch with July Summers" in the **Memo** field.

    j. Enter "94.10" as the **AMOUNT**.

    k. Click **Save and new**.

3. To record purchase of stamps with a credit card:

    a. Select **Add new** in the **Choose a payee** dropdown menu.

        i.   Enter "USPS" as the **Name**.

        ii. Select **Vendor** as the **Type**.

        iii. Click **Save**.

    b. Select **Global Credit Card** as the account to be credited.

    c. Enter the current date as **Payment date**.

    d. Select **MasterCard** as the **Payment method**.

    e. Leave **Ref. No.** blank.

    f. In the **Account details** section, select **Office Expense** as the **ACCOUNT**.

    g. Enter "84" as the **AMOUNT**.

    h. Click **Save and close**.

PAYING VENDOR BALANCES

Eventually vendors must be paid! Most companies pay vendors in batches. A check run might be processed twice a month in a smaller company. Check runs would likely be processed more frequently in larger companies.

In a manual system, checks are prepared and then entered in the cash disbursements journal. The totals of the journal are posted to the general ledger and each transaction is posted to the appropriate vendor's subsidiary ledger.

In QBO, bill payment transactions are automatically posted to the general ledger and the vendor subsidiary ledger when the transaction is saved.

Companies can pay bills using cash, checks, or credit cards. Paying vendor balances by check is the most common payment method in small- to medium-sized companies.

There are two methods for recording payments of vendor balances in QBO. Payments of one or more vendor **bills** can be batch processed through the **Pay Bills** window. Payment of one or more **bills** to a single vendor can be processed through the Vendor Center.

Paying Multiple Vendor Bills

Click the ✚ icon on the icon bar.

Click **Pay Bills** to open the **Pay Bills** window.

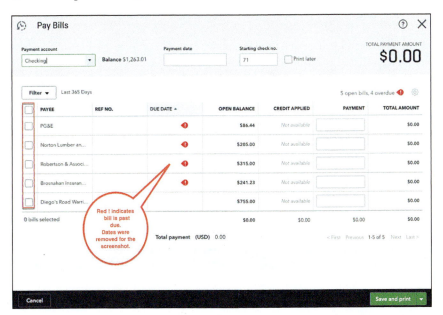

There is a lot to do on this screen so take your time!

You must identify the **payment account** being used (checking, credit card, etc.) and the **Payment date**. If you choose to pay by check, QBO will display a **Starting check no.** That can be changed, if needed.

You can limit the number of items displayed by opening the **Filter** dropdown menu.

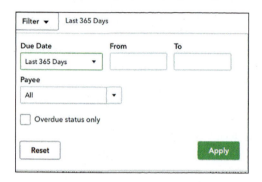

Filtering is available (by due date or by vendor name). For vendor names, your choice is limited, however, to either all vendors or one specific vendor.

Bills to be paid are selected by checking the box to the left of the specific **bill**. If you want to see the details of a specific **bill**, you can double-click the **Payee** name. QBO will display the original **bill**.

If there are any available credits, the amounts will be displayed in the **Credit Applied** field when the vendor is selected for payment. Vendor credits are covered in Chapter 6.

The total amount to be paid is displayed on the screen. The balance remaining in the account used to pay the **bill** is also displayed. The window might look something like this if two bills were paid:

> **BEHIND THE SCENES** If multiple bills from the same vendor have been selected for payment, QuickBooks Online will automatically combine the amounts and create a single check for that particular vendor.

In this class, you should click **Save and close** to record the payments without printing physical checks.

Paying One or More Bills from a Single Vendor

Payment of one or more **bills** from a single vendor can be processed through the Vendor Center.

Click **Expenses** on the navigation bar.
Click **Brosnahan Insurance** on the **Vendors** tab.

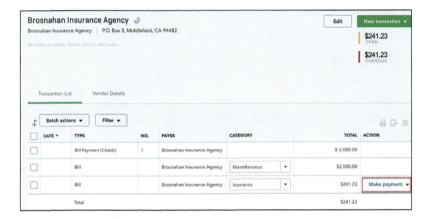

Click **Make payment** next to the $241.23 amount.

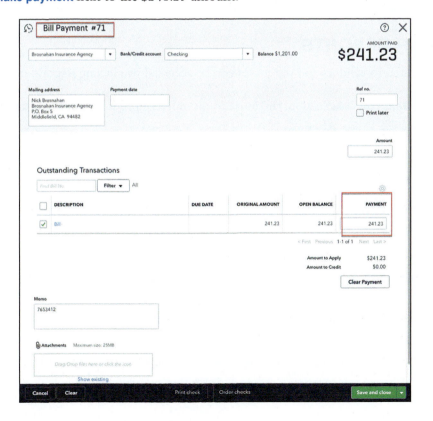

Note that QBO automatically creates a **Bill Payment** transaction. Partial payments can be recorded by changing the amount in the **PAYMENT** field.

> **BEHIND THE SCENES** If multiple **bills** were outstanding for Brosnahan, all would appear as **Outstanding Transactions** on the **Bill Payment** screen. One or more could then be selected for payment with a single check.

PRACTICE
EXERCISE

Record payment of bills for Craig's Design and Landscaping.
(Craig's Design pays several vendor balances.)

1. Click the ⊕ icon on the icon bar.

2. Click **Pay Bills**.

3. **Make a note** of the balance due to **Robertson & Associates**.

4. Select **Checking** as the **Payment account** and the current date as the **Payment date**.

5. Leave the **Starting check no.** as 71.

   a. **TIP:** If you didn't log out after the last Practice Exercise, use 75 as the **Starting check no.**

6. Place a checkmark next to **Norton Lumber** and **Robertson & Associates.**

7. **Make a note** of the total amount paid.

8. Click **Save and close**.

QuickCheck
4-2

> Assume you selected 5 bills to be paid in a single run. Three of the bills were to the same vendor. How many checks would QBO create? (Answer at end of chapter.)

VENDOR REPORTS

Reports related to vendors and purchases can be accessed by clicking **Reports** on the navigation bar.

In the **What You Owe** section, the most commonly used reports would most likely be:

- **Accounts payable Aging Summary**

- **Unpaid Bills**

In the **Expenses and Purchases** section, the most commonly used reports would likely be:

- **Transaction list by Vendor**

- **Check Detail**

PRACTICE
EXERCISE

Prepare reports on payables for Craig's Design and Landscaping.
(Craig's Design needs an A/P Aging and wants a check register.)

1. Prepare an A/P aging.

   a. Click **Reports**.

   b. Click **Accounts payable aging summary** in the **What You Owe** section.

   c. Change date to the current date and click **Run report**.

(continued)

2. Prepare a check register.

   a. Click **Reports**.

   b. Click **Check Detail** in the **Expenses and Vendors** section.

   c. Change **Report period** to **All Dates**.

   d. Click **Customize**.

   e. Click **Rows/Columns**.

   f. Click **Change columns**, if necessary.

   g. Remove the check next to **Clr**.

       i. NOTE: Checks not marked as **Clr** are still outstanding (haven't cleared the bank).

   h. Click **Run report**.

   i. **Make a note** of the account debited in the journal entry underlying the check to Tony Rondonuwu.

3. Click **Dashboard** to exit the window.

Accounts Payable (A/P)

Three checks would be created.

ANSWER TO
QuickCheck
4-1
ANSWER TO
QuickCheck
4-2

CHAPTER SHORTCUTS

Add a vendor
1. Click **Expenses** on the navigation bar
2. Click the **Vendors** tab to open the Vendor Center
3. Click **New Vendor**

Edit a vendor
1. Open Vendor Center
2. Click vendor name
3. Click **Edit**

Inactivate a vendor
1. Open Vendor Center
2. Open the dropdown menu in the **Action** column for the vendor to be inactivated
3. Select **Make inactive**

Record a check
1. Click the ➕ icon on the icon bar
2. Click **Check** in the **Vendors** column

Record a credit card charge
1. Click the ➕ icon on the icon bar
2. Click **Expense** in the **Vendors** column

Record payments to vendors on account balances
1. Click the ➕ icon on the icon bar
2. Click **Pay Bills** in the **Vendors** column

Set up a new credit term
1. Click the **gear** icon on the icon bar
2. Click **All Lists**
3. Click **Terms**

CHAPTER REVIEW (Answers available on the publisher's website.)

Matching

Match the term or phrase (as used in QuickBooks Online) to its definition.

1. Bill   5. Vendor
2. 1099 vendor   6. Net 15
3. Bill Payment   7. Bill No
4. Display Name   8. Check

_____ transaction type used for recording invoices received from vendors

_____ vendor invoice number

_____ transaction type used to record payments to vendors on account

_____ individual or company from whom goods or services are purchased

_____ an individual or company that receives payments that must be reported to the IRS

_____ a type of payment term

_____ transaction type used to record up front payments to vendors

_____ vendor identifier

Multiple Choice

1. A purchase of a computer, on account, would be recorded in the _____ section of a **bill** in QBO.
   a. Item details
   b. Fixed assets
   c. Account details
   d. Computer Equipment

2. Vendors
   a. can be deleted as long as there are no outstanding amounts due to the vendor.
   b. can be deleted at any time.
   c. can be inactivated at any time.
   d. can be inactivated as long as there are no outstanding amounts due to the vendor.

3. When a purchase made with a credit card is recorded in QBO,
   a. cash is credited.
   b. a liability account is credited (Account Payable account type).
   c. a liability account is credited (Credit Card account type).
   d. a liability account is credited (Other Current Liability account type).

4. Payments to vendors can be entered _____.
   a. using the Check transaction type
   b. using the Bill Payment transaction type
   c. using the Expense transaction type
   d. using Check, Bill Payment, or Expense transaction types

5. Which of the following statements is true?

a. You can only have one account with an **account type** of **Accounts Payable** in QBO.

b. You can have multiple accounts payable accounts for use in recording vendor bills and tracking vendor balances in QBO but they must each have a different name and they must all have an "Accounts Payable" **account type**.

c. You can have multiple accounts payable accounts in QBO but only the default Accounts Payable account created by Intuit can be used when entering bills or bill payments.

d. Vendor balances cannot be tracked in QBO.

ASSIGNMENTS

Background information: Martin Smith, a college student and good friend of yours, had always wanted to be an entrepreneur. He is very good in math so, to test his entrepreneurship skills, he decided to set up a small math tutoring company serving local high school students who struggle in their math courses. He set up the company, Math Revealed!, as a corporation in 2018. Martin is the only owner. He has not taken any distributions from the company since it opened.

The business has been successful so far. In fact, it's been so successful he has decided to work in his business full time now that he's graduated from college with a degree in Mathematics.

He has decided to start using QuickBooks Online to keep track of his business transactions. He likes the convenience of being able to access his information over the Internet. You have agreed to act as his accountant while you're finishing your own academic program.

He currently has a number of regular customers that he tutors in Pre-Algebra, Algebra, and Geometry. His customers pay his fees by cash or check after each tutoring session but he does give terms of Net 15 to some of his customers. He has developed the following fee schedule:

Name	Description	Rate
Refresher	One-hour session	$40 per hour
Persistence program	Two one-hour sessions per week	$75 per week
Crisis program	Five one-hour sessions per week	$150 per week

The tutoring sessions usually take place at his students' homes but he recently signed a two-year lease on a small office above a local coffee shop. The rent is only $200 per month starting in January 2019. A security deposit of $400 was paid in December 2018.

The following equipment is owned by the company:

Description	Date placed in service	Cost	Life	Salvage Value
Computer	7/1/18	$3,000	36 months	$300
Printer	7/1/18	$ 240	24 months	$ 0
Graphing Calculators (2)	7/1/18	$ 294	36 months	$ 60

All equipment is depreciated using the straight-line method.

As of 12/31/18, he owed $2,000 to his parents who initially helped him get started. They are charging him interest at a 6% annual rate. He has been paying interest only on a monthly basis. His last payment was 12/31/18.

Assignment 4A

Math Revealed!

Assignments with the MBC **are available in myBusinessCourse.**

Over the next month or so, he plans to expand his business by selling a few products he believes will help his students. He has already purchased a few items:

Category	Description	Vendor	Quantity On Hand	Cost per unit	Sales Price
Books and Tools					
	Geometry in Sports	Books Galore	20	12	16
	Solving Puzzles: Fun with Algebra	Books Galore	20	14	18
	Getting Ready for Calculus	Books Galore	20	15	20
	Protractor/Compass Set	Math Shack	10	10	14
	Handheld Dry-Erase Boards	Math Shack	25	5	9
	Notebooks (pack of 3)	Paper Bag Depot	10	15	20

1/3/19

✓ Since Martin is expanding his business, he decides to purchase a general liability insurance policy from Protector Insurance Company. The annual premium is $480. It covers the period 1/1-12/31/19. You write a check (#1101) to pay the full year premium amount. (You add Protector Insurance as a vendor without adding any detail information.) You will make an adjustment to recognize insurance expense for January at the end of the month. (**TIP:** You will be doing this as part of Chapter 5's assignment.)

✓ Martin is moving into his new space today. The furniture arrives in the morning. The total cost of the desk, large study table, and eight chairs Martin ordered from Frank's Furniture is $360. A bill, dated 1/3 (#ST8990) for the total amount, is included with the shipment. The terms are Net 30.

- You set up a new account called Office Furniture (Account #185). (**HINT:** This account should have a **Fixed Asset account type**. You decide to record depreciation on all fixed assets in a single account so you don't check the **Track depreciation of this asset** box.

- You also set up the new vendor:

  Frank's Furniture

  2174 Hardwood Street

  Sacramento, CA 95822

✓ Martin also purchases two more computers and three more calculators since he's doing more tutoring at his new location. The equipment, purchased from Paper Bag Depot, costs $1,197 in total ($441 for the three calculators and $756 for the two computers). Martin expects the calculators and computers to last three years. Martin uses a new credit card to make the purchase.

- You set up the general ledger account for the new credit card first. You use Prime Visa Payable as the account name and 220 as the account number. (**HINT:** Don't forget to select the appropriate **account type**.)

- You also set up a new vendor for the card.

  Prime Visa Company

  55 Wall Street

  New York, NY 10005

  Terms: Net 15

- You enter the credit card charge using 1/3 as the date. **TIP:** Use the **Expense** form to record credit card charges.

✓ You pay January's rent ($200) with check #1102. The landlord is Pro Spaces.

1/4/19

✓ Martin purchases some graphing paper, pencils, and some 8.5" × 11" dry-erase boards from Math Shack for $182.79, on account (Invoice #3659). He is tracking all tutoring supplies as an asset. At the end of the month, he'll determine the value of the supplies on hand and you'll make any necessary adjustments. The terms are Net 15.

1/8/19

✓ Martin hands you the receipt for the $20 of gas he purchased at Cardinal Gas & Snacks using his VISA credit card and you enter the credit card charge in QBO.

- You save the new vendor without adding any additional vendor details.

1/11/19

✓ You take a look at the **Unpaid Bills** report in the **What You Owe** section of **Reports**. It looks like some of the bills were due on 12/31! You know that can't be true so you look through the unpaid bill file. You correct the terms on each of the bills as follows:

- Kathy's Coffee—Net 15
- Math Shack—Net 15
- Paper Bag Depot—Net 30

TIP: Click on the appropriate bills in the **Unpaid Bills** report, enter the terms, and click **Save and close**.

✓ Since these are the normal terms for these three vendors, you also change the terms in the vendor records.

- While you're in the Vendor Center, you go ahead and add terms to Sacramento Utilities (Net 30).

✓ You pay all bills due on or before 1/20 from the Checking account.

- There should be three bills totaling $512.79. Start with check #1103 (There will be two **checks**).

1/16/19

✓ You receive two bills in the mail, which you record in QBO.

- One of the bills, dated 1/16, is from Sacramento Utilities. The January bill (#01-59974) total is $85. The bill is due in 30 days.
- The other bill is from Parent's Survival Monthly, a parenting magazine targeting parents with teenage children. Martin had placed an ad with them set to appear in next Sunday's paper. The total cost is $80 (vendor invoice #12213, dated 1/16). The payment terms are Net 15.

1/18/19

✓ Martin asks you to contact Frank's Furniture and order some shelving for the new space. He wants a unit that includes open shelves and some drawers. You call and talk to the representative who gives you an estimate of $649. That sounds reasonable to you and you place the order. The expected arrival date is 1/30.

1/22/19

✓ Although the Mathmagic Clinic was a success overall, there was one small incident. One of the friends of Martin who helped with the tutoring tripped over the feet of one of the students and fell into the study table. He ended up with a gash on his left hand. He went to the 24 Hour Quick Stitch Clinic and had his hand bandaged up. Luckily, he didn't require any stitches. The cost of the visit was $220 and the clinic gave Martin a bill, dated 1/19 (#121521).

- The 24 Hour Quick Stitch Clinic's address is 7500 Medical Boulevard, Sacramento, CA 95822. The phone number is 916-222-9999. The terms are Net 10.
  - **HINT:** You'll need to set up a new term.
- You decide to expense the cost to Miscellaneous Expense (Account 699).

1/23/19

✓ Your friend Samantha Levin helped Martin out at the clinic last Saturday by checking students in and out. Martin doesn't expect to hire her as an employee but if you pay her more than $600 during the year, you'll need to file a 1099 for her at year-end. You decide to get everything set up just in case she's paid over the threshold.

  • You set up a new general ledger account. You decide to name the account "Contract labor" and use account #605. You make it a subaccount of Labor costs and you use **Cost of labor** as the **detail type**.

  • You also set Samantha up as a vendor. Her address is 901 Angles Lane, Sacramento, CA 95822. Her phone number is 916-654-4321.

    ○ You set her up as a 1099 vendor. Her social security number (**Business ID number**) is 222-33-6666.

✓ Samantha had agreed to a $15 per hour pay rate. She helped out for four hours so you write her a check (#1105) for $60.

1/24/19

✓ Martin hands you another gas receipt for $22. He purchased the gas at Cardinal Gas & Snacks using his credit card today. You record the charge in QBO.

1/25/19

✓ You pay all bills due on or before 2/4/19.

  • There should be four bills totaling $810. Start with check #1106.

✓ Martin brings in coffee drinks from Moon Coffee as a treat for getting through the first month in the new space. He hands you the receipt for $8.75. (He used the credit card to buy the coffee.) You decide to charge the coffee to a new account called "Staff Relations" (a labor cost). You use 608 as the account number.

1/30/19

✓ The shelving unit is delivered and installed by Frank's Furniture. Martin is impressed by the quality of the product. The actual price is the $649 you were originally quoted. The invoice # is ST9998, dated 1/30, and the terms are Net 30.

✓ Martin has been working hard and asks you to write him a check for $1,500. (Use check #1110.)

  • You set Martin Smith up as a vendor first.

    949 Ambitious Street

    Sacramento, CA 95822

    916-131-4679

  • **HINT:** This is a corporation so a payment to Martin (other than salary or reimbursement) is a dividend. Use 345 as the account number. (**HINT:** QBO doesn't have a **detail type** for dividends. Use **Partner Distributions** as a substitute.)

Check numbers as of 1/31

Checking account balance:. $2,872.21
Accounts Payable:. . . . .$ 734.00
Net income (January only):. $3,634.25

Reports to create for Chapter 4:

All reports should be in portrait orientation.

• Journal—1/01 through 1/31.

  ▪ Include only these transaction types: Check, Bill, Bill Payment (Check), Expense.

- Vendor Balance Detail (as of 1/31)
- Profit and loss statement (January only)
- Vendor Contact List
  - Columns (in order) should be Vendor, Address, Phone Numbers, Terms, Track 1099

**Salish Software
Solutions**

Background information: Sally Hanson, a good friend of yours, double majored in Computer Science and Accounting in college. She worked for several years for a software company in Silicon Valley but the long hours started to take a toll on her personal life.

Last year she decided to open up her own company, Salish Software Solutions (a corporation). Sally currently advises clients looking for new accounting software and assists them with software installation. She also provides training to client employees and occasionally troubleshoots software issues.

She has decided to start using QuickBooks Online to keep track of her business transactions. She likes the convenience of being able to access financial information over the Internet. You have agreed to act as her accountant while you're working on your accounting degree.

Sally has a number of clients that she is currently working with. She gives 15-day payment terms to her corporate clients but she asks for cash at time of service if she does work for individuals. She has developed the following fee schedule:

Name	Description	Rate
Select	Software Selections	$500 flat fee
Set Up	Software Installation	$ 50 per hour
Train	Software training	$ 40 per hour
Fix	File repair	$ 60 per hour

Sally rents office space from Alki Property Management for $800 per month.

The following furniture and equipment is owned by Salish:

Description	Date placed in service	Cost	Life	Salvage Value
Office Furniture...........	6/1/18	$1,400	60 months	$200
Computer	7/1/18	$4,620	36 months	$300
Printer..................	5/1/18	$ 900	36 months	$ 0

All equipment is depreciated using the straight-line method.

As of 12/31/18, she owed $3,500 to Dell Finance. The monthly payment on that loan is $150 including interest at 5%. Sally's last payment to Dell was 12/31/18.

Over the next month or so, Sally plans to expand her business by selling some of her favorite accounting and personal software products directly to her clients. She has already purchased the following items.

Item Name	Description	Vendor	Quantity On Hand	Cost per unit	Sales Price
Easy1	Easy Does it	Abacus Shop	15	$100	$175
Retailer...........	Simply Retail	Simply Accounting	2	$400	$700
Contractor........	Simply Construction	Simply Accounting	2	$500	$800
Organizer	Organizer	Personal Solutions	25	$ 25	$ 50
Tracker	Investment Tracker	Personal Solutions	25	$ 20	$ 40

1/2/19

✓ You pay January's rent ($800) to Alki Property Management with check #1101.

✓ Sally recently decided to purchase business insurance from Albright Insurance Company. The policy was effective as of 1/1/19. You write a check (#1102) to pay the full year premium amount ($1,800).

- You add Albright Insurance as a vendor without adding any detail information.
- You will make an adjustment to recognize insurance expense for January at the end of the month. (**TIP:** You will be doing this as part of the Chapter 5 assignment.)

✓ You notice that payment terms aren't set up for many of Salish's vendors. You change the records as follows:

- Abacus Shop—Net 15
- Paper Bag Depot—Net 30
- Personal Software—Net 15
- Sacramento Light & Power—Net 30
- Simply Accounting—Net 15
- Western Phone Company—Net 30

1/3/19

✓ Sally receives the credit card she applied for last month.

- You set up the general ledger account for the new credit card. You use Capital 3 Visa Payable as the account name and 220 as the account number. (**HINT:** Don't forget to select the appropriate **account type**.)
- You also set up a new vendor for the card.

   ○ Capital Three
     58 Wall Street
     New York, NY 10005
     Terms: Net 15

✓ Sally had completely run out of office supplies at the end of December so she uses her VISA card to purchase paper, pens, and file folders at Paper Bag Depot. You enter the credit card charge of $500 using the **Expense** form. You're not sure how long the supplies will last but you're sure they won't all be used in January. You will take an inventory at the end of January to see how much was used this month. (**TIP:** You will do this in the homework for Chapter 5.)

1/4/19

✓ You receive two bills in the mail, which you record in QBO.

- One of the bills (#01-59974), dated 1/4, is from Sacramento Light & Power. The bill total is $105 and is due in 30 days. The bill is for January utilities.
- The other bill (#8911-63) is from Western Phone Company for Sally's January cell phone service. The $108.95 bill, dated 1/4, has payment terms of Net 30.

1/8/19

✓ Sally purchases some new computer software today from Abacus Shop. The software costs $840 and will help Sally track her installation projects. She expects it to last 2 years (no salvage value). Abacus gives you a bill (#8944-11) with 15-day payment terms.

- You set up a new account called Computer Software (#184). You decide to record all depreciation in a single accumulated depreciation account, so you don't check the **Track depreciation of this asset** box. You'll record depreciation at the end of the month.

1/14/19

✓ You take a look at the **Unpaid Bills** report in the **What You Owe** section of **Reports**. It looks like some of the bills were due on 12/31! You know that can't be true so you look through the unpaid bill file. You correct the payment terms on each of the **bills** dated 12/31 as follows:

- Abacus Shop—Net 15
- Personal Software—Net 15
- Simply Accounting—Net 15
- **TIP:** Click each invoice on the **Unpaid Bills** report to open the bill form. Enter the terms and save.

✓ You pay all bills due on or before 1/21/19 from the Checking account.

- There should be three bills totaling $1,235. Start with check 1103.

1/16/19

✓ You receive a bill from Entrepreneur, a local magazine targeting small business owners. Sally had placed an ad in January's magazine for the upcoming workshop. The total cost is $150 (vendor invoice #12213, dated 1/16). The payment terms are Net 10. (**TIP:** You'll need to create a new payment term.)

- Entrepreneur Magazine
  534 American River Drive
  Sacramento, CA 95822

✓ Sally asks you to order a large storage cabinet from Rikea. She needs to have a storage area for the inventory she plans to sell starting in February. You call and talk to a sales representative who gives you an estimate of $1,500. That sounds reasonable to you and you place the order. The expected arrival date is 1/30.

✓ Sally uses her credit card to pay for the space she rented at Hacker Spaces for Friday's workshop. You record the $300 charge. This is a new type of expense for Salish Software so you set up two new accounts.

- You add a primary account "Workshop Costs" with 660 as the account number and a subaccount "Space rental expense" (#661). You use **Other Miscellaneous Service Cost** as the **detail type** for each account.

✓ Just before closing, you get a call from Hacker Spaces. They made a mistake on the fee. It should have been $600 for the space. You transfer the call to Sally and, although she's unhappy, she agrees to make another credit card payment. She did think the fee was almost too good to be true. You record the $300 charge.

1/22/19

✓ Although the Picking the Right Software workshop was a great success overall, there was an unexpected additional expense. Sally ended up breaking one of Hacker Spaces' tables when she was trying to get the room set up. You write Hacker Spaces a check (#1106) for $200 to cover the cost of replacing the table.

- You decide to expense the cost to Space rental expense.

1/24/19

✓ Your friend Oscar Torres helped Sally out at the workshop last Friday. Sally doesn't expect to hire him as an employee but you know that if you pay him more than $600 during the year, you'll need to file a 1099 for him at the end of the year. You decide to get everything set up just in case he's paid over the threshold.

- You set up a new general ledger account. You decide to name the account "Workshop Helpers" with 665 as the account number. You make it a subaccount of Workshop Costs. You use **Cost of Labor** as the **detail type**.
- You also set Oscar up as a vendor. His address is 901 Luna Drive, Sacramento, CA 95822. His phone number is 916-654-4321.
  - ○ You set him up as a 1099 vendor. His social security number (**Business ID number**) is 222-33-4444.

✓ Oscar had agreed to work for $20 per hour pay rate. He helped out for six hours so you write him a check (#1107) for $120.

✓ Sally has lunch with the IT director for Metro Markets, a large grocery chain. She is hoping to do some work for the company in the future. She uses her credit card to pay for the $110, very nice, lunch at The Blue Door. You record the charge to Client relations expense.

- Nothing is decided at the lunch so you don't set up Metro Markets as a customer.

1/28/19

✓ You pay all bills due on or before 2/11/19.

- There should be four bills totaling $1,203.95. Start with check #1108.

1/30/19

✓ The storage cabinets are delivered and installed by Rikea. The final price is the $1,500 you were originally quoted. The invoice # is RK65541, dated 1/30, and the terms are Net 30. You expect the cabinets to last for 5 years.

- Rikea
  25 Bigbox Lane
  Sacramento, CA 95822

✓ Sally has been working hard and asks you for a $2,500 check. (Use check #1112.)

- You set Sally Hanson up as a vendor first.
  14 Technology Drive
  Sacramento, CA 95822
  916-346-9258

- **TIP:** This is a corporation so a payment to Sally (other than salary or reimbursement) is a dividend. Use 345 as the account number. (HINT: QBO doesn't have a **detail type** for dividends. Use **Partner Distributions** as a substitute.)

Check numbers as of 1/31

Checking account balance:. $7,871.05
Accounts Payable:. $1,500.00
Net income (January only):. $7,086.05

Reports to create for Chapter 4:

All reports should be in portrait orientation; Fit to one page wide

- Journal—1/01 through 1/31.
  - Include only these transaction types: Check, Bill, Bill Payment (Check), Expense.

- Vendor Balance Detail (as of 1/31)

- Profit and loss statement (January only)

- Vendor Contact List
  - Include these columns in this order: Vendor, Address, Phone Numbers, Terms, Track 1099

APPENDIX 4A REPORTING 1099 VENDOR ACTIVITY

Companies are required to report certain types of payments to the Internal Revenue Service (IRS) annually using Form 1099-MISC. 1099 vendors include attorneys, landlords, and independent contractors. Independent contractors are, in general, individuals who provide services to the general public through an independent business. Payments to independent contractors are reported as nonemployee compensation on 1099s.

For each type of payment, the IRS sets annual threshold amounts. Only payments to vendors that exceed the threshold, in total during a calendar year, need to be reported.

As noted in the "Adding a Vendor" section of this chapter, 1099 vendors can be identified, along with the required tax information, in the **Vendor Information** window when a new vendor is created. Users can update 1099 information about existing vendors by clicking **Vendors** on the navigation bar, clicking the vendor name, and clicking **Edit**.

To prepare 1099s, click **Expenses** on the navigation bar and select the **Vendors** tab.

Click **Prepare 1099s**.

Click **Let's get started**.

The address and tax identification number of the company filing the 1099s are reviewed and edited if necessary. Click **Save** after updating any information.

Click **Next**.

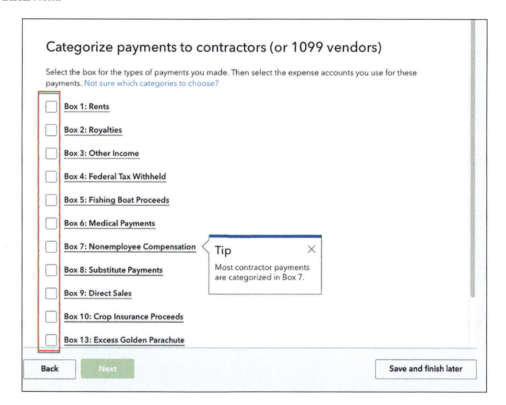

The 1099-MISC form can be used for reporting multiple types of payments to vendors. Each type of payment (category) is entered in a different box on the 1099 form. In this screen, the user selects the type of payments that will be reported. For each **Box** identified, the user is also required to indicate the account used to record the payments. The screen might look something like this for the test drive company.

> **BEHIND THE SCENES** "Bookkeeper" has been identified for **Box 7 Nonemployee Compensation**. Note that wages paid to employees who perform bookkeeping functions would not be reported on 1099s.

Click **Next** to review 1099 vendor details (address, tax identification number).

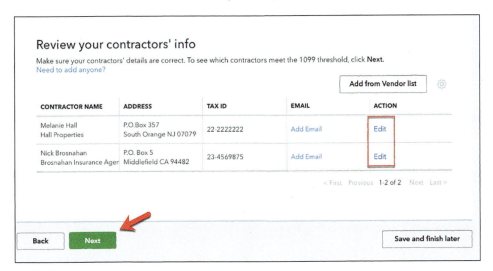

Hall Properties will not appear in your test drive company. Certain changes were made to the file for illustration purpose.

Edits can be made to vendor information on this screen. Any edits here will also update the vendor record.

Click **Next** to review vendors who were paid amounts over the IRS threshold during the calendar year.

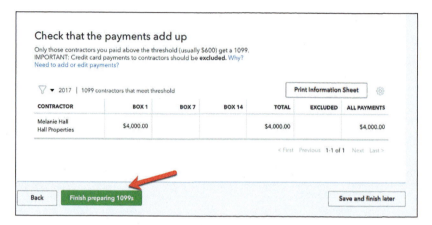

Click **Finish preparing 1099s** to review options for filing. Intuit provides filing services for a fee or users can prepare the forms independently.

End-of-Period Activity
(Service Company)

After completing Chapter 5, you should be able to:

1. Reconcile bank and credit card accounts.

2. Make adjusting journal entries.

3. Create and modify financial statement reports.

4. Close an accounting period.

BEFORE ISSUING FINANCIAL STATEMENTS

Sales, purchases, cash receipts, and cash payments make up the vast majority of transactions in a company. You've already learned how most of those standard transactions are entered in QBO and you've seen how QBO does a lot of the work related to posting and tracking those transactions for you. As we discussed in Chapter 1, though, the accuracy and the usefulness of all that data are still dependent on the operator(s) of QBO.

For most companies, the primary financial reports (such as the profit and loss statement and the balance sheet) are prepared monthly. It's at the end of the month, then, that the accountant needs to make sure that:

- All accounting transactions have been recorded.

- No accounting transactions have been duplicated.

- All accounting transactions have been recorded in the proper accounts.

- All accounting transactions are recognized in the proper accounting period.

There is, unfortunately, no foolproof method for ensuring the accuracy of the financial statements. There are some tools though. They include:

- Reconciling account balances to external sources.
    - Cash accounts to bank statements.
    - Vendor payable balances to vendor statements.
    - Debt balances to lender reports.
- Reconciling account balances to internal sources.
    - Physical count of supplies on hand to supplies account balance.
    - Physical count of inventory to inventory account balance.
    - Timesheets for the last period of the month to salaries payable account if all salaries have not been paid as of the end of a period.
- Reviewing accounts for reasonableness.

Normal balance The side (debit or credit) on which increases to the account are recorded.

Contra account An account with the opposite normal balance as other accounts of the same type.

    - Most account balances should reflect their **normal** balance (assets should have debit balances, **contra** assets should have credit balances, expenses should have debit balances, etc.).
    - Relationships between accounts should make sense. For example, payroll tax expense shouldn't be higher than salaries expense!
    - Account balances that are significantly higher or lower than the prior month should be investigated.

As a result of all this reconciliation and review, I can virtually **guarantee** you that adjustments will need to be made! Without even thinking very hard, I know you can come up with a few examples.

They might include:

- Recording bank charges that you weren't aware of until you saw the bank statement.

- Adjusting the Supplies on Hand account to record supplies used during the period.

- Adjusting revenue accounts to ensure that all revenue reported is earned revenue and all earned revenue is recognized.

- Recording depreciation expense for the period.

- Accruing expenses that weren't recorded through the normal payable process (interest for example).

RECONCILING BANK AND CREDIT CARD ACCOUNTS

Bank Reconciliations

QBO has an account reconciliation tool that can actually be used for any balance sheet account other than Accounts Receivable, Accounts Payable, Undeposited Funds, and Retained Earnings. That's a useful tool for companies that take advance deposits, for example. In this textbook, we'll only be using the tool for bank and credit card reconciliations.

To access the reconciliation tool, click the **gear** icon on the icon bar.

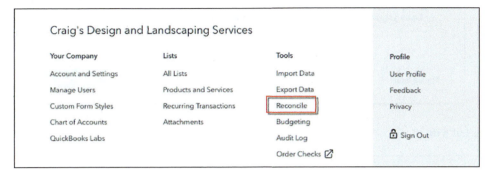

Click **Reconcile**.

 HINT: You can also access the reconciliation tool by clicking **Accounting** on the navigation bar and selecting the **Reconcile** tab.

The first time you use the reconcilation function, you'll need to move through a few informational screens.

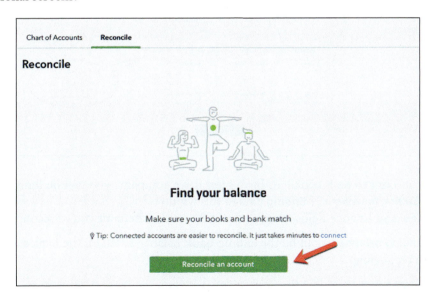

Click **Reconcile an account**.

Click **Let's do it**.

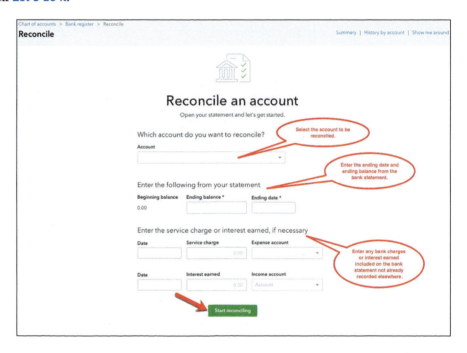

Select the account to be reconciled. In the test drive company, you will be limited to entering an **Ending balance** and **Ending date** in this window.

The date and balance fields **must** agree to the bank statement you're reconciling.

- The **Ending balance** would be the ending **bank** balance listed on the bank statement you're reconciling.

- The **Ending date** would be the ending date listed on the bank statement.

In your homework company file, you will also be able to enter bank charges or interest income amounts that appear on the bank statement. You can use the dropdown menus to select the general ledger account you want debited for service charges or credited for interest income. If you had already entered these transactions, you would leave the fields blank.

Click **Start reconciling**.

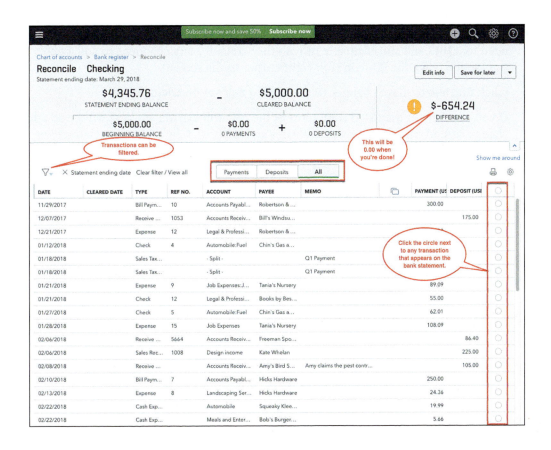

> **BEHIND THE SCENES** Take a look at the column titles on the right side of the
> **All** tab. These are set up from the bank's point of view. You'll notice that the far
> right column is titled **DEPOSIT**. A debit to cash to record a bank deposit on the
> company's books is a credit (liability) on the bank's books since they now owe you
> that amount. Although the column to the left of **DEPOSIT** is titled **PAYMENT**, any
> journal entries crediting the cash account would be listed here as well.

There are three tabs on the screen. Transactions in the account being reconciled that have
not been cleared in a prior reconciliation are listed on the **All** tab.

To reconcile the account, click the circle next to any transaction on this screen that also
appears on the bank statement. These are the transactions that "cleared" the bank. Any
unclicked transactions represent outstanding checks or deposits in transit.

  HINT: It's sometimes easier to use the **Payments** and **Deposits** tabs (instead of
the **All** tab) when reconciling. The **PAYMENTS** tab includes only those transactions (**checks**, **bill payments**, **transfers**, or **journal entries**) that credit the cash
account. The **DEPOSITS** tab includes the transactions (**deposits**, **transfers**, or
journal entries) that debit the cash account.

A few hints that might help with the reconciliation process:

- If you can't complete the reconciliation, you can click the **Save for later** button in the
  top right corner of the screen. QBO will save all your work until you return to complete the reconciliation.

- You can leave the reconciliation window open and create (or edit) a transaction if you need to. QBO will automatically refresh the screen for any changes. To add a new transaction, click the ➕ icon (top right corner of the screen).

- Click **Edit Info** to make changes to the **Ending balance** or **Ending date**.

- If you click any of the listed transactions, the row will expand and you will be able to change certain data fields (generally dates and memos). Click **Edit** to open the form and make more substantial changes. It will look something like this:

- QBO automatically filters the list to only include those uncleared transactions dated prior to the statement ending date (the only transactions that **could** have cleared the bank assuming all transactions are dated correctly).

  - If you only want to display certain types of transactions, click the funnel above the far left column.

- You can change the sort order of either **Checks and Payments** or **Deposits and Other Credits** by clicking the column headings.

When you've reconciled the account, the **Difference** field in the top right section of the screen will equal zero. Only then should you click the **Finish Now** button.

> **!** **WARNING: Do not click the Finish Now button if you haven't finished the reconciliation (the difference isn't zero). QBO will give you a warning if you try but if you persist, it will allow you to "reconcile" without actually reconciling. That would leave what my former accounting professors would call a "dangling" credit or debit. Of course QBO won't actually allow you to create an unbalanced transaction so it will either debit (or credit) an account called Reconciliation Discrepancies for the Difference amount. You'd then have to fix that later.**

Once you've reconciled the account, the following screen will appear:

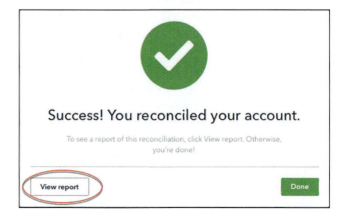

To view the reconciliation report, click **View report**. The report includes lists (by type) of all cleared transactions and all uncleared transactions. Appendix 5B goes over the reconciliation report in detail.

Reconciliation reports are also accessible in the **For My Accountant** section of **Reports**.

Reconcile the bank account for Craig's Design and Landscaping.
(Craig's Design receives its bank statement. The ending balance is $4,345.76. There were no bank service charges included on the statement.)

1. Click the **gear** icon on the icon bar.

2. Click **Reconcile**.

3. Click **Reconcile an account**.

4. Click **Let's do it**.

5. Select **Checking** as the **Account**.

6. Enter the current date as the **Ending Date** and "4,345.76" as the **Ending Balance**.

   a. Since you're working in the test drive company and dates in that company are constantly being updated, you need to enter the date you're actually doing the reconciliation.

7. Click **Start reconciling**.

8. Click the **Payments** tab and check the circles next to the first ten checks.

   a. The checks you're marking as cleared should start with a $300 check and end with a $250 check.

9. Click the **Deposits** tab and check the circles next to the first four deposits.

   a. The first deposit you check as cleared should be for $175. The last one should be for $105.

10. **Difference** should be 0.00.

11. Click **Finish Now**.

12. Click **View report**.

13. **Make a note** of the total for checks cleared in your reconciliation.

14. Click **Dashboard** to close the window.

PRACTICE EXERCISE

Fixing Bank Reconciliation Errors

At the time this book was written, Intuit had just announced the future addition of an "Undo Reconciliation" feature. When the feature is operational, a supplement to the book will be made available to you through the Supplements page of the text website and myBusinessCourse. There will be a video in myBusinessCourse to guide you as well.

The following instructions can be used if your company file does not include the new feature and you need to correct your bank reconciliation.

- Option 1: You can change the status of **all** transactions that you reconciled so that you can start over. To do that:

  - Click the **gear** icon on the icon bar and select **Chart of Accounts**.

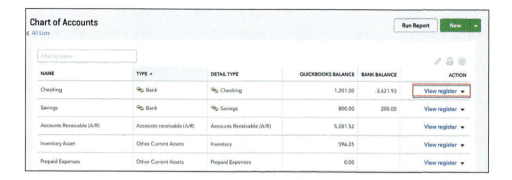

■ Click **View register** in the **ACTION** column for the account you want to work on.

■ For each transaction included in the period you were reconciling, click the field (between **DEPOSIT** and **BALANCE**), that contains an **R** or a **C** and click until the field is blank.

○ In this field, **R** means **Reconciled** and **C** means **Cleared**. A transaction is automatically assigned **C** status when it's first marked in the reconciliation process. (Transactions accepted into QBO through a download from a company's financial institution would also be marked **C**.) When the reconciliation process is finished, the **C** is automatically changed to **R**. A blank means the transaction is still available for reconciliation.

● Option 2: You can change the status of specific transactions that were reconciled incorrectly. Follow the directions given in Option 1 but only change the status for the transactions you know have been reconciled improperly.

> **WARNING:** It can be very difficult to successfully use Option 2. Each time you change the reconciliation status of a transaction, QBO changes the **Beginning Balance** of the account. If all transactions are unreconciled (Option 1), the **Beginning Balance** should be the same as the beginning balance on your bank statement and all the transactions on the statement should be again available for reconciliation. If you only change the status of some of the transactions, the **Beginning Balance** won't match and some of the items on the bank statement won't appear on the screen since they weren't unreconciled. This can be very confusing when you try to redo the reconciliation.

Credit Card Reconciliations

You learned in Chapter 4 how company credit cards are handled in QBO. A separate account is set up (**Credit Card account category**) and individual card transactions are posted to the account as they occur. There are a number of credit card forms (**transaction types**). One thing they all have in common though is that because they are not **bills** or **vendor credits** they do not show up in the **Pay Bills** screen. That's a good thing since companies don't pay individual credit card charges; they pay the credit card statement balance.

At some point, though, the statement balance must be paid. QBO provides a few options. All options are automatically offered after the credit card reconciliation process is complete.

> **BEHIND THE SCENES** It's important to reconcile credit card account activity to the statement because there aren't a lot of controls on credit cards. Whoever holds the card can generally use the card. Companies need to make sure that all charges are legitimate. Companies would normally require employees with access to credit cards to submit original receipts for all purchases.

The process for reconciling a credit card account is very similar to the bank reconciliation process.

The reconciliation tool is easily accessed by clicking the **gear** icon on the icon bar and choosing **Reconcile**.

In the **Reconcile an account** window, the credit card account should be selected.

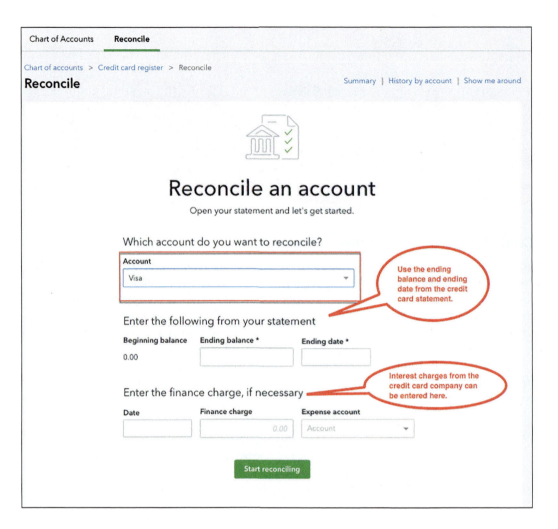

The dates and amounts entered on the initial screen are from the statement being reconciled. Interest or late fee charges should also be entered in this window if they haven't been previously recorded.

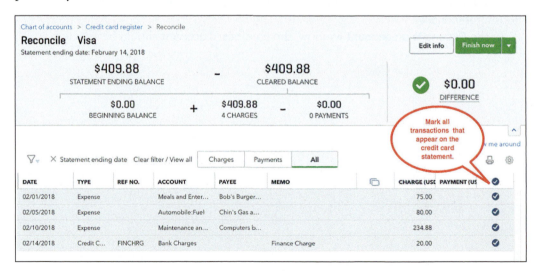

All displayed transactions that agree to items listed on the credit card statement should be checked (marked).

> **BEHIND THE SCENES** If you discover that there's an error on one of the recorded **Charges** or **Payments** while you're in the reconciliation process, you can click the transaction to edit the form. You can also leave the reconciliation screen open while you create a new transaction. The new transaction will automatically appear in the reconciliation screen once it's saved.

Once the statement is reconciled, the following screen will appear:

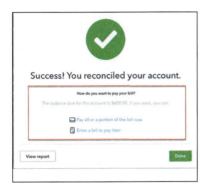

If the **Pay all or a portion of the bill now** option is selected, a **Check** form will automatically appear. The credit card company name would be selected in the payee field.

If **Enter a bill to pay later** is selected, a **Bill** form will automatically appear. The appropriate vendor would need to be selected. QBO will automatically enter the credit card liability account in the distribution section of the form (in the **Account details** section).

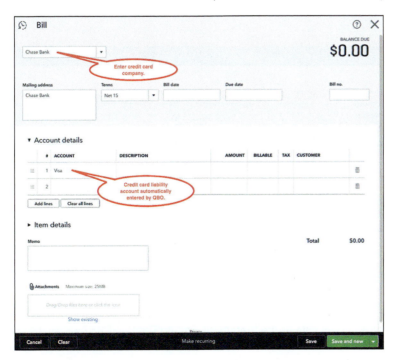

HINT: Remember, credit cards are issued either by banks (VISA or Master-Card credit cards for example) or by companies (like Macy's or Union 76 credit cards). You will need to set up the company that issued the credit card as a vendor in QBO.

Once the **Bill** is completed and saved, it would appear on the **Pay Bills** screen and would be included in the Accounts Payable account.

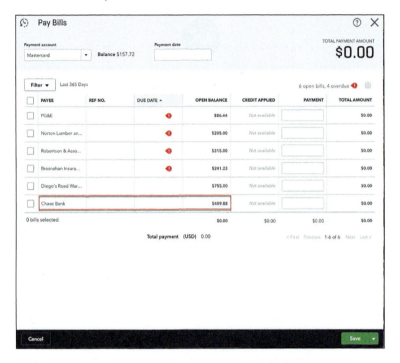

QuickCheck
5-1

What journal entry does QBO make if you select the **Enter a bill for payment later** option after reconciling a credit card?

PRACTICE
EXERCISE

Reconcile Craig's Design and Landscaping's credit card statement.
(Craig's Design received its December statement from Global Credit. The ending statement balance is $157.52. There were no service charges.)

1. Click the **gear** icon on the icon bar.

2. Click **Reconcile**.

3. Select **MasterCard** as the **Account**.

4. Enter the current date as the **Statement Ending Date** and "157.72" as the **Ending Balance**.

5. Click **Start reconciling**.

6. Check the circles next to all transactions.

   a. **TIP:** Checking the circle at the top of the far right column will mark all circles.

(continued)

7. **Difference** should be 0.00.

8. **Make a note** of the amount of the transaction on the **Payments** tab.

9. Click **Finish Now**.

10. Select **Enter a bill to pay later**.

    a. Set up a vendor for the bank that issued the card.

       i. Click **Add New** in the **Vendor** dropdown menu.

       ii. Click ➕ **Details**

       iii. Vendor name is "Global Credit, Inc." (**Company** and **Display** names)

           "1000 Wall Street

           New York, NY 10000"

       iv. **Terms** are **Net 15**.

       v. Click **Save**.

11. Make sure **MasterCard** shows as the **ACCOUNT** in the **Bill**.

12. Enter "CC Stmt" as the **Bill No.**

13. Click **Save and close**.

14. Click **Done**.

15. Click **Dashboard** to close the window.

MAKING ADJUSTING JOURNAL ENTRIES

All transactions are recorded as journal entries, right? You only have to look at a **Journal** report in QBO to see that all the **Invoices**, **Checks**, **Bills**, **Bill Payments**, etc. are listed (and they're in journal entry form, too).

    Adjusting **journal entries** are simply journal entries that are made to adjust account balances. Although they can be made at any time during an accounting period, the majority of them are made at the end of an accounting period.

    In a manual system, adjusting journal entries are created in the general journal. The entries are then posted to the general ledger.

    In QBO, adjusting journal entries are created in an electronic version of the general journal. They are posted automatically to the general ledger.

    The form used to create an adjusting entry (**Journal Entry** transaction type) is accessed by clicking the ➕ icon on the icon bar.

Journal entry An entry of accounting information into a journal.

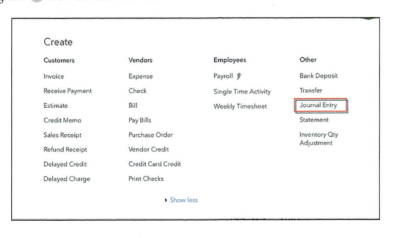

Select **Journal Entry** in the **Other** column.

Journal Entry #1								⑦ ✕

Journal date

Journal no.
1

	#	ACCOUNT	DEBITS	CREDITS	DESCRIPTION		NAME	
≡	1							🗑
≡	2							🗑
≡	3							🗑
≡	4							🗑
≡	5							🗑
≡	6							🗑
≡	7							🗑
≡	8							🗑

Add lines   Clear all lines

Memo

Cancel   Make recurring   Save   Save and new ▼

To complete the form, you need to enter the accounts and amounts involved.

Although you **can** use the **Journal Entry** form to create entries in accounts receivable, accounts payable, and cash accounts, it's generally better to use the standard forms for transactions that affect those accounts.

> **BEHIND THE SCENES** If you do make an adjusting journal entry to accounts receivable (or payable), you would need to enter the name of the customer (vendor) in the **NAME** field so that the subsidiary ledger is updated.

Here are some "good practice" points for working with adjusting entries:

- Include a brief description of the transaction in the **Memo** field of the form for future reference.

- Make one entry per type of adjustment. In other words, don't make one big entry with lots of different types of transactions on it. Companies should keep documentation to support adjusting journal entries and it's easier to match the entry to the documentation if you keep the entries simple.

The mechanics of recording adjusting journal entries in QBO are very simple. To help with the hardest part (knowing what adjustments need to be made), here's a list of common monthly entries for service companies:

- Depreciation
- Accrual of:
    - Unpaid salaries
    - Interest or other charges for which a vendor bill has not yet been received
    - Unbilled revenue
- Expiration (consumption) of
    - Prepaid expenses
    - Supplies on hand
- Recognition of deferred revenue as earned

Record some adjusting journal entries for Craig's Design and Landscaping.
(Craig's Design records month-end adjustments for depreciation on office equipment and for supplies used.)

1. Click the + icon on the icon bar.

2. Click **Journal Entry** (in the **Other** column).

3. Record depreciation expense of $225 for the current month.

   a. Enter the current date as the **Date**. You can leave the **Journal no.** as 1.

   b. In the first row, select **Depreciation** as the debit **ACCOUNT** and enter "225" in the **DEBITS** column. **TIP:** Select the one listed as an **Other Expense account type**.

      i. Enter "Current month depreciation" in the **DESCRIPTION** field.

   c. In the second row, click **Add new** in the **ACCOUNT** field to add an **Accumulated Depreciation** account.

      i. Select **Fixed Asset** as the **account type** and **Accumulated Depreciation** as the **detail type**.

      ii. Select **Accumulated Depreciation** as the **Name**.

      iii. Click **Save and Close**.

      iv. Enter "225" in the **CREDITS** column for **Accumulated Depreciation**.

      v. The **Description** field should have been automatically filled.

   d. Click **Save and new**.

4. Record supplies on hand. Count of supplies on hand totaled $450. Craig's doesn't have a Supplies on Hand account set up yet.

   a. Enter the current date as the **Date**. Leave the **Journal no.** as 2.

   b. In the first row, click **Add new** in the **ACCOUNT** field to add a Supplies on Hand account.

      i. Select **Other Current Asset** as the **account type** and **Other Current Assets** as the **detail type**.

      ii. Enter "Supplies on Hand" as the **Name**.

      iii. Click **Save and Close**.

   c. Enter "450" in the **DEBITS** column for the first line.

      i. Enter "Supplies on hand at end of the month" in the **DESCRIPTION** field.

   d. In the second row, select **Supplies** as the **ACCOUNT** (make sure you're picking the **expense** account) and enter "450" in the **CREDITS** column.

   f. Click **Save and close**.

PREPARING FINANCIAL STATEMENTS

As you know, there are four basic financial statements:

- **Balance sheet**
- Profit and loss statement (**Income statement**)
- Statement of retained earnings (or **Statement of stockholders' equity**)
- **Statement of cash flows**

Balance sheet A financial statement showing a business's assets, liabilities, and stockholders' equity as of a specific date.

Income statement A financial statement reporting a business's sales revenue and expenses for a given period of time.

Statement of stockholders' equity A financial statement presenting information regarding the events that cause a change in stockholders' equity during a period. The statement presents the beginning balance, additions to, deductions from, and the ending balance of stockholders' equity for the period.

Statement of cash flows A financial statement showing a firm's cash inflows and cash outflows for a specific period, classified into operating, investing, and financing activity categories.

You can prepare a balance sheet, profit and loss statement, and statement of cash flows automatically in QBO. In this course, we'll only be looking at the balance sheet and profit and loss statement.

> **BEHIND THE SCENES** QBO's Statement of Cash Flows can contain some inaccuracies. For example, activity in short-term loans is classified in the operating activity section instead of the investing activity section. Although it's still a useful tool for management, it's generally better to prepare the cash flow statement manually.

The financial statements are accessed by clicking **Reports** on the navigation bar. The most common reports are found in the **Business Overview** section.

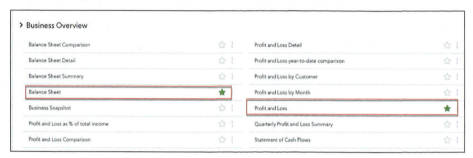

Statements can be prepared on the accrual or the cash basis. QBO allows for a number of other modifications to be made to reports. For example, here is the main modification bar for a **Balance Sheet** report.

Other modifications can be made by clicking **Customize**.

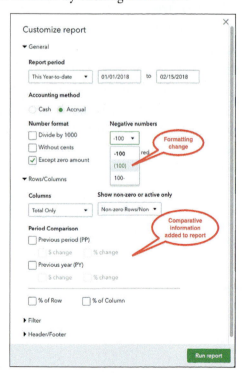

In the **Customize** sidebar, the format of numbers can be changed and additional information (comparative amounts or percentages) can be added.

Financial statements may be distributed to:

- Owners
- Management
- Lenders
- Potential investors
- Regulatory agencies

They should be clear and professional in appearance. There are a few standard reporting conventions to consider:

- Assets are generally reported in descending order of liquidity (how quickly or easily they can be converted to cash).
- Liabilities are generally reported in descending order of their priority for payment.
- Revenue and expenses are generally reported in order of dollar amount (highest to lowest).
- Categories are sorted first; then individual accounts within each category.

> **BEHIND THE SCENES** There are no absolute rules for presentation, particularly in the order of accounts on the profit and loss statement. For instance, there are some accounts that are generally reported last (like depreciation expense and miscellaneous expense) regardless of the dollar amount. As the accountant, your responsibility is to organize the information in the clearest and most meaningful manner possible.

QBO doesn't have an easy way to change the account order. In your homework assignment, you'll be using account numbers. Account numbers can be changed to reorder the accounts. Another option for companies using QBO is to export the statements to Excel and reorder the accounts there. Exporting reports to Excel will be covered in Chapter 12.

PRACTICE EXERCISE

Prepare year-end financial statements for Craig's Design and Landscaping.
(Craig's Design needs a balance sheet and profit and loss statement.)

1. If you didn't log out of QBO after the last practice exercise, you'll need to sign out now to clear your previous transactions. Log back in to continue.

2. Review balance sheet.
   a. Click **Reports** on the navigation bar.
   b. Click **Balance Sheet** in the **Favorites** section.
   c. Use the current date in both date fields.
   d. Click **Customize**.
   e. In the **General** tab, select **(100)** in the dropdown for **Negative numbers**.
   f. In the **Rows/Columns** tab, click **Non-zero** for both rows and columns in the **Show non-zero or active only** dropdown menu.
   g. Click **Run Report**.

(continued)

> h.   **Make a note** of the balance in **Accounts Receivable**.
>
> > i.   Click **back to report list**. It's in blue right above the **Report period** field in the top left corner.
>
> 2.   Review the income statement.
>
> > a.   Click **Profit and Loss** in the **Favorites** section.
> >
> > b.   Select **All Dates** in the report period dropdown menu.
> >
> > c.   Click **Run report**.
> >
> > d.   **Make a note** of the total for **NET INCOME**.
> >
> > e.   Select **Cash** as the **Accounting method**.
> >
> > f.   Click **Run report**.
> >
> > g.   **Make a note** of the total for **Net Income** on the cash basis.
> >
> > h.   Click **Dashboard** to close the report window.

CLOSING A PERIOD

There are really two types of period closings:

- Closing a period after financial statements are prepared and distributed (generally every month).

- Year-end closing (closing the books at the end of the company's legal year [fiscal year]).

Closing an Accounting Period

When we talk about closing an accounting period, we are usually simply talking about not making any additional entries to that accounting period. An additional small bill might come in that relates to the period or we might discover that we made a small error in a reconciliation affecting the closed period, but, once financial statements have been prepared and distributed, we generally don't want to go back and make changes. Instead, we simply record those transactions in the current period.

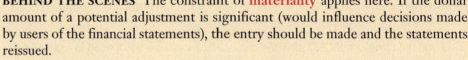

> **BEHIND THE SCENES**   The constraint of **materiality** applies here. If the dollar amount of a potential adjustment is significant (would influence decisions made by users of the financial statements), the entry should be made and the statements reissued.

Materiality An accounting guideline that states that insignificant data that would not affect a financial statement user's decisions may be recorded in the most expedient manner.

So what does all this have to do with QBO? QBO actually gives us a tool that's useful here.

As I'm sure you've noticed by now, QBO will let you enter any date you want for transactions. Many of my students (and clients) have spent hours trying to reconcile their financial statements and it turns out they simply entered a wrong date on a transaction or two.

QBO allows you to set a **Closing Date** in your company file. When a closing date is set, QBO will warn you if you try to enter a transaction dated prior to that date. You can override the warning but at least it's there.

Closing dates are set in **Account and Settings**.

Click the **gear** icon on the icon bar.

Select **Account and Settings** and open the **Advanced** tab.

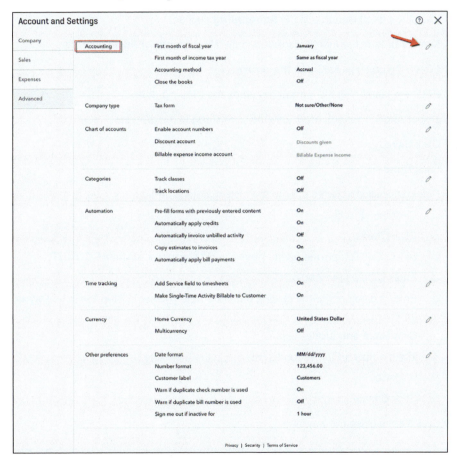

Click the **pencil** icon in the top right corner of the **Accounting** section.

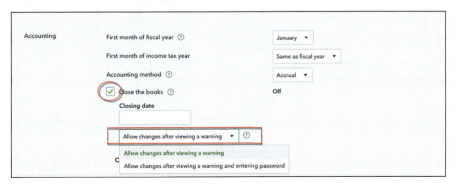

Check the box next to **Close the books** and enter a **Closing date**.

You can pick one of two options. You can require a password to make changes or you can simply allow changes to be made after a warning is posted. In a company with multiple employees, a password would be important.

EXERCISE

Set a closing date for Craig's Design and Landscaping.
(Craig's Design sets a closing date in QBO.)

1. Click the **gear** icon on the icon bar.

2. Click **Account and Settings**.

3. Click the **Advanced** tab.

4. Click the **pencil** icon to edit the **Accounting** section.

5. **Make a note** of the month displayed in the **First month of fiscal year** field.

6. Check the box next to **Close the books**.

7. Enter the last day of the current month as the **Closing date**.

8. Select **Allow changes after viewing a warning** in the dropdown menu.

9. Click **Save**.

10. Click **Done**.

11. Enter a transaction dated prior to the closing date to verify.

    a.　Click the ➕ icon.

    b.　Click **Check**.

    c.　Select **Cal Telephone** as the **payee** and **Telephone** as the **ACCOUNT**.

    d.　Enter $200 as the **AMOUNT**.

    e.　Enter a date prior to the closing date (the date you set in Step 7) as the **Payment date**.

    f.　Click **Save and close**.

    g.　**Make a note of** the second sentence in the message.

    h.　Click **No**.

    i.　Click **Cancel**.

12. Click **Yes** to close the window.

Year-end Closing

Closing process A step in the accounting cycle in which the balances of all temporary accounts are transferred to the Retained Earnings account, leaving the temporary accounts with zero balances.

When a company file is originally set up, you must enter the first month of the fiscal (legal) year. QBO uses that date in reporting and budgeting. It also uses that date to automatically close (clear) all revenue and expense account types (Income, Cost of Goods Sold, Expense, Other Income, and Other Expense) to an equity account at the end of the year. The **closing process** is done automatically by QBO.

> **BEHIND THE SCENES** To close temporary accounts, QBO doesn't create an entry that's visible in the Journal. It does, however, change the reports. For example, let's say a company started business on 3/1/18 and their year-end was 12/31/18. For all reports dated between 3/1/18 and 12/31/18, revenues and expenses for the period would be reported on the profit and loss statement. A total for net income or loss would show as a single line item on the balance sheet in the equity section.
>
>   On 1/1/19, the reports would automatically change. None of the 2018 revenue and expense activity would appear on the profit and loss statement. Unless there were already some entries posted on 1/1/19, the profit and loss statement would show net income of $0.00. On the balance sheet, the net income (or loss) line (related to 2018 transactions) would also no longer appear. Instead, Retained Earnings would have been credited (or debited) for the 2018 operating results.

Although QBO appropriately closes out revenue and expense accounts at year-end, there still may be some final housekeeping entries that need to be made. These entries vary depending on the type of entity.

- For proprietorships: Most proprietorships set up separate capital investment and draw accounts (equity accounts) so that activity for the year is visible on the balance sheet. If so, those accounts should be closed out to an Owner's Equity at the beginning of a new year. Retained Earnings should also be closed out to Owner's Equity. (Sole proprietorships would not normally maintain a retained earnings account.)

- For partnerships: Most small partnerships set up separate capital investment, draw, and capital balance accounts (equity accounts) for each partner. If so, the capital investment, draw, and Retained Earnings accounts should be closed out to each partner's capital balance account at the beginning of a new year.

- For corporations: Most corporations set up a dividends account (equity account) so that current-year distributions to shareholders are visible on the balance sheet. If so, the dividend account should be cleared out to Retained Earnings at the beginning of a new year.

Credit Card Payable		XXX	
Accounts Payable			XXX

ANSWER TO

QuickCheck

5-1

CHAPTER SHORTCUTS

Reconcile an account

1. Click **gear** icon
2. Click **Reconcile**

Record adjusting journal entries

1. Click ➕ icon
2. Click **Journal Entry**

Matching

Match the term or phrase (as used in QuickBooks Online) to its definition.

1. journal entry
2. statement ending date
3. reconciled
4. charge
5. cleared
6. payment
7. fiscal year
8. close date

_____ company's legal year

_____ status of a bank transaction marked as cleared **during** the reconciliation process

_____ date set by user; used to limit entry of transactions dated prior to that date

_____ date of statement received from bank

_____ title of column in the credit card reconciliation screen listing all debits to the account being reconciled

_____ status of bank transaction that has been marked as cleared as part of a completed reconciliation

_____ transaction type used for recording an adjusting entry

_____ title of column in the credit card reconciliation screen listing all credits to the account being reconciled

Multiple Choice

1. All transactions posted to an account being reconciled will appear on the bank reconciliation screen in QBO EXCEPT
   a. cleared transactions and uncleared transactions recorded through a general journal entry.
   b. cleared transactions.
   c. uncleared transactions.
   d. uncleared **bill payment** transactions.

2. Which of the following accounts **could** be reconciled using the reconciliation tool in QBO? (Select all that apply. Assume all of the accounts listed were in the company's chart of accounts.)
   a. Cash (Bank account type)
   b. Prepaid Expenses (Other Current Asset account type)
   c. Accounts Payable (Accounts Payable account type)
   d. Unearned Revenue (Other Current Liability account type)

3. The **Journal** report includes _____.
   a. all accounting transactions no matter where (how) they were recorded
   b. only those accounting transactions recorded in the **Journal Entry** form
   c. only accounting transactions recorded through certain forms
   d. only accounting transactions NOT recorded in the **Journal Entry** form

4. When a credit card statement is reconciled,

    a. the user can elect to create a **bill** for the statement balance.

    b. the user can elect to write a **check** for the statement balance.

    c. the user can elect to retain the balance in the credit card liability account.

    d. the user can elect any of the three options listed.

5. On the first day of a new fiscal year, QBO automatically closes

    a. all temporary accounts.

    b. all revenue and expense accounts.

    c. all revenue, expense, and equity accounts.

    d. all revenue, expense, and dividend accounts.

ASSIGNMENTS

Assignment 5A

Math Revealed!

Assignments with the MBC **are available in myBusinessCourse.**

Background information: Martin Smith, a college student and good friend of yours, had always wanted to be an entrepreneur. He is very good in math so, to test his entrepreneurship skills, he decided to set up a small math tutoring company serving local high school students who struggle in their math courses. He set up the company, Math Revealed!, as a corporation in 2018. Martin is the only owner. He has not taken any distributions from the company since it opened.

The business has been successful so far. In fact, it's been so successful he has decided to work in his business full time now that he's graduated from college with a degree in Mathematics.

He has decided to start using QuickBooks Online to keep track of his business transactions. He likes the convenience of being able to access his information over the Internet. You have agreed to act as his accountant while you're finishing your own academic program.

He currently has a number of regular customers that he tutors in Pre-Algebra, Algebra, and Geometry. His customers pay his fees by cash or check after each tutoring session but he does give terms of Net 15 to some of his customers. He has developed the following fee schedule:

Name	Description	Rate
Refresher	One-hour session	$40 per hour
Persistence program	Two one-hour sessions per week	$75 per week
Crisis program	Five one-hour sessions per week	$150 per week

The tutoring sessions usually take place at his students' homes but he recently signed a two-year lease on a small office above a local coffee shop. The rent is only $200 per month starting in January 2019. A security deposit of $400 was paid in December 2018.

The following equipment is owned by the company:

Description	Date placed in service	Cost	Life	Salvage Value
Computer	7/1/18	$3,000	36 months	$300
Printer	7/1/18	$ 240	24 months	$ 0
Graphing Calculators (2)	7/1/18	$ 294	36 months	$ 60

All equipment is depreciated using the straight-line method.

As of 12/31/18, he owed $2,000 to his parents who initially helped him get started. They are charging him interest at a 6% annual rate. He has been paying interest only on a monthly basis. His last payment was 12/31/18.

Over the next month or so, he plans to expand his business by selling a few products he believes will help his students. He has already purchased a few items:

Category	Description	Vendor	Quantity On Hand	Cost per unit	Sales Price
Books and Tools					
	Geometry in Sports	Books Galore	20	12	16
	Solving Puzzles: Fun with Algebra	Books Galore	20	14	18
	Getting Ready for Calculus	Books Galore	20	15	20
	Protractor/Compass Set	Math Shack	10	10	14
	Handheld Dry-Erase Boards	Math Shack	25	5	9
	Notebooks (pack of 3)	Paper Bag Depot	10	15	20

1/31/19

✓ You decide to reconcile the bank statement for January. You get the following information from the bank's website:

CITY BANK OF SACRAMENTO
51 Capital Avenue
Sacramento, CA 95822 (916) 585-2120

Your Name Math Revealed!
3835 Freeport Blvd
Sacramento, CA 95822
Account # 1616479

January 31, 2019

	CREDITS	CHARGES	BALANCE
Beginning Balance, January 1			$2,845.00
1/4, Check 1102—Pro Spaces		$200.00	2,645.00
1/7, Check 1101—Protector Insurance		480.00	2,165.00
1/11, Deposit	$ 430.00		2,595.00
1/22, Check 1100—Gus Ranting		20.00	2,575.00
1/22, Deposit	1,335.00		3,910.00
1/29, Check 1104—Math Shack		487.79	3,422.21
1/29, Check 1107—Paper Bag Depot		150.00	3,272.21
1/30, Deposit	1,845.00		5,117.21
1/30, Check 1109—Frank's Furniture		360.00	4,757.21
Ending Balance, 1/31			$4,757.21

• **TIP:** Since this is the first time the checking account has been reconciled in QBO, the 12/31 balance will show as a deposit.

✓ You also receive the credit card statement in the mail. You reconcile the card and set up the balance for payment to **Prime Visa Company** later. Use JanCC as the **Bill no**.

PRIME VISA COMPANY
55 Wall Street
New York, NY 10005

Your Name Math Revealed!
3835 Freeport Blvd
Sacramento, CA 95822
Account # 212456770439

January 31, 2019

	PAYMENTS	CHARGES	BALANCE
Beginning Balance,			$ 0.00
1/3—Paper Bag Depot		$1,197.00	1,197.00
1/8—Cardinal Gas & Snacks		20.00	1,217.00
1/22—Cardinal Gas & Snacks		22.00	1,239.00
1/25—Moon Coffee		8.75	1,247.75
Ending Balance, 1/31			$1,247.75

Minimum Payment Due: $10.00   **Payment Due Date: February 15**

✓ Martin asks you to give him a summary of the hours you worked in January. He agrees to pay you $20 per hour for the 10 hours you worked on his accounting. You are only doing this temporarily since you have some extra time so you set yourself up as a 1099 vendor and write yourself a check for the $200. The check number is 1111. You consider this a professional service expense.

- Use 333-44-5555 as your **Business ID number** and 2119 Abacus Drive as your address. Use your home city, state to complete the address.

✓ You make adjusting journal entries for the month of January as needed. (Start with Journal no. 2.) You carefully consider the following:

- Math Revealed! used the straight-line method to determine depreciation expense for all office equipment.

  ○ Monthly depreciation expense for the equipment purchased prior to 12/31 is $91.50. (Computer $75; Printer $10; Calculators $6.50)

  ○ Math Revealed! purchased $360 of furniture on 1/3. You expect the furniture to last 3 years, with no salvage value. You take a full month depreciation on furniture.

  ○ Two computers ($756) and three calculators ($441) were also purchased on 1/3. You expect the computers to have a 3-year life (no salvage value) and the calculators to have a 3-year life ($90 salvage value). You take a full month depreciation on the equipment.

  ○ On 1/30, shelving was installed. The cost of the shelving was $649. You expect the shelving to last for the term of the lease (24 months). You estimate the salvage value at $49 at the end of the two years. You started using the shelving on February 1.

- You check the supplies on hand. You estimate that $80 of supplies were used during January.

- The insurance policy premium paid in January was $480. The policy term is 1/1-12/31/19.

- You check to make sure that all the revenue recorded in January was earned during the month.

  ○ You realize that the amount paid by Teacher's College was for a workshop to be held in February.

  ○ You also take a look at Invoice #1009 to Annie Wang. Half of the $300 billed on 1/14 was for February tutoring.

  ○ **TIP:** Consider whether you need a new account here.

- Martin has agreed to pay his parents interest on the $2,000 they loaned him to get the business started. The last payment was 12/31/18. The annual interest rate (simple interest) on the loan is 6%. You forgot to pay them in January. You call and let them know that the check will come in February.

  ○ **TIP:** Just because you didn't pay it in January doesn't mean you don't owe it in January. Consider whether you need a new account here.

Check numbers as of 1/31

Checking account balance: . . . . $ 2,672.21
Accounts Payable: $1,981.75
Net income (January only): $1,522.00

Reports to create for Chapter 5:

All reports should be in portrait orientation.

- Journal—1/31 transactions only
- Balance Sheet (as of 1/31)
- Profit and loss statement (January)

**Assignment
5B**

**Salish Software
Solutions**

MBC

Background information: Sally Hanson, a good friend of yours, double majored in Computer Science and Accounting in college. She worked for several years for a software company in Silicon Valley but the long hours started to take a toll on her personal life.

Last year she decided to open up her own company, Salish Software Solutions (a corporation). Sally currently advises clients looking for new accounting software and assists them with software installation. She also provides training to client employees and occasionally troubleshoots software issues.

She has decided to start using QuickBooks Online to keep track of her business transactions. She likes the convenience of being able to access financial information over the Internet. You have agreed to act as her accountant while you're working on your accounting degree.

Sally has a number of clients that she is currently working with. She gives 15-day payment terms to her corporate clients but she asks for cash at time of service if she does work for individuals. She has developed the following fee schedule:

Name	Description	Rate
Select	Software Selections	$500 flat fee
Set Up	Software Installation	$ 50 per hour
Train	Software training	$ 40 per hour
Fix	File repair	$ 60 per hour

Sally rents office space from Alki Property Management for $800 per month.

The following furniture and equipment is owned by Salish:

Description	Date placed in service	Cost	Life	Salvage Value
Office Furniture............	6/1/18	$1,400	60 months	$200
Computer	7/1/18	$4,620	36 months	$300
Printer...................	5/1/18	$ 900	36 months	$ 0

All equipment is depreciated using the straight-line method.

As of 12/31/18, she owed $3,500 to Dell Finance. The monthly payment on that loan is $150 including interest at 5%. Sally's last payment to Dell was 12/31/18.

Over the next month or so, Sally plans to expand her business by selling some of her favorite accounting and personal software products directly to her clients. She has already purchased the following items.

Item Name	Description	Vendor	Quantity On Hand	Cost per unit	Sales Price
Easy1	Easy Does it	Abacus Shop	15	$100	$175
Retailer...........	Simply Retail	Simply Accounting	2	$400	$700
Contractor........	Simply Construction	Simply Accounting	2	$500	$800
Organizer	Organizer	Personal Solutions	25	$ 25	$ 50
Tracker	Investment Tracker	Personal Solutions	25	$ 20	$ 40

1/31/19

✓ You talk to Sally about getting paid for the work you're doing. You suggest $25 an hour and she agrees. You are only doing this temporarily since you have some extra time so you set yourself up as a 1099 vendor and write yourself a check for the 10 hours you worked in January ($250). The check number is 1113. You consider this a professional service expense.

- Use 999-88-7777 as your Business ID number and 3056 Abacus Drive as your address. Use your home city, state to complete the address.

✓ You decide to reconcile the bank statement for January. You get the following information from the bank's website:

SACRAMENTO CITY BANK
1822 Capital Avenue
Sacramento, CA 95822 (916) 585-2120

Your Name Salish Software Solutions
3835 Freeport Blvd
Sacramento, CA 95822
Account # 855922   **January 31, 2019**

	PAYMENTS	CHARGES	BALANCE
Beginning Balance, January 1			$10,500.00
1/3, Check 1102—Albright Insurance		$1,800.00	8,700.00
1/4, Check 1101—Alki Property Mgmt		800.00	7,900.00
1/10, Deposit	$ 630.00		8,530.00
1/16, Check 1103—Abacus Shop		200.00	8,330.00
1/18, Deposit	2,475.00		10,805.00
1/19, Check 1104—Personal Software		135.00	10,670.00
1/19, Check 1105—Simply Accounting		900.00	9,770.00
1/23, Check 1106—Hacker Spaces		200.00	9,570.00
1/26, Check 1107—Oscar Torres		120.00	9,450.00
1/30, Deposit	$2,200.00		11,650.00
Service charge		$ 20.00	11,630.00
Ending Balance, 1/31			$11,630.00

- **TIP:** Since this is the first time the checking account has been reconciled in QBO, the 12/31 balance will show as a deposit.

✓ You also receive the credit card statement in the mail. You reconcile the card and set up the balance for payment later. Use JanCC as the Bill no.

CAPITAL THREE
58 Wall Street
New York, NY 10005

Your Name Salish Software Solutions
3835 Freeport Blvd
Sacramento, CA 95822
Account # 646630813344   **January 31, 2019**

	PAYMENTS	CHARGES	BALANCE
Beginning Balance,			$ 0.00
1/3—Paper Bag Depot		$500.00	500.00
1/16—Hacker Spaces		300.00	800.00
1/16—Hacker Spaces		300.00	1,100.00
1/24—The Blue Door		110.00	1,210.00
Ending Balance, 1/31			$1,210.00

Minimum Payment Due: $10.00   **Payment Due Date: February 15**

✓ You make adjusting journal entries for the month of January as needed. (Start with Journal no. 2.) You carefully consider the following:

- Salish Software Solutions used the straight-line method to determine depreciation expense for all fixed assets.
  - ○ None of the assets purchased prior to 12/31 were fully depreciated. **TIP:** Use the information provided in the table included in Background Information at the top of this assignment to determine the monthly amount.
  - ○ Sally paid $840 for software on 1/8. She expected the software to last two years, with no salvage value. The software was not placed in service until 1/8 so you decide to take 75% of a full month's depreciation.
  - ○ The storage cabinets were installed on 1/30. The cost was $1,500. Sally expects the cabinets to last for five years. You don't think the cabinets will have any resale value at the end of the five years. Sally started using the cabinets on February 1.
- You check the supplies on hand. You estimate that $225 of supplies were used during January.
- The insurance policy premium paid in January was $1,800. The policy term is 1/1-12/31/19.
- You check to make sure that all the revenue recorded in January was earned during the month.
  - ○ You ask Sally about the Butter and Beans installation work. She says that she has completed about half the work (20 of the 40 hours billed on Invoice 1009 for $2,000).
  - ○ You also take a look at Invoice #1011 to Albus Software. The workshop will be held in mid-February.
  - ○ **TIP:** Consider whether you need to create a new account here.
- Sally's last payment to Dell Finance was 12/31/18. That payment included interest through 12/31. The next payment of $150 is due on February 1. The annual interest rate (simple interest) on the loan is 5%.
  - ○ **TIP:** Think about what that February 1st payment will cover. Does any of the amount relate to January activity? You may need to create a new account.

Check numbers as of 1/31

Checking account balance: $7,601.05
Accounts Payable: $2,710.00
Net income (January): $2,735.22

Reports to create for Chapter 5:

All reports should be in portrait orientation; fit to one page wide

- Journal—1/31/19 transactions only
- Balance Sheet (as of 1/31)
- Profit and loss statement (January only)

APPENDIX 5A GETTING IT RIGHT

Most accountants work the hardest (use their brains the most!) at the end of an accounting period. They know the income statement for the period should accurately reflect the earnings (or loss) for the period. They know the balance sheet as of the period end should accurately reflect the assets owned and the liabilities owed by the company. The difficulty doesn't lie in knowing the basic concepts. The difficulty lies in knowing what the "accurate" amounts are.

Most students have the most difficulty with the assignments for Chapter 5 and Chapter 8 for the same reason. You have check numbers to refer to, which will hopefully help, but if your numbers don't match those numbers, how do you figure out where you went wrong?

Here are some suggestions for finding your mistakes:

- Start by checking dates.
  - Entering an incorrect date is the **single most common** cause of student errors (and student headaches!). QBO enters default dates when you first open a form. It defaults to the current date when you start entering transactions during a work session. If you change the date on the first invoice, it will default to that new date when you enter the second invoice. If you open a new form, however, it will default back to the current date. Accounting is date driven, so your financial statements won't match the check figures if you enter a transaction in the wrong month. First thing to do? Pull a report of transactions dated BEFORE the first transaction date in the assignment and then one of transactions dated AFTER the last transaction date of the assignment. Make sure you're only checking for transactions that **you** entered. (There were some transactions entered in the initial setup of the company file you are using for your homework. Those should **not** be changed.)

- Really **LOOK** at the balance sheet.
  - The account balances will be positive if they reflect the normal balance for that type of account. Are any of the amounts on your balance sheet negative numbers? If so, should they be negative? If they are contra accounts, the answer would be yes. If there are no negative amounts on your balance sheet, should there be? Again, if you have any contra accounts, the answer would be yes. Accumulated depreciation is a contra account so, if entries were made correctly, it would show as a negative number on the balance sheet. If accumulated depreciation isn't negative, you might have mixed up your debits and credits when making an entry. That's easy to do. Double-click on the amount, then double-click on the underlying entry(ies) and make the necessary corrections.
  - Don't worry about errors in Cash, A/R, or A/P until you are comfortable with the other balances. This is double-entry bookkeeping so if one account is wrong, then at least one other account is also wrong. It's hard to find errors in cash, A/R, and A/P due to the sheer volume of transactions that affect these accounts. SO: if you don't match the check figures, see if you can find the other account(s) that is (are) also off. If you can find and correct the other error(s), these accounts will, of course, fix themselves!
  - Pay particular attention to other current assets and to liabilities other than accounts payable. Are they adjusted properly? Does the supplies on hand account equal the check number given to you? Does the balance in prepaid insurance represent the cost of future (unused) insurance coverage? Should there be any interest accrued on debt? Keep asking questions.

- Really **LOOK** at the profit and loss statement.
  - Again, look for negative amounts that shouldn't be negative. There are some contra revenue and expenses accounts, of course. Sales discounts and purchase discount accounts are two examples of contra accounts that you'll be working with in future chapters.
  - Look at the detail for accounts that just look "odd." Is rent expense higher than income? That could happen, of course, but probably not in this class!

- If you're still off, you're going to have to do some detective work. Try to narrow down the possible errors first.

    - For example, let's say your A/R number is **higher** than the check figure given for A/R. You wouldn't start by looking for unrecorded invoices or cash sales. Why? Because missing invoices or cash sales wouldn't overstate A/R. You **would** start by looking for unrecorded customer payments or customer credits. Look through the assignment (day by day) and agree any customer payments or credits described to the payment and credit memo transaction types listed in your journal.

    - Another example—Let's say your cash number is **lower** than the check number given for cash. You might start by looking for undeposited checks by making sure there isn't a balance in the undeposited funds account. You might also look for duplicated customer payments. Then look through the assignment (day by day) and agree any payment transactions to check, expense, and bill payment transaction types listed in your journal.

    - Don't give up. Keep checking transactions. You'll find the error.

- I have one other suggestion. It's listed last here only because students tend to waste a lot of time looking for a specific amount when the difference is often the sum of several errors. That being said, sometimes you just get lucky! So, determine the difference between the check figure and your total. Is the number divisible by 9? You may have a transposition error (for example, you entered 18 instead of 81). Is the difference equal to the amount of a transaction? Maybe you forgot to enter it (or entered it on the wrong date). Is the difference equal to twice one of your transactions? You may have entered a journal entry backwards (watch those debits and credits!).

APPENDIX 5B UNDERSTANDING THE RECONCILIATION REPORT

The purpose of a bank reconciliation is to make sure the amount reported as cash in the balance sheet is accurate. Reconciliations are performed by comparing activity reported on statements received from the bank (an external source of information) to activity recorded internally in the cash general ledger account. Because internal information is being reconciled to external information, bank reconciliations are considered part of a company's internal control system.

There will, invariably, be differences between what's recorded in the general ledger and what's reported on the bank statement.

Differences that represent **errors** are considered permanent differences. Permanent differences must be corrected before the reconciliation process is considered complete. If the error was made by the company, an adjusting entry would be made. If the error was made by the bank institution, a correction would be in the bank's records. Permanent differences are relatively uncommon.

Temporary differences, on the other hand, are very common. Temporary differences occur when a transaction is recorded by the company **before or after** that transaction is recorded by the bank.

Here are some examples:

- A check to a vendor is recorded by the company (cash is credited) when the check is issued. The check is sent to the vendor, the vendor records receipt of the check, and the vendor deposits the amount in its bank account. In the final step, the vendor's bank requests and receives the cash from the company's bank to cover the check. This process can occur over several days or even weeks.

- A check from a customer is received by the company. The customer payment is recorded (cash is debited) immediately but the checks are not deposited with the bank until a later date.

- The bank charges a monthly service fee to the company's account. The company records the fee after the bank statement is received.

Most temporary (timing) differences are resolved before the bank statement is reconciled. As long as a transaction is recorded in the same accounting period (usually a month), any timing difference won't be an issue.

The two most common types of temporary differences are:

- Outstanding checks—Checks that were recorded by the company but had not been presented to the company's bank for payment as of the statement date.

- Deposits in transit—Deposits that were recorded by the company but had not yet been deposited at the bank as of the statement date.

The reconciliation report in QBO provides information about the differences that remain as of the statement date.

The top section of a reconciliation report looks something like this:

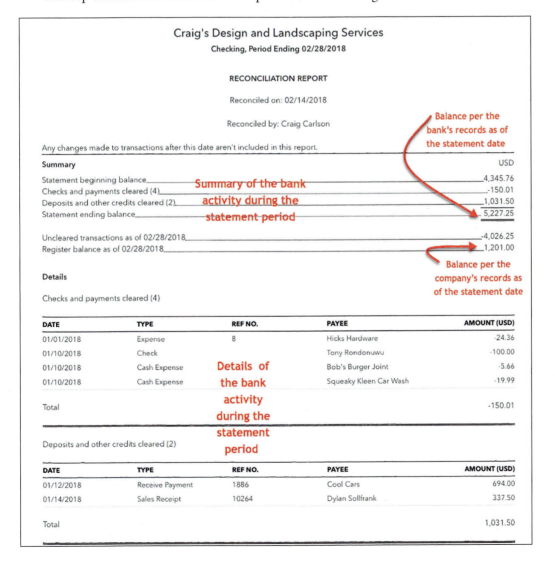

This section includes all of the transactions that were "matched" during the period. Although all of the transactions listed here were recorded in the bank's records during the current period, they could have been recorded in the company's records during the current period or in a prior period. If they were recorded in the company's books during a prior period, they would have been listed as outstanding checks in the prior reconciliation.

The balance in the company's cash account as of the statement date is also listed in this section.

The bottom section of a reconciliation report looks something like this:

Additional Information

List of all the timing differences as of the statement date

Uncleared checks and payments as of 02/28/2018

DATE	TYPE	REF NO.	PAYEE	AMOUNT (USD)
01/11/2018	Check	70	Chin's Gas and Oil	-185.00
01/11/2018	Cash Expense		Chin's Gas and Oil	-52.14
01/12/2018	Bill Payment	11	Hall Properties	-900.00
01/13/2018	Check	2	Mahoney Mugs	-18.08
01/13/2018	Expense	13	Hicks Hardware	-215.66
01/15/2018	Cash Expense		Bob's Burger Joint	-3.86
01/16/2018	Bill Payment	1	Brosnahan Insurance Agency	-2,000.00
01/17/2018	Bill Payment	3	Books by Bessie	-75.00
01/17/2018	Check	Debit	Squeaky Kleen Car Wash	-19.99
01/17/2018	Refund	1020	Pye's Cakes	-87.50
01/18/2018	Expense	108	Tania's Nursery	-46.98
01/18/2018	Cash Expense		Chin's Gas and Oil	-63.15
01/18/2018	Bill Payment	45	Tim Philip Masonry	-666.00
01/18/2018	Bill Payment	6	PG&E	-114.09
01/19/2018	Check	75	Hicks Hardware	-228.75
01/19/2018	Expense	76	Pam Seitz	-75.00
01/22/2018	Cash Expense		Tania's Nursery	-23.50
02/02/2018	Credit Card Credit			-900.00
Total			**Outstanding check total**	-5,674.70

Uncleared deposits and other credits as of 02/28/2018

DATE	TYPE	REF NO.	PAYEE	AMOUNT (USD)
01/17/2018	Receive Payment	2064	Travis Waldron	103.55
01/17/2018	Receive Payment		Freeman Sporting Goods:55 Twin Lane	50.00
01/17/2018	Deposit			218.75
01/18/2018	Deposit			408.00
01/19/2018	Deposit			868.15
Total			**Deposits in transit total**	1,648.45

All of the timing differences are listed in this section—outstanding checks and deposits in transit. This list includes all the transactions that had been recorded in the company's books but had not been recorded by the bank as of the statement date. Some of the transactions were recorded by the company during the statement period. Others were recorded by the company during a prior period. These would have been timing differences in the prior reconciliation as well.

The final step is to reconcile the bank statement balance to the book balance.

Although QBO doesn't include this in the report, the reconciliation summary you learned in your introduction to financial accounting course can be created using the data in the reconciliation report. It would look something like this:

Balance per bank	$5.227.25
Add: Deposits in Transit	1,648.45
Less: Outstanding Checks	5,674.70
Balance per book	$1,201.00

QuickBooks

Merchandising Companies

In this section, we'll primarily be looking at how QuickBooks Online handles the unique needs of merchandising companies. However, some of the new processes and procedures you will learn can be, and are, also used by service companies.

Accounting in a merchandising company is a little more complex. For example, inventory purchases and sales need to be accounted for and sales tax may need to be collected and remitted.

Merchandising companies are also, generally, larger than service companies. That means more employees, including more employees involved in accounting functions. Although **internal controls** are important in **any** company, the complexity and size of merchandising companies make the review and development of internal control systems even more important.

Two of the primary purposes of a good internal control system are:

- To safeguard assets.
- To ensure the accuracy of financial records.

QBO has some features that can be part of a good internal control system.

CONTROLS IN QUICKBOOKS ONLINE

Limiting User Access

Many merchandising companies have multiple employees involved in the record-keeping functions. Those employees must, of course, have access to the accounting software. Allowing every employee **full** access to the software, however, presents opportunities for **fraud**.

Fraud Any act by the management or employees of a business involving an intentional deception for personal gain.

© 2019 Cambridge Business Publishers

QBO allows individual users to be limited in access to particular areas of the program and even to functions within those areas. QBO requires that at least one user, the administrator, have access to all functions. The administrator sets up the other users.

> **BEHIND THE SCENES** The person who created the company file is automatically set up as the administrator. Because you created the homework company file, you are the administrator.

To set up new users, click the **gear** icon on the icon bar.

Click **Manage Users**.

> **WARNING: New users cannot be set up in the test drive. You can, however, use the following instructions to set up users in your homework company file.**

All current users are displayed (contact name and email address) on the first screen. Individuals added as **Users** would normally include company owners and/or other company employees. Companies can also give their outside accountants access to their files through this screen.

In QuickBooks Online Plus (the version provided to you), a company can add up to 5 **Users** and 2 **Accountants** at no additional fee. (An unlimited number of users with restricted access can be added at no fee.) Up to 25 users with access to accounting functions can be added for an additional monthly fee.

Current users can be added or edited through the **Manage Users** screen.

To add a user, click **New**.

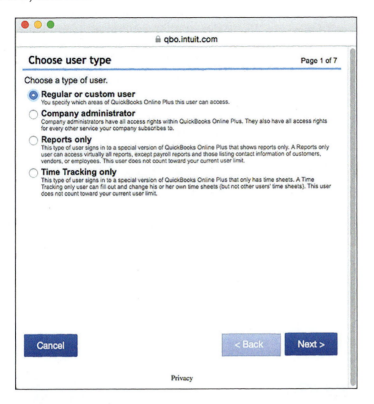

The type of user is selected first. **Regular or custom user** would be selected for employees who perform accounting functions. (**Reports only** and **Time Tracking only** users will not be covered in this textbook.)

Click **Next.**

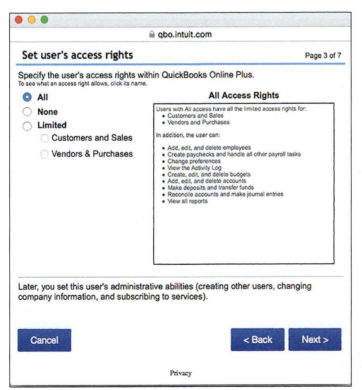

On this next screen, the administrator can limit the number of areas of access.

For example, if **Limited/Customers and Sales** is selected, the user is restricted to accessing sales related functions. The rights and limitations are identified on the right side of the screen.

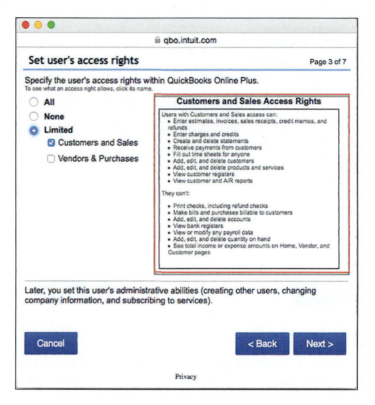

Click **Next**.

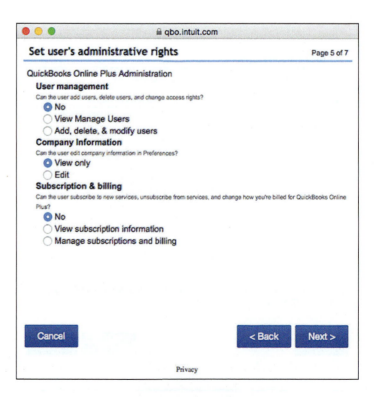

Administrative rights can be given to users if appropriate.

Click **Next**.

In the final screen, the email address of the new user is entered.
     Click **Next**.

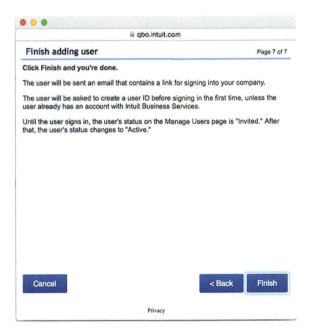

An invitation is sent to the new user automatically. The process is completed when the new user logs in and creates his or her user ID.

     The process is more streamlined when adding an **Accountant** to the list of users. After the accountant's email address is entered, the invitation is sent. The accountant must simply log in to complete the process.

> **BEHIND THE SCENES** There are no screens for limiting access and rights for **Accountants**. Accountant users will have administrator rights.

Editing, Monitoring and Deleting Users

To edit, monitor, or delete a user, open the **Manage Users** screen. (Click the **gear** icon to access the link.)

Clicking **Activity** allows the administrator to view all user activity in chronological order. Activity would include log ins, transactions added or edited, setting changes, etc. Activity can also be accessed using the reports introduced in the next section.

Reporting on Transaction History

QBO tracks all significant changes to transactions including the name of the user entering or modifying the transaction. Several reports are available.

   The **Audit Log** is accessed by clicking the **gear** icon in the icon bar and selecting **Audit Log** in the **Tools** column. The **Audit Log** provides detail on the history of every transaction. On the main page, transactions are listed in chronological order. Certain information is listed for every transaction (name of user initiating transaction, entry date, amounts, etc.). An initial entry is identified as **Added**. Any revisions are flagged as **Edited**. The log can be sorted by user, date, amount, or name. Links to the transactions are provided.

   Further details about each transaction can be obtained by clicking the **View** link. For edited transactions, the changes made to the transaction are clearly highlighted.

   If a closing date has been set in a company file, an **Exceptions to Closing Date** report can be created. The report lists only those prior period transactions that were changed after the closing date and includes the name of the user making the change. The **Exceptions to Closing Date** report, if available, is located in the **For My Accountant** section of **Reports**.

   Reports, obviously, can't prevent fraud. However, the fact that these reports are available acts as a fraud deterrent because employees know they are identified (by user name) with all transactions they enter (or change).

SECTION OVERVIEW

Chapter 6 will cover the sales cycle in a merchandising company.
Chapter 7 will cover the purchase cycle in a merchandising company.
Chapter 8 will cover end of change to end-of-period accounting in a merchandising company.

6 Sales Activity
(Merchandising Company)

After completing Chapter 6, you should be able to:

1. Set up sub-customers.

2. Set up sales taxes.

3. Manage customer shipping addresses.

4. Set up and edit inventory items.

5. Record various types of customer discounts.

6. Record pending sales transactions.

7. Write off uncollectible accounts.

8. Record customer credit card payments.

9. Record early payment discounts taken by customers.

10. Process customer checks returned by the bank due to insufficient funds in the customer's bank account.

11. Prepare sales reports by inventory item.

12. Create customer statements.

WHAT IS THE SALES CYCLE IN A MERCHANDISING COMPANY?

- Get orders.

- Fill orders.

- Bill for the products.

- Collect the sales price.

The sales cycle in a merchandising company, as you can see, is similar to that of a service company and many of the accounting functions are the same. There are some differences though. In this chapter, we'll cover those differences. We'll also cover some more advanced topics that apply to both service and merchandising companies.

MANAGING CUSTOMERS

Setting up and editing customers is covered in Chapter 3. This section covers:

- Setting up sub-customers

- Entering sales tax information for customers.

- Entering shipping information for customers.

Setting Up Sub-Customers

Customers may have multiple locations or subsidiaries and they may want **invoices** to reflect the specific location or subsidiary being charged.

This can be accommodated by setting up a parent customer with **sub-customers** in QBO. The relationship is identified in the **sub-customers** record.

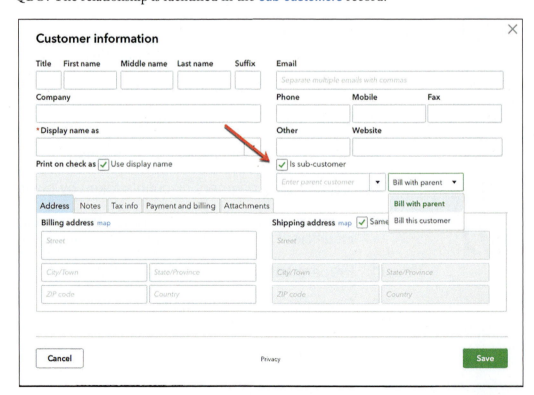

There are two options available when setting up **sub-customers**.

- **Bill with parent**—If this option is selected, **invoices** created for the **sub-customer** will be included on any **statements** created for the parent customer. In addition, when recording payments received directly from the parent, any outstanding invoices for the **sub-customer** will appear in the **receive payment** window.

- **Bill this customer**—If this option is selected, **invoices** created for the **sub-customer** will not be included on any **statements** created for the parent customer. In addition, any outstanding invoices for the **sub-customer** would not appear in the **receive payment** window if the payment was received from the parent customer.

Customers and Sales Tax

Many states levy a tax on purchases of tangible products by consumers (users) of those products. The tax is called a "sales" tax because it is charged to the customer at the point of sale.

Unless a merchandising company is selling to a reseller (a company that will, in turn, sell to consumers) or a tax-exempt entity, the seller is responsible for collecting the tax from their customers and remitting the taxes to the taxing authorities.

A new sales tax feature was added to QBO in the fall of 2017, which greatly automated the management of sales taxes. Once the appropriate taxing jurisdictions are added, QBO will automatically update the rates and agency information.

Whether or not QBO calculates tax on a **particular** charge on an invoice or sales receipt is determined by two things:

- First, is the customer a consumer, a reseller, a tax-exempt entity?
  - QBO relies on the information included on the **Tax info** tab in the customer record.

- Second, if the customer is a consumer and not tax-exempt, does the charge represent a sale of a taxable item?
  - QBO relies on the information included in the **item** record.

The **amount** of tax, if any, QBO charges on a taxable item is primarily determined by the company's address (physical location and legal address) and the customer's address.

> **BEHIND THE SCENES** Almost all states (currently 45 of them) impose a tax on sales. All sales of taxable products or services to non-exempt customers located in the same state as the company are subject to tax. Determining when a company must collect sales taxes on taxable sales to customers in **other** states can be difficult. The basic rule is this: If the company has a **presence** (called nexus) in the state (people or property), the company must collect sales taxes on sales to non tax-exempt customers in that state. The actual rules about how many people or how much property is enough to establish nexus and which products and services are taxable vary from state to state. QBO users are responsible for knowing the rules.

The sales tax liability account automatically updates when an invoice or sales receipt including taxable sales is completed. Sales tax payable accounts can't be edited or deleted in QBO.

Setting up Sales Taxes

Overall management of sales taxes is done through the **Sales Tax Center**.

WARNING: Intuit rolled out the new sales tax feature in the fall of 2017. This new feature, as described in the next few sections of this chapter, should be available in all academic licenses.

However, as of April 2018, the sales tax feature was still not operational in the test drive company. Practice Exercises will include detailed instructions for entering sales taxes in Craig's Landscaping and Design. You will not be able to use the screenshots in the next two sections to help you in the Practice Exercises. You will be able to use them to help you with your homework.

Click **Taxes** on the navigation bar to get started.

Click **Set up sales tax**.

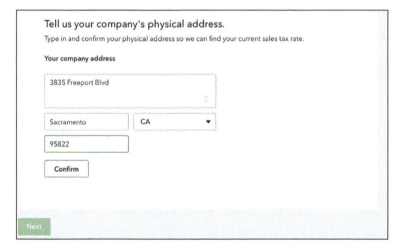

QBO may have 1automatically completed the address fields but if not, you would need to type in the address and click **Confirm**.

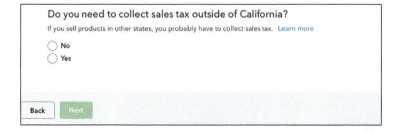

If **Yes** is selected, the user will be able to select additional tax jurisdictions. QBO updates the list regularly. In this course, you will only be selling in California, so select **No** and click **Next**.

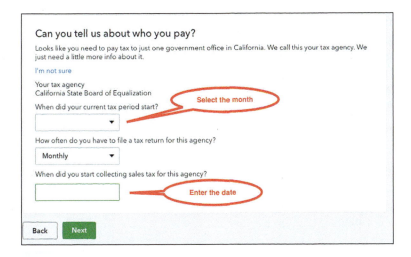

QBO automatically includes a list of possible tax agencies in this screen. Users would select the appropriate agencies if there is more than one option. Other information that must be entered in this screen is:

- First month of the current tax period

- The company's filing frequency (monthly, quarterly, annually)

- Date the company first started collecting sales taxes during the current tax period for the listed agency

Click **Next** to complete the setup and return to the **Sales Tax Center**.

The setup of sales taxes is now complete. QBO has automatically created the appropriate tax agency (based on the company's physical address) and the appropriate tax rates for the company.

As of the date this textbook was written, no amount will be displayed in the Sales Tax Center until the reporting period has ended and the tax is now due.

In future updates, it's expected that once taxable activity has been recorded, the Sales Tax Center will expand to include up to three sections:

- **Due This Month—**
  - List of taxes that are currently due (reporting period ended)

- **Upcoming**
  - List of taxes being accrued for the next period (not yet due)

- **Past Due**
  - List of unpaid, past due taxes

Managing the Tax Status of Customers

When sales tax is set up in a company file, QBO will assume all new and existing customers are taxable.

QBO uses the customer location in determining the appropriate tax rate. The shipping address entered in the customer record is considered the physical location. If no shipping address is entered, QBO will use the billing address. If no address is entered in the customer record, no sales tax will be calculated on sales forms (**invoices** or **sales receipts**) unless the user adds an address in one of the address fields on the form.

For non-taxable customers (for example resellers of products) the tax status must be identified as tax exempt in the customer record.

Click **Sales** on the navigation bar and select the **Customers** tab.

Click a customer name.

Click **Edit** to open the customer record.

On the **Tax info** tab of the customer record, the **This customer is tax exempt** field should be checked. A reason for the tax exemption must be selected in the dropdown menu. The customer's taxpayer identification number is entered in the **Exemption details** field.

The customer record for a reseller might look something like the screenshot above.

> **BEHIND THE SCENES** Individual states set the rules for taxability of organizations and taxability of transactions with those organizations. Users would need to know those state rules in order to select an appropriate reason for not collecting sales tax.

Set up a tax-exempt customer for Craig's Design and Landscaping.
(Craig's Design wants to set up a new Sacramento customer.)

1. Set up a new Sacramento customer, a reseller of concrete.

   a. Click **Sales** on the navigation bar.

   b. Click the **Customers** tab.

   c. Click **New Customer**.

   d. In the **Customer Information** window:

      i. Enter "Sacramento Supplies" in the **company** and **display name as** fields.

      ii. Enter "1122 Main Street, Sacramento CA 95822" on the **Address** tab.

      iii. Uncheck **This customer is taxable** on the **Tax info** tab and enter 91-4444772. **TIP:** In your homework company, you would check **This customer is tax** exempt and would select the reason for the exemption in addition to entering the customer's taxpayer identification number.

   e. Click **Save**.

Shipping Addresses

Merchandising companies often ship products to locations with addresses different from the customer's billing address. Billing **and** shipping addresses can be maintained in QBO.

Both addresses are entered in the **Customer Information** window.

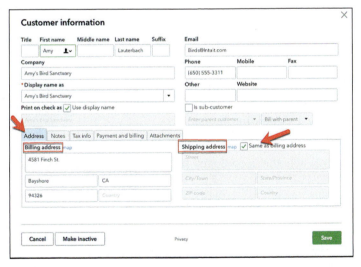

If the billing and shipping addresses are the same, you can check the **Same as billing address** field in the **Shipping address** section of the window. (The shipping address fields will be grayed out if **Same as billing address** is checked.)

Manage shipping addresses for customers of Craig's Design and Landscaping.
(Craig's Design needs to enter a shipping address for Amy's Bird Sanctuary.)

1. Click **Sales** on the navigation bar.

2. Click the **Customers** tab.

3. Click **Amy's Bird Sanctuary**.

(continued)

Specific identification method An inventory costing method involving the physical identification of goods sold and goods remaining and costing these amounts at their actual costs.

First-in, first-out (FIFO) method An inventory costing method that assumes that the oldest (earliest purchased) goods are sold first.

Last-in, first-out (LIFO) method An inventory costing method that assumes that the newest (most recently purchased) goods are sold first.

Weighted average cost method An inventory costing method that calculates an average unit purchase cost, weighted by the number of units purchased at each price, and uses that weighted-average unit cost to determine the cost of goods sold for all sales.

Periodic inventory A system that records inventory purchase transactions; the Inventory account and the cost of goods sold account are not updated until the end of the period when a physical count of the inventory is taken.

Perpetual inventory A system that records the cost of merchandise inventory in the Inventory account at the time of purchase and updates the Inventory account for subsequent purchases and sales of merchandise as they occur.

---

4. Click **Edit**.

5. Uncheck the **Same as billing address** box.

6. Enter the shipping address as:

   "2580 Bluebird St.

   Bayshore, CA 94326"

7. **Make a note** of the street name for Amy's billing address.

8. Click **Save**.

MANAGING ITEMS (MERCHANDISING COMPANY)

The biggest single difference between service and merchandising companies is, of course, inventory. There are several systems used by merchandising companies to track inventory (**periodic** and **perpetual**) and a number of acceptable methods used to value inventory (**specific identification**, **FIFO**, **LIFO**, **weighted average**, etc.).

Merchandising companies can use QBO whether they choose to use **periodic** or **perpetual** inventory systems. However, the program is most effectively used as a perpetual tracking system. QBO values inventory using the FIFO method.

A company will need to set up an item for each and every product that it sells. There are two **item types** that can be used for inventory:

- **Inventory part**
  - Used for products that a company sells, maintains in inventory, **and** tracks using a perpetual inventory system.

- **Non-inventory part**
  - Used for products that a company sells, maintains in inventory, but doesn't track.
    - Generally insignificant items.
    - More frequently used by manufacturing companies.
  - Used for products that a company purchases to order and doesn't maintain in inventory.
  - Can be used in a periodic tracking system.

Setting Up Inventory Items

The process for setting up **inventory items** is similar to the process for setting up **service items**. Click the **gear** icon on the icon bar.

Click **Products and Services**.

Click **New** to add an **inventory item**.

The initial window for adding items looks something like this:

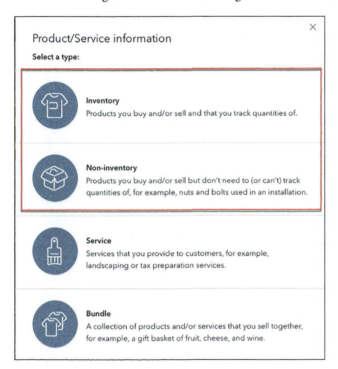

Setting Up Non-inventory Part Items

Click **Non-inventory**.

When a new item is set up as a non-inventory part, the screen initially looks like this:

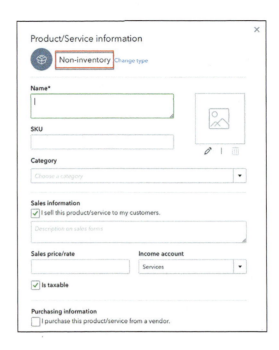

A **name** must be assigned. Items can be identified using names or numbers. SKUs (identifier codes) are optional.

Users can elect to attach **items** to a **category**. See Chapter 3 for help with **categories**.

If the **item** is sold to customers (the most likely scenario in service and merchandising companies), additional information is needed.

A check in the box next to **I sell this product/service to my customers** opens the necessary additional fields for entering:

- A description of the item to appear on sales forms

- A default sales price/rate

- The general ledger account to be credited in a sales transaction (debited if a credit memo is issued)

If the sale of a specific product or service **item** is **ever** taxable, certain information must be included in the **item** record.

First, the **Is taxable** box must be checked.

When **Is taxable** is checked, additional fields will be displayed. A **Sales tax category** must be selected and the type of product (or service) must be identified in the **What you sell** dropdown menu.

The tax status section of an **item** in your homework company might look something like this:

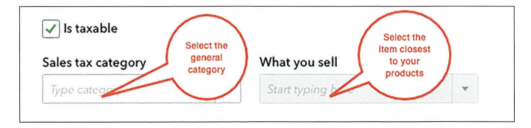

If a particular **customer** is non-taxable, the customer tax status will automatically override the **item** tax status when an **invoice** or **sales receipt** is created. You can also manually override the default **item** tax status, if needed, when preparing **invoices** or sales **receipts**.

In most merchandising companies, **non-inventory parts** are purchased from vendors.
Check the box next to **I purchase this product/service from a vendor** to display additional fields related to purchase transactions.

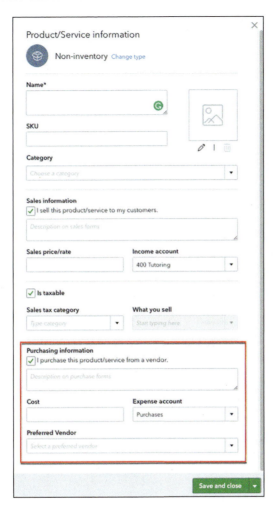

A default **cost** and **description** should be entered. The **cost** field is a default amount automatically displayed when an **item** is added to a purchase transaction. The actual cost, if different, would be entered before saving the transaction.

The associated general ledger account (**Expense** account) should be selected. The **Expense account** selected will be debited for the purchase price when **non-inventory parts** are purchased (and credited if **items** are returned).

> **BEHIND THE SCENES** There are a lot of possibilities here. The company might record all purchases of non-inventory parts in an inventory account or in a Purchases (expense) account if the company uses a periodic inventory system. If the non-inventory part costs are insignificant, the company might record the purchases directly to a parts expense account.

A **preferred vendor** can also be entered in the **item** record. The benefit of entering a **preferred vendor** will be covered in Chapter 7.

Setting Up Inventory Items

Inventory part items are also set up by clicking **New** in the **Products and Services** list. **Inventory** is selected as the type.

The screen looks like this:

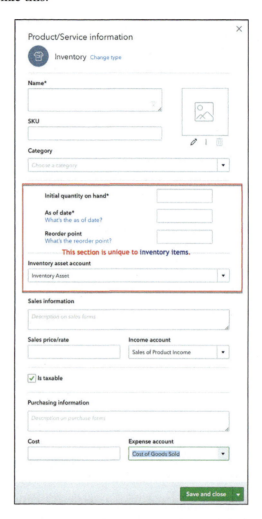

The **inventory item Name** is entered in the top section along with the **category** (if used). There's additional information **required** in the next section.

- **Initial quantity on hand** and **As of date**
  - Although these fields are required even when a brand new item is created, they are primarily used when an existing company is converted to QBO from the desktop version of QuickBooks. In your homework company files, beginning inventory quantities were imported to QBO. When new items are created, enter 0 as the **initial quantity on hand** and the current date as the **As of date**.

- **Inventory asset account**
  - The account selected here will be debited when **inventory items** are purchased and credited when **inventory items** are returned. The account selected would be an asset account (**current asset account type**) because inventory is tracked using a perpetual tracking system in QBO.

You can also set a reorder point for inventory part items in this section. A reorder point indicates the lowest level of inventory that should be maintained. Reorder points will be discussed further in Chapter 7.

BEHIND THE SCENES Reorder points are used by management to determine when to place orders. Setting a reorder point does not generate a transaction.

The Sales information section of the window is identical to the sales section for non-inventory items.

- Description to appear on sales forms is entered.

- Default sales price/rate is entered.

- Income account is selected.
    - This is the general ledger account that will be credited for the revenue generated by the sale.

    Is taxable should be checked if the sale of the inventory item is **ever** taxable to a customer. If checked, a sales tax category must be selected and the type of product (or service) must be identified in the What you sell dropdown menu

    The Purchasing information section appears identical to the purchasing section for **non-inventory items**. The description used in purchase transactions and the default **cost** is entered. The Expense account selected here, however, will be debited for the cost of the inventory item when it's sold, not when it's purchased.

BEHIND THE SCENES The Expense account selected for inventory part items would normally have a cost of goods sold account type. Most merchandising companies prepare multi-step income statements. QBO automatically reports all cost of goods sold accounts directly below income accounts on the profit and loss report and appropriately includes a gross profit subtotal so the account type is important.

QBO automatically creates the following journal entry when an inventory part is purchased:

Inventory (using the asset account specified in item setup)

Accounts payable (or cash)

QBO automatically creates the following journal entry when an inventory part is sold:

Accounts Receivable (or Undeposited Funds if cash sale)

Cost of goods sold (using the expense account specified in item setup)

Revenue (using the income account specified in item setup)

Inventory (using the inventory asset account specified in item setup)

Sales tax payable (if sale was subject to sales tax)

A preferred vendor can also be entered in the inventory item record. The benefit of entering a preferred vendor will be covered in Chapter 7.

Click Save and close to complete the setup.

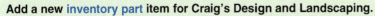

Add a new inventory part item for Craig's Design and Landscaping.

(Craig's Design has decided to sell small sprinkler systems. It expects to purchase the systems from Glorious Growers for $75 and sell them for $140. The company will be selling the product to consumers.)

PRACTICE
EXERCISE

(continued)

1. Click the **gear** icon on the icon bar.

2. Click **Products and Services**.

3. Click **New**.

4. Click **Inventory**.

5. Enter **item name** as "Sprinkler System."

6. Click **category** and select **Add new**.

7. Enter "Garden products" as the **category name**.

8. Click **Save**.

9. Enter "0" as the **Initial quantity on hand** and the current date as the **As of Date**.

10. Select **Inventory Asset** as the **inventory asset account**, if necessary.

11. Enter "5" as the **Reorder point**.

12. Enter "Small sprinkler system" in the **Sales information** field.

13. Leave **Inventory asset** as the **Inventory asset account**.

14. Enter "140" as **Sales price/rate**.

15. Select **Sales of Product Income** as the **income account**, if necessary.

16. Leave checkmark next to **Is taxable**. **TIP:** In your homework company, you would also need to select the **sales tax category** and the **type of product**.

17. Enter "Small sprinkler system" in the **Purchasing information** field.

18. Enter "75" as the **cost**.

19. Select **Cost of Goods Sold** as the **Expense account**, if necessary.

20. Select Hicks Hardware as the **Preferred Vendor**.

21. **Make a note** of the profit Craig's Design will make on each small sprinkler system it sell.

22. Click **Save and close**.

RECORDING SALES REVENUE

Merchandising companies, like service companies, make cash and credit sales. We learned how to record **invoices** and **sales receipts** in Chapter 3. In this chapter, we're going to cover:

- Customer discounts

- Delayed charges and credits

- Handling uncollectible accounts

None of the above are unique to merchandising companies. The processes outlined below would be used in service companies as well.

Customer Discounts

Companies often give discounts to customers. They might include:

- Price breaks for large orders
- Discounts for nonprofits, senior citizens, students

Price breaks and customer-specific discounts can be entered directly on sales forms (**Invoices** and **sales receipts**) if the **Discount** feature is activated.

Activating Sales Discounts

To activate **discounts**, click the **gear** icon on the icon bar and click **Account and Settings**.

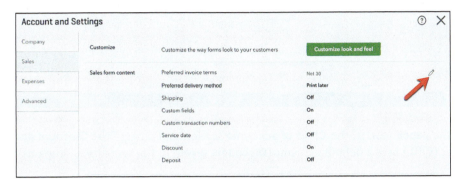

On the **Sales** tab, click the **pencil** icon in the **Sales form content** section.

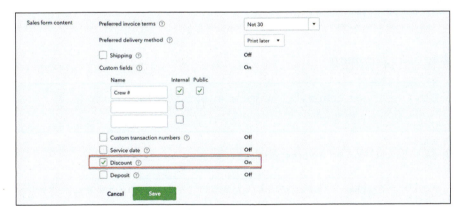

Put a checkmark in the box next to **Discount** to turn the feature on and click **Save**. A discount field will now be available on all sales forms.

Users must then identify the account to be debited for the amount of the discount. This is done on the **Advanced** tab of **Account and Settings**.

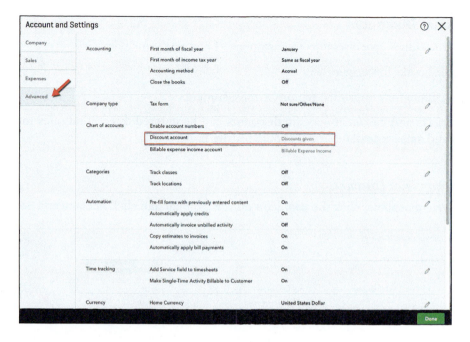

Click the **pencil** icon in the **Chart of accounts** section and change the **Discount account** as needed. (QBO uses a default account (**Discounts given**) in the test drive company.)

> **BEHIND THE SCENES** Sales discounts are normally reported as contra revenue accounts. For proper reporting, the account linked to **Discounts** should have an **Income account type**.

Recording Sales Discounts

 HINT: The instructions below use an **invoice** form as an example. The process would be the same for **sales receipts**.

To include a discount on an **invoice**, click the ⊕ icon on the icon bar.

Click **Invoice**.

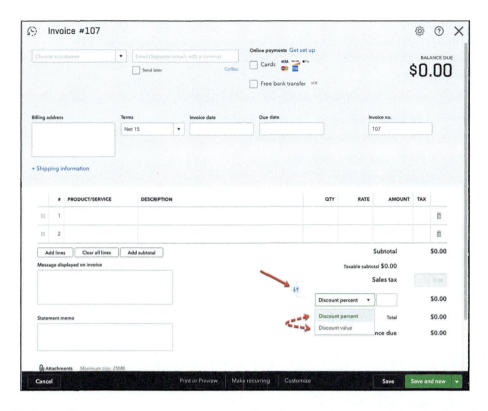

Either a discount percent or amount can be given to a customer. Use the dropdown menu to make the selection.

The default in QBO is to calculate tax, if any, on the invoice total before any discount. If the discount should be applied first, click the **arrows** icon next to the discount field. When the discount field appears above the tax field, QBO will calculate tax on the balance net of the discount. The screen would look something like this:

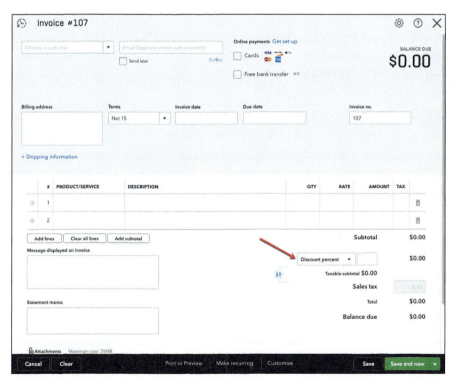

PRACTICE
EXERCISE

Set up and give sales discounts in Craig's Design and Landscaping.
(Craig's Design has decided to give 10% sales discount on landscape installation at Dukes Basketball Camp.)

1. Activate sales discounts. (The feature may already be activated in your test drive company. Go through Steps 1a to 1c to make sure.)

   a. Click the **gear** icon on the icon bar.

   b. Click **Account and Settings**.

   c. Open the **Sales** tab.

   d. Click the **pencil** icon in the **Sales form content** section.

   e. **Make a note** of the options available in the **Preferred delivery method** dropdown menu.

   f. Place a checkmark next to **Discount**.

   g. Click **Save**.

2. Link the discount to a general ledger account.

   a. Click the **Advanced** tab. (You should still be in the **Account and Settings** screen.)

   b. Click the **pencil** icon in the **Chart of accounts** section.

   c. Open the **Discount account** dropdown menu.

   d. Select **Add new**.

   e. Select **Income** as the **Account Type** and **Discounts/Refunds Given** as the **Detail Type**.

   f. Use "Sales Discounts" as the **Name**.

   g. Click **Save and close**.

   h. Click **Save**.

   i. Click **Done**.

3. Create an invoice for Dukes Basketball Camp (40 hours of Landscape Installation at $50 per hour with a 10% discount applied before tax). Landscape Installation at Craig's Design is taxable.

   a. Click the ➕ on the icon bar.

   b. Click **Invoice**.

   c. Select **Dukes Basketball Camp** as the customer.

   d. Select **Net 30** as the **Terms** and enter the current date as the **Invoice date**.

   e. Select **Pump** as the **PRODUCT/SERVICE** and enter "40" as the **QTY**.

   f. Leave the rate at 15.

   g. Enter "10" in the **Discount percent** field.

   h. **Make a note** of the balance due.

   i. Switch the order of the tax and discount fields so that the discount appears before the tax field.

   j. The balance due should be $583.20.

   k. Click **Save and close**.

Delayed Charges and Delayed Credits

There are times when a company wants to be able to track a sales transaction that is in process but not yet completed. Here are two examples:

- A customer places an order for some products. The order has not yet been shipped.

- A customer requests a credit for damaged merchandise but the merchandise has not yet been returned.

Neither of these is an accounting transaction because the accounting equation hasn't changed yet. The customer order won't be an accounting transaction until the product is shipped or delivered. The customer credit won't be an accounting transaction until the company actually receives the damaged merchandise.

There are many examples of pending transactions that a company might want to track. The company could, of course, track them outside of their accounting system but it's most efficient to be able to have information available in the system.

Delayed charges and **delayed credits** are options available in QBO for tracking pending transactions. Both of these are **non-posting** transactions. A **non-posting** transaction does not create a journal entry and with pending transactions, we don't want a journal entry. The information is available in the system but account balances are not affected.

Delayed charge or **delayed credit** forms are accessed by clicking the ➕ icon on the icon bar.

Recording and Processing Delayed Charges

When a customer places an order that will not be fulfilled immediately, a **delayed charge** can be created. A **delayed charge** form looks something like this:

Remember, a **delayed charge** does not create a journal entry and it does not affect account balances. For example, here is the account balance for a customer with a **delayed charge**.

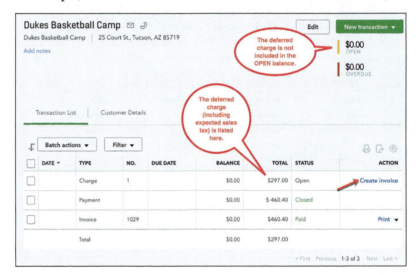

When the product is shipped or the work completed, the user clicks **Create invoice** to change the **delayed charge** to an **invoice**.

The final **invoice** might look something like this:

> **BEHIND THE SCENES** Sales taxes and sales discounts are not available on **delayed charges**. Both fields are available when the **delayed charge** is converted to an **invoice**.

Recording and Processing Delayed Credits

A **delayed credit** is created if a user wants to track a credit that will be available to a customer at some future date. For example, if a company promised a customer a 10% discount on an **invoice** IF the customer provided two referrals within a two-week period, that could be set up as a **delayed credit**. If and when the customer provided the referrals, the credit would be applied.

A **delayed credit** form looks something like this:

Delayed credits, like **delayed charges**, are **non-posting** transactions so account balances are not affected. The balance of a customer with a **delayed credit** would look something like this:

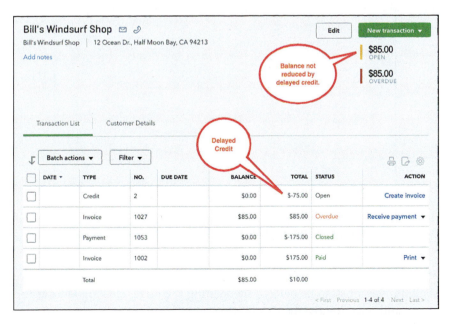

Probably the most efficient way to process a **delayed credit** once the transaction is completed is to apply it to an outstanding **invoice**. Instead of clicking **Start invoice**, the user opens an existing invoice. To display the **delayed credit**, click the small **<** icon in the top right corner of the **invoice** to open the sidebar. (The **<** changes to **>** when the sidebar is open.) It would look something like this:

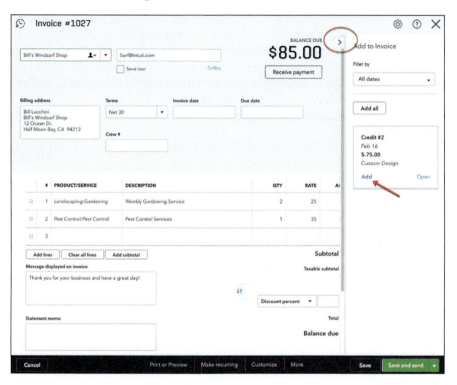

Click **Add** to apply the credit to the **invoice**. After application, the **invoice** would look something like this:

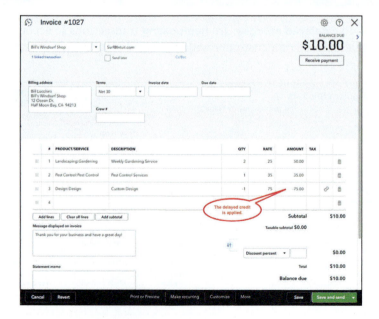

Managing Non-posting Transactions

Non-posting transactions can be deleted by opening the form, clicking **More** at the bottom of the screen, and selecting **Delete**.

For a list of all **delayed credit** and **delayed charge** transactions, click **Reports** on the navigation bar.

Select **Transaction List by Date** in the **For My Accountant** section.

Click **Customize** and open the **Filter** section.

Put a checkmark by **Transaction Type** and select **non-posting**.

Click **Run report**.

Set up a delayed charge for Craig's Design and Landscaping.

(Craig's Design has agreed to a fee of $400 for some gardening work to be done in August and wants to get the invoice set up in QBO. The work will be invoiced when the work is performed.)

1. Create the **delayed charge**.

    a.   Click the ➕ icon on the icon bar.

    b.   Click **Delayed Charge**.

    c.   Click **Wedding Planning by Whitney** as the **Customer**.

    d.   Enter the current date as the **Invoice date**.

    e.   Select **Trimming** as the **PRODUCT/SERVICE**.

    f.   Enter "400" as the **AMOUNT**.

    g.   Click **Save and close**.

2. Create the **invoice** from the **delayed charge**.

    a.   Click **Sales** on the navigation bar.

    b.   Click the **Customers** tab.

    c.   In the dropdown menu in the **ACTION** column for Wedding Planning by Whitney, click **Create Invoice**.

    d.   Click **Add** in the **Charge #1** box in the sidebar.

    e.   Leave the terms as **Net 30**.

    f.   Enter "8/1/18" as the **Invoice date**.

    g.   Click **Save and close**.

PRACTICE EXERCISE

Recording Uncollectible Accounts

Unfortunately, companies don't always collect the balances owed to them by their customers. Merchandisers will often try to get the product back when the customer defaults but, depending on the type and value of the products sold, that may not be feasible or even possible.

If the company has exhausted all reasonable collection methods, the invoice must be written off. Deleting or voiding the invoice in QBO would not be good accounting. The company did make the sale and should show the revenue. They should also report that uncollectible sales (recorded as **bad debt expenses**) are a real cost of selling on credit.

There are two methods for accounting for uncollectible accounts: the **allowance method** and the **direct write-off method**. Only the allowance method is acceptable under generally accepted accounting principles.

Allowance Method Refresher

Under the allowance method, an estimate of the amount of uncollectible receivables is made at the end of an accounting period. The initial entry to establish an allowance for those amounts is:

Bad debt expense The expense stemming from the inability of a business to collect an amount previously recorded as receivable. It is normally classified as a selling or administrative expense.

Allowance method An accounting procedure whereby the amount of bad debts expense is estimated and recorded in the period in which the related credit sales occur.

Direct write-off method An accounting procedure whereby the amount of bad debts expense is not recorded until specific uncollectible customer accounts are identified.

| | Bad debt expense | | |
| | Allowance for doubtful accounts | | |

The allowance account is a contra asset account (contra to accounts receivable). Accounts receivable net of the allowance is referred to as the net realizable value of receivables (amount that the company actually expects to collect or "realize"). When a **specific** customer account is determined to be uncollectible, the account is written off. The entry is:

| | Allowance for doubtful accounts | | |
| | Accounts receivable | | |

If a previously written off amount is subsequently received, the entry is:

| | Cash | | |
| | Allowance for doubtful accounts | | |

At the end of each accounting period, the allowance account is adjusted to reflect the amount that is currently considered uncollectible. For example, if the end of period balance in the allowance account is estimated to be too low, the entry is:

| | Bad debt expense | | |
| | Allowance for doubtful accounts | | |

Direct Write-off Method Refresher

Companies that historically do not have many uncollectible accounts often use the direct write-off method. Under this method, bad debt expense is only recognized when a specific customer account is determined to be uncollectible. This method violates generally accepted accounting principles but is sometimes used when the amount of bad debts is insignificant.

The entry is:

| | Bad debt expense | | |
| | Accounts receivable | | |

QuickCheck
6-1

> Which accounting principle is violated under the direct write-off method?

Either the allowance or the direct write-off method can be used in QBO.

If the allowance method is used, the entry to set up or adjust the allowance account should be made as a general journal entry (**Journal entry transaction type**). See Chapter 5 if you need help with making adjusting journal entries.

The actual write-off of an invoice (under either the allowance or direct write-off method) can be done by creating a **credit memo** recognizing the bad debt and then applying the **credit memo** to the uncollectible **invoice**.

The first step is to set up the necessary accounts. Under either method, a Bad Debt Expense account is necessary. Under the allowance method, an Allowance for Doubtful Accounts is also necessary. Remember, the Allowance account is a contra asset account.

Click the **gear** icon on the icon bar and select **Chart of Accounts**.

- For the bad debt expense account, the **account type** would be **Expenses** and the **detail type** would be **Bad Debts**.

- For the Allowance account, both the **account type** and the **detail type** would be **Accounts Receivable (A/R)**.

- **Accounts Receivable (A/R)** is chosen as the **account type** so that the Allowance account will appear with Accounts Receivable in the balance sheet.

The second step is to set up a new **item**. Remember, every line on any sales transaction (other than discounts and sales tax) is an **item**. To create the credit memo, you'll need an **item**.

Click the **gear** icon on the icon bar and select **Products and Services**.

Click **New** and select **Service**. (A **service item** is normally selected for any non-product related fee or charge.)

The **item** might be set up something like this if the company uses the direct write-off method of recording uncollectible accounts:

If the allowance method is used, the **income** account selected should be **Allowance for Doubtful Accounts**.

> **BEHIND THE SCENES** It might seem counter-intuitive to select an asset or expense account in the **income** field of the **service item** setup. QBO automatically credits the account selected here when an **invoice** or **sales receipt** is collected. QBO automatically debits the account selected here when a **credit memo** is created. Because write-offs are entered through **credit memos**, you're identifying the account to be debited when the **credit memo** is prepared. For uncollectible accounts, the debit account should be either bad debt expense or the allowance account, depending on the method used.

Once the **service item** is created and the appropriate general ledger accounts are set up, the user can create a **credit memo** to record the write-off. The **credit memo** is then applied to the uncollectible **invoice**. (The application is automatic if the **automation** feature is turned on in **Account and Settings**. The **credit memo** must be manually applied if **automation** is turned off.)

The process is demonstrated in the next practice exercise.

Record an uncollectible account at Craig's Design and Landscaping.

(Jeff's Jalopies has gone bankrupt. Craig's Design and Landscaping has very few uncollectible accounts and has elected to use the direct write-off method to account for bad debts.)

(continued)

PRACTICE
EXERCISE

1. Set up the appropriate account.

    a.   Click the **gear** icon on the icon bar.

    b.   Click **Chart of Accounts**.

    c.   Click **See your Chart of Accounts**.

    d.   Click **New**.

    e.   Select **Expenses** as the **account type** and **Bad Debts** as the **detail type**.

    f.   Enter "Bad Debt Expense" as the **name**.

    g.   Click **Save and close**.

2. Set up the new **service item**.

    a.   Click the **gear** icon on the icon bar.

    b.   Click **Products and Services**.

    c.   Click **New**.

    d.   Select **Service**.

    e.   Enter "Write off" as the **name**.

    f.   Select **Add new** as the **Category**.

        i.   Enter "Other Charges" as the **Name** and click **Save**.

    g.   Enter "Write off of uncollectible account" in the **description** field.

    h.   Select **Bad Debt Expense** as the **Income Account**.

    i.   Uncheck the **Is taxable** box.

    j.   Click **Save and close**

3. Create a credit memo.

    a.   Click the ➕ icon on the icon bar.

    b.   Select **credit memo**.

    c.   Select **55 Twin Lane** as the **name**.

    d.   Use the current date.

    e.   Select **Write off** as the **PRODUCT/SERVICE** and enter "85" as the amount.

    f.   Click **Save and close**.

4. Since the **automation** feature is on by default in the test drive company, the **credit memo** will automatically be applied to the 55 Twin Lane account.

RECORDING PAYMENTS FROM CUSTOMERS

Chapter 3 outlines the process for recording cash (or check) payments from customers. This chapter covers:

- Customer payments by credit card

- Customer checks returned by the bank due to insufficient funds (NSF checks)

- Early payment discounts

Customer Payments by Credit Card

Most retail stores accept credit cards as a form of payment. Credit card payments are considered **almost** the equivalent of cash. "Almost" because:

- The company pays a fee to the financial institution processing credit card receipts for the company (commonly called the merchant bank) on all credit card receipts.

- The merchant bank generally makes the deposits directly to the merchandiser's account (net of any fees) within a few days in batches that correspond to the credit card type (VISA, MasterCard, etc.).

Credit card payments can be received at the time of sale or as payment on an account balance.

> **HINT:** Users can purchase a credit card processing service through QBO. Credit card receipts are processed automatically when entered. The processes described below assume that the company does **not** have that service.

Recording Receipt of Customer Credit Card Payment

Most companies receive credit card receipts from the merchant bank within a few days so sales paid by credit card, at point of sale, are normally recorded as **Sales Receipts** (cash sales). The type of credit card used (VISA, MasterCard, etc.) is selected as the payment method. QBO allows users to enter the credit number and expiration date. We will not be entering that information in this class.

When customers use credit cards to pay account balances, the payment is recorded through the **Receive Payment** window (similar to payments of account balances by cash or check). The type of credit card used (VISA, MasterCard, etc.) is selected as the payment method.

Record customer credit card transactions for Craig's Design and Landscaping.
(The merchant bank is America's Bank. The transaction fee is 3% of credit card receipts.)

PRACTICE EXERCISE

1. Record cash sale using a credit card. (Cool Cars pays $200 to purchase some garden lights.)
   a. Click the icon on the icon bar.
   b. Click **Sales Receipt**.
   c. Select **Cool Cars** as the customer.
   d. Use the current date.
   e. Select **Visa** as the **Payment method**.
   f. Make sure Undeposited Funds appears in the **Deposit to** field.
   g. Select **Lighting** as the **Product/Service**.
   h. Enter a **QTY** of "5" and a **RATE** of "$20."
   i. Select **California** as the **sales tax rate**.
   j. **Make a note** of the tax rate for California. **TIP:** In your homework company, the tax rate will not be visible to you.
   k. **Amount received** should show as $108.00.
   l. Click **Save and close**.

2. Record customer payment of an account balance with a credit card. (Mark Cho pays his $314.28 invoice balance with a credit card.)
   a. Click the icon on the icon bar.
   b. Click **Receive Payments**.
   c. Select **Mark Cho** as the customer.

> d. Use the current date.
>
> e. Select **Visa** as the **Payment method**.
>
> f. Make sure Undeposited Funds appears in the **Deposit to** field.
>
> g. Enter "314.28" as the **Amount received**.
>
> h. Click **Save and close**.

 WARNING: **The next practice exercise uses the transactions just entered. If you logged out or timed out after the last practice exercise, you'll need to reenter the above transactions before moving forward.**

"Depositing" Credit Card Receipts

As you learned in Chapter 3, unless the default preference is changed, QBO debits **Undeposited Funds** for all payments received from customers through **Sales Receipt** or **Payment** forms. The receipts are transferred, in batches that correspond to the actual deposit amounts, from the **Undeposited Funds** account to the cash account through the **Bank Deposit** form.

The same considerations must be made for credit card receipts. The merchant bank makes deposits to the merchandiser's bank account in batches (grouped by credit card type), net of any transaction fees charged. The deposit in QBO for credit card receipts should be made in corresponding batches, net of the fees. Checks and cash receipts should not be included on the same deposit form in QBO as credit card receipts because they would show as separate transactions on bank statements.

Recording a deposit of credit card receipts is done using the **Bank Deposit** form accessed by clicking the ⊕ icon on the icon bar. The screen looks something like this when there are receipts that have not yet been deposited:

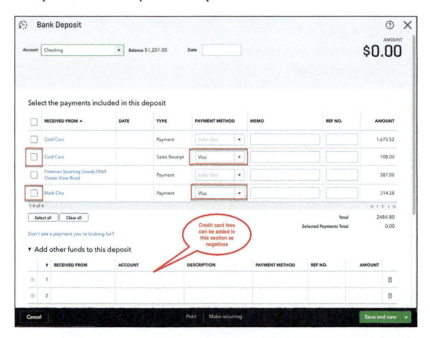

The user should mark (check) all receipts of the same credit card type for deposit.

Credit card fees are entered in the **Add New Deposits** section. To record the fee, the merchant bank is entered in the **RECEIVED FROM** field. The account used to record merchant bank fees should be selected in the **ACCOUNT** field. The fee is entered as a negative number in the **AMOUNT** field.

The screen would look something like this:

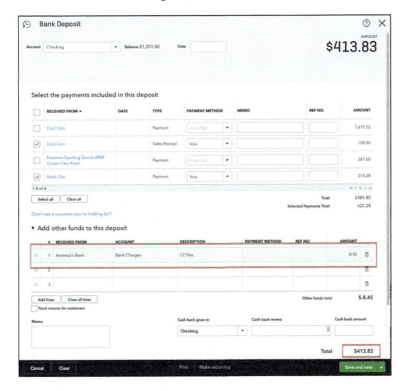

> **BEHIND THE SCENES** Remember, the default journal entry underlying a deposit transaction includes a debit to the Bank account indicated for the total deposit amount and a credit to the Account(s) indicated on the deposit form. Credit card processing fees are expenses. Entering the amount as a negative tells QBO to debit, not credit, the **ACCOUNT** for the merchant fees.

 HINT: QBO has a built-in calculator feature that can be useful here. The feature is activated by entering a number and then a mathematical operator (+, −, * or /). Ignore the **This value is out of range** warning that appears when you enter the operator. The message will disappear when you enter the next number.

If the transaction fee amount is not known when the deposit is initially recorded in QBO, the deposit form can be edited later (fees added) so that the net amount agrees to the amount actually received from the merchant bank.

 WARNING: The following practice exercise uses transactions entered in the last exercise. If you logged out or timed out after the last practice exercise, you'll need to complete that exercise again before moving forward.

<table>
<tr><td>**PRACTICE**
EXERCISE</td><td>

Make a deposit of credit card receipts for Craig's Design and Landscaping.
(Craig's Design processes its VISA credit card receipts.)

1. Click the ➕ icon on the icon bar.

2. Click **Bank Deposit**.

3. Select **Checking** as the bank account, if necessary.

4. Use the current date.

5. Check all VISA transactions displayed in the **Select Existing Payments** section.
   a. **Selected Payments Total** should be $422.28.

6. Enter the credit card fees in the **Add New Deposits** section.
   a. Enter "America's Bank" as a vendor in the **RECEIVED FROM** field.
      i. Add without additional detail.
   b. Select **Bank Charges** as the **ACCOUNT**.
   c. Enter "Credit card fees" in the **DESCRIPTION** field.
   d. Enter the 3% transaction fee "($12.67)" as a negative in **AMOUNT** field.

7. **Total** should be $409.61.

8. Click **Save and close**.

</td></tr>
</table>

Early Payment Discounts

Companies often give customers discounts if credit sales are paid before the due date. Any available early payment discounts are included as part of the credit terms listed on the invoice.

Examples of credit terms with early payment discounts include:

- 2/10, Net 30
  - Discount of 2% of the invoice total if paid within 10 days of the due date. Balance is due in full 30 days from the invoice date.

- 1/15, Net 45
  - Discount of 1% of the invoice total if paid within 15 days of the due date. Balance is due in full 45 days from the invoice date.

All credit terms used by the company (for customers OR vendors) are set up in the **Terms** lists accessed by clicking the **gear** icon on the icon bar and selecting **All Lists**. Setting up **terms** was covered in Chapter 3.

The credit terms granted to a **specific** customer are entered on the **Payment and billing** tab of the customer record. These credit terms are automatically included on invoices prepared for the customer. They can be changed on a specific invoice if necessary.

Although credit terms can be created in QBO that include early payment discounts, there is currently no mechanism for recording early payment discounts in the **Receive Payment** form.

> **BEHIND THE SCENES** Because early payment discounts should not be recognized until the customer actually takes the discount, the user cannot enter the discount that **might** be taken on the original invoice.
>
> A user could possibly edit the original invoice when the payment is received. However, this would not be an acceptable choice if the original invoice was recognized in a prior period. (Editing the invoice would automatically change the prior period's financial statements.)

Instead, a **credit memo** for the amount of the discount taken by the customer is created and applied when the customer's payment is recorded.

To create a **credit memo**, an **item** is needed so the first step would be to create a new **service item**.

Click the **gear** icon on the icon bar and select **Products and Services**. Click **New** and **Service**.

The new **Item** might be set up something like this:

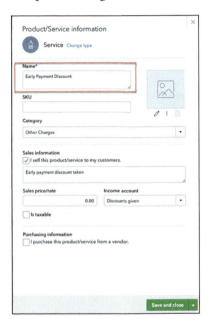

When a customer takes an early payment discount, the **credit memo** should be created for the discount amount before the payment is recorded. (This assumes the user is applying credit memos manually. If the **automation** feature is turned on, it shouldn't matter which step is done first.) Refer back to Chapter 3 for help with applying credits to customer **invoices**.

The credit memo is then applied to the **invoice** when the payment is recorded.

PRACTICE
EXERCISE

Record an early payment discount taken by a customer of Craig's Design and Land-scaping.

(Geeta Kalapatapu took a 2% early payment discount ($12.58) when she paid Invoice #1033.)

1. Turn off the **automation** feature to allow for manual application of credit memos.

   a.   Click the **gear** icon on the icon bar.

   b.   Click **Account and Settings** screen.

   c.   Click the **Advanced** tab.

(continued)

  d. Click the **pencil** icon in the **Automation** section.

  e. Remove the checkmark next to **Automatically apply credits**.

  f. Click **Save**.

  g. Click **Done**.

2. Set up a **service item** for early payment discounts.

  a. Click the **gear** icon on the icon bar.

  b. Select **Products and Services**.

  c. Click **New**.

  d. Select **Service**.

  e. Enter "Early Payment Discount" as the **Name**.

  f. Select **Add new** as the **Category**.

  g. Enter "Other Charges" as the **Name**.

  h. Click **Save**.

  i. Enter "Early payment discount" as the **Description**.

  i. Select **Discounts given** as the **Income account**.

  j. Uncheck **Is taxable**.

  k. Click **Save and close**.

3. Create a **credit memo** for Geeta Kalapatapu in the amount of $12.58 for the early payment discount taken on Invoice 1033.

  a. Click the ➕ icon on the icon bar.

  b. Select **Credit Memo**.

  c. Select **Geeta Kalapatapu** as the customer.

  d. Use the current date.

  e. Select **Early Payment Discount** as the **PRODUCT/SERVICE**.

  f. Enter "12.58" in the **AMOUNT** field.

  g. Click **Save and close**.

4. Record Geeta's check for $616.52.

  a. Click the ➕ icon on the icon bar.

  b. Select **Receive Payment**.

  c. Select **Geeta Kalapatapu** as the customer.

  d. Use the current date as the **Payment date**.

  e. Enter "Check" as the **Payment method** and "10987" as the **Reference no.**

  f. Enter "616.52" as the **Amount received**.

  g. Place checkmarks in the boxes next to **Invoice 1033** and the **credit memo** you created in Step 3.

  h. Make sure the **PAYMENT** amount shows as 629.10 for the **invoice** and 12.58 for the **credit memo**.

  i. The **Amount to Apply** should show as $629.10.

  j. Click **Save and close**.

Customer Checks Returned by Bank Due to Insufficient Funds (NSF Checks)

Every company that accepts checks from customers accepts a risk that the customer does not have sufficient funds in the bank to cover the check.

When customer checks are returned NSF (non-sufficient funds), the companies will normally either:

- Attempt to redeposit the check OR

- Write off the invoice as a bad debt OR

- Re-invoice the customer (for the amount of the check plus processing fees).

Regardless of the choice made, an NSF check must be recorded in the accounting records along with any fees associated with the NSF check.

Remember, when the customer check was originally recorded in QBO, the entry was:

Undeposited Funds			
Accounts receivable (or income)			

When the check was deposited, the amount was transferred from Undeposited Funds to the Cash account. Cash is now overstated by the amount of the NSF check. The entry underlying the invoice created will need to affect (credit) the Cash account not an income account.

> **BEHIND THE SCENES** The process for handling NSF checks described below assumes that the company will attempt to collect the full amount. A new invoice is created for the amount of the NSF check and any processing fees the company might decide to charge the customer. If the company later decides that the amount is uncollectible, the following procedures should still be followed so that there is a record of the NSF check associated with the customer. The new invoice should then be written off as described earlier in the "Recording Uncollectible Accounts" section of this chapter.

Recording a Customer NSF (Bounced) Check and Associated Fees

The most efficient process in QBO is to set up two new **service items** that can be used to record an **invoice** charging the customer for the bounced check amount and any fees.

- **Bounced Check Amount**—used to invoice the customer for the check amount. The appropriate bank account would be selected as the income account associated with this item.

- **Processing Fee**—used to invoice the customer for any processing fees charged by the company. Most companies would select the Bank Service Charges expense account as the associated income account for this item.

BEHIND THE SCENES The underlying entry for the new **invoice** would then be:

	Accounts Receivable		
	Checking		
	Bank Service Charges		

The credit to cash offsets the original deposit amount. (The amount that didn't clear the bank.) The credit to Bank Service Charges offsets any fees charged by the company's bank. Fees charged by the bank would normally be entered through the bank reconciliation process or by journal entry.

**PRACTICE
EXERCISE**

Record a bounced check and related fees for Craig's Design and Landscaping.
(The check received from Travis Waldron for $81 was returned marked NSF. Craig's Design charges its customers $25 for processing bounced checks. Craig's Design intends to pursue collection of the $81.)

1. Set up the new **service items**.
   a. Click the **gear** icon on the icon bar.
   b. Click **Products and Services**.
   c. Click **New**.
   d. Select **Service**.
   e. Enter "Bounced Check" as the **name**.
   f. Select **Other Charges** as the **category**.
      i. Set up the **Other Charges category** if needed.
   g. Enter "Check returned for insufficient funds" in the **sales information** field.
   h. Select **Checking** as the **Income Account**.

(continued)

   i.   Remove the checkmark next to **Is taxable**.

   j.   Click **Save and new**.

   k.   Enter "Processing Fee" as the **name**.

   l.   Select **Other Charges** as the **category**.

   m. Enter "Fee for processing NSF check" in the **sales information** field.

   n.   Select **Bank Charges** as the **Income Account**.

   o.   Remove the checkmark next to **Is taxable**.

   p.   Click **Save and close**.

2. Create an **invoice**.

   a.   Click the ➕ icon on the icon bar.

   b.   Select **Invoice.**

   c.   Select **Travis Waldron** as the **name**.

   d.   Use the current date.

   e.   Select **Bounced Check** as the **PRODUCT/SERVICE** and enter "81" as the **AMOUNT**.

   f.   On the next line, select **Processing fee** as the **PRODUCT/SERVICE** and enter "25" as the **AMOUNT**.

   g.   The **Balance due** should show as $106.

   h.   Click **Save and close**.

CUSTOMER REPORTS

The sales and receivables reports in QBO used by merchandising companies are generally the same as those used by service companies (introduced in Chapter 3). However, the **Sales Product/Service Summary** report used by a merchandising company would normally include cost of goods sold and gross margin (gross profit) fields for inventory part items. A report of inventory item sales (included in the **Sales and Customers** section of **Reports**) would look something like this:

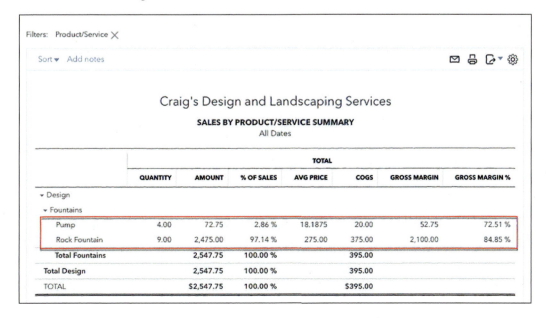

Filters: Product/Service ✕

Craig's Design and Landscaping Services

SALES BY PRODUCT/SERVICE SUMMARY

All Dates

	QUANTITY	AMOUNT	% OF SALES	AVG PRICE	COGS	GROSS MARGIN	GROSS MARGIN %
▾ Design							
▾ Fountains							
Pump	4.00	72.75	2.86 %	18.1875	20.00	52.75	72.51 %
Rock Fountain	9.00	2,475.00	97.14 %	275.00	375.00	2,100.00	84.85 %
Total Fountains		2,547.75	100.00 %		395.00		
Total Design		2,547.75	100.00 %		395.00		
TOTAL		$2,547.75	100.00 %		$395.00		

One useful report that we haven't looked at yet is the **Collections Report**. The report lists the invoice and due dates and can be helpful when making collection calls to tardy customers! The report is available in the **Who Owes You** section of **Reports**. The report looks something like this:

Craig's Design and Landscaping Services

COLLECTIONS REPORT

DATE	TRANSACTION TYPE	NUM	DUE DATE	PAST DUE	AMOUNT	OPEN BALANCE
▾ Amy's Bird Sanctuary (650) 555-3311						
12/30/2017	Invoice	1021	01/29/2018	18	459.00	239.00
Total for Amy's Bird Sanctuary					**$459.00**	**$239.00**
▾ Bill's Windsurf Shop (415) 444-6538						
12/04/2017	Invoice	1027	01/03/2018	44	10.00	10.00
Total for Bill's Windsurf Shop					**$10.00**	**$10.00**
▾ Freeman Sporting Goods:55 Twin Lane (650) 555-0987						
12/04/2017	Invoice	1028	01/03/2018	44	81.00	81.00
01/12/2018	Invoice	1005	02/11/2018	5	54.00	4.00
Total for Freeman Sporting Goods:55 Twin Lane					**$135.00**	**$85.00**
▾ Jeff's Jalopies (650) 555-8989						
12/30/2017	Invoice	1022	01/29/2018	18	81.00	81.00
Total for Jeff's Jalopies					**$81.00**	**$81.00**
▾ John Melton (650) 555-5879						
12/27/2017	Invoice	1007	01/26/2018	21	750.00	450.00
Total for John Melton					**$750.00**	**$450.00**
▾ Kookies by Kathy (650) 555-7896						
12/03/2017	Invoice	1016	01/02/2018	45	75.00	75.00
Total for Kookies by Kathy					**$75.00**	**$75.00**
▾ Red Rock Diner (650) 555-4973						
11/13/2017	Invoice	1024	12/13/2017	65	156.00	156.00
Total for Red Rock Diner					**$156.00**	**$156.00**
▾ Shara Barnett:Barnett Design (650) 557-1289						
01/07/2018	Invoice	1012	02/06/2018	10	274.50	274.50
Total for Shara Barnett:Barnett Design					**$274.50**	**$274.50**
▾ Sushi by Katsuyuki (505) 570-0147						
01/12/2018	Invoice	1018	02/11/2018	5	80.00	80.00
Total for Sushi by Katsuyuki					**$80.00**	**$80.00**
TOTAL					**$2,020.50**	**$1,450.50**

PRACTICE
EXERCISE

Prepare various sales and receivable reports for Craig's Design and Landscaping.
(Craig asks for information about sales over the last two months. He also wants to see which customers have unpaid balances.)

1. Click **Reports** on the navigation bar.
   a. Click on **Sales by Product/Service Summary** in the **Sales and Customers** section.
   b. Select **All Dates** in the **Report period** dropdown menu.
   c. Click **Customize**.
   d. Click **Filter**.
   e. Check the box next to **Product/Service** and select **Pump** and **Rock Fountain**.
   f. Click **Run report**.
   g. **Make a note** of the **COGS** amount for **Rock Fountain**.

(continued)

2. Click **Back to report list**.

   a.   Click **Collections Report** in the **Who owes you** section.

3. Click **Dashboard** to close the window.

Customer Statements

Companies will often send statements to customers on a monthly basis. Statements, for the most part, are simply summaries of activity over some period of time. They generally include a beginning balance, a list of all invoices and payments during the period, and an ending balance. Statements can be an effective way of communicating with customers.

For internal control purposes, most companies will not pay from a statement. (Companies choose to only pay from original invoices to avoid the risk of making duplicate payments.) For that reason, statements rarely include new charges (amounts not previously billed using an invoice). The most common exception would be finance charges assessed on past-due balances. We will not cover finance charges in this course.

Statements can be prepared in QBO and are easily accessed by clicking the ➕ icon on the icon bar and selecting **Statement** in the **Other** column.

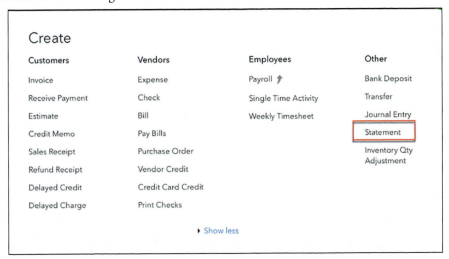

The screen looks something like this:

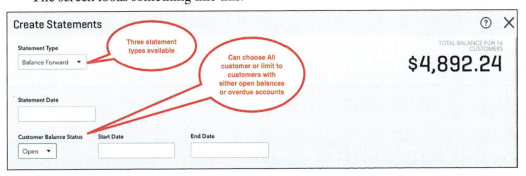

A statement date is entered. A company can choose the data that will appear on the statements by selecting one of the options in the **Statement Type** dropdown menu.

●   **Open item**—All open transactions are displayed.

●   **Balance forward**—The ending balance from the prior period and all current period transactions are displayed.

- Transaction Statement—Transactions during the period are listed in two columns. The Amount column includes any invoices or sales receipts. The Received column includes payments received.

The company can also choose which customers will receive statements. In the Customer Balance Status dropdown menu, options are available to select only customers with balances or only customers with overdue balances. Specific customers can be selected in the Recipients List section.

PRACTICE
EXERCISE

Prepare statements for Craig's Design and Landscaping.

(Craig's Design decides to send statements to all customers with unpaid balances.)

1. Click the ➕ icon on the icon bar.

2. Click Statement.

3. Select Balance Forward as the Statement type.

4. Use the current date.

5. Select Overdue as the Customer Balance Status.

6. Leave default dates.

7. Click Apply.

8. Click Print or Preview at the bottom of the screen to view statements.

9. Click Close (bottom left corner).

10. Click Cancel (bottom left corner of the window).

ANSWER TO
QuickCheck
6-1

The matching (expense recognition) principle.

CHAPTER SHORTCUTS

Activate sales tax

1. Click Taxes in the navigation bar

2. Click Set up sales tax

Add item (inventory part, non-inventory part, service)

1. Click the gear icon on the icon bar

2. Click New

Create a delayed charge

1. Click the Plus icon

2. Click Delayed Charge

Create a delayed credit

1. Click the Plus icon

2. Click Delayed Credit

CHAPTER REVIEW (Answers available on the publisher's website.)

Matching

Match the term or phrase (as understood in QuickBooks Online) to its definition.

1. inventory part

2. statement

3. discount

4. delayed charge

5. bounced check

6. non-inventory part

7. delayed credit

8. nexus

_____ transaction type used for recording a pending sale

_____ product available for sale that is not being tracked in a perpetual tracking system

_____ sufficient physical presence

_____ percentage or dollar amount reduction in charge to customer

_____ transaction type used for recording a pending customer credit

_____ report sent to customer to summarize activity for a period

_____ product available for sale that is being tracked in a perpetual tracking system

_____ customer check returned by bank due to insufficient funds in account

Multiple Choice

1. When a **customer** makes a purchase using his or her credit card, it would normally be recorded as a(n):
    a. invoice.
    b. bill.
    c. sales receipt.
    d. credit card charge.

2. When a bounced customer check is recorded, which account should QBO credit for the amount of the customer check?
    a. Cash (or Checking)
    b. Bad debt expense
    c. Accounts payable
    d. Unearned revenue
    e. Undeposited funds

3. The inventory valuation method used by QBO is:
    a. FIFO
    b. LIFO
    c. Specific identification
    d. Weighted average
    e. Any of the above can be selected by the user.

4. Which form might be used to record a customer order before the items are shipped?
    a. Delayed Charge
    b. Delayed Credit
    c. Invoice
    d. Sales Receipt

5. Credit card processing fees charged by merchant banks _____.
    a. can be recorded when the deposit is recorded
    b. can be recorded using a journal entry
    c. can be recorded when the fee is known by editing the deposit transaction
    d. All of the above are options for recording credit card fees.

ASSIGNMENTS

Background information: Martin Smith, a college student and good friend of yours, had always wanted to be an entrepreneur. He is very good in math so, to test his entrepreneurship skills, he decided to set up a small math tutoring company serving local high school students who struggle in their math courses. He set up the company, Math Revealed!, as a corporation in 2018. Martin is the only owner. He has not taken any distributions from the company since it opened.

The business has been successful so far. In fact, it's been so successful he has decided to work in his business full time now that he's graduated from college with a degree in mathematics.

He has decided to start using QuickBooks Online to keep track of his business transactions. He likes the convenience of being able to access his information over the Internet. You have agreed to act as his accountant while you're finishing your own academic program.

He currently has a number of regular customers that he tutors in Pre-Algebra, Algebra, and Geometry. His customers pay his fees by cash or check after each tutoring session but he does give terms of Net 15 to some of his customers. He has developed the following fee schedule:

Name	Description	Rate
Refresher	One-hour session	$40 per hour
Persistence program	Two one-hour sessions per week	$75 per week
Crisis program	Five one-hour sessions per week	$150 per week

The tutoring sessions usually take place at his students' homes but he recently signed a two-year lease on a small office above a local coffee shop. The rent is only $200 per month starting in January 2018. A security deposit of $400 was paid in December 2018.

The following equipment is owned by the company:

Description	Date placed in service	Cost	Life	Salvage Value
Computer	7/1/18	$3,000	36 months	$300
Printer	7/1/18	$ 240	24 months	$ 0
Graphing Calculators (2)	7/1/18	$ 294	36 months	$ 60

All equipment is depreciated using the straight-line method.

As of 12/31/18, he owed $2,000 to his parents who initially helped him get started. They are charging him interest at a 6% annual rate. He has been paying interest only on a monthly basis. His last payment was 12/31/18.

Over the next month or so, he plans to expand his business by selling a few products he believes will help his students. He has already purchased a few items:

Category	Description	Vendor	Quantity On Hand	Cost per unit	Sales Price
Books and Tools					
	Geometry in Sports	Books Galore	20	12	16
	Solving Puzzles: Fun with Algebra	Books Galore	20	14	18
	Getting Ready for Calculus	Books Galore	20	15	20
	Protractor/Compass Set	Math Shack	10	10	14
	Handheld Dry-Erase Boards	Math Shack	25	5	9
	Notebooks (pack of 3)	Paper Bag Depot	10	15	20

2/1/19

✓ Now that Martin is selling more products, you know that Math Revealed! will need to start collecting sales taxes so you click **Taxes** on the navigation bar and activate the sales taxes feature.

- You use 3835 Freeport Blvd, Sacramento, CA 95822 as the address.

- You do not expect to sell any products to out-of-state customers.

- You check and find out you will be required to file monthly. Your current tax period starts with February.

- You indicate that taxes will be collected starting 2/1/19. **TIP:** You must enter as 02/01/2019

✓ Martin comes in early with some great news. A new Center for High Academic Achievement has just opened in downtown Sacramento with a satellite campus in Elk Grove, CA. The space is supported and staffed by the local high schools. The director of the new program, Michelle Farman, has contacted Martin and asked him to provide materials that could be purchased by students enrolled in their program.

- You first set the Center up as the **parent customer**.

  Center for High Academic Achievement

  3635 Freeport Blvd

  Sacramento, CA 95822

  (916) 855-5558

  Terms are Net 30

- You check the **This customer is tax exempt** on the **Tax Info** tab. The Center is a reseller of the materials and isn't subject to tax. You enter the Center's resale number (SRY-333-444444) in the **Exemption details** field.

- You also set up both locations as **sub-customers** and select the **Bill with parent** option. You use the same company name, billing address, terms, and reseller number for both locations. You use "Downtown" and "Elk Grove" as the **display names**. (**TIP:** If you check **sub-customer** first and select Center for High Academic Achievement as the **parent**, the address fields will be automatically filled. You will need to enter the **display** and **company names**. You will also need to enter the **Terms** and complete the **Tax info** tab.)

  ○ For the Downtown location, the shipping address is the same as the billing address.

  ○ For the Elk Grove location, the shipping address is 445 Forest Drive, Elk Grove, CA 95624.

2/5/19

✓ You edit the records of all **inventory items** in the **products and services** list, identifying them as taxable.

✓ You use **Retail** as the **Sales tax category** and select **School and educational instructional materials** in the **What you sell** field.

2/6/19

✓ Martin delivers supplies as promised to both locations of the Center for High Academic Achievement. You prepare separate invoices for:

- Downtown shipment
  ○ 5 each of the following books:
    ❑ Geometry in Sports (**Sports**)
    ❑ Solving Puzzles: Fun with Algebra (**Puzzles**)
    ❑ Getting Ready for Calculus (**Ready**)
  ○ Invoice #1013 totals $270.
- Elk Grove shipment
  ○ 3 each of the following books:
    ❑ Geometry in Sports (**Sports**)
    ❑ Solving Puzzles: Fun with Algebra (**Puzzles**)
  ○ Invoice #1014 totals $102.

✓ You receive a check in the mail from Jon Savidge for $750 in payment of invoice #1010. (Check #3359, dated 2/6)

✓ You realize that Kim Kowalski still hasn't paid the remaining $100 due on Invoice #1001. You had called her a month ago and she had promised to pay the balance by the end of January. You give her a call. She apologizes and drives over with a check for $100. (Check #198, dated 2/6)

2/8/19

✓ Martin gives you the detail for the tutoring sessions since the first of February.

- You complete **sales receipts** (starting with #107) for the customers who paid using their credit card. **TIP:** Make sure you select **Credit Card** as the **Payment method**.
  - ○ Alonso Luna—5 **Refresher** sessions—$200
  - ○ Marcus Reymundo—2 **Refresher** sessions—$80
- You complete invoices for the following customers:
  - ○ Paul Richard—3 weeks of the **Crisis** program starting 2/5—$450 (Invoice #1015)
  - ○ Debbie Han—4 weeks of the **Crisis** program starting 2/1—$600 (Invoice #1016)

✓ You deposit the credit card receipts received today and the two checks received on 2/6. (**TIP:** You'll be making two deposits. One for the credit card receipts. One for the checks.)

- The cash and check deposit totals $850.
- The bank charges a 2% fee on all credit card sales. You record the fee and charge it to the **Bank Service Charges** account. You select **City Bank of Sacramento** in the **RECEIVED FROM** field.
- The credit card deposit totals $274.40 (after the fee).

2/12/19

✓ Martin delivers another order to the Downtown location of the Center for High Academic Achievement.

- You prepare the invoice (#1017) for $474.
  - ○ 10 Geometry in Sports (**Sports**)
  - ○ 8 Solving Puzzles: Fun with Algebra (**Puzzles**)
  - ○ 5 Getting Ready for Calculus (**Ready**)
  - ○ 5 Protractor/Compass sets (**Kit**)

✓ You receive checks in the mail from:

- Center for High Academic Achievement—$372 in payment of invoices #1013 and #1014. Check #9758844 **TIP:** You only need to select the parent customer (**Center for High Academic Achievement**) when you receive the payment since the **bill with parent** option was selected in the customer setup for the locations.
- Marley Roberts—$75.00, Check #1731

2/15/19

✓ The Downtown location of the Center for High Academic Achievement returns two of the protractor/compass sets (**Kit**). Both sets had broken compasses! Martin will be returning the compasses to Math Shack later.

- You create a $28 credit memo (CM1017) and send it to the Center.

2/19/19

✓ The Teacher's College workshop was a huge success. One of the teachers Martin met there asked him whether he'd be willing to put on a similar workshop next Friday (2/23). The teacher explains that this is for an independent group of educators and asks Martin if he'd consider discounting the Educator Workshop fee. Martin agrees to give the group a 10% discount on the $1,000 fee. (The fee is lower than the previous workshop because Martin will be making fewer speeches!) **TIP:** You'll need to enter the discount when you prepare the sales form.

- You set up a new account (Sales Discounts) to track discounts given to customers. You use #490 as the account number. **TIP:** Discounts are contra revenue accounts. Make sure you pick the correct **account type**.
- You turn on the **Discount** feature on the **Sales** tab of **Account and Settings**.
- You select the new **sales discount** account in the **Chart of accounts** section in the **Advanced** tab of **Account and Settings**.
- You don't want to forget to send the invoice next week so you create a **Delayed Charge** (#100).
  - The new customer is:

    Dynamic Teaching

    2121 Parallel Street

    Sacramento, CA 95822

    Dynamic Teaching is subject to sales taxes.

    Terms Net 30

2/20/19

✓ You receive notice from the bank that the $100 check from Kim Kowalski that was recorded on 2/6 (deposited on 2/9) was returned for insufficient funds. You call Kim and she lets you know that she closed her bank account. She agrees to pay a $20 processing fee. She decides to pay the full $120 with her credit card.

- You set up two **service items**. Neither of the **items** are taxable. You classify them both in a new **category** called Other Charges.
  - For the first **service item** (Bounced Check) you use "Check returned for insufficient funds" as the **description**. You wouldn't need a default price here. **TIP:** Think about the account you want credited for the check amount.
  - For the second **service item** (Processing Fee), you use "Processing fee on NSF check" as the **description** and you select **Bank service charges** as **the income account.** You enter $20 as the default **sales price/rate** for the processing fee.
- You record her payment using sales receipt #109. (**TIP:** The only items on the sales receipt will be the **Bounced check** and **Processing fee** items.)

> **BEHIND THE SCENES** This transaction can seem complicated. It might help to remember that the journal entry underlying this **sales receipt** is DR Undeposited Funds; CR Cash; CR Bank Service Charges.

✓ You process the credit card receipt right away. The deposit amount (after the 2% fee) is $117.60.

2/23/19

✓ Martin holds another Mathmagic Clinic. This time 40 students show up, almost double last month's attendance! You tell Martin he might want to think about hiring an assistant or two. Martin says he might think about doing that in March.

- All the students pay in cash—$20 each for the tutoring.
- Some of the students also purchase some supplies, with cash. You sell:
  - 10 Handheld dry-erase boards (**Dry Erase**)
  - 5 Notebook packs (**Notebook**)

- ○ 3 Protractor/Compass sets (**Kit**)
- You create one **sales receipt** (#110), using Drop-In as the customer.
  - ○ The **sales receipt** total is $1,051.14 (including sales tax). **TIP:** If the sales tax amount is zero, you probably forgot to enter the address when setting up the Drop In customer. Use 3835 Freeport Blvd, Sacramento, CA 95822.
- ✓ The bank is open late today so you deposit the cash received at the Clinic and the checks received on 2/12. The deposit totals $1,498.14.

2/25/19

- ✓ You create the invoice for the workshop Martin put on for the Dynamic Teaching group from the **delayed charge** you created on the 19th. You remember to give the customer the promised discount of 10%. Invoice #1018 totals $900.
- ✓ One of the students from the Mathmagic Clinic on the 24th (Isla Parker) returns the **Kit** she purchased. The compass broke the first time she used it! You write her a check (#1112) for the full $15.16 cost of the set plus sales tax. (**TIP:** Refunds are given using **refund receipts**. RR101.)
  - Her address is 1164 Rosa Drive, Sacramento, CA 95822.
  - Martin is definitely going to talk to Math Shack about the quality of the sets. If they can't find a better substitute he may need to find another supplier.
- ✓ Martin gives you the detail for the tutoring sessions held after 2/18.
  - You create invoices (starting with Invoice #1019) for:
    - ○ Navi Patel—Two weeks of **Crisis** starting 2/15—$300. Net 15
    - ○ Eliot Williams—One week of **Persistence** starting 2/18—$75.
- ✓ Martin decides to take a few days off so no tutoring sessions are held from 2/25 to 2/28.

2/27/19

- ✓ You receive a check in the mail (# 9759115) from the Center for High Academic Achievement for $446 in payment of Invoice #1117. They took the credit for the returned Geometry Kits. **TIP:** Check the **invoice** and **credit memo** boxes first. The **Amount received** field should automatically show as $446. Entering the check amount first can result in issues applying the credit.
- ✓ You deposit the check right away.
- ✓ You review the Collections Report. Invoice #1005 to Marcus Reymundo has been outstanding since 1/20. You try calling him but discover that his phone has been disconnected. You decide to write off the balance of $40 to bad debt expense. Math Revealed uses the direct write-off method because it has historically had very few uncollectible accounts. You consider bad debt expense to be a sub-account of **Marketing Costs**.
  - **TIP:** You'll need to set up a new account and then a new non-taxable **service item**. You set up the bad debt account as a **sub-account** of **Marketing Costs**. Use 638 as the account number.
  - You create a **credit memo** (CM1005) for the $40 write-off.
  - You apply the credit to Invoice #1005 through the **receive payment** form.

Check numbers 2/28

Checking account balance: $5,743.19
Accounts receivable: $2,625.00
Total cost of goods sold (February): . . . . . . $ 765.00
Net income (February) $3,648.00

Reports to create for Chapter 6:

All reports should be in portrait orientation.

- Journal—February transactions only
- Sales by Product/Service Summary (February)
- A/R Aging Detail (2/28)

Background information: Sally Hanson, a good friend of yours, double majored in Computer Science and Accounting in college. She worked for several years for a software company in Silicon Valley but the long hours started to take a toll on her personal life.

Last year she decided to open up her own company, Salish Software Solutions (a corporation). Sally currently advises clients looking for new accounting software and assists them with software installation. She also provides training to client employees and occasionally troubleshoots software issues.

She has decided to start using QuickBooks Online to keep track of her business transactions. She likes the convenience of being able to access financial information over the Internet. You have agreed to act as her accountant while you're working on your accounting degree.

Sally has a number of clients that she is currently working with. She gives 15-day payment terms to her corporate clients but she asks for cash at time of service if she does work for individuals. She has developed the following fee schedule:

Name	Description	Rate
Select	Software Selections	$500 flat fee
Set Up	Software Installation	$ 50 per hour
Train	Software training	$ 40 per hour
Fix	File repair	$ 60 per hour

Sally rents office space from Alki Property Management for $800 per month.

The following furniture and equipment is owned by Salish:

Description	Date placed in service	Cost	Life	Salvage Value
Office Furniture............	6/1/18	$1,400	60 months	$200
Computer	7/1/18	$4,620	36 months	$300
Printer...................	5/1/18	$ 900	36 months	$ 0

All equipment is depreciated using the straight-line method.

As of 12/31/18, she owed $3,500 to Dell Finance. The monthly payment on that loan is $150 including interest at 5%. Sally's last payment to Dell was 12/31/18.

Over the next month or so, Sally plans to expand her business by selling some of her favorite accounting and personal software products directly to her clients. She has already purchased the following items.

Item Name	Description	Vendor	Quantity On Hand	Cost per unit	Sales Price
Easy1	Easy Does it	Abacus Shop	15	$100	$175
Retailer...........	Simply Retail	Simply Accounting	2	$400	$700
Contractor........	Simply Construction	Simply Accounting	2	$500	$800
Organizer	Organizer	Personal Solutions	25	$ 25	$ 50
Tracker	Investment Tracker	Personal Solutions	25	$ 20	$ 40

2/1/19

✓ Now that Sally is ready to start selling products, you realize that you'll need to set up sales taxes in QBO so you click **Taxes** on the navigation bar to activate the sales tax feature.

- You use 3835 Freeport Blvd, Sacramento, CA 95822 as the company address.

- You do not expect to sell any products to out-of-state customers.
- You contact the Board of Equalization and find out Salish Software will need to report monthly. Your current tax period starts with February.
- You enter 2/1/19 as the starting date for tax collection. **TIP:** You must enter as 02/01/2019

✓ You also take a look at the **inventory items** in your **Products and Services** list. You see that the tax status needs to be updated. You edit each **item**, using **Retail** as the **Sales tax category** and selecting **Taxable Retail Items** in the **What you sell** field.

2/4/19

✓ A friend of Sally's, Rey Butler, has been doing very well in his financial management firm Reyelle Consulting. He has an office in Roseville and a recently opened office in Davis. He gives Sally a call to ask about purchasing some electronic tools to sell to his customers. Sally suggests that he try the **Organizers** and **Investment Trackers**.

- You first set Reyelle up as the **parent customer**.
  Reyelle Consulting
  3200 Bullish Lane
  Sacramento, CA 95822
  (916) 558-4499
  Terms are Net 30
- Don't forget to check the **This customer is tax exempt** field in the **Tax info** tab. Reyelle is a reseller of the materials and isn't subject to tax. You enter the company's resale number (SRY-424-424242) in the **Exemption details** field.
- You also set up both locations as **sub-customers** and select the **Bill with parent** option. You use the same billing address, terms, and reseller number for both locations. You use "Roseville" and "Davis" as the **display names**. (**TIP:** If you check **sub-customer** and select Reyelle Consulting as the **parent**, the address fields will be automatically filled. You will need to enter the **display** and **company names**. You will also need to enter the **Terms** and complete the **Tax info** tab.)
  - For the Roseville location, the shipping address is the same as the billing address.
  - For the Davis location, the shipping address is 2911 Equity Street, Davis, CA 95616.

2/6/19

✓ Sally delivers the software disks to both Reyelle locations. You prepare separate **invoices** for:
- Roseville shipment
  - 5 each of the following books:
    - **Organizer**
    - **Tracker**
  - Invoice 1013 totals $450.
- Davis shipment
  - 3 each of the following books:
    - **Organizer**
    - **Tracker**
  - Invoice 1014 totals $270.

✓ You receive two checks in the mail. Both are dated 2/6.
- Check # 22443359 from Butter and Beans for $2,000. (Invoice 1009).
- Check #86115 from Fabulous Fifties for $500. (Invoice 1010)

2/8/19

✓ Sally gives you her client work hours for the past week and you prepare the invoices as follows:

- Fabulous Fifties—10 hours of **Set Up**—$500. Invoice 1015
- Alki Deli—10 hours of **Set up** and 5 hours of **Train**—$700. Invoice 1016

✓ One of the owners of mSquared Enterprises (a local general contractor) stops in to ask about construction accounting software. Sally gives her a demonstration of **Contractor** and she's impressed. She uses her credit card to purchase the software.

- You complete a **sales receipt** (#106) to record the $1,082.50 purchase (tax included).
- You set the company up with the following address:
  - ○ 595 Newbuild Avenue
    Sacramento, CA 95822

✓ You deposit the credit card receipts received today and the two checks received on 2/6. (**TIP:** You'll be making two deposits. One for the credit card receipt. One for the checks.)

✓ o   The check deposit totals $2,500.

✓ o   The credit card deposit should total $1,060.85 (after the fee).

- ○ The bank charges a 2% fee on all card sales. You charge the fee to the **Bank Service Charges** account. You select **Sacramento City Bank** in the **RECEIVED FROM** field.

2/12/19

✓ Sally delivers another order to the Davis location of Reyelle Consulting. The **Trackers** are selling quickly. Reyelle also decides to purchase a few of the **Easy Does It** programs for its Davis location. It has a few clients that own very small businesses and the **Easy Does It** program would be sufficient for their needs.

- You prepare the invoice (#1017) for $1,400.
  - ○ 10 **Trackers**
  - ○ 5 **Easy1**

✓ You receive a $300 check, dated 2/12, in the mail from Dew Drop Inn (Check 89946). (Invoice 1012)

- You call Harry over at Dew Drop to ask about the $200 balance. He says they've had some issues recently. A guest at the hotel got stuck in the elevator for 16 hours and is now suing for emotional distress. He'll try to get the balance to you by the end of February.
- You deposit the check right away.

✓ Sally tells you that she was talking to the staff at Fabulous Fifties. They mentioned that they knew some people who might be interested in getting some help picking out new accounting software. Sally offers them a $50 referral fee for any new software selection clients that they steer her way. You go ahead and set up a **delayed credit** (#101). You use **Select** as the **item**. (**TIP:** You'll need to override the $500 default price.)

2/15/19

✓ The Roseville location of Reyelle's returns one of the **Organizer** disks because it was damaged. Sally finds another damaged disk in the storage cabinet. She'll return both to Personal Software sometime next week.

- You create a $50 credit memo (CM1013).

✓ You get a call from the bank. Dew Drop Inn's check for $300 was returned for insufficient funds. You call Harry. He apologizes and agrees to pay a $30 processing fee. He uses his credit card to cover the $330 total.

- You set up two **service items**. Neither of the **items** are taxable. You classify them both in a new **category** called Other Charges.
  - For the first **service item** (Bounced Check), you use "Check returned for insufficient funds" as the **description** and you select **Checking** as the **Income account**. You don't need to set a default price
  - For the second **service item** (Processing Fee) you use "Processing fee on NSF check" as the **description** and you select **Bank Service Charges** as the **Income account**. You enter $30 as the default **sales price/rate** for the processing fee.
- You record Harry's payment using **sales receipt** #107. **TIP:** The only **items** on the sales form will be the **Bounced Check** and **Processing Fee**.

> **BEHIND THE SCENES** This transaction can seem complicated. It might help to remember that the journal entry underlying this **sales receipt** is DR Undeposited Funds; CR Cash; CR Bank Service Charges.

✓ You process the credit card payment right away. The deposit amount (after the 2% fee) is $323.40

2/18/19

✓ The Effective Troubleshooting workshop was a huge success. At the end of the workshop, Albus' CEO (Anatoly Deposit) tells Sally that he mentioned the workshop to James Gooden, a business acquaintance, from Cezar Software who is very interested in presenting a similar workshop. Anatoly suggests giving James a call.

✓ Sally calls James Gooden right away. James would like to host the workshop at their facility this coming Friday (the 22nd). James explains that Cezar Software creates software programs used by nonprofit organizations. He's hoping that there might be some kind of nonprofit discount available. Sally agrees to offer a 25% discount on the $2,500 fee.

- You turn on the **Discount** feature on the **Sales** tab of **Account and Settings**.
- You decide to use QBO's default account (Discounts Given). You select that account in the **Advanced** tab of **Account and Settings**.
  - You notice it doesn't have an account number so you edit the account (in the **Chart of Accounts** list) to add account number 490.
  - **TIP:** You may need to wait for QBO to activate the account before you can add the account number. You can proceed with the assignment. Make sure to go back though to add the account number.
- You don't want to forget to send the invoice so you create a **Delayed Charge** (#100) for the full $2,500 (**Tips**). You'll enter the discount when you invoice Cezar.
  - The new customer is:
    Cezar Software
    8644 Technology Avenue
    Sacramento, CA 95822
    Terms Net 30

2/20/19

✓ You receive checks in the mail from the following customers, all dated 2/20

- Albus Software—Check 755566, $2,500 for Invoice 1011
- Fabulous Fifties—Check 415161, $500 for Invoice 1015
- Alki Deli—Check 71144, $700 for Invoice 1016

✓ You record the checks and take them down to the bank. The deposit totals $3,700.

2/22/19

✓ Sally gives you her work schedule since 2/8. You create the following invoices.

- You create invoices (starting with Invoice #1018) for:
  - ○ Metro Market—**Select**—$500
    - ❑ Metro Market is a new client. It was referred to Salish by Fabulous Fifties.
      - ● Metro Market
        210 Admiral Way
        Sacramento, CA 95822
        Net 15
  - ○ Alki Deli—5 hours of **Train**—$200
  - ○ Butter and Beans—12 hours of **Train**—$480
  - ○ Fabulous Fifties—12 hours of **Set Up** and 4 hours of **Train**—$760

✓ After the **invoice** for Fabulous Fifties is created, you remember that they have a **delayed credit** available. You open Invoice #1021 and apply the credit. The **Balance due** now shows as $710.00. (**TIP:** You need to expand the sidebar on the right side of the window in order to see the **delayed credit**.)

✓ Sally tells you she's taking a few days off (2/25 to 2/28) to visit family in Chicago.

2/25/19

✓ You create the **invoice** for the workshop Sally put on for Cezar Software from the **delayed charge** you created on the 18th. You remember to give the customer the promised discount of 25%. Invoice # 1022 totals $1,875.

2/27/19

✓ You receive a check (# 9759115) in the mail from Reyelle Consulting-Roseville for $400 in payment of Invoice 1013. The check was dated 2/27. Reyelle took the credit for the returned **Tracker** disk. **TIP:** Check the **invoice** and **credit memo** boxes first. The **Amount** received field should automatically show as $400. Entering the check amount first can result in issues applying the credit.

✓ You deposit the check right away.

✓ You get a call from Harry at Dew Drop Inn. The lawsuit has bankrupted his company. He apologizes but lets you know there are no assets remaining to cover the balance owed to Salish. You decide to write off the $200 to bad debt expense. Salish Software uses the direct write-off method because it has historically had very few uncollectible accounts.

- You set up a bad debt expense account as a **sub-account** of Marketing Costs. You use account #638.
- You create a new **service item** (Write off) and include it in the **Other Charges** category. The new **service item** is not taxable.
- You create a **credit memo** for the $200 write off. (You use WO1012 as the **Credit Memo no.**)
- You apply the credit to Invoice 1005 through the **receive payment** form.

> **BEHIND THE SCENES** This transaction can seem complicated. It might help to remember that the journal entry underlying the **credit memo** is DR Bad Debt Expense; CR Accounts Receivable.

Check numbers 2/28

Checking account balance:. $15,585.30
Account receivable:. . . . . $ 5,435.00

Total cost of goods sold (February):. . . . . . $ 1,535.00
Net income . . . . $ 6,301.75

Reports to create for Chapter 6:

All reports should be in portrait orientation

- Journal—February transactions only
- Sales by Product/Service Summary (February)
- A/R Aging Detail (2/28)

Purchasing Activity
(Merchandising Company)

Objectives

After completing Chapter 7, you should be able to:

1. Record the purchase of inventory by check.

2. Set up reorder points for inventory items.

3. Create and edit purchase orders.

4. Record the receipt of inventory with or without a vendor bill.

5. Enter and apply vendor credit memos.

6. Take early payment discounts on payments to vendors.

7. Prepare inventory and purchase order reports.

WHAT IS THE PURCHASE CYCLE IN A MERCHANDISING COMPANY?

- Place an order for products.

- Receive the products.

- Receive a bill for the products.

- Pay the vendor.

The single biggest cost in service companies is usually labor. The single biggest cost in merchandising companies is usually inventory.

Proper inventory management is critical to the success of a merchandising company because:

- It costs money to store inventory.
  - Costs include warehouse rent, insurance, utilities, security, interest, etc.

- Inventory held too long can become obsolete.
  - It's hard to charge full price (or sometimes any price!) for last year's model.

- You can't sell what you don't have.
  - Customers who can't find what they want to buy are not happy customers!

To determine the optimal level of product inventory, management needs information about sales volume, accessibility of products, product returns, gross margins, etc. That information frequently comes from the accounting system.

In this chapter, we will cover transactions related to the purchase and management of inventory. We'll also add some topics that apply to both service and merchandising companies.

PURCHASING INVENTORY

In Chapter 3 and again in Chapter 6, we covered how the various **items** (**service**, **inventory part**, and **non-inventory part items**) are used in the sales cycle. In this chapter, we look at how **inventory part items** are used in the purchase and end of period cycles.

In summary, every **inventory part item** represents a product purchased and sold by the merchandising company. General information about each product is stored in the inventory part record. That information includes:

- The standard sales price

- The expected unit cost

- The asset account (normally the inventory account) that should be debited if the item is purchased for future sales

- The income account that should be credited if the item is sold

- The expense account (cost of goods sold account) that should be debited if the item is sold

In addition, information about inventory quantities and values is maintained by QBO for each **inventory part item** including the quantity and value of units ordered, received, sold, and on hand.

Using **items** allows a company to maintain considerable detail without creating a gigantic chart of accounts. For example, a retail store might have only one income account called "Sales Revenue" but it can still generate a report that lists sales quantities and dollars for each and every product sold in the store. A retail store might also have only one inventory (asset) account but it can still track how many units are on hand at any point in time for each individual product.

In order to maintain that detail, of course, all transactions related to products must be recorded using **items**. That includes purchase and adjustment transactions as well as sales transactions.

> **WARNING:** **Bill**, **Check**, **Expense Purchase Order**, **Vendor Credit** and **Credit Card Credit** forms all have two distribution sections. One section is labeled **Account Details** and one is labeled **Item Details**. In order to properly adjust the subsidiary ledgers, the **Item Details** section must always be used when entering inventory transactions. Charging a purchase to the "Inventory" account on the **Account details tab** <u>will</u> result in a debit to the asset but will not properly adjust the inventory quantity in the subsidiary ledgers.

Paying at Time of Purchase

In most cases, merchandise inventory is **not** purchased by going directly to the supplier's location and paying at time of purchase BUT it could be. This might happen if the company needs to ship an order to a customer right away and it doesn't have sufficient products on hand to fill the order.

A company might pay for inventory at time of purchase using a check or credit card. The only difference between entering checks or credit card charges for inventory purchases and entering checks and credit charges for other purchases is the section used to identify the account distribution. We'll use a purchase by check to demonstrate using the appropriate section. (Refer to Chapter 4 for a refresher on entering credit card charges.)

If a company writes a check for the purchase, the **check** form is accessed by clicking the ⊕ icon on the icon bar and selecting **Check** in the **Vendors** column.

> **BEHIND THE SCENES**   Remember:
> - The vendor name, date, and amount of purchase are all used by QBO to credit the bank account and to prepare the check (if checks are printed directly from QBO).
> - The distribution section of the form is used to identify the debit account(s) in the underlying journal entry.

Purchases of inventory must be entered on the **Item details** section.

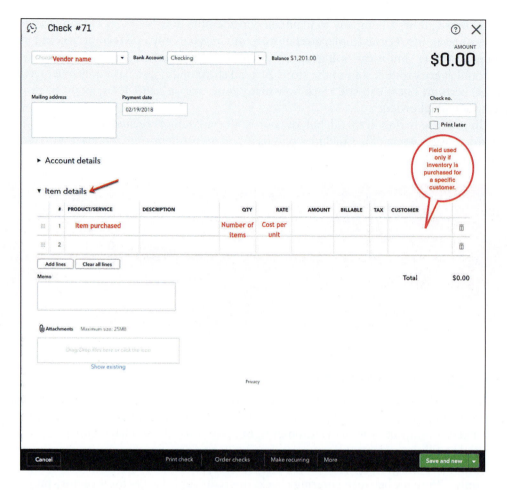

If an **item** is being purchased for a specific customer, the customer name can be included in the **Item** row.

When distributions are entered on the **Item details** section (and the form is saved), QBO automatically:

- Debits the asset account specified in the **item** setup for the amount of the purchase.

- Updates the quantity records for the item purchased.

PRACTICE
EXERCISE

Purchase inventory for Craig's Design and Landscaping with a check.
(Purchased five **Fountain Pumps** for $65 to have on hand.)

1. Click the ➕ icon on the icon bar and select **Check**.

2. Select **Norton Lumber and Building Materials** as the vendor.

3. Enter "71" as the check number.

    a. You may have to close the sidebar to access the full form. Click the **>** on the left edge of the sidebar to close it.

4. Use the current date as the **Payment date**.

5. Open the **Item details** section (lower half of the screen) by clicking the **triangle** next to **Item details**.

6. Select **Pump** as the **PRODUCT/SERVICE** and enter "5" as the **QTY**.

7. Enter "65" as the **AMOUNT**.

8. **Make a note** of the **RATE** calculated by QBO.

9. Click **Save and close**.

Ordering Inventory

Setting Reorder Points

At the beginning of this chapter, we reviewed some important considerations in inventory management.

- Inventory levels should be high enough that customer orders can be promptly filled.

- Inventory levels should be low enough that costs and the risks of obsolescence are minimized.

Management generally puts considerable effort into determining what inventory level is appropriate for each product. As part of that process, they determine the **minimum** amount of product they should have on hand at any point in time to safely meet customer demand. When the quantity on hand reaches that minimum level, an order for more inventory is placed with the vendor. The minimum level is called the reorder point.

A reorder point can be set for every inventory part item in QBO. Reports can then be generated that list products that should be ordered based on current inventory levels.

The reorder point is set in the **inventory part item** record. (As a reminder, the **item** records are accessed by clicking the **gear** icon on the icon bar and selecting **Products and Services**. Clicking **Edit** in the **Action** column for a specific item opens the **item** record.) The screen looks something like this:

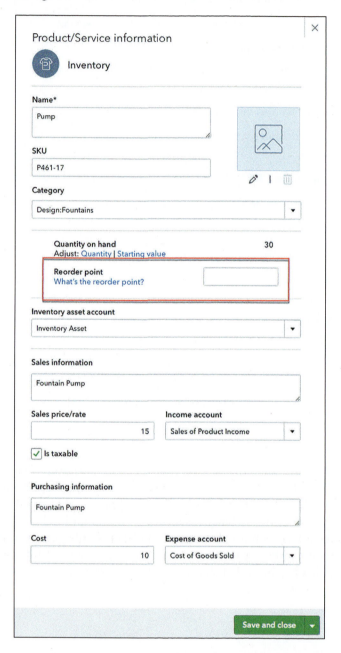

The reorder point is entered in the **Reorder Point** field in the middle of the screen.

Inventory part items that have quantities on hand less than the reorder point (or have quantities of 0) are highlighted at the top of the Products and Services Center.

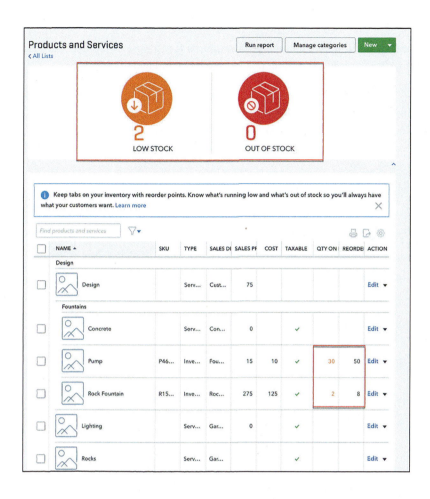

BEHIND THE SCENES The words "stock" and "inventory" are often used interchangeably. In manufacturing companies, the word "stock" is sometimes used to refer specifically to finished goods held for sale. The word "inventory" is generally used to refer either to finished goods held for sale or any of the materials used to manufacture those goods. QBO uses stock and inventory interchangeably.

Reports can be created to assist employees responsible for ordering inventory.

To create a stock status report, select **Run report** in the **More** dropdown menu on the Products and Services Center screen. Customize the report by adding **Reorder Point** as a **Rows/Columns** field and removing **Price** as a **Rows/Columns** field. Filter the report by including only **inventory part items**.

The customized report will look something like this after you complete the practice exercise:

Craig's Design and Landscaping Services

STOCK STATUS REPORT

PRODUCT/SERVICE	TYPE	DESCRIPTION	COST	QTY ON HAND	REORDER POINT
Design:Fountains:Pump	Inventory	Fountain Pump	10.00	25.00	50.00
Design:Fountains:Rock Fountain	Inventory	Rock Fountain	125.00	2.00	8.00
Landscaping:Sprinklers:Sprin...	Inventory	Sprinkler Heads	0.75	25.00	25.00
Landscaping:Sprinklers:Sprin...	Inventory	Sprinkler Pipes	2.50	31.00	25.00

PRACTICE
EXERCISE

Edit inventory part items to include reorder points for Craig's Design and Landscaping.
(Craig's Design wants to set reorder points for pumps and rock fountains.)

1. Edit inventory part items.

    a. Click the **gear** icon on the icon bar.

    b. Select **Products and Services**.

    c. In the **Pump** row, click **Edit**.

        i. Enter "50" as the **Reorder point**.

        ii. Click **Save and close**.

    d. In the **Rock Fountain** row, click **Edit**.

        i. Enter "8" as the **Reorder point**.

        ii. Click **Save and close**.

    e. In the **Sprinkler Heads** and **Sprinkler Pipes** rows, click **Edit**.

        i. Enter 25 as the **reorder point** for both.

2. Prepare a custom Stock Status report.

    a. In the Products and Services screen, click **Run report** in the **More** dropdown menu.

    b. Click **Customize**.

    c. Open the **Rows/Columns** section.

        i. Click **Change Columns**.

        ii. Check the **Reorder Point** field and uncheck the **Price** field.

    d. Open the **Filter** section.

        i. Check **Product/Service**.

        ii. In the **Product/Service** dropdown menu, check:

            1. **Design:Fountains:Pump**

            2. **Design:Fountains:Rock Fountain**

            3. **Landscaping:Sprinklers:Sprinkler Heads**

            4. **Landscaping:Sprinklers:Sprinkler Pipes**

    e. Open the **Header/Footer** section.

        i. Change the **Report title** to "Stock Status Report".

    f. Click **Run Report**.

    g. **Make a note** of the **QTY ON HAND** for **Sprinkler Heads**.

3. Click **Dashboard** on the navigation bar.

Creating Purchase Orders

Once the company decides how many of each item need to be purchased, the suppliers are contacted. Many suppliers will not fill an order without written documentation (a purchase order) from their customer. Even when the supplier doesn't require written documentation, most companies create purchase orders as part of their internal control system.

Although ordering inventory is not an accounting transaction, a good accounting software program will include a purchase order tracking system so that management knows, at all times, how many units are on their way. Purchase orders are tracked in QBO for informational purposes only. No journal entry is recorded in QBO when a purchase order is created.

Why isn't ordering inventory an accounting transaction?	**Quick**Check **7-1**

The use of purchase orders is a **setting** (preference) in QBO. In the test drive company, the setting is turned on. To verify, click the **gear** icon on the icon bar and select **Account and Settings**. Open the **Expenses** tab. **Use purchase orders** must be set to **On** for the feature to be available to use.

The **purchase order** form is accessed by clicking the ➕ icon on the icon bar and selecting **Purchase Order** in the **Vendors** column.

The form looks like this:

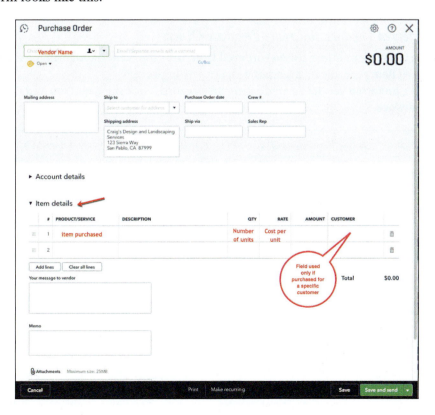

You need to enter the vendor name and the **items** being ordered to complete the form.

If an **item** is being purchased for a specific customer, the customer name can be included in the **Item** row for tracking purposes.

BEHIND THE SCENES QBO will automatically enter the default cost when an inventory part item is selected. The unit cost can be changed at this point, if appropriate. The cost can also, of course, be changed later when the vendor bill is received.

PRACTICE EXERCISE

Creat purchase orders for Craig's Design and Landscaping.

(Management decides to order 20 **Sprinkler Heads** and 10 **Sprinkler Pipes**.)

1. Click the ⊕ icon on the icon bar and select **Purchase Order**.

2. Select **Tania's Nursery** as the vendor.

3. Use the current date as the **Purchase Order date**.

4. In the **Item details** section:

   a. Select **Sprinkler Heads** as the **PRODUCT/SERVICE** and enter "20" as the **QTY**.

      i. Use the default **Rate**.

   b. In the next row, select **Sprinkler Pipes** as the **PRODUCT/SERVICE** and enter "10" as the **QTY**.

      i. Use the default **Rate**.

5. **Make a note** of the **Total** for the order as calculated by QBO.

6. Click **Save and close**.

Using Preferred Vendors To Create Purchase Orders

If **items** are always (or almost always) ordered from the same vendor, identifying a **preferred vendor** in the **item** record can streamline the ordering process.

To add a **preferred vendor** to an existing **item** record, click the **gear** icon and click **Products and Services**.

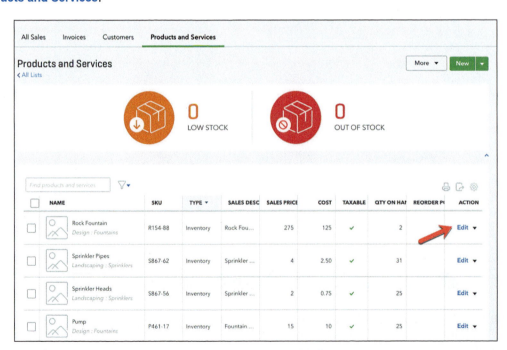

Click **Edit** in the **ACTION** column of the **item**.

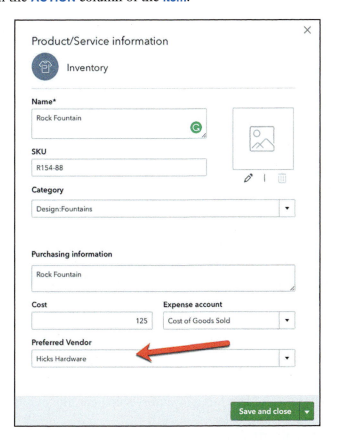

Select the **Preferred Vendor** and click **Save and close** to exit the **item** record.

Once the **preferred vendor** for an **item** has been identified, users can select **reorder** in the dropdown menu (**ACTION** column) for that **item** to open a new purchase order.

The vendor name and terms fields and the **item** to be ordered will automatically fill.

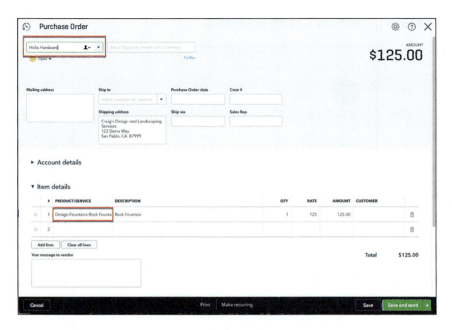

Quantities and rates can be edited; additional **items** can be added.

Receiving Ordered Inventory

RECEIVING ORDERED INVENTORY **WITH** A BILL

When a vendor bill is received with the inventory shipment, the **purchase order** information is transferred to a **bill** in QBO.

Click **Expenses** on the navigation bar.

Click the **Vendors** tab to open the Vendor Center.

Locate the appropriate **vendor** and click **Create bill** in the **Action** column.

The screen will look something like this:

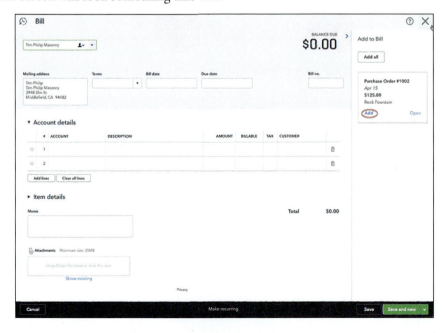

In the sidebar on the right side of the screen, click **Add** to transfer the information from the **purchase order** to the **bill**.

> **HINT:** The **purchase order** can be opened from this screen to make any necessary changes before the information is transferred.

The **bill** will look something like this after the information is transferred over. The **Bill no.**, **Bill date**, and **Terms** should be added. Additional charges can also be added to the **bill** as needed.

Click **Save** to link the **purchase order** to the **bill**.

The form would now look something like this:

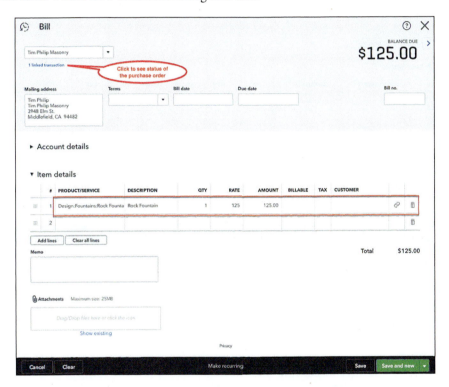

To see the changed status of the purchase order, click **SAVE**.

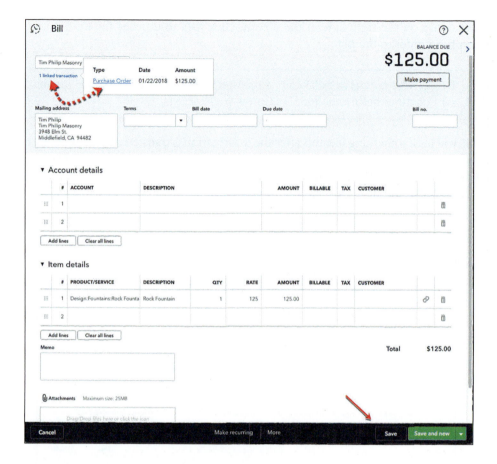

Click **1 linked transaction** and click **Purchase Order**.

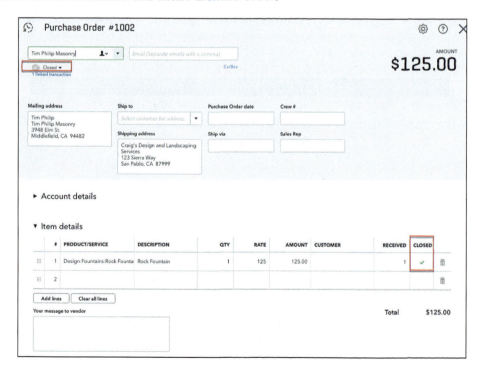

The status of the **purchase order** changes to **Closed** when the transfer is complete.

PRACTICE
EXERCISE

Receive ordered inventory with a bill for Craig's Design and Landscaping.
(Items ordered on PO #1002 from Tim Philip Masonry received in full with a bill (#5011-33) for $130.00—slightly higher than expected.)

1. Click **Expenses** on the navigation bar.

2. Click the **Vendors** tab to open the Vendor Center.

3. In the **Action** column in the row for **Tim Philip Masonry**, select **Create Bill**.

4. Click **Add** in the sidebar on the right side of the screen to transfer the **purchase order** information to the **bill** form.

5. Select **Net 30** in the **Terms** field.

6. Use the current date as the **Bill date**.

7. Enter "5011-33" as the **Bill no.**

8. In the **Item details** section, change the **AMOUNT** to "130."

9. Click **Save and close**.

RECEIVING PARTIAL SHIPMENTS

It's not unusual for a vendor to fill an order in multiple shipments. This would happen when:

- Ordered materials are coming from different locations.

- Vendors are out of stock of a particular item when the first shipment is sent but are able to send the backordered items at a later date.

QBO will track partially filled orders so that users can properly record inventory purchases as they're received.

To record a partial shipment, click the **Plus** icon on the icon bar and select **Bill**. Enter the vendor's name.

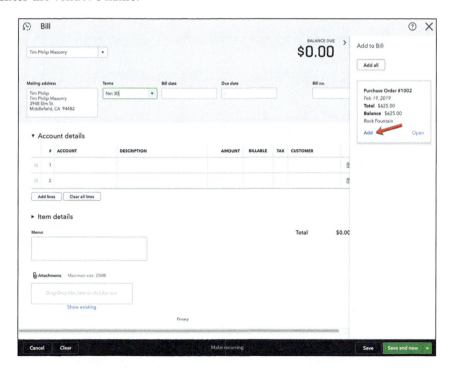

Click **Add** in the sidebar to transfer information from the **purchase order** to the **bill**.

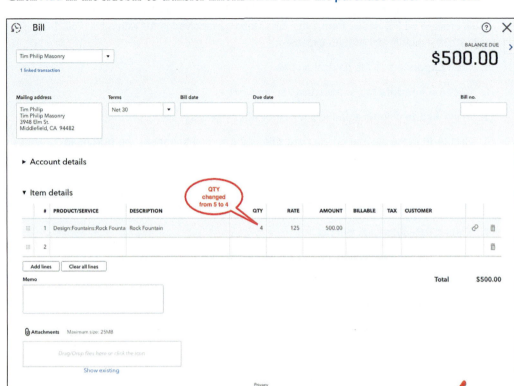

Enter the actual quantity received in the **QTY** field and click **Save**. (The **bill** form will still be open.)

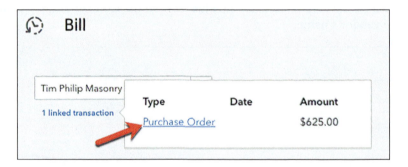

To see the status of the purchase order, click **1 linked transaction** and select **Purchase order**.

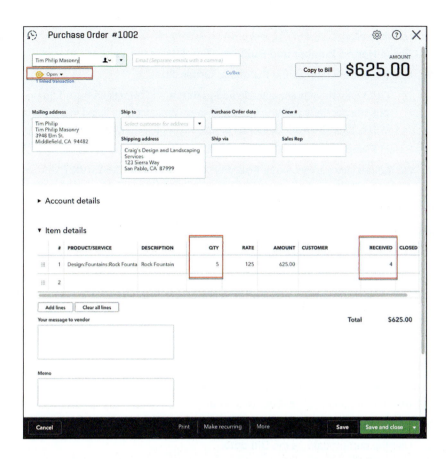

The purchase order will now display a **RECEIVED** column and the **purchase order** will remain open.

When the remaining items are received a new **bill** can be created from the original **purchase order**.

To create a report of all open purchase orders, click **Reports** on the navigation bar and select **Open Purchase Order Detail**.

(continued)

Receive a partial shipment of ordered inventory for Craig's Design and Landscaping. (Five of the eight fountain pumps ordered on PO #1005 from Norton Lumber and Building Materials received with a bill (#46464).)

PRACTICE EXERCISE

1. Create a **purchase order** for eight **fountain pumps** and three **rock fountains**.

   a.   Click the ➕ icon on the icon bar.

   b.   Click **Purchase order**.

(continued from previous page)

    c. Select **Norton Lumber and Building Materials** as the **Vendor**.

    d. Use the current date as the **Purchase Order date**.

        i. QBO may have automatically added **items** and quantities based on previous transactions with the vendor. If there are amounts listed in the purchase order, click **Clear all lines** just below the section to remove them.

    e. Select **Pump** as the **PRODUCT/SERVICE** and enter "8" as the **QTY**.

    f. On the next line, select **Rock Fountain** as the **PRODUCT/SERVICE** and enter "3" as the **QTY**.

    g. Click **Save and close**.

2. Enter the bill for the items received:

    a. Click the ➕ icon on the icon bar.

    b. Click **Bill**.

    c. Select **Norton Lumber and Building Materials** as the **Vendor**.

        i. QBO may automatically add amounts in the **Item details** section of the **purchase order** based on previous transactions with the vendor. If these amounts are added, click the **trash** icon in the far right column of the rows to remove them.

    d. Click **Add** in the sidebar on the right side of the screen to transfer the **purchase order** information (PO #1005) to the **bill** form.

    e. Select **Net 30** in the **Terms** field.

    f. Use the current date as the **Bill date**.

    g. Enter "46464" as the **Bill no.**

    h. In the **Item details** section, change the **QTY** for **Fountain Pumps** from 8 to 5.

    i. Change the **QTY** for **Rock Fountains** from 3 to 0.

    j. **Make a note** of the new **Total**.

    k. Click **Save and close**.

3. Receive the backorder items.

    a. Click the ➕ icon on the icon bar.

    b. Click **Bill**.

    c. Select **Norton Lumber and Building Materials** as the **Vendor**.

        i. Select **Net 30** in the **Terms** field.

        ii. Use the current date as the **Bill date**.

        iii. Enter "46468" as the **Bill no**.

    d. Click the **trash** icon in the far right column for any rows automatically added by QBO.

    e. Click **Add** in the sidebar on the right side of the screen to transfer the remaining items to the **bill**.

    f. **Make a note** of the **Total** amount.

    g. Click **Save**.

    h. Click **1 linked transaction**.

    i. Click **Purchase order**.

    j. Each **item** should have a checkmark in the **Closed** column.

    k. Click **Save and close**.

RECEIVING ORDERED INVENTORY **WITHOUT** A BILL

Merchandising companies need to update their inventory records as soon as purchased goods arrive so that their inventory on hand quantities are accurate. However, many suppliers include a packing slip (detailing the products and quantities included in the carton) with their shipments but no bill. The vendor's invoice (detailing costs) frequently arrives after the shipment. This might be done:

- As part of a supplier's internal control system.
- Because a supplier's warehouse or store is physically separate from the supplier's accounting office.

QBO does not currently have a feature that allows the company to record an increase in inventory and the creation of a related liability in the accounting records without a **bill** being created.

To keep inventory quantities updated, the company would normally create a **bill** using the anticipated costs. The **bill** would then be updated (with actual costs and vendor reference numbers) when the vendor invoice was finally received.

It would be good practice to make a note of the packing slip number in the **Memo** box of the **bill**. This should make it easier to match the final bill to the draft bill created in QBO from the packing slip.

Managing Purchase Orders

QBO automatically "closes" purchase orders when all of the **items** have been received.

Sometimes a company might need to manually close a purchase order. This might happen when:

- The supplier is unable to ship any of the items.
- The company decides to order from a different supplier.

Closing a purchase order is a housekeeping task. There are no underlying journal entries!

Manually Closing Purchase Orders

To manually close a purchase order, the **Purchase Order** form must be open.

Purchase orders can be found by clicking **Reports** in the navigation bar and selecting **Open Purchase Order List** in the **Expenses and Vendors** section.

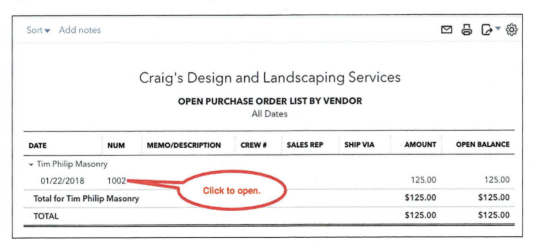

Click the purchase order number of the **purchase order** you want to manually close.

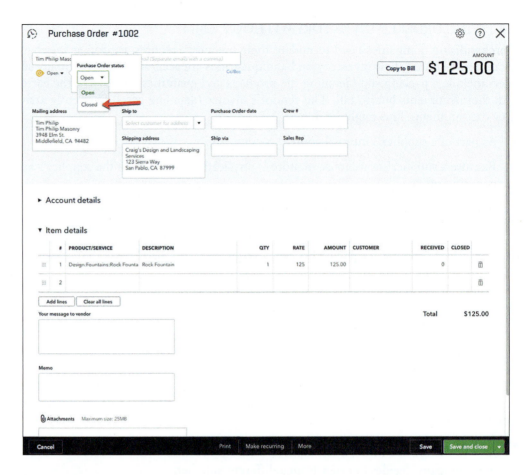

Select **Closed** on the purchase order status dropdown menu to close the order.

PRACTICE
EXERCISE

Manually close a purchase order for Craig's Design and Landscaping.
(Craig's Design decides it doesn't need the Rock Fountain ordered from Tim Philip Masonry on PO #1002.)

1. **TIP:** If you didn't log out of the test drive company after the last practice exercise, log out to clear out previous transactions. Log back in to continue.

2. Click **Reports** on the navigation bar.

3. Click **Open Purchase Order List** in the **Expenses and Vendors** section.

4. Click PO #1002.

5. Click **Open** (directly under the vendor name field) to access the **Purchase Order status** dropdown menu.

6. Select **Closed**.

7. Click **Save and close**.

Ordering Inventory Without Using the Purchase Order System

Given the importance of maintaining proper inventory levels, most companies want to track the status of orders they've placed with suppliers (purchase orders) and choose to use the purchase order system outlined above.

Companies that do not use purchase orders can still, of course, use QBO!

VENDOR CREDITS

Vendors issue credit memos for a variety of reasons. Those reasons might include the following:

- Goods were returned.

- There was an error on a previously issued bill.

- To give a "good faith" allowance when a customer isn't satisfied with goods or service.

Vendor credits aren't unique to merchandising companies. Service and manufacturing companies would also use the procedures outlined here.

Entering Credits from Vendors

Credit memos from vendors are recorded in QBO as transaction type **Vendor Credit**. (Remember: a credit issued to a customer is transaction type **Credit Memo**.)

To access the vendor credit form, click the ✚ icon on the icon bar and select **Vendor Credit**.

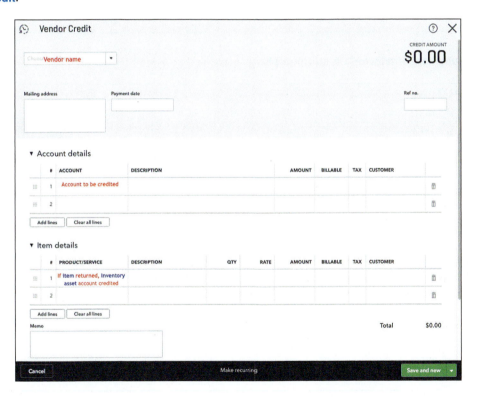

You'll need to enter the vendor name, date of the credit memo (identified as **Payment date** in QBO), reference number (that number often incorporates the original bill number), and the account that should be credited. The form includes some familiar sections (**Account details** and **Item details**).

Vendor credits received for returned **inventory items** or overbillings on **inventory items** would be entered in the **Item details** section. All other vendor credits would be entered in the **Account details** section.

Vendor credits are tracked in the vendor subsidiary ledger. All available credits will be displayed in the vendor record (**transaction list** tab) whenever future vendor payments are being processed.

Applying Credits from Vendors

To apply a **vendor credit**, click **Expenses** on the navigation bar.

Click the **Vendors** tab to open the Vendor Center. Click the **vendor** to be paid to open the vendor record.

The **transaction list** tab would look something like this:

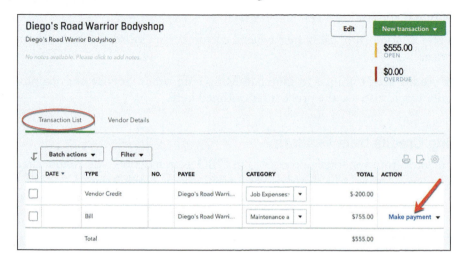

Make payment is selected on an open **bill**.

If there are available credits, QBO will automatically apply them. The **credit** can be deselected if the user elects to retain the credit for future use.

Vendor credits can also be applied through the **pay bills** screen.

Click the ➕ icon on the icon bar.

Select **Pay bills**.

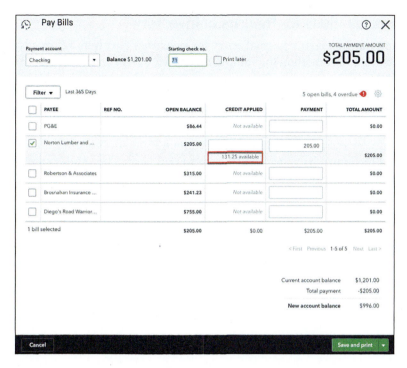

Available credits will be displayed for all vendors selected (checked).

If any of the available credit amount is manually entered in the **CREDIT APPLIED** field, the **PAYMENT** amount will automatically adjust.

Enter a vendor credit for Craig's Design and Landscaping.

(Craig's Design receives a credit memo from Craig's. They had been overcharged for some repair work done by Diego's.)

PRACTICE EXERCISE

1. Record the **vendor credit**.

   a. Click the ➕ icon on the icon bar and select **Vendor Credit**.

   b. Select **Diego's Road Warrior Bodyshop** as the **Vendor**.

   c. Use the current date as the **Payment date**.

   d. On the **Account details** section, select **Equipment Repairs** as the **ACCOUNT**.

   e. Enter "Overcharge" in the **DESCRIPTION** field.

   f. Enter "200" as the **AMOUNT**.

   g. Click **Save and close**.

2. Apply the **vendor credit**.

   a. Click **Expenses** on the navigation bar.

   b. Click the **Vendors** tab to open the Vendor Center.

   c. Click **Make Payment** in the **Action** column of **Diego's Road Warrior Bodyshop**.

   d. Select **Checking** as the payment method.

   e. Use the current date as the **payment date**.

   f. Make sure that both the **credit** and the **bill** are checked.

   g. Click **Save and close**.

   h. **Make a note** of the check amount.

Special Considerations for Returns of Inventory

Understanding the underlying journal entry for inventory part item returns is important.

QBO uses the FIFO method for valuing inventory. When an item is returned (through a **vendor credit**), QBO credits the inventory account for the cost in the oldest FIFO layer. That may or may not agree to the amount on the vendor credit. If it doesn't agree, QBO will automatically debit (or credit) the difference to the costs of goods sold account for that **item**.

To illustrate, let's assume we return one Fountain Pump to Norton Lumber and Building Material. The pumps had cost us $10 each to purchase. The **vendor credit** would look like this if Norton only gave us a $9 credit for the return.

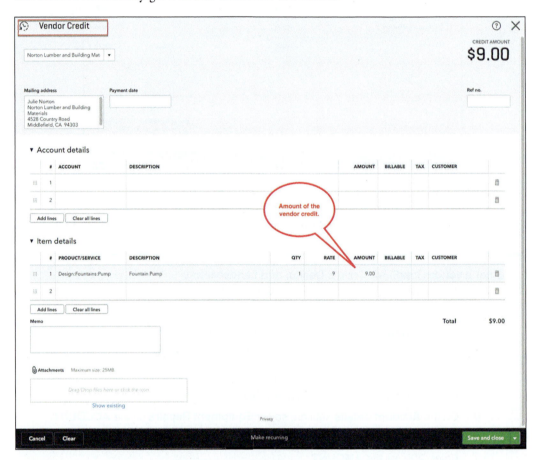

To see how the inventory valuation is impacted, click **Reports** on the navigation bar. Select **Inventory Valuation Detail** in the **Sales and Customers** section. Change the dates to see transactions over the last thirty days. Click **Run report**.

The **Inventory Valuation Detail** report should look something like this:

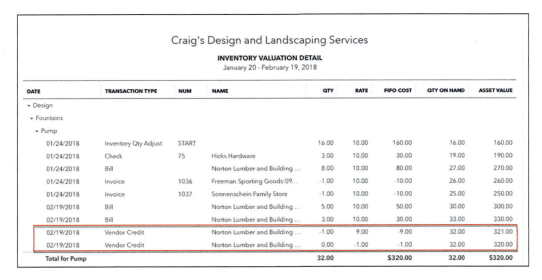

DATE	TRANSACTION TYPE	NUM	NAME	QTY	RATE	FIFO COST	QTY ON HAND	ASSET VALUE
▾ Design								
▾ Fountains								
▾ Pump								
01/24/2018	Inventory Qty Adjust	START		16.00	10.00	160.00	16.00	160.00
01/24/2018	Check	75	Hicks Hardware	3.00	10.00	30.00	19.00	190.00
01/24/2018	Bill		Norton Lumber and Building ...	8.00	10.00	80.00	27.00	270.00
01/24/2018	Invoice	1036	Freeman Sporting Goods:09...	-1.00	10.00	-10.00	26.00	260.00
01/24/2018	Invoice	1037	Sonnenschein Family Store	-1.00	10.00	-10.00	25.00	250.00
02/19/2018	Bill		Norton Lumber and Building ...	5.00	10.00	50.00	30.00	300.00
02/19/2018	Bill		Norton Lumber and Building ...	3.00	10.00	30.00	33.00	330.00
02/19/2018	Vendor Credit		Norton Lumber and Building ...	-1.00	9.00	-9.00	32.00	321.00
02/19/2018	Vendor Credit		Norton Lumber and Building ...	0.00	-1.00	-1.00	32.00	320.00
Total for Pump				**32.00**		**$320.00**	**32.00**	**$320.00**

Two lines appear for the transaction. The first line shows a reduction of 1 unit at a FIFO cost of $9 (the amount of the credit). The second line shows an adjustment to the FIFO cost of an additional $1. This represents the difference between the credit of $9 and the oldest FIFO layer cost of $10 per unit.

To see the underlying journal entry, click **vendor credit**.

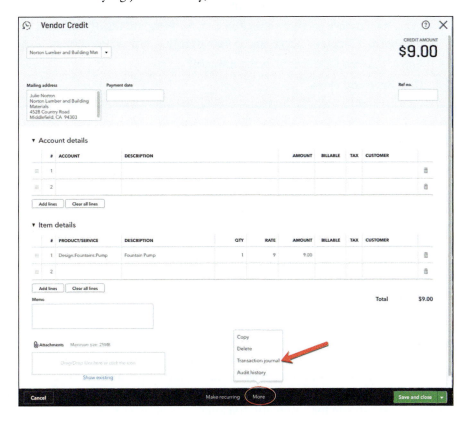

Click **More** and select **Transaction Journal**.

In the entry, Inventory Asset has been credited for $10, Accounts Payable has been debited for $9, and the $1 difference has been debited to Cost of Goods Sold.

Enter a vendor credit for return of inventory for Craig's Design and Landscaping. (One damaged Fountain Pump was returned to Norton Lumber.)

1. Record the vendor credit for return of inventory.

   a. Click the ➕ icon on the icon bar and select **Vendor Credit**.

   b. Select **Norton Lumber and Building Materials** as the **Vendor**.

   c. Use the current date as the **Payment date**.

   d. In the **Item details** section, select **Pump** as the **PRODUCT/SERVICE**. **TIP:** You may need to click the triangle next to **Item details** to expand the section.

   e. Enter "1" as the **QTY** and "9" as the **AMOUNT**.

   f. Click **Save and close**.

PAYING VENDOR BALANCES

We covered the basics of paying vendor account balances in Chapter 4. In this chapter, we cover

- Applying vendor credits.

- Taking early payment discounts on payments to vendors.

Applying vendor credits when paying bills was covered in the "Vendor Credits" section of this chapter. In this section, we'll look at early payment discounts.

Although early payment discounts can be small in dollar amount, the return is quite high. For example, a common payment term is 2%/10, net 30. The customer gets a reduction of 2% off the bill just for paying 20 days early. The effective interest rate earned on that discount is almost 37%! Most companies want to take those discounts whenever possible.

Although vendor payment terms are set in the vendor record, QBO does not currently have a feature that allows users to track **bills** by discount date or to automatically apply any allowable early payment discounts when a **bill** is paid. There are some tools that can be used, though, as a substitute for automatic tracking.

Early Payment Discounts

Setting Up Early Payment Discount Terms

Before we start, let's review the process for setting up payment terms.

Click the **gear** icon on the icon bar and select **All Lists**.

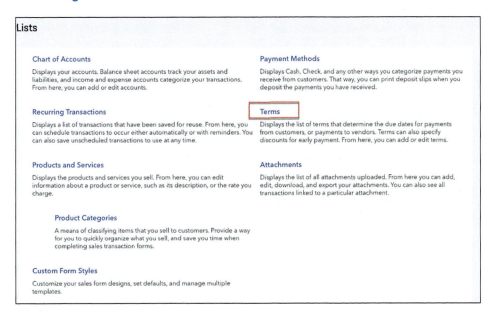

Click **Terms** and click **New**.

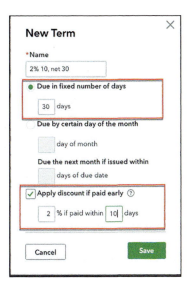

A payment term of 2% 10, net 30 means that the bill is due in full in 30 days. However, if you pay within 10 days you get a discount of 2%. The screenshot above shows how that payment term would be set up in QBO.

Tracking Bills with Early Payment Discounts

For tracking early payment discounts, it's fairly easy to create a custom report that can be used to identify discount opportunities.

Click **Reports** on the navigation bar. Select **Unpaid Bills** in the **What You Owe** section.

Click **Customize**. Open **Rows/Columns** and click **Change columns**. Check **Terms** to add that column to the report. **Past Due** and **Due Date** columns could be removed. The order of the columns could also be rearranged. The changes might look something like this:

Open **Filter** on the **Customization** sidebar.

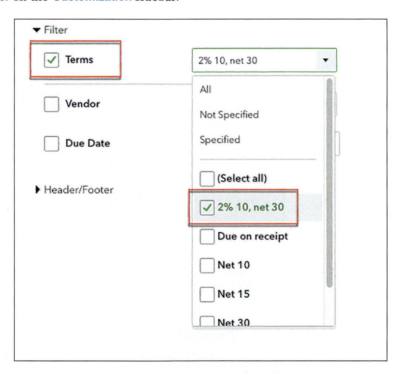

Check **Terms** and select all terms that include early payment discounts. The report title could be changed in **Header/Footer**.

Click **Run Report**. The report might look something like this:

The report can then be scanned for available discounts.

Taking Available Early Payment Discounts

As noted earlier, QBO does not currently have a feature that allows users to automatically apply available early payment discounts when a **bill** is paid.

> **BEHIND THE SCENES** Although it would be possible to enter the amount of the early payment discount as a line item in the **bill**, early payment discounts should not be recognized until it is certain that payment will be made within the payment terms.

What users can do is create a **vendor credit** in the amount of the discount just before the payment is processed.

The **vendor credit** would then be applied to the **bill** when payment was recorded.

> **BEHIND THE SCENES** Under GAAP, discounts related to the purchase of inventory are properly accounted for as a reduction of the cost in inventory. QBO does not have the capacity to handle that level of complexity. As long as the error in inventory values (due to these discounts) is not material (not significant), crediting cost of goods sold for early payment discounts on inventory items is acceptable.

Record payment of a bill with an early payment discount for Craig's Design and Landscaping.

(Robertson & Associates has changed its credit terms to 2%/10, net 30. Craig's intends to take the discount as allowed on the $315 bill currently due to Robertson.)

1. Set up the new terms.

    a.   Click the **gear** icon on the icon page.

    b.   Click **All Lists**.

PRACTICE EXERCISE

(continued)

(continued from previous page)

     c. Click **Terms**.

     d. Click **New**.

     e. Enter "2% 10, net 30" as the **Name**.

     f. Toggle **Due in Fixed number of days**.

     g. Enter "30" in the **days** field.

     h. Check the **Apply discount if paid early** box.

     i. Enter "2" in the **%** field and "10" in the **days** field.

     j. Click **Save**.

2. Add the new terms to Robertson & Associates' vendor record.

     a. Click **Expenses** on the navigation bar.

     b. Click the **Vendors** tab to open the Vendor Center.

     c. Click **Robertson & Associates**.

     d. Click **Edit**.

     e. Under **Terms**, select **2% 10, net 30**.

     f. Click **Save**.

     g. Click the **Transaction List** tab. (You should still be in the vendor record.)

     h. Click the $315 open bill.

     i. Select **2% 10, net 30** in the **Terms** field.

     j. Click **Save and close**.

3. Create the **vendor credit**.

     a. Click the ➕ icon on the icon bar and select **Vendor Credit**.

     b. Select **Robertson & Associates** as the **Vendor**.

     c. Use the current date as the **Payment date**.

     d. On the **Account details** section, select **Miscellaneous** as the **ACCOUNT**.

        i. If the discount is related to a purchase of inventory, a cost of goods sold account would be more appropriate.

     e. Enter "2% early payment discount on $315 bill" in the **DESCRIPTION** field.

     f. Enter "6.30" as the **AMOUNT**.

     g. Click **Save and close**.

4. Pay the discounted bill.

     a. Click **Expenses** on the navigation bar.

     b. Click the **Vendors** tab to open the Vendor Center.

     c. Click **Make Payment** in the **Action** column for **Robertson & Associates**.

     d. Select **Checking** as the payment method.

     e. Use the current date as the **payment date**.

        i. In this example, it is likely that the payment date is more than 10 days past the invoice date. Since the test drive company dates are constantly changing, we'll have to accept some departures from reality!

     f. Make sure that both the **credit** and the **bill** are checked.

     g. **Make a note** of the amount of the check.

     h. Click **Save and close**.

VENDOR REPORTS

We reviewed some of the standard vendor and payables reports in Chapter 4. For this chapter, we're most interested in inventory and purchase reports.

Inventory valuation reports are accessed through the **Sales and Customers** section of **Reports**. A commonly used inventory report is:

- **Inventory Valuation Summary**
  - A report of quantity, average cost, and total cost of units on hand, by item.

Inventory purchase reports are accessed through the **Expenses and Vendors** section of **Reports**. Commonly used reports include:

- **Open Purchase Order List**
  - List of all unfilled purchase orders

- **Purchases by Product/Service**
  - A report of purchases, by **item**, including information about quantity, unit cost, and vendor.

- **Purchases by Vendor Detail**
  - A report of purchases, by vendor, including information about **items**, quantity, and unit cost.

Prepare reports on inventory and purchases for Craig's Design and Landscaping.
(Craig's Design wants an inventory valuation report and a report of all open purchase orders.)

1. Click **Reports** on the navigation bar.
   a. Click **Inventory Valuation Summary** in the **Sales and Customers** section.
   b. **Make a note** of the four columns included in the report.
   c. Click **Dashboard** to close the report screen.

PRACTICE EXERCISE

Because there is no change in the accounting equation when an order is placed.

ANSWER TO QuickCheck 7-1

CHAPTER SHORTCUTS

Record vendor credit memos
1. Click the ✚ icon on the icon bar
2. Click **Vendor Credit**

Record purchase orders
1. Click the ✚ icon on the icon bar
2. Click **Purchase Order**

CHAPTER REVIEW (Answers available on the publisher's website.)

Matching

Match the term or phrase (as used in QuickBooks Online) to its definition.

1. vendor credit
2. item details
3. make payment
4. open purchase orders list

5. reorder point
6. purchase order
7. stock
8. Inventory Valuation Summary

_____ inventory

_____ dropdown option in vendor center used to open a bill payment form

_____ section of a form used to identify distribution of inventory charges or credits

_____ transaction type used to record credit memos received from vendors

_____ report summarizing the quantity and value of inventory items

_____ report of all unfilled purchase orders

_____ order for goods sent to vendor

_____ minimum desired quantity of inventory to have on hand

Multiple Choice

1. A liability is recorded in QBO when:
   a. inventory is ordered from the supplier.
   b. a vendor bill for inventory is paid.
   c. inventory is received with a bill from the supplier.
   d. inventory purchases are made by check.

2. Vendor credits _____.
   a. must be manually applied to specific bills by the user
   b. are automatically applied to bills by QBO when bill is paid
   c. are automatically applied by QBO when vendor credit is entered

3. If some of the items on a purchase order have been received,
   a. the purchase order is automatically marked as "closed" by QBO.
   b. the purchase order must be manually updated by checking the **CLOSED** column for each item received.
   c. the purchase order remains open until the bill has been paid.
   d. the purchase order remains open until all items have been received or the user manually closes the purchase order.

4. QBO uses the _____ method of valuating inventory.
   a. FIFO
   b. LIFO
   c. weighted average
   d. Any of the above methods can be used in QBO.

5. To take an early payment discount on a vendor bill, _____.

    a. a vendor credit can be created for the amount of the discount and applied to the bill when paid

    b. the potential discount can be included on the **bill** (in **Terms**)

    c. Both *a* and *b* are possible in QBO.

ASSIGNMENTS

Background information: Martin Smith, a college student and good friend of yours, had always wanted to be an entrepreneur. He is very good in math so, to test his entrepreneurship skills, he decided to set up a small math tutoring company serving local high school students who struggle in their math courses. He set up the company, Math Revealed!, as a corporation in 2018. Martin is the only owner. He has not taken any distributions from the company since it opened.

    The business has been successful so far. In fact, it's been so successful he has decided to work in his business full time now that he's graduated from college with a degree in mathematics.

    He has decided to start using QuickBooks Online to keep track of his business transactions. He likes the convenience of being able to access his information over the Internet. You have agreed to act as his accountant while you're finishing your own academic program.

    He currently has a number of regular customers that he tutors in Pre-Algebra, Algebra, and Geometry. His customers pay his fees by cash or check after each tutoring session but he does give terms of Net 15 to some of his customers. He has developed the following fee schedule:

Assignment 7A

Math Revealed!

MBC

Assignments with the MBC are available in **myBusinessCourse.**

Name	Description	Rate
Refresher	One-hour session	$40 per hour
Persistence program	Two one-hour sessions per week	$75 per week
Crisis program	Five one-hour sessions per week	$150 per week

The tutoring sessions usually take place at his students' homes but he recently signed a two-year lease on a small office above a local coffee shop. The rent is only $200 per month starting in January 2018. A security deposit of $400 was paid in December 2017.

    The following equipment is owned by the company:

Description	Date placed in service	Cost	Life	Salvage Value
Computer	7/1/18	$3,000	36 months	$300
Printer	7/1/18	$ 240	24 months	$ 0
Graphing Calculators (2)	7/1/18	$ 294	36 months	$ 60

All equipment is depreciated using the straight-line method.

    As of 12/31/18, he owed $2,000 to his parents who initially helped him get started. They are charging him interest at a 6% annual rate. He has been paying interest only on a monthly basis. His last payment was 12/31/18.

    Over the next month or so, he plans to expand his business by selling a few products he believes will help his students. He has already purchased a few items:

Category	Description	Vendor	Quantity On Hand	Cost per unit	Sales Price
Books and Tools					
	Geometry in Sports	Books Galore	20	12	16
	Solving Puzzles: Fun with Algebra	Books Galore	20	14	18
	Getting Ready for Calculus	Books Galore	20	15	20
	Protractor/Compass Set	Math Shack	10	10	14
	Handheld Dry-Erase Boards	Math Shack	25	5	9
	Notebooks (pack of 3)	Paper Bag Depot	10	15	20

2/1/19

✓ You pay the February rent to your landlord, Pro Spaces, (Check #1112 $200).

✓ You also mail a check to Martin's parents for the interest owed to them for January (Check #1113). (**TIP:** Look at the balance sheet if you've forgotten the interest amount due to Martin's parents.)

- You write the check to Richard Sorensen (Martin's dad). The address is 5406 Hawthorne Ave, Seattle, WA 98107. The terms are Net 30.

2/7/19

✓ Martin went to a Math Educators Conference in Los Angeles last weekend. He used the credit card to pay for:

- Gas for the trip $45 (LA Gasoline Stop)
- Hotel room (2 nights) $380 (Good Sleep Inn)
- Meals $150 (Good Sleep Inn)

✓ You enter the credit card charges in QBO, using 2/3 as the date, and charge them to Professional development expense, a new labor cost account (#604). You use **Office/General Administrative Expenses** as the **Detail Type**. (**TIP:** The **Labor costs** expense group includes any costs related to employees, not just wages.)

2/8/19

✓ Since Martin has started selling products, you decide to enter reorder points for the items currently in QBO. You enter reorder points of 20 for the books (**Puzzles**, **Sports**, and **Ready**), 15 for the protractor/compass kits and dry-erase boards, and 8 for the notebooks.

✓ You want to keep track of any orders you place so you turn on the purchase order feature in the **Expense** tab of **Account and Settings**. You check the **Custom transaction numbers** box.

✓ You look at the inventory items on hand and see that some of the items are below the reorder point.

✓ You prepare PO 100 and order the following from Books Galore:

- 15 each of **Puzzles** and **Sports**
- 10 **Ready**
- The PO total is $540.

✓ You also place an order with Math Shack (PO 101 for $100) for 10 of the protractor/compass sets (**Kit**).

2/12/19

✓ Martin learned about a new product at the Math Educators Conference he attended in Los Angeles. It's a low-cost handheld game console that can be loaded with a variety of educational math games. His plan is to sell the consoles and the software packs to local middle schools. They can then be loaned out to students that need extra help with math but can't afford personal tutoring. He has found the following supplier:

- Cartables, Inc.

  1390 Freestone Road

  San Diego, CA 92104

  Main Phone: (619) 378-5432

- You see that Cartables allows a 2% discount if the payment is made within 10 days. You set up a new term in the **All Lists** menu of the **gear** icon window. You name it "2% 10, net 30."

- You decide to set up a new category called "Math Games" for the new product line.

- New items are:

- ○ Console (Description—Game Console)—Expected cost $225; Selling price $350

- ○ Fractions (Description—Parts of a Whole)—Expected cost $35; Selling price $50

- ○ Equations (Description—Equal or Not?)—Expected cost $35; Selling price $50

- ○ Ratios (Description—Ratios and Proportions)—Expected cost $35; Selling price $50

- ○ Each new **inventory part item**:

  - ❑ Will have a reorder point of 3

  - ❑ Will be recorded in the **130 Inventory Asset** account

  - ❑ Will use account **420 Sales of Product Income** and **500 Cost of Goods Sold** as the **Income** and **Expense** accounts, respectively.

  - ❑ Is taxable. You use **Retail** as the **Sales tax category** and select **Schools Education and Instruction Materials** in the **What you sell** dropdown menu.

  - ❑ Has Cartables as the **preferred vendor**.

  - ❑ **TIP:** Enter 0 as the **initial quantity on hand** and 2/12/19 as the **As of date**. You'll be entering purchases of the **items** when they are received

- • You prepare a purchase order (#102) for the first Cartables order—5 consoles and 5 each of the three game packs. The PO totals $1,650.00.

✓ You receive the 10 **Kits** from Math Shack ordered on PO 101. There was no bill included in the shipment. You go ahead and enter a bill using the expected costs and terms. The bill total is $100.

2/14/19

✓ You receive the following bills in the mail:

- • Sacramento Utilities February bill (for heat and light) #9976—$95.15 dated 2/14. The terms are Net 30.

- • Horizon Phone February bill #121–775 for $40.28 dated 2/14. You charge the amount to the Utilities Expense account. The terms are Net 30.

  - ○ Horizon Phone, Inc.

    2345 Corporate Way

    Sacramento, CA 95822

✓ You pay all bills due on or before 2/15.

- • There are two bills to be paid. The total amount is $1,332.75. The first check number is 1114.

2/15/19

✓ You receive the books ordered from Books Galore. All **items** were received except for the 15 **Sports** books. Bill # 2117 for $360.00 was included. The terms are Net 30.

2/19/19

✓ The order from Cartables (PO 102) comes in today. All items are received. A bill (#949444-55) for $1,650.00 is included with the shipment. You make a note to yourself to remember to pay the amount by 3/1 so that you can take advantage of the 2% discount.

✓ You receive the bill dated 2/19 from Math Shack for the 10 **Kits** received on 2/12. The bill (#M58822) is for $110, which is a little higher than expected. You call Math Shack and they let you know that they had to find a new supplier for the **Kits** and the price went up. You adjust the bill you already recorded in QBO accordingly (date and amount). **TIP:** Consider using the search feature to find the Math Shack bill.

> **BEHIND THE SCENES** Most users prefer to enter the bill date, rather than the receive date, when recording vendor invoices so that the payable records are more accurate. (Due dates are generally based on the invoice date.) The difference in dates may affect the FIFO layer(s). However, this would normally be an insignificant amount.

2/21/19

✓ Martin sees a great new book when he stops by Books Galore. The book is called "Using Modeling to Make Better Decisions." He purchases 10 of them to hold for resale, using check #1116. The total cost is $170.00.

- You set up the new **inventory item** using "Modeling" as the **item** name and "Using Modeling to Make Better Decisions" as the description. The cost is $17 each. You set the sales price at $25 after discussing it with Martin and the reorder point at 5. (**TIP:** Make sure you link the new **item** to a **category** and set the **item** as taxable.) These are retail sales of school educational materials.

2/26/19

✓ Martin returns the 3 broken **Kits** to Math Shack. They reassure him that they have found a new supplier. They prepare a credit memo, which he brings back to the office. You record the credit (#R2525-8) for $30.00.

✓ You and Martin meet at Dick's Diner for lunch and a short meeting. You decide to bring him a $1,000 dividend check (Check # 1117). It's less than last month because you're a bit concerned about the big bill from Cartables. You want to take advantage of the discount, which means you need to pay the bill tomorrow.

✓ The lunch at Dick's Diner comes to $19.50. You use the credit card to pay the bill.

- You charge the lunch to **608 Staff Relations**.

✓ Martin reviews the inventory on hand when he gets back from the meeting.

- He places an order with Books Galore (PO 103) for the following:
  - ○ 10 each **Puzzles** and **Ready**
  - ○ He decides not to order **Sports** yet. He's still waiting for the backordered shipment from PO 100.
- He places an order with Math Shack (PO #104) for 8 **Kits**.

✓ You enter both purchase orders in QBO. The total for PO 103 is $290.00. The total for PO 104 is $80.00.

2/27/19

✓ You receive a bill (#3330) for $450 in the mail from a consulting firm, Les & Schmidt, LLC. Martin had hired the company to create a business plan for him Les & Schmidt completed the work in February. The bill is dated 2/27. The bill is due in 30 days. (**TIP:** This is a professional service.)

- The address for Les & Schmidt is 25 Norton Way, Sacramento, CA 95822.

✓ You decide to pay all bills due on or before 3/10 PLUS any bills with early payment discounts expiring before 3/10.

✓ You start by creating a **vendor credit** to record the early payment discount you will be taking on the Cartables bill. The discount is 2% of the total $1,650 due. You use "DISC" as the **Ref no.**

- Since the early payment discount applies to inventory purchases, you charge the amount to a new **Cost of Goods Sold** account—"Purchase discounts." You use 510 as the account number and **Supplies & Materials—COGS** as the **detail type**.

✓ You pay three bills. You apply credits on two of them. The total of the three checks, after taking the credits, is $2,346. The first check number is 1118. **TIP:** The check total shows up in the **PAYMENT** column.

✓ You write a check (#1121) to Martin's parents (Richard Sorensen) for February interest. Martin also asks you to include a $100 principal payment in the check. He wants to start paying his parents back.

✓ You plan to take a few days off so you prepare and mail the March rent check (#1122) to your landlord (Pro Spaces).

- **TIP:** The matching (expense recognition) principle applies here.

Check numbers 2/28

Checking account balance:. . . . . $ 374.44
Inventory: $2,691.00
Accounts Payable: . . . .$ 945.43
Net income (February): $2,292.07

Reports to create for Chapter 7:

All reports should be in portrait orientation.

- Journal—2/01 through 2/28.
  - Transaction types: Check, Expense, Bill, Vendor Credit, Bill Payment
- Inventory Valuation Summary as of 2/28
- Open purchase orders
- A/P Aging Summary as of 2/28

Background information: Sally Hanson, a good friend of yours, double majored in Computer Science and Accounting in college. She worked for several years for a software company in Silicon Valley but the long hours started to take a toll on her personal life.

Last year she decided to open up her own company, Salish Software Solutions (a corporation). Sally currently advises clients looking for new accounting software and assists them with software installation. She also provides training to client employees and occasionally troubleshoots software issues.

She has decided to start using QuickBooks Online to keep track of her business transactions. She likes the convenience of being able to access financial information over the Internet. You have agreed to act as her accountant while you're working on your accounting degree.

Sally has a number of clients that she is currently working with. She gives 15-day payment terms to her corporate clients but she asks for cash at time of service if she does work for individuals. She has developed the following fee schedule:

Salish Software Solutions

Name	Description	Rate
Select	Software Selections	$500 flat fee
Set Up	Software Installation	$ 50 per hour
Train	Software training	$ 40 per hour
Fix	File repair	$ 60 per hour

Sally rents office space from Alki Property Management for $800 per month.

The following furniture and equipment is owned by Salish:

Description	Date placed in service	Cost	Life	Salvage Value
Office Furniture.	6/1/18	$1,400	60 months	$200
Computer	7/1/18	$4,620	36 months	$300
Printer.	5/1/18	$ 900	36 months	$ 0

All equipment is depreciated using the straight-line method.

As of 12/31/18, she owed $3,500 to Dell Finance. The monthly payment on that loan is $150 including interest at 5%. Sally's last payment to Dell was 12/31/18.

Over the next month or so, Sally plans to expand her business by selling some of her favorite accounting and personal software products directly to her clients. She has already purchased the following items.

Item Name	Description	Vendor	Quantity On Hand	Cost per unit	Sales Price
Easy1	Easy Does it	Abacus Shop	15	$100	$175
Retailer.	Simply Retail	Simply Accounting	2	$400	$700
Contractor.	Simply Construction	Simply Accounting	2	$500	$800
Organizer	Organizer	Personal Solutions	25	$ 25	$ 50
Tracker	Investment Tracker	Personal Solutions	25	$ 20	$ 40

2/1/19

✓ You pay the February rent ($800) to your landlord, Alki Property Management (Check #1114).

✓ You also make the $150 monthly loan payment to Dell Finance. **TIP:** Think about what the payment is covering.

2/4/19

✓ Now that Sally has started selling products, you decide to enter reorder points for the items currently in QBO. You enter reorder points of 20 for **Tracker** and **Organizer**; 10 for **Easy1**; and 2 for **Contractor** and **Retailer**. (**Contractor** and **Retailer** are expensive so Sally doesn't want too many of those on the shelf!)

✓ You want to keep track of any orders you place so you turn on the purchase order feature in the **Expense** tab of **Account and Settings**. You check the **Custom transaction numbers** box.

✓ Sally has decided to go to a seminar on new accounting software being held in San Francisco on Friday and Saturday of this week. She asks you to use the credit card to pay the $175 registration fee to the AAASP (American Association of Accounting Software Providers). You enter the credit card charges in QBO. **TIP:** This is a type of professional development.

2/7/19

✓ You receive the following bills in the mail:

• Sacramento Light and Power's February bill (for heat and light) #01-84443—$105.00 dated 2/7. The terms are Net 30.

• Western Phone February bill #8911-64 for $105.75 dated 2/7. The terms are Net 30.

2/8/19

✓ You look at the inventory items on hand and see that some of the **items** are below the reorder point.

✓   You prepare PO 100 and order 15 each of **Organizer** and **Tracker** from Personal Software. The PO total is $675.

2/11/19

✓   You pay the balance due to Capital Three ($1,210) with check #1116.

✓   Sally had a great time at the software seminar last weekend. You record the credit card receipts she brings in for her travel expenses:

- Hotel and Saturday breakfast—The Franciscan—$235.85

- Gas—Bell Gas—$35

- Friday Dinner—Top Of The Hill—$42.66

- You consider the travel costs to be part of the cost of attending the seminar and you use 2/11 as the date for the charges.

✓   Sally places an order for two **Contractor** packages and one **Retailer** package from Simply Accounting. You create PO 101 for the $1,400 purchase.

- You decide to give the vendor a call about their payment terms. The item costs are high and you're hoping to get some kind of early payment discount. Simply Accounting agrees to give Salish terms of 2% 10, net 10. You add a new **Term** to the **Terms** list in QBO. You change the payment terms in the vendor record.

2/12/19

✓   Sally was very impressed with a couple of the new products demonstrated by Abacus Shop at the AAASP Conference in San Francisco. The company has created appointment and client management systems for various types of professional firms. Sally decides to offer the products to her Sacramento clients.

- You decide to set up a new **category** called "Management Products" for the new product line.

  ○ Since the product line is expanding, you decide to organize the product categories a bit. You change the name **Products** to "Accounting Products." You edit **Organizer** and **Tracker** to include them in the new "Management Products" **category**.

  ○ **TIP:** Select **Manage categories** in the **More** dropdown menu of **Products and Services** to make the changes.

- Each new **inventory part item**:

  ○ Will have a reorder point of 1.

  ○ Will be recorded in the **130 Inventory Asset** account.

  ○ Will use account **420 Sales of Product Income** and **500 Cost of Goods Sold** as the **Income** and **Expense** accounts, respectively.

  ○ Is taxable. You use **Retail** as the **Sales tax category** and select **Taxable Retail Items** in the **What you sell** dropdown menu.

  ○ **TIP:** Enter 0 as the **initial quantity on hand** and 2/12/19 as the **As of date**. You'll be entering purchases of the **items** when they are received.

- The new **items** are:

  ○ Legal (Description—Manage Your Law Firm)—Expected cost $350; Selling price $500

  ○ Medical (Description—Manage Your Medical Practice)—Expected cost $350; Selling price $500

  ○ Engineering (Description—Manage Your Engineering Firm)—Expected cost $350; Selling price $500

✓   You prepare a purchase order (#102) for the three new products—2 of each. The PO to Abacus totals $2,100.

2/15/19

✓ You receive the shipment from Personal Software for **items** ordered on PO 100. All **items** were received except for 2 of the **Trackers**. No bill was included with the shipment. You go ahead and create a **bill** using the expected costs and terms. The total is $635. **TIP:** Don't forget to **Add** the purchase order information from the sidebar of the **bill**.

2/19/19

✓ The order from Simply Accounting (PO 101) comes in today. All items are received. A bill (#65411-8) for $1,400 is included with the shipment. You make a note to yourself to remember to pay the amount within the discount period so that you can take advantage of the 2% discount.

✓ You receive the bill from Personal Software for the **Organizers** and **Trackers** received on 2/15. You open the **bill** to make the edits. The bill (#744466) is for $641.50 and is dated 2/15/19 (the date the shipment was received). The **Trackers** were slightly more than expected ($20.50 per unit instead of $20). You call Personal Software and they apologize for not letting you know about the price change sooner. **TIP:** Consider using the Find feature to locate the bill.

✓ Sally returns the two damaged **Organizer** disks from last week. Personal Software sends over a credit memo (RR6122-44) for $50, which you record. **TIP:** This is a vendor credit.

2/21/19

✓ You receive the shipment from Abacus Shop for all **items** ordered on PO 102. The bill (TAS 25344) for $2,100 has terms of Net 15.

✓ You ask Sally whether she wants you to follow up on the 2 **Trackers** that weren't received in the Personal Software shipment on 2/15. She says she'll go ahead and call Personal Software to cancel the backorder. You close PO 100 in QBO.

2/22/19

✓ You and Sally meet at Roscoe's for lunch and a short meeting before she takes off for Chicago. You decide to bring her a $2,500 dividend check (Check # 1117). You're a bit concerned about the big bill coming due from Abacus Shop and you ask her to wait before cashing the check. She agrees.

✓ The lunch at Roscoe's comes to $28.50. You use the credit card to pay the bill.

• You decide to set up a new account. **Staff meetings expense**, a subaccount of **600 Labor Costs** to track the cost of staff meetings. You use **Office/General Administrative Expenses** as the **Detail Type** and 608 as the account number.

✓ Sally takes a few minutes to review the inventory on hand when she gets back from lunch.

• She places an order with Abacus for 5 **Easy1s**. You record the PO (#103) for $500.

2/27/19

✓ You receive a bill (#3330) for $550 in the mail from an accounting firm, Dovalina and Diamond, LLC. Sally hired the company to do a two-year financial projection. The work was completed in February. She thinks she may need to either borrow some money from a bank or attract investors in order to grow as quickly as she'd like. The bill, is dated 2/27. The bill is due in 30 days. (**TIP:** This is a professional service.)

• The address for Dovalina and Diamond is 419 Upstart Drive, Sacramento, CA 95822.

✓ You decide to pay all bills due on or before 3/5 PLUS any bills with early payment discounts expiring before 3/5.

• You start by creating a **vendor credit** to record the early payment discount you will be taking on the Simply Accounting bill. You use 65411-8D as the **ref no**. The discount is 2% of the total $1,400 due.

○ Since the early payment discount applies to inventory purchases, you charge the amount to a new **Cost of Goods Sold** account—"Purchase discounts." You use 510 as the account number and **Other Costs of Services—COS** as the **Detail Type**.

- You pay three bills. You apply credits on two of them. The total of the three checks is $3,463.50. The first check number is 1118. **TIP:** The check total shows up in the **PAYMENT** column.

✓ You plan to take a few days off so you prepare and mail the March rent check (#1121) to your landlord (Alki Property Management).

- **TIP:** The matching (expense recognition) principle applies here.

Check numbers 2/28

Checking account balance:.. $6,661.80
Inventory: $6,981.50
Account payable:. $2,860.75
Net income (February): $4,251.99

Reports to create for Chapter 7:

All reports should be in portrait orientation

- Journal (2/1-2/28)
  - Transaction types: Check, Expense, Bill, Vendor Credit, Bill Payment
- Inventory Valuation Summary as of 2/28
- Open purchase orders
- A/P Aging Summary as of 2/28

End-of-Period and Other Activity

(Merchandising Company)

After completing Chapter 8, you should be able to:

1. Adjust inventory quantities.

2. Pay sales taxes.

3. Record non-customer cash receipts.

4. Record transfers between bank accounts.

5. Inactivate and merge accounts.

6. Add comments to reports.

All of the "end of period" procedures we covered in Chapter 5 apply to merchandising companies as well as service companies. Bank accounts must be reconciled. Adjusting journal entries must be made. Remember: end of period procedures are focused on making sure the financial records are as accurate as possible. The financial statements should give internal and external users a fair picture of:

- The operations of the company for the period (profit and loss statement).

- The financial position of the company at the end of the period (balance sheet).

There are a few additional procedures unique to merchandising companies that we'll cover in this chapter.

- Inventory adjustments

- Managing sales taxes

We'll also look at a few procedures and QBO features not covered in previous chapters:

- Recording non-customer cash receipts

- Recording bank transfers

- Inactivating and merging accounts

- Adding comments to reports

ADJUSTING INVENTORY

As you know, QBO features a perpetual inventory tracking system for inventory part items so quantities are automatically updated when goods are received, sold, or returned.

If life were perfect, the inventory quantities in QBO would **always** equal inventory quantities on hand (physically in the store or warehouse). Unfortunately, we know that that isn't always the case. Differences can occur because of:

- Theft

- Unrecorded transactions (sales, item receipts, returns by customers, or returns to vendors)

- Damaged goods

In addition to needing to know the quantity on hand for valuing inventory, companies must have an accurate record of how many of each of their products they have available to sell. That's part of a good inventory management system. I'm guessing a few of you have asked a clerk about a book you can't find on the shelf at your favorite bookstore. The clerk looks the book up in the store's computer system and it says that they should have two in stock. You go back to the shelves with the clerk and neither of you can find the book. It may just be misplaced or it may have been stolen but both you and the clerk have wasted time looking for it and you're a disappointed customer. The more accurate the inventory records, the smoother the operation and the more accurate the financial statements. So, periodically, the inventory on hand is physically counted and the inventory records are adjusted as necessary.

Counts can be taken at any point during a year but are usually taken, at a minimum, at the end of the year. (Companies that need audited financial statements **must** take a count, with auditors present, at the end of the year.) Counts are frequently taken more often (quarterly, for example). It's usually a big job to take a physical inventory count so many companies don't count inventory monthly. If there hasn't been a history of significant inventory adjustments, taking an annual physical inventory count is probably sufficient. (If you're in the bookstore business and you have lots of books on shelves, you might want to consider more frequent counts!)

To get a good inventory count, it's usually best to take the count when products aren't moving (not being sold or received). Many companies take inventory counts after closing or on weekends. Counters are given a list of products and the unit of measure that should be used to count the products (units, cartons, pounds, etc.). As a control, the count sheets should not list the expected quantity. Why? For one thing, it's just too easy to see what you think you **should** see (i.e., what the count sheet says)!

Once the physical inventory count is taken, the count sheets are compared to the accounting records. Significant variations should be investigated. Documentation (particularly packing slips) related to transactions occurring close to the count date can often provide useful information. Goods might have been received or shipped out earlier or later than the customer invoice or vendor bill dates used in the accounting system. In practice, physical inventory counts usually involve a lot of recounts.

Once the company is confident that they've got a good count and all known transactions have been recorded, the accounting records are adjusted to the count.

In QBO, count sheets are available in the **Sales and Customers** section of **Reports**.

The **Physical Inventory Worksheet** looks something like this:

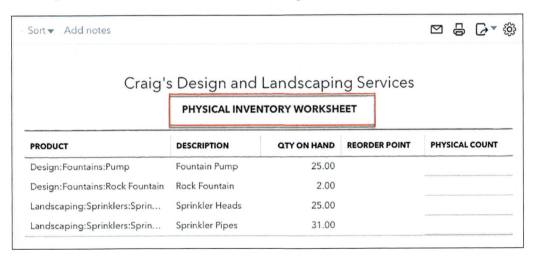

The worksheet can easily be modified by clicking **Customize**. For example, a company that uses SKU numbers would likely want those included on the count sheet. The **QTY ON HAND** column should be removed. **REORDER POINT** isn't necessary for a count and could be removed.

> ✳ **HINT:** You might have noticed that the date for the worksheet can't be changed. The count sheets must be printed on the day the count is taken.

After the count sheets are completed, the listed counts are compared to the inventory quantities in QBO. As noted earlier, recounts are normally requested if the counts vary significantly from the perpetual records.

Once the company determines that the count is accurate, any necessary inventory adjustments are recorded through the **Inventory Qty Adjustment** form accessed by clicking the icon in the icon bar.

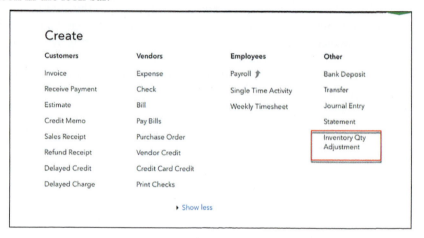

The form looks like this:

The **Adjustment date** would be the date of the inventory count. The **Inventory adjustment account** is the choice of management. Most companies debit or credit inventory adjustments to an account with a **cost of goods sold account type**. The offset account is, of course, the inventory (asset) account.

The **inventory part** items to be adjusted are selected in the **PRODUCT** column.

> **WARNING: Occasionally, QBO will not allow users to select a product in the Inventory Quantity Adjustment screen. In that case, use the following workaround:**
>
> 1. **Exit out of the Inventory Quantity Adjustment screen.**
> 2. **Click the gear icon on the icon bar.**
> 3. **Click Products and Services.**
> 4. **In the far left column, check the box next to the items to be adjusted.**
> 5. **Select Adjust Quantity in the Batch actions dropdown menu. (The menu is on the right side of the list near the top.)**

The form will look something like this when **items** have been selected:

QBO automatically updates the **QTY ON HAND** with the current quantity in the **item** record. Users enter the quantity from the count sheet as the **NEW QTY**.

Once the **Inventory Qty Adjustment** form is saved, QBO adjusts both the quantity and the value of **items** selected in the form. The oldest FIFO layer is used to determine the amount of the value adjustment.

An **Inventory Valuation Detail** report customized to show only the **items** adjusted in the Practice Exercise to follow would look something like this:

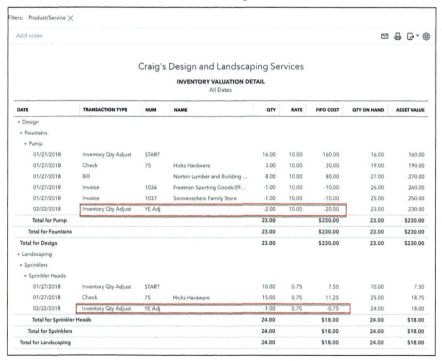

BEHIND THE SCENES Under GAAP, inventory values must be adjusted when the reported cost is less than the market value (usually defined as replacement cost). This is known as the "lower of cost or market" rule. Currently, QBO does not have a feature allowing users to change values for inventory to comply with the lower of cost or market rule. As an alternative, companies could create a contra asset account and record an allowance to cover the difference between cost and market.

Inventory starting values (values entered when the company was first set up in QBO), on the other hand, **can** be adjusted with or without changing quantities. This is done by selecting **Adjust starting value** in the **ACTION** column for the specific **item** in the **Products and Services** list.

PRACTICE
EXERCISE

Adjust inventory for Craig's Design and Landscaping.

(Inventory was counted today. All of the counts agreed to the QBO records except for Fountain Pumps (there were only 23 pumps) and Sprinkler Heads (there were only 24).)

1. Click the ➕ icon on the icon bar.

2. Click **Inventory Qty Adjustment**.

3. Enter the current date as the **Adjustment date**.

4. Select **Add new** in the **Inventory adjustment account** field.

   a.   Select **Cost of Goods Sold** as the **Account Type**.

   b.   Select **Supplies & Materials—COGS** as the **Detail Type**.

   c.   Enter "Inventory adjustments" as the **Name**.

   d.   Click **Save and close**.

5. Enter "YE Adj" as the **Reference no.**

6. In the first row, select **Pump** in the **PRODUCT** field and enter "23" as the **NEW QTY**.

   a.   **TIP:** If you are unable to select a product in the field, use the workaround described in the WARNING box in this section.

7. In the second row, select **Sprinkler Heads** in the **PRODUCT** field and enter "24" as the **NEW QTY**.

8. Click **Save and close**.

9. Click **Reports** on the navigation bar.

10. Click **Physical Inventory Worksheet** in the **Sales and Customers** section.

11. **Make a note** of the **QTY ON HAND** for **Rock Fountains** and **Sprinkler Pipes**.

MANAGING SALES TAXES

Sales taxes are remitted to taxing authorities on a periodic basis—generally annually, quarterly, or monthly, depending on the size of the company. Remember, the tax is on the consumer but the responsibility to collect and remit the tax is on the seller. In most states, sellers are responsible for remitting to the tax authorities the amount they **should** have charged (which hopefully agrees with the amount they actually **did** charge!).

BEHIND THE SCENES In most cases, a company is required to report and remit sales taxes when the tax is **charged** to the customer (accrual method). Some states allow a company to remit the tax when it's **collected** from the customer (cash method). The default in QBO is the "charged" date (the date of the invoice or sales receipt). Currently, QBO only calculates sales tax liabilities based on the accrual method. If users change the accounting method to Cash basis in Accounts and Settings after sales taxes have been activated, QBO will continue to calculate tax liabilities on the accrual method. If users set the accounting method to cash basis **before** sales taxes are activated, users will need to calculate sales taxes manually (no automatic calculation by QBO). In the example below, and in the homework assignments, the default (charged) date will be used.

At the end of a tax-reporting period, a report should be prepared detailing sales and sales taxes charged, by taxing jurisdiction, and reviewed.

The **Sales Tax Liability**, **Taxable Sales Summary**, and **Taxable Sales Detail** reports are accessible in the **Sales tax** section of **Reports**.

The **Sales Tax Liability** report will look something like this if **All Dates** is selected in the **Report period** field:

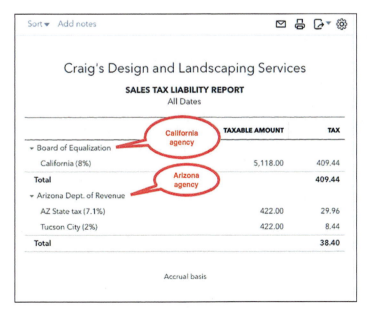

This report lists taxable sales by jurisdiction. This report would be used to prepare the various tax reports that are filed with the state and local tax agencies.

> **BEHIND THE SCENES** For control purposes, the company should carefully review its tax reports. Remember, QBO is reporting what happened, not what **should** have happened.

The **Taxable Sales Summary** report lists taxable sales by product. Drilling down on any of the **items** listed allows you to see the specific sales included in the total. The report would look something like this if **All dates** was selected as the **Report period**.

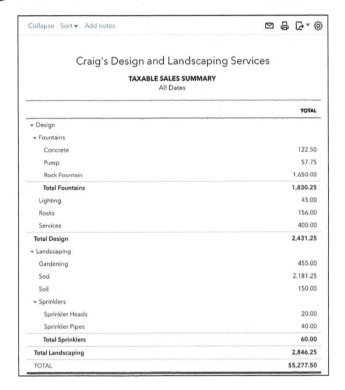

Remitting Sales Tax Liabilities

Sales tax functions (like tax payments and adjustments) are accessed through the Sales Tax Center.

Your homework company uses the current version of sales tax processing covered in Chapter 6. The test drive company has not yet been updated and still uses the older version. To help you with your homework, the following descriptions and screenshots are from the newer version. There will be no Practice Exercises for this section.

Click **Taxes** on the navigation bar.

> **BEHIND THE SCENES** QBO automatically sets up a separate liability account **(Other currently liability account type)** for each sales tax agency. When sales taxes are paid, QBO automatically debits the appropriate liability account. These accounts cannot be changed in any way or deleted.

If any taxes are due **as of the current date** (the date the user accesses the window), the amount will be shown in the **Due this month** section.

Any open tax period (taxes not yet due) will be listed in the **Upcoming** section. Tax amounts will not be listed for open periods.

Click **View Return** to start the tax payment (remittance) process.

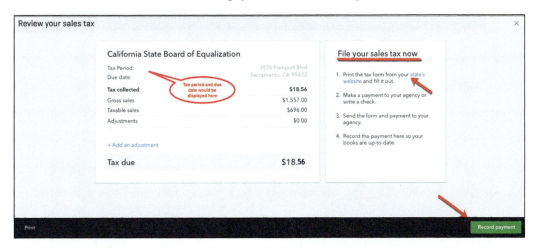

Users have a chance to review or adjust the return on this screen. Users can also click the link in the **File your sales tax now** section to access the appropriate form.

Click **Record payment**.

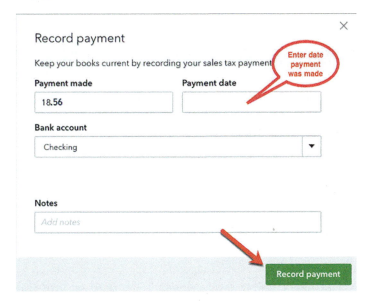

Enter the date and bank account to be charged. Click **Record payment** to enter the transaction. (The **transaction type** for tax remittances is **Sales Tax Payment**.)

Click **Record payment**.

Click the payment date to see the transaction detail.

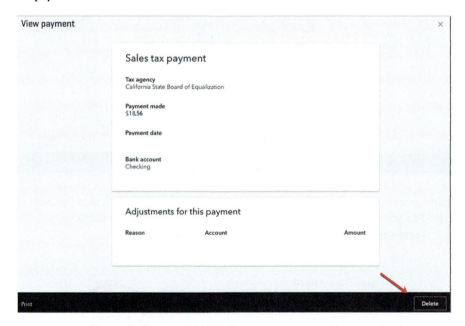

Once a **Sales Tax Payment** has been recorded, it can be deleted but not adjusted.

Adjusting Sales Tax Liabilities

The liability might need to be adjusted because:

- QBO wasn't yet updated for a recent rate change.

- A specific customer was inadvertently overcharged or undercharged for sales tax.

- The company is located in a state that levies an additional tax (called an excise tax) on the **seller**.

> **BEHIND THE SCENES** Excise taxes are generally based on gross sales revenue. Excise taxes cannot be entered as a sales tax item because they are not charged to the customer. They are an expense of the seller.

Although sales tax payments can't be adjusted after they are recorded, adjustments **can** be made on the **Review your sales tax** screen before the payment is processed.

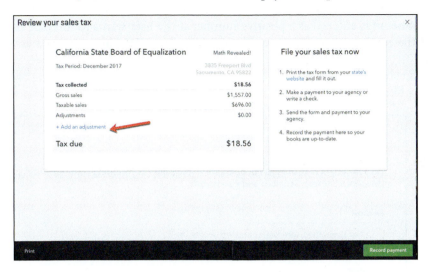

Click ⊕ **Add an adjustment**

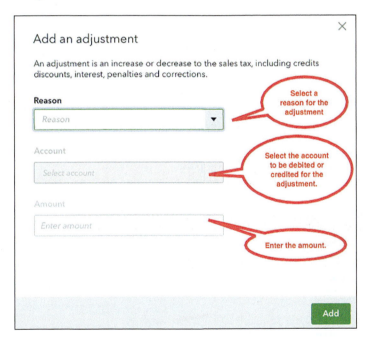

A reason for the adjustment must be selected from one of the following options.

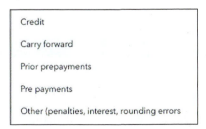

The account to be charged for the amount of the adjustment is entered in the **Account** field.

Adjustments due to corrections of errors would normally be charged to a miscellaneous expense or income account. Rounding errors and adjustments for excise taxes would normally be charged to a business tax expense account.

The **Amount** is entered as a positive number if the user wants to increase the tax payment. If the payment amount should be decreased the **Amount** is entered as a negative number.

An adjustment to increase the amount to be paid by $0.04 (rounding) would look something like this:

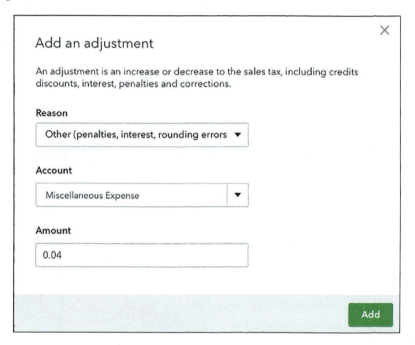

Click **Add** to adjust the tax amount to be paid.

Users have a chance to review the payment amount on the next screen.

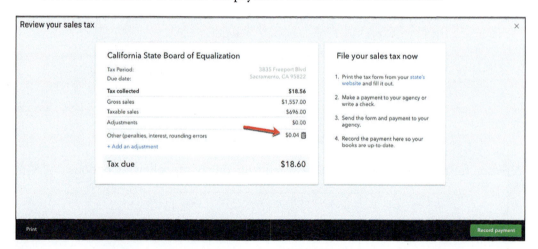

Click **Record payment**.

The payment date and bank account to be used is entered on the next screen. The information is updated by clicking **Record payment** again.

The **View payment** screen would look something like this:

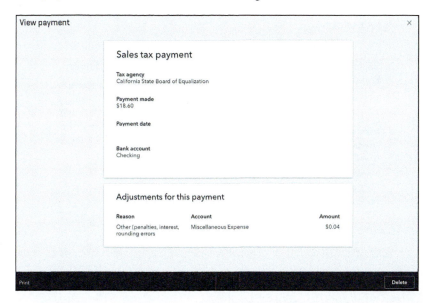

> **BEHIND THE SCENES** If a customer was overcharged, the company would generally want to reimburse the customer, if possible, by issuing a check or credit memo. If a customer was undercharged, the company might choose to invoice the customer for the tax. In that case, the company would need to set up an **item** for uncollected tax. That **item** would, of course, be non-taxable.

Deleting Sales Tax Payments

Although **sales tax payments** can't be edited once they've been recorded, they can be deleted.

The sales tax liability is automatically restored when **sales tax payments** are deleted. The user can then record the correct payment.

To delete the payment, click **Taxes** on the Navigation bar.

Click **History**.

Click **View return**.

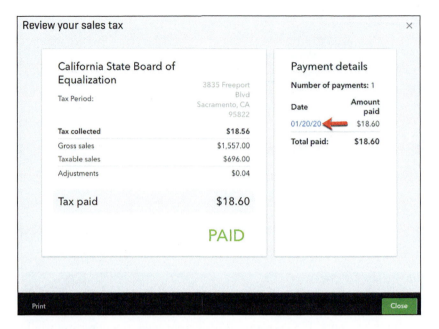

Click the payment date.

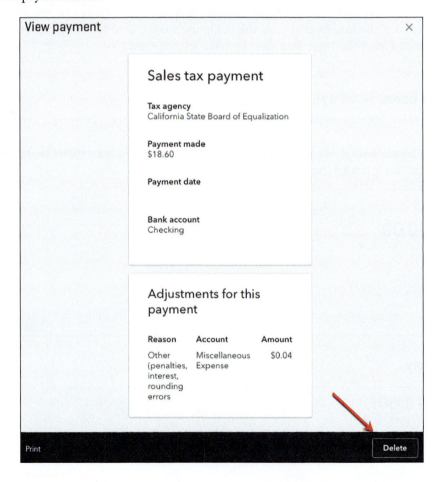

Click **Delete**.

Sales Tax Payment transactions can also be deleted by drilling down (clicking) on the transaction in journal reports.

The transaction screen would look something like this.

Click **Delete Payment**.

ENTERING CASH RECEIPTS FROM NON-CUSTOMERS

In companies, most cash receipts come from customers. (At least we hope they do!) There are other sources of cash though:

- Borrowings

- Sales of company stock

- Sales of property or equipment

- Etc.

In previous chapters, all cash receipts were entered through one of the following forms:

- Sales Receipts
    - Used for cash sales to customers
- Payments
    - Used for cash payments by customers on account receivable balances

As you know, the default debit account in the underlying entry for both **sales receipt** and **payment** transactions is **Undeposited Funds**, an asset account. Receipts are later transferred from **Undeposited Funds** to the appropriate **Bank** account through the **Deposit** form.

When cash is received from non-customers, the amounts are entered **directly** into the **Deposit** form.

The **Deposit** form is opened by clicking the ➕ icon on the icon bar and selecting **Bank Deposit**.

If there are pending undeposited funds, the initial screen will look like this:

The appropriate bank account should be selected and the deposit **Date** entered.

Non-customer receipts would be added in the **Add New Deposits** section of the form. The payer's name should be selected in the **RECEIVED FROM** field and the account to be credited should be selected in the **ACCOUNT** field.

> **BEHIND THE SCENES** Deposits should be grouped to correspond to the actual bank deposits. If a non-customer receipt is being deposited with customer receipts, both types should be recorded in the same make deposits form.

Multiple entries can be recorded for one non-customer receipt. The **Total** must, of course, equal the amount that's being deposited. An example is provided as part of the Practice Exercise that follows. The final screen from that exercise would look something like this:

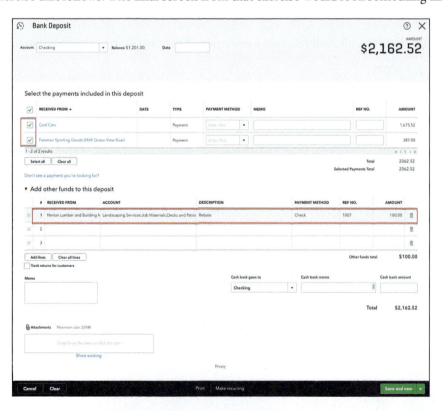

PRACTICE
EXERCISE

Record a non-customer cash receipt for Craig's Design and Landscaping.
(Craig's Design received a $100 rebate check from one of its vendors (Norton Lumber). Craig's deposited it along with a few checks from customers.)

1. Click the ➕ icon on the icon bar.

2. Click **Bank Deposit**.

3. Check the boxes next to the two payments listed in the **Select the payments included in the deposit** section.

   a. **Make a note** of the customer names appearing in the **RECEIVED FROM** column.

4. In the **Add other funds to this deposit** section:

   a. Select **Norton Lumber and Building Materials** in the **RECEIVED FROM** column (first line).

   b. Select **Decks and Patios** as the **ACCOUNT**.

   c. Enter "Rebate" as the **DESCRIPTION**.

   d. Select **Check** as the **PAYMENT METHOD**.

   e. Enter "1007" as the **REF NO.**

   f. Enter "100" as the **AMOUNT**.

5. The **Total** should be $2,162.52.

6. Click **Save and close**.

RECORDING BANK TRANSFERS

Many companies maintain more than one bank account. Other than the general checking account, a company will frequently have a separate checking account for payroll. They might also open a savings or a money market account to earn some interest on funds not needed for immediate operations.

If the accounts are with the same bank, transfers between accounts can generally be made either electronically (through the bank's website) or by phone.

In QBO, electronic or phone transfers are recorded using the **Transfer** form. The **Transfer** form is accessed by clicking the ➕ icon on the icon bar and selecting **Transfer** in the **Other** column. The screen looks like this:

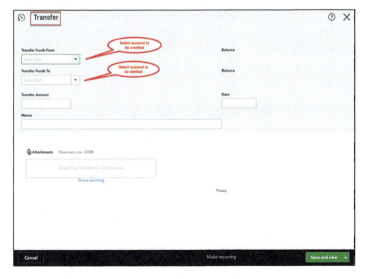

The account selected in the **Transfer Funds From** field represents the account to be credited. The account selected in the **Transfer Funds To** field represents the account to be debited. QBO will display the current balances in each account selected.

The amount to be transferred is recorded in the **Transfer Amount** field. The **date** must also be entered.

PRACTICE EXERCISE

Transfer funds between accounts for Craig's Design and Landscaping.
(Craig's Design decides to open a money market account with a $500 transfer from checking.)

1. Click the ➕ icon on the icon bar.

2. Click **Transfer.**

3. Select **Checking** in the **Transfer Funds From** dropdown menu.

4. Make a note of the number of **Bank** accounts listed in the dropdown menu.

5. Select **Add new** in the **Transfer Funds To** dropdown menu.

    a. Select **Bank** as the **Account Type.**

    b. Select **Money Market** as the **Detail Type.**

    c. Leave the **Name** as **Money Market.**

    d. Click **Save and Close.**

6. Enter "500" as the **Transfer Amount.**

7. In the **Memo** field, enter "Opened new money market account."

8. Click **Save and close.**

INACTIVATING AND MERGING GENERAL LEDGER ACCOUNTS

Companies generally set up their initial chart of accounts based on expected activities and informational needs. As companies grow and change, the chart of accounts usually expands. Often it expands substantially. An effective chart of accounts contains only those accounts that provide useful detail for owners and managers.

Periodically, a company should take a look at the structure of its chart of accounts to make sure it still meets the needs of the company. We already know how to group accounts. Accounts can be moved from one group to another (within the same account type) and "header" accounts can be added or deleted. But what do we do with accounts that are no longer needed or useful?

Accounts cannot be permanently deleted but QBO does provide two tools for managing unused accounts:

- Temporarily deleting accounts ("inactivating" the account)
    - A deleted account isn't available for use in future transactions.
        - It's also unavailable for filtering or searching.
    - A deleted account can be re-activated if necessary.
    - Deleted temporary (revenue and expense) accounts **will** appear on reports when appropriate.
- Merging accounts

- An account is deleted after all activity in the account is transferred to an existing account identified by the user.
- Merging an account is permanent (can't be undone!).

Deleting (Inactivating) an Account

Deleting an account is an option when a company needs to maintain detail about past transactions. Let's use an example. Let's say five years ago, a barbershop sold shampoo in addition to cutting hair. It has since discontinued selling products because of the high cost of maintaining inventory. The barbershop no longer needs the inventory account or the cost of goods sold account. It might, however, need that information in the future. That might be the case if it is ever audited or if it decides to reconsider merchandise sales.

Deleting an Account with a Zero Balance

Deleting an account with a zero balance is a relatively simple process.

To delete the account in QBO, click the **gear** icon on the icon bar and select **Chart of Accounts**.

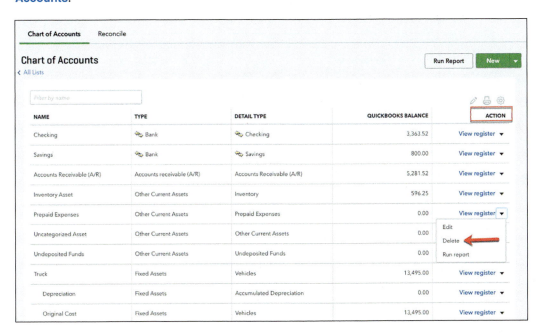

In the **ACTION** column of the account you want to delete, select **Delete**. QBO will ask you to confirm your decision. Once an account has been deleted, it is no longer visible on the default **Chart of Accounts** screen.

Reactivating Deleted Accounts

Accounts can be undeleted (reactivated). The simplest process is to click the **gear** icon and select **Chart of Accounts**.

Once the account list is open, click **Run Report** and **Customize**.

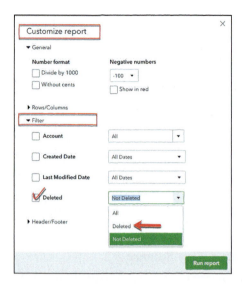

Open the **Filter** section and check the **Deleted** box. In the dropdown menu, select **Deleted**.

When the report is run, only deleted accounts will be displayed. The report should look something like this:

Click the account you want to reactivate.

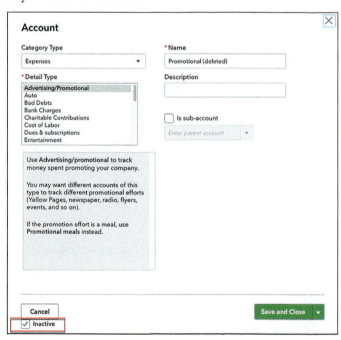

Unchecking the **Inactive** box makes the account available for use. Click **Save and Close** to complete the process.

Deleting an Account with a Non-zero Balance

QBO allows users to delete accounts with balances. The user process is the same as the process for deleting accounts without balances described in the previous section. It's important, though, for the user to understand what happens to those account balances.

If the account to be deleted is a permanent (balance sheet) account, QBO will display the following message:

If **Yes** is selected, QBO will automatically make a journal entry to clear the account (bring it to zero). The offset account used is **Opening Balance Equity** (an **equity account type**). For example, if a user deleted Prepaid Insurance and that account had a $200 debit balance, QBO would make the following entry:

	Opening Balance Equity	200	
	Prepaid Insurance		200

If the account to be deleted is a temporary (revenue or expense) account, no journal entry will be made. The account (identified as a deleted account) would still appear on profit and loss reports with the balance at the point it was deleted. For example, if Rent Expense with a balance of $500 was deleted, it would continue to appear on profit and loss reports as Rent Expense (deleted) through the end of the year.

If accounts with balances at the time of deletion are reactivated, the transaction detail prior to the deletion will be visible. The entry made by QBO to zero out permanent accounts, however, will NOT be reversed. The reactivated account will show a zero balance.

Merging Accounts

Merging an account would be the best option when an account does not (and maybe never did) provide useful detail. Let's use another example. Let's say the accountant for a barbershop set up separate general ledger accounts for every **service item**. There was an account for shampoos, another for haircuts, another for beard trims, etc. Those accounts were unnecessary because the revenue detail is already available by using the **Sales by Item** reports. It would make sense, then, to merge some or all of those accounts.

Merging an account really means transferring activity out of the account you no longer wish to use INTO an appropriate existing account. There needs to be two accounts: The "transferor account" (the account you want to eliminate) and the "transferee account" (the account that you intend to keep).

To merge an account, the Chart of Accounts list must be open. In the **ACTION** column of the "transferor account" (the account you want to eliminate) select **Edit**.

Change the **Name** of the account to the name of the "transferee account" (the account you intend to keep). The name must be **identical** or you'll create a new account.

When you click **Save and close**, QBO will give you the following message:

Clicking **Yes** will **permanently** delete the transferor account. All transactions posted to the account will now appear in the transaction detail of the remaining account.

Manage the chart of accounts in Craig's Design and Landscaping.
(The Promotional expense account is deleted and the Bookkeeper and Accounting expense accounts are merged.)

1. Click the **gear** icon on the icon bar.

2. Click **Chart of Accounts**.

3. Click **See your Chart of Accounts**, if necessary.

4. Delete an account.

   a. In the **ACTION** column for **Promotional** expense, click the arrow next to **Run Report** and select **Delete**.

   b. Click **Yes**.

5. Merge an account.

   a. In the **ACTION** column for **Bookkeeper** expense, click the arrow next to **Run Report** and select **Edit**.

   b. Change the **Name** to "Accounting."

      i.   Make sure you enter the name exactly as noted. If you have any differences, QBO will simply change the name.

   c. Click **Save and close**.

   d. Click **Yes** at the prompt to merge.

      i.   If this prompt doesn't appear, you most likely made a spelling error when you entered the account name. Go back to step 5a.

   e. **Make a note** of the parent account for **Accounting**.

6. Click **Dashboard** to exit out of the **Chart of Accounts** window.

ADDING NOTES TO REPORTS

At the end of an accounting period, after all adjustments have been made, the accountant should be comfortable with the balances in each of the accounts on the financial statements. For many accounts, there are subsidiary ledgers or worksheets that provide documentation. For example, agings (by customer or by vendor) support accounts receivable and accounts payable account balances. Bank reconciliations support cash balances. **Sales by item** reports provide support for revenue and cost of goods sold amounts.

For other accounts (such as prepaid or unearned revenue accounts), there may not be any standard, formal documentation. For control purposes (and in case of memory lapses!), the accountant would want to document the balances in those accounts as well.

QBO has included a feature in all reports that allows the user to add notes to reports. This feature can be very useful to accountants as part of the end of period process. For example, instead of preparing an offline worksheet detailing the components of Prepaid Expenses, the accountant can simply include that detail in the balance sheet for the period by adding a note to the report.

Other uses of this feature might include:

• Adding a note to an **inventory valuation summary** report, reminding the reader that a particular **item** is nearing obsolescence.

- Adding a note to an **open purchase order** report, reminding the reader to contact the vendor and determine the status of a backorder.

A report must be open before notes can be added.

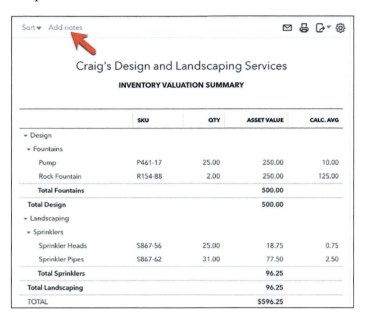

Clicking **Add notes** on the report menu bar adds a new field at the bottom of the report.

Reports that contain notes can be printed, emailed, or saved as a PDF file. The notes will appear at the bottom of the report.

Reports with notes can also be saved for future reference by clicking **Save customization** at the top of the report window.

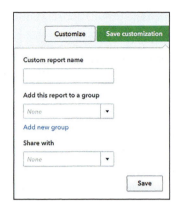

A unique name should be given to the saved report. Customized reports can be saved in groups and can also be restricted to certain users.

For example, an **inventory valuation summary** report might be saved in a group of inventory reports accessible to all users. Customization would look something like this:

Saved reports are accessed by clicking **Reports** on the navigation bar and selecting the **Custom Reports** tab.

All saved reports will be displayed by group on the **My Custom Reports** tab.

Saved reports can be edited and modified.

PRACTICE
EXERCISE

Add a comment to a report.
(Craig's Design adds a note to the balance sheet related to the cost of its truck.)

1. Click **Reports** on the navigation bar.

2. Click **Balance Sheet** in the **Favorites** section.

3. **Make a note** of the balance in **Accounts Payable (A/P)**.

(continued)

4. Click **Add notes**.

5. In the notes field, type "Cost to refit the truck is not yet included in the Truck account balance."

6. Click **Save customization**.

7. Enter "Balance Sheet with Notes" as the **Customer report name**.

8. Click **Add new group**.

9. Enter "Month End Reports" as the **New group name**.

10. Click **Add**.

11. Select **All** in the **Share with** dropdown menu.

12. Click **Save**.

13. Click **Dashboard** to exit out of reports.

CHAPTER SHORTCUTS

Adjust inventory quantities
1. Click the **+** icon on the icon bar
2. Click **Inventory Qty Adjustment**

Record payment of sales tax
1. Click **Sales tax** on the navigation bar
2. Click **Review return** next to the taxing jurisdiction name

Record non-customer cash receipt
1. Click the **+** icon on the icon bar
2. Click **Bank Deposit**

Record bank transfer
1. Click the **+** icon on the icon bar
2. Click **Transfer**

Delete an account
1. Click **gear** icon on the icon bar
2. Click **Chart of Accounts**
3. Select **Delete** in the **Action** column of the account to be deleted

Merge two accounts
1. Click **gear** icon on the icon bar
2. Click **Chart of Accounts**
3. Select **Edit** in the **Action** column of the account to be merged
4. Change the name of the account

CHAPTER REVIEW (Answers available on the publisher's website.)

Matching

Match the term or phrase (as used in QuickBooks Online) to its definition.

1. quantity on hand
2. inventory quantity adjustment
3. custom report
4. transfer
5. merging
6. add other funds to this deposit
7. deleted account
8. sales tax liability report

_____   number of inventory part items available

_____   transaction type used to record cash transfers between bank accounts

_____   section of the bank deposit form used to record non-customer cash receipts

_____   tool used to transfer all activity from one account into another account

_____   transaction type used to record quantity corrections to inventory part items

_____   account that is unavailable for posting or searching

_____   saved report that may include manually entered user comments

_____   report of taxable sales revenue and related tax amount by jurisdiction

Multiple Choice

1. Adjustments to inventory can be made in QBO:
    a. to the current quantity of inventory on hand only.
    b. to the current value of inventory on hand only.
    c. to both the current value and current quantity of inventory on hand.

2. When sales tax is charged to a customer, the amount is credited to _____.
    a. an accounts payable account type
    b. an income account type
    c. an other current liability account type
    d. a sales tax payable account type

3. It is possible, in QBO, to:
    a. delete an account by merging the account with another.
    b. permanently delete any account.
    c. permanently delete revenue or expense accounts.
    d. separate two accounts that have been merged.

4. A deleted account in QBO:
    a. can be used in transactions.
    b. can be used to filter reports.
    c. can be used in the search function.
    d. None of the above statements are true.

5. Recording proceeds from a bank loan could be done:
    a. through a general journal entry.
    b. by entering a deposit.
    c. either by creating a general journal entry or by entering the transaction as a deposit.

ASSIGNMENTS

**Assignment
8A**

**Math
Revealed!**

Background information: Martin Smith, a college student and good friend of yours, had always wanted to be an entrepreneur. He is very good in math so, to test his entrepreneurship skills, he decided to set up a small math tutoring company serving local high school students who struggle in their math courses. He set up the company, Math Revealed!, as a corporation in 2018. Martin is the only owner. He has not taken any distributions from the company since it opened.

The business has been successful so far. In fact, it's been so successful he has decided to work in his business full time now that he's graduated from college with a degree in mathematics.

He has decided to start using QuickBooks Online to keep track of his business transactions. He likes the convenience of being able to access his information over the Internet. You have agreed to act as his accountant while you're finishing your own academic program.

He currently has a number of regular customers that he tutors in Pre-Algebra, Algebra, and Geometry. His customers pay his fees by cash or check after each tutoring session but he does give terms of Net 15 to some of his customers. He has developed the following fee schedule:

Name	Description	Rate
Refresher	One-hour session	$40 per hour
Persistence program	Two one-hour sessions per week	$75 per week
Crisis program	Five one-hour sessions per week	$150 per week

The tutoring sessions usually take place at his students' homes but he recently signed a two-year lease on a small office above a local coffee shop. The rent is only $200 per month starting in January 2019. A security deposit of $400 was paid in December 2018.

The following equipment is owned by the company:

Description	Date placed in service	Cost	Life	Salvage Value
Computer	7/1/18	$3,000	36 months	$300
Printer	7/1/18	$ 240	24 months	$ 0
Graphing Calculators (2)	7/1/18	$ 294	36 months	$ 60

All equipment is depreciated using the straight-line method.

As of 12/31/18, he owed $2,000 to his parents who initially helped him get started. They are charging him interest at a 6% annual rate. He has been paying interest only on a monthly basis. His last payment was 12/31/18.

Over the next month or so, he plans to expand his business by selling a few products he believes will help his students. He has already purchased a few items:

Category	Description	Vendor	Quantity On Hand	Cost per unit	Sales Price
Books and Tools					
	Geometry in Sports	Books Galore	20	12	16
	Solving Puzzles: Fun with Algebra	Books Galore	20	14	18
	Getting Ready for Calculus	Books Galore	20	15	20
	Protractor/Compass Set	Math Shack	10	10	14
	Handheld Dry-Erase Boards	Math Shack	25	5	9
	Notebooks (pack of 3)	Paper Bag Depot	10	15	20

2/28/19

✓ You call Martin at home and tell him that the bank balance is very low. He meets with his banker at City Bank of Sacramento and explains the situation. The bank agrees to provide a $2,500 loan at 6% based on Martin's personal credit. The loan is set up to be repaid over a 12-month period ($215.17 per month including interest). You record the deposit of $2,500 into the company's checking account. **TIP:** You're going to need to set up a new account for this loan. Think carefully when choosing the **account type**.

✓ Your friend, Samantha Levin, agrees to come in to help Martin count the inventory on hand.

• She counts the inventory at the end of the day and gives you this list:

Taken by Samantha Levin	Inventory Count Sheet—2/28	Unit of Measure	Quantity on Hand
Books and Tools			
	Dry Erase boards	Items	13
	Kit	Items	12
	Modeling	Items	10
	Notebooks	Packages of 3	3
	Puzzles	Items	19
	Ready	Items	20
	Sports	Items	2
Math Games			
	Console	Items	5
	Equations	Items	5
	Fractions	Items	5
	Ratios	Items	5

✓ You do a few rechecks to make sure the count is correct, which it is. You adjust the inventory quantities in QBO to agree to the count. **TIP:** You can either add all products to the **inventory adjustment** window and change only those **items** that differ from the count, or you can compare the count sheet provided above to the Product/Service List in QBO first and then add only those **items** that need adjustment to the window.

- You talk to Martin about the shortages. He believes that some of the items were probably used by the tutors during the Mathmagic Clinic. You decide to charge the inventory adjustment to a new "Teaching supplies expense" account (a sub-account of **Office Costs**). You use account number 642.

- You use FebInvAdj as the **reference no.**

- **TIP:** To check your accuracy, click **Save**. Click **More** and select **Transaction journal**. The total adjustment should be $40.

✓ Because Samantha is willing to stay a bit longer, you ask her to count the supplies on hand. She tells you that there is $52.79 worth of office supplies on hand. You adjust the supplies accounts appropriately.

✓ It took Samantha only two hours to count the inventory and supplies. You write her a check (#1123) for $30 ($15 per hour) and charge the amount to the **Contract Labor** account.

✓ You get ready to pay your sales tax liability.

- You review your **Sales Tax Liability** report. The total tax liability for February sales is $17.98. (Most of your product sales were made to the Center for Academic Excellence, a reseller of the products.)

- You remit your taxes using Check #1124.

  ○ **TIP:** QBO will not allow you to use the normal process for remitting sales tax payments (as outlined in the chapter) if you're completing this assignment before March 2019. If that's the case, create a **check** to the Board of Equalization instead and charge the **California State Board of Equalization Payable** account for the $17.98.

After month end:

✓ You receive the February bank statement. You see that the bank charged a $20 processing fee for the NSF check from Kim Kowalski. You enter the charge when you reconcile the statement to your records.

CITY BANK OF SACRAMENTO
51 Capital Avenue
Sacramento, CA 95822 (916) 585-2120

Your Name Math Revealed!
3835 Freeport Blvd
Sacramento, CA 95822
Account # 1616479   **February 28, 2019**

	CREDITS	CHARGES	BALANCE
Beginning Balance, January 1			$4,757.21
2/1, Check 1103, Kathy's Coffee		$ 25.00	4,732.21
2/1, Check 1105, Samantha Levin		60.00	4,672.21
2/4, Check 1110, Martin Smith		1,500.00	3,172.21
2/4, Check 1112, Pro Spaces		200.00	2,972.21
2/8, Deposit	$ 274.40		3,246.61
2/8, Deposit	850.00		4,096.61
2/12, Check 1106, 24 Hour Quick Stitch		220.00	3,876.61
2/12, Check 1108, Parent's Survival Monthly		80.00	3,796.61
2/20, Deposit	117.60		3,914.21
2/20, Check 1111, Student		200.00	3,714.21
2/20, Check 1115, Sacramento Utilities		85.00	3,629.21
2/20, Check 1114, Prime Visa Company		1,247.75	2,381.46
2/20, Charge for Kowalski NSF Check		100.00	2,381.46
2/20, Service fee		20.00	2,361.46
2/23, Deposit	1,498.14		3,759.60
2/25, Check 1112		15.16	3,744.44
2/27, Deposit	446.00		4,190.44
2/27, Check 1122, Pro Spaces		200.00	3,990.44
2/28, Deposit	2,500.00		6,490.44
Ending Balance, 2/28			$6,490.44

✓ You receive the credit card statement in the mail. You start to reconcile the account and notice that there's a gas charge for $21 that you haven't recorded. Martin apologizes for not submitting the receipt. You record the charge, finish the reconciliation, and set up the balance for payment later. **TIP:** You can click the ➕ icon to add the gas charge without leaving the reconciliation.

PRIME VISA COMPANY
55 Wall Street
New York, NY 10005

Your Name Math Revealed!
3835 Freeport Blvd
Sacramento, CA 95822
Account # 212456770439   **February 28, 2019**

	PAYMENTS	CHARGES	BALANCE
Beginning Balance, January 1			$1,247.75
2/7—Good Sleep Inn		$530.00	1,777.75
2/7—LA Gasoline Stop		45.00	1,822.75
2/15—Payment	$1,247.75		575.00
2/20—Cardinal Gas & Snacks		21.00	596.00
2/27—Dick's Diner		19.50	615.50
Ending Balance, 2/28			$ 615.50

Minimum Payment Due: $10.00   **Payment Due Date: March 15**

✓ You review the account balances and make additional adjusting journal entries for February (dated 2/28) as needed, carefully considering the following:

- Your last loan payment was made on 2/27 and covered interest through 2/28.
- You review your revenue and unearned revenue accounts to make sure all earned revenue (and only earned revenue) is recognized.
  - ○ For the revenue account, you check to make sure that the tutoring sessions billed in February were completed in February. All the income billed in February was earned in February so you don't make any adjustments.
  - ○ For Unearned revenue, you review the entries made in January. The unearned revenue for Annie Wang at the end of January was for sessions held in February. The unearned revenue for Teacher's College was for a workshop held in February. You make the appropriate entry to properly recognize any February revenue.
- You look at the adjusting journal entries made in January. You make entries for depreciation and prepaid accounts as needed.
  - ○ TIP: For depreciation, you will need to add depreciation for the shelving placed in service on 2/1. The cost was $649. You think the shelving will have a $49 salvage value. You depreciate it over the lease term (24 months). Don't forget to depreciate all the items purchased in prior months. The depreciation amount for those items will be the same as the entry in January.
  - ○ TIP: For prepaids, look at all the prepaid accounts on the balance sheet. Should any of them be adjusted? Look at the profit and loss statement. Are there expenses recorded that shouldn't be recognized in February? Are there expenses that should have been recorded but haven't been? It's often very helpful to be able to compare months when doing month-end work. Consider customizing the profit and loss report by changing the dates to 1/1 to 2/28 and selecting Months in the Display columns by dropdown menu.
- You realize you forgot to pay yourself for work done in February. You create an account called "Accrued Expenses" (Account #221) and record the $300 due you for your accounting work. (TIP: Use other current liabilities as the detail type.)

✓ You review your chart of accounts.

- You aren't using the Exam Proctoring account (Account #410) so you delete the account (make it inactive).
- You decide to move the $450 paid to Les & Schmidt for the marketing study out of Professional Fees and into a new Marketing Expense account. You use account #632.

Check numbers 2/28

Checking account balance:......................$ 2,806.46
Net income for the two months ending 2/28:.......$ 4,805.82
Total assets: $14,036.75
Total liabilities: ....$ 6,260.93

Reports to create for Chapter 8:

All reports should be in portrait orientation.

- Journal (2/28 entries only)
- Balance Sheet as of 2/28
- Profit and Loss for February (with year to date column included)
- Inventory Valuation Summary as of 2/28
- Bank Reconciliation Summary 2/28

Background information: Sally Hanson, a good friend of yours, double majored in Computer Science and Accounting in college. She worked for several years for a software company in Silicon Valley but the long hours started to take a toll on her personal life.

Last year she decided to open up her own company, Salish Software Solutions (a corporation). Sally currently advises clients looking for new accounting software and assists them with software installation. She also provides training to client employees and occasionally troubleshoots software issues.

She has decided to start using QuickBooks Online to keep track of her business transactions. She likes the convenience of being able to access financial information over the Internet. You have agreed to act as her accountant while you're working on your accounting degree.

Sally has a number of clients that she is currently working with. She gives 15-day payment terms to her corporate clients but she asks for cash at time of service if she does work for individuals. She has developed the following fee schedule:

Assignment
8B

**Salish Software
Solutions**

MBC

Name	Description	Rate
Select	Software Selections	$500 flat fee
Set Up	Software Installation	$ 50 per hour
Train	Software training	$ 40 per hour
Fix	File repair	$ 60 per hour

Sally rents office space from Alki Property Management for $800 per month.
The following furniture and equipment is owned by Salish:

Description	Date placed in service	Cost	Life	Salvage Value
Office Furniture............	6/1/18	$1,400	60 months	$200
Computer	7/1/18	$4,620	36 months	$300
Printer..................	5/1/18	$ 900	36 months	$ 0

All equipment is depreciated using the straight-line method.

As of 12/31/18, she owed $3,500 to Dell Finance. The monthly payment on that loan is $150 including interest at 5%. Sally's last payment to Dell was 12/31/18.

Over the next month or so, Sally plans to expand her business by selling some of her favorite accounting and personal software products directly to her clients. She has already purchased the following items.

Item Name	Description	Vendor	Quantity On Hand	Cost per unit	Sales Price
Easy1	Easy Does it	Abacus Shop	15	$100	$175
Retailer...........	Simply Retail	Simply Accounting	2	$400	$700
Contractor.........	Simply Construction	Simply Accounting	2	$500	$800
Organizer	Organizer	Personal Solutions	25	$ 25	$ 50
Tracker	Investment Tracker	Personal Solutions	25	$ 20	$ 40

2/28/19

✓ Sally meets with her banker at Sacramento City Bank. She wants to have easy access to funds in case a good opportunity comes along. The banker explains that with a line of credit, Sally can borrow as much as she needs up to the credit line maximum. Only interest (on any unpaid balance) will be due on a monthly basis although Sally can make principal payments at any time. The bank agrees to provide Sally with a $5,000 line. Interest will be set at 6%. Interest payments will be due on the last day of the month. The line will have a term of one year. Sally doesn't borrow on the line today but you set up the account so it's ready for the future. **TIP:** Think carefully when choosing the **account type**.

✓ Oscar Torres agrees to come in to count the inventory on hand.

- He counts the inventory at the end of the day and gives you this list:

Taken by Oscar Torres	Inventory Count Sheet—2/28	Unit of Measure	Quantity on Hand
Accounting Products			
	Contractor	Items	3
	Easy1	Items	10
	Retailer	Items	3
Management Products			
	Engineering	Items	2
	Legal	Items	2
	Medical	Items	2
	Organizer	Items	28
	Tracker	Items	19

- You do a few rechecks to make sure the count is correct, which it is.

- You're a little surprised that so many **Organizers** are missing. You discuss it with Sally but neither of you can come up with an explanation. You decide to keep a closer eye on the storage cabinet in the future.

- You make an adjustment for the inventory count, charging the differences to a new **cost of goods sold type** account called Inventory Adjustments (#509). You use Feb-InvAdj as the **reference no**. **TIP:** You can either add all products to the **inventory adjustment** window and change only those **items** that differ from the count or you can compare the count sheet provided above to the Product/Service List in QBO first and then add only those **items** that need adjustment to the window.

- **TIP:** To check your accuracy, click **Save**. Click **More** and select **Transaction journal**. The total adjustment should be $95.

✓ You go ahead and look at the amount of office supplies there are on hand. You estimate the cost at $225.

✓ It took Oscar an hour to count the inventory. You write him a check (#1122) for $30 and charge the amount to a new Contract labor expense account (#609). You set it up as a subaccount of **Labor Costs**.

✓ You get ready to pay your sales tax liability.

- You review your **Sales Tax Liability** report. The total tax liability for February sales is $82.50.

- You remit your taxes using Check # 1123.

  ○ **TIP:** QBO will not allow you to use the normal process for remitting sales tax payments (as outlined in the chapter) if you're completing this assignment before March 2019. If that's the case, create a check to the **Board of Equalization** instead and charge the **California State Board of Equalization Payable** account for the $82.50.

After month end:

✓ You receive the credit card statement in the mail. You start to reconcile the account and notice that there's a $21.85 charge from Screamin' Beans Coffee that you haven't recorded. Sally searches through her desk and finds the receipt for 2/5. She had taken a couple of people from Butter and Beans out for coffee. You consider this a client relations expense. **TIP:** You can click the ➕ icon to add the charge without leaving the reconciliation.

✓ You finish the reconciliation and set up the balance for payment later. You use Feb19 as the **Bill no**.

PRIME VISA COMPANY
55 Wall Street
New York, NY 10005

Your Name Salish Software Solutions
3835 Freeport Blvd
Sacramento, CA 95822
Account # 646630813344

February 28, 2019

	PAYMENTS	CHARGES	BALANCE
Beginning Balance,			$1,210.00
1/31, Payment	$1,210.00		0.00
2/4, AAASP		$175.00	175.00
2/5, Screamin' Beans		21.85	196.85
2/11, Top Of The Hill		42.66	239.51
2/11, Bell Gas		35.00	274.51
2/11, The Franciscan		235.85	510.36
2/22, Roscoe's		28.50	538.86
Ending Balance, 2/28			$ 538.86

Minimum Payment Due: $10.00   **Payment Due Date: March 15**

✓ You receive the February bank statement. You see that the bank charged a $20 processing fee for the NSF check from Dew Drop Inn. You enter the charge when you reconcile the statement to your records.

SACRAMENTO CITY BANK
1822 Capital Avenue
Sacramento, CA 95822 (916) 585-2120

Your Name Salish Software Solutions
3835 Freeport Blvd
Sacramento, CA 95822
Account # 855922

February 28, 2019

	CREDITS	CHARGES	BALANCE
Beginning Balance, February 1			$11,630.00
2/1, Check 1114, Alki Property Management		$ 800.00	10,830.00
2/1, Check 1100, Marie Elle		75.00	10,755.00
2/1, Check 1113, Student		250.00	10,505.00
2/4, Check 1108, Abacus Shop		840.00	9,665.00
2/6, Check 1115, Dell Finance		150.00	9,515.00
2/6, Check 1111, Western Phone Company		108.95	9,406.05
2/8, Deposit	$1,060.85		10,466.90
2/8, Deposit	2,500.00		12,966.90
2/12, Check 1112, Sally Hanson		2,500.00	10,466.90
2/12, Check 1109, Entrepreneur Magazine		150.00	10,316.90
2/12, Deposit	300.00		10,616.90
2/14, Check 1110, Sacramento Light & Power		105.00	10,511.90
2/15, Deposit	323.40		10,835.30
2/15, Check returned for insufficient funds		300.00	10,535.30
2/18, Fee for NSF check		20.00	10,515.30
2/18, Check 1116, Capital Three		1,210.00	9,305.30
2/20, Deposit	3,700.00		13,005.30
2/27, Deposit	400.00		13,405.30
Ending Balance, 2/28			$13,405.30

✓ You review the account balances and make additional adjusting journal entries for February (dated 2/28) as needed, carefully considering the following:

- You review your revenue and unearned revenue accounts to make sure all earned revenue (and only earned revenue) is recognized.
  - For the revenue accounts, you check with Sally to make sure that all the hours and fees billed in February were completed in February. All the income billed in February was earned in February so you don't need to defer any of that revenue.
  - For **Unearned revenue**, you review the entries made in January. The unearned revenue for Butter and Beans at the end of January was for the remaining 20 hours of work billed on Invoice 1009. Sally lets you know that all that work has now been completed. The unearned revenue for Albus Software was for a workshop held in February. You make the appropriate entry to properly recognize February revenue.
- You look at the adjusting journal entries made in January. You make entries as needed.
  - **TIP:** For depreciation, you will need to add depreciation for the cabinets placed in service on February 1st. The cost was $1,500. Sally doesn't think there will be any resale value at the end of the service life. You depreciate the cabinets over the service life (5 years). Don't forget to depreciate all the items purchased in prior months. The depreciation amount for those items will be the same as the entry(ies) in January.
  - **TIP:** You made the last payment to Dell Finance on 2/1. The $150 payment covered January interest ($14.58) and reduced the loan balance by $135.42.
  - **TIP:** For prepaids, look at all the prepaid accounts on the balance sheet. Should any of them be adjusted? Look at the profit and loss statement. Are there expenses recorded that shouldn't be recognized in February? Are there any expenses that weren't recorded that should be? It's often very helpful to be able to compare months when doing month-end work. Consider customizing the **profit and loss** report by changing the dates to 1/1 to 2/28 and selecting **Months** in the **Display columns by** dropdown menu. It's often very helpful to be able to compare months when doing month-end work. Consider customizing the **profit and loss** report by changing the dates to 1/1 to 2/28 and selecting **Months** in the **Display columns by** dropdown menu.
- You realize you forgot to pay yourself for work done in February. You create an account called "Accrued Expenses" (Account # 221) and record the $350 due you for your accounting work.
✓ You review your chart of accounts.
  - You see that QBO has created a new **Cost of Goods Sold** account (Inventory Shrinkage). You realize this was created by default when you made your inventory adjustment entry. You decide to use the default account set up by QBO so you merge 509 Inventory Adjustments into the Inventory Shrinkage account. You want to keep the account number.
    - **TIP:** You will need to edit the Inventory Adjustment account by changing the name to Inventory Shrinkage and removing the account number. Then you can go back in and add the account number.

Check numbers 2/28

Checking account balance:. . . . .$ 6,529.30
Net income for the two months ending 2/28: . . . .$ 9,540.09
Total assets: $30,168.30
Total liabilities:. . . . .$ 7,128.21

Reports to create for Chapter 8:

- Journal (2/28 entries only)
- Balance Sheet as of 2/28
- Profit and Loss for February (with year to date column included)

- Inventory Valuation Summary as of 2/28
- Bank Reconciliation Summary 2/28

APPENDIX 8A DOWNLOADING BANK TRANSACTIONS INTO QBO

One of the most time-saving features of QBO is the ability to download banking and credit card transactions directly into the company file.

Although you will not be able to use this feature in the homework file, you can get a feel for the process in the test drive company.

Click **Banking** on the navigation bar. The screen will look something like this:

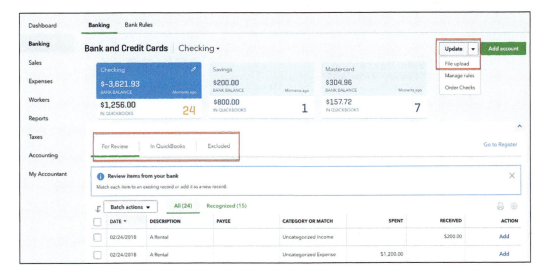

There are three fictitious accounts connected to the test drive company (Mastercard, Checking, and Savings).

Transactions are automatically downloaded nightly from most financial institutions although some institutions limit the number of downloads. Transactions can also be downloaded on demand by selecting **File upload** on the **Update** dropdown menu

For each connected account, downloaded transactions first appear on the **For Review** tab.

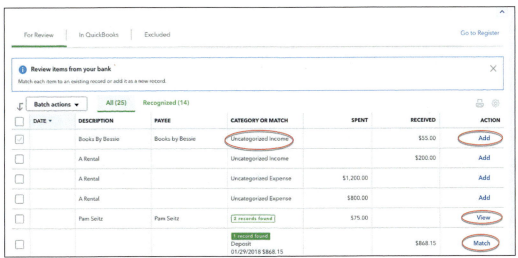

When transactions are downloaded, QBO will attempt to assign a **category** (account) to the transaction based on the name of the company or the description. If a similar transaction has occurred in the past, QBO will display a suggested **match**. QBO will select **uncategorized income** or **uncategorized expense** as the account when no suggestion or match is possible.

Clicking anywhere in the transaction row opens a more detailed window. For transactions without a **match**, the window would look something like this:

The user can change the account distribution in this screen by clicking the dropdown menu in the **category** field. If the transaction should be debited or credited to multiple accounts, the user can click **Split**.

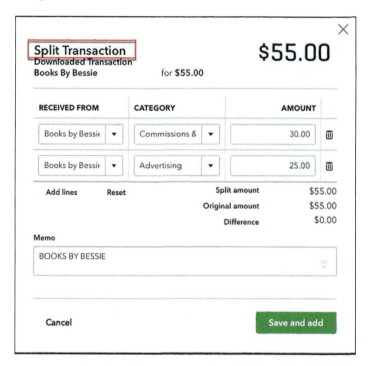

If **Find match** is toggled, QBO will open a list of transactions of the same type (deposit or withdrawal). The user can then select a similar transaction. If **Transfer** is toggled, the transaction can be moved to a different balance sheet account. **Transfer** could be used to record a loan payment or payment of a credit account balance.

For transactions with a **Match**, the detailed screen will look something like this:

Users can open the matched transaction for further review. Users can also look for other **matches** or use the **Transfer** option. If **Add** is toggled, the user can select an account or use **Split** to select multiple accounts.

Once the user is satisfied with the account (category) distribution, clicking **Add** or **Match** posts the transaction to QBO.

Added or **matched** transactions appear on the **In QuickBooks** tab.

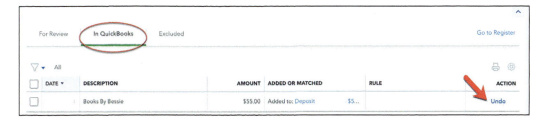

If a user incorrectly added or matched a transaction, clicking **Undo** will return the transaction to the **For Review** tab.

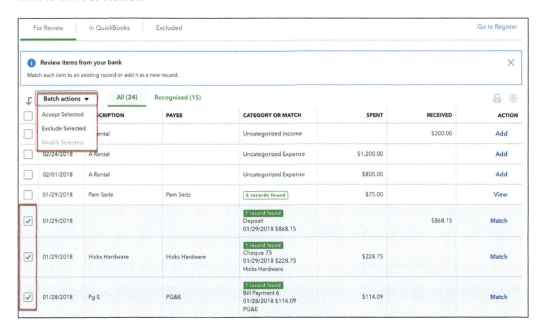

Reviewed transactions can be added to QBO in batches. A check is placed in each reviewed row, and **Accept Selected** is chosen in the **Batch actions** dropdown menu.

Occasionally, duplicate transactions will be downloaded into QBO. Using the **Exclude Selected** batch option will move the transactions to the **Excluded** tab. **Excluded** transactions can be deleted.

Setting Banking Rules

Users can set **rules** to guide QBO in managing downloaded transactions. To set rules, click **Banking** on the navigation bar and select the **Bank rules** tab.

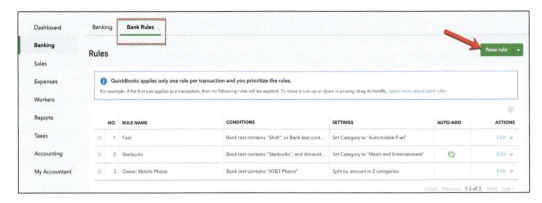

Three rules have been set in the test drive company.

Click **New rule** to create another option.

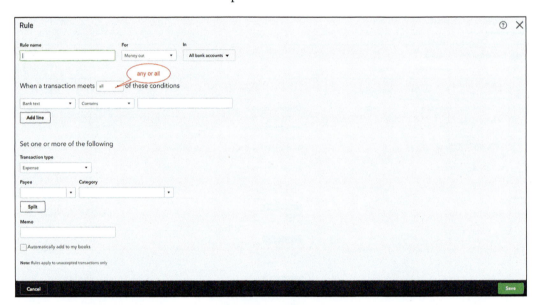

Rules can be set to apply to certain types of transactions or to transactions in certain accounts. Up to five conditions can be set and up to three results defined.

For each transaction, however, only one rule will be applied. The order in which the rules are listed on the **Rules** list determines the priority of application.

QuickBooks

SECTION FOUR

Paying Employees, Project Costing, and Billing for Time

Employee related functions (hiring, managing, paying, evaluating, terminating, etc.) are some of the most complex functions in business. They are also some of the most important. There aren't many businesses that can be successful over the long term if they don't have a strong employee base.

In accounting for payroll, the primary focus is on:

- Calculating, processing, and recording employee compensation.
- Recording, reporting, and remitting payroll taxes and employee benefits.

Those two processes may look straightforward but, as anyone who has worked in payroll could tell you, they can be very complex.

In Chapter 9 of this section, we'll cover basic payroll functions that would be used in all types of companies (service, merchandising, and manufacturing).

In Chapter 10, we will be covering how time records are used in various types of industries. Construction companies, law firms, accounting firms, architectural firms, and custom shops are just a few examples of the types of companies that would need the ability to track worker time. They need this information in managing their business. In many cases, they also need this information for billing purposes.

BEFORE WE MOVE FORWARD

Most of you are familiar with payroll either through prior accounting classes or through your own work experience but the following review of terms and concepts might be helpful.

Compensation

- Employees are usually paid in the form of a salary (usually stated as an annual or monthly amount) or an hourly wage. They can also be paid bonuses, commissions, overtime, etc. The total amount earned by an employee during a pay period is called the employee's **gross pay**. The amount of the paycheck (gross pay less taxes and other withholdings) is called the employee's **net pay**.

- Employers normally pay employees on a set payroll schedule. The schedule can be monthly, semi-monthly, weekly, etc.

Gross pay The amount an employee earns before any withholdings or deductions.

Net pay The amount of an employee's paycheck, after subtracting withheld amounts.

Payroll Taxes

- There are federal, state, and local payroll taxes. Some are the responsibility of the employer, some are the responsibility of the employee, and some are a shared responsibility of both employer and employee.

- Most payroll taxes are calculated as a percentage of a base amount. The percentage and the base will depend on the specific payroll tax.

- Federal taxes include:
  - Federal income (FIT)—Employee tax
  - FICA (Social Security and Medicare)—Shared tax (both employer and employee pay) except for the additional Medicare tax on compensation over $200,000 that is only paid by the employee.
  - Federal unemployment (FUTA)—Employer tax

- State taxes (for California as an example) include:
  - State income (SIT)—Employee tax
  - State unemployment (SUI)—Employer tax
  - Employment training (ETT)—Employer tax
  - State disability (SDI)—Employee tax

> **BEHIND THE SCENES** Employers are also required to maintain worker's compensation insurance in most states. In some states, that is paid through state government programs. In others, insurance coverage is purchased from private insurance carriers and would be entered and paid as a bill. In states that allow a company to be self-insured, a reserve would be accrued as a liability for potential claims.

Benefits

- Employers often provide benefits to employees. These might include:
  - Paid time off—might include sick, vacation, and family leave time
  - Medical insurance plan—can be fully or partially paid by employer
  - Retirement plan—can be fully or partially paid by employer

9

Payroll Activity

After completing Chapter 9, you should be able to:

1. Add and edit salaried and hourly employees.

2. Add and edit payroll items.

3. Create paychecks and payroll tax liability checks.

4. Create and modify payroll and payroll tax reports.

Objectives

WHAT IS THE PAYROLL CYCLE?

- Hire employees and obtain their tax information.

- Track employee time if appropriate.

- Calculate compensation and withholdings for each employee for the pay period.

- Distribute paychecks to employees with information about current and year-to-date payroll information.

- Calculate employer taxes.

- Remit employee withholdings and employer taxes.

- File required tax reports with federal and state taxing authorities.

In a manual system, managing employees and processing payroll is very labor intensive. If any employees are paid on an hourly basis, employees must submit timesheets used in calculating compensation. Withholdings and deductions must be determined for each employee before paychecks can be prepared. Employer taxes must be calculated and tax forms must be completed. And, of course, payroll transactions must be journalized and entered into the general ledger. These functions are done in all types of companies (service, merchandising, and manufacturing).

In QBO, various payroll services are available that calculate employee withholdings and employer taxes, create paychecks, and update the general ledger automatically. There are even software programs available from other vendors that allow for remote online entry of time by employees directly into QBO.

PAYROLL PLANS AVAILABLE IN QBO

Federal and state payroll tax rates and wage thresholds change fairly regularly. In a small company with limited accounting staff, it can be difficult to stay current with those changes. For an additional monthly fee, users can subscribe to one of QBO's payroll plans.

- Basic Payroll Plan
    - Automatically updates tax rates and withholding tables from federal and state taxing authorities.
    - Automatically calculates taxes and other deductions as part of creating employee paychecks.
    - Allows users to track paid time off, contributions to retirement plans, and various types of employee deductions.

- Enhanced Payroll Plan
    - Includes all features from the Basic Payroll plan.
    - Automatically completes federal and most state payroll tax returns and allows users to electronically file and pay taxes.
    - Allows users to print W-2s at year end.

Direct deposit of employee paychecks is available in both plans.

Most users subscribe to one of the payroll plans. Withholding, remitting, and reporting payroll taxes correctly is a critical business function and having accurate and up-to-date tax information is essential.

BEFORE WE START

The trial version of QBO that is provided for academic use by Intuit does not include access to either of the payroll plans so you will not be able to use the payroll features in the home-work assignments. You will, however, be able to learn about the payroll functions available in QBO using the test drive company. QBO uses Collins Paint and Wallpaper Services instead of Craig's Design and Landscaping Services in the payroll function. The screens are slightly different in a fully activated payroll system in QBO but the basic setup is the same.

TURNING ON PAYROLL

 HINT: At the time this book was written, Intuit was considering changing **Workers** to **Employees** in the navigation bar. This would be a name change only. The features and procedures should not have changed.

To turn on the payroll function in the test drive, click **Workers** in the navigation bar.

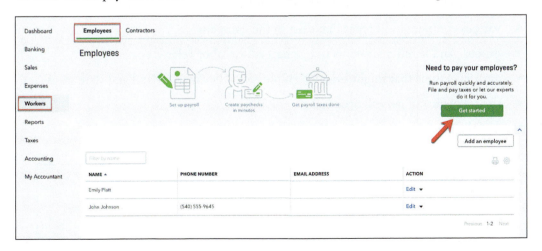

Click **Get Started**.

! **WARNING: You may experience some difficulty opening the test drive payroll function. It may take a minute or two to open payroll after you click Get Started or you may get a "technical difficulties" error message. Clearing your browser cache normally solves the problem. For information about how to delete temporary Internet files in your browser, go to https://community.intuit.com/articles/1145697-how-do-i-clear-the-temporary-internet-files-cache**

Once payroll has been turned on, the **My Payroll** screen (the Employee Center) screen will look like this:

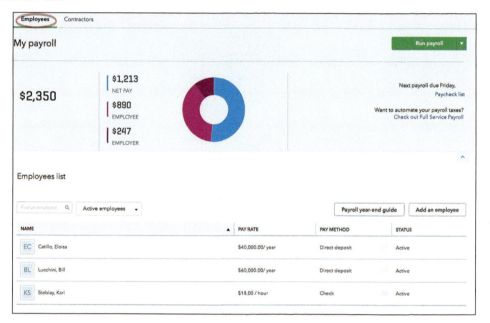

MANAGING PAYROLL SETTINGS

Before payroll can be processed, users must identify:

- various compensation types that exist in the company
- expense and liability accounts to be charged for labor related costs
- any deductions that might exist for employees other than federal and state taxes
- the frequency of payroll processing

Most of the payroll settings are set in the payroll preferences window in QBO.
Click the **gear** icon on the icon bar.

Click **Payroll Settings**.

> **!**   **WARNING: The payroll settings link will not be available unless payroll has been turned on. Refer back to the Before We Start section of this chapter for instructions. Remember, if you close the test drive company at any point, you will need to turn payroll back on to complete the Practice Exercises in this chapter.**

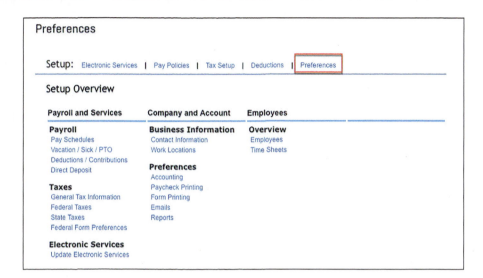

Setting Accounting Preferences for Payroll

Setting accounting preferences is a good place to start.

     Click the **Preferences** tab.

Click **Accounting Preferences**.

To simplify the process, we're going to use quite a few of the QBO default settings. Click **Next**.

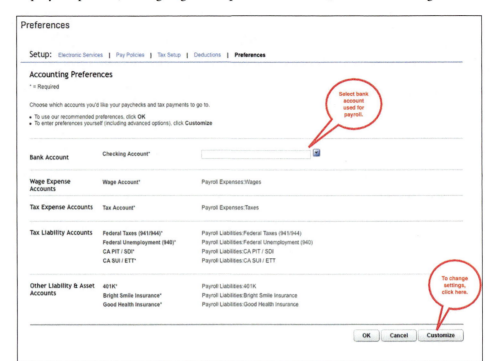

In **Accounting Preferences**, all of the general ledger accounts needed to make payroll entries are identified.

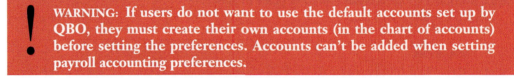

> **!** **WARNING: If users do not want to use the default accounts set up by QBO, they must create their own accounts (in the chart of accounts) before setting the preferences. Accounts can't be added when setting payroll accounting preferences.**

In its simplest form, the journal entry behind paychecks in QBO is:

    Wages and salaries expense
    Employer payroll taxes expense
        Payroll Taxes Payable
        Cash

The first account identified in the screen is the **Bank Account**. The payroll system in QBO recognizes (records) wages and salaries when they are paid so the account selected here will be credited when paychecks are recorded.

BEHIND THE SCENES Under GAAP (matching principle), labor expenses must be recognized when the salaries and wages are **earned** by the employees. If the "earned" accounting period is different from the "paid" accounting period, journal entries are required in QBO. For example, if salaries for the pay period January 16 to January 31 are paid on February 10th, a journal entry would be created to recognize (record) the payroll in January. That entry can then be reversed to offset the entry created when the payroll is processed in QBO on February 10th. Reversing entries are discussed further in Chapter 12.

In the **Wage Expense Accounts** section of the **Accounting Preferences** screen, the account(s) to be debited for wages and salaries expense is(are) identified. In the test drive company, all labor is charged to **Wages**, a subaccount of **Payroll Expenses**. Users can select a different account here as long as it's already set up in the chart of accounts.

In the **Tax Expense Accounts** section of the **Accounting Preferences** screen, the account(s) to be debited for employer payroll tax expenses is(are) identified. In the test drive company, all employer payroll taxes are charged to **Taxes**, a subaccount of **Payroll Expenses**. Again, users can select a different account here as long as it's already set up in the chart of accounts.

Both of these sections can be customized by clicking **Customize**.

There are now two new additional options for accounting for wages. Instead of debiting **Wages** for all employee compensation:

- different accounts can be used for different groups of employees.
  - Can also be for different individual employees

- different accounts can be used for different types of wages
  - Salary, hourly, overtime, sick leave, etc.

Similarly, there are two additional options for accounting for employer payroll taxes. Instead of debiting **Taxes** for all employer taxes:

- different accounts can be used for different groups of employees.
  - Can also be for different individual employees

- different accounts can be used for different types of taxes
  - Federal, state, etc.

There are fewer options in the **Tax Liability Accounts** and **Other Liability & Asset Accounts** sections of the **Accounting Preferences** screen.

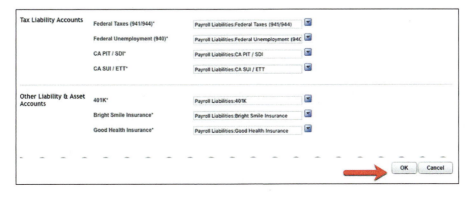

Users can either use the default accounts or select an alternate account(s).

A single general ledger account can be used for more than one wage expense, payroll tax expense, or liability account.

Click **OK** to save the account choices.

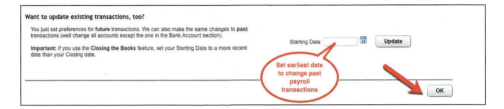

An option in the final screen allows users to change the accounts used for past transactions as well as future transactions.

Click **OK** to return to the **Preferences** screen.

Setting Pay Policies

Click the **Pay Policies** tab.

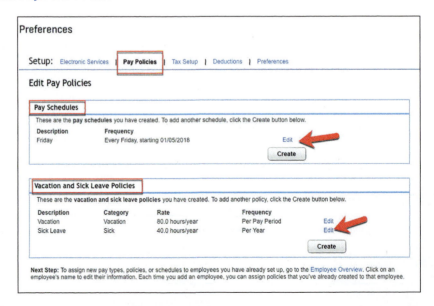

Payroll frequencies and vacation and sick leave policies are identified in the **Pay Policies** screen.

The default pay schedule is weekly. To change the schedule, click **Edit**.

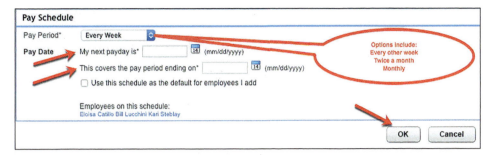

The pay frequency is set in the **Pay Period** dropdown menu. The options are:

- Every week

- Every other week

- Twice a month

- Monthly

The expected date of the next payroll is entered as is the period covered by the next paycheck.

Clicking **OK** displays a **confirmation schedule** of the next four pay periods.

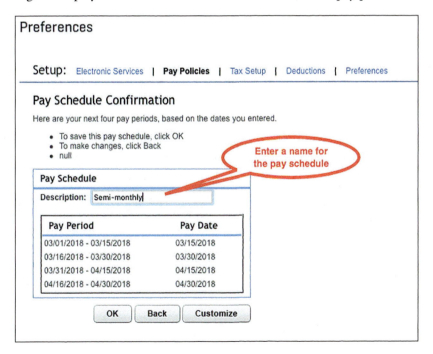

If the pay periods listed are incorrect, users can click **Back** to reset the payroll frequency, next payday, or next pay period. A name for the **pay schedule** is entered in this window.

Clicking **OK** again saves the settings.

Users can have multiple pay schedules. This would be necessary if, for example, some employees are paid weekly and others are paid semi-monthly (twice a month). Click **Create** on the **Edit Pay Policies** screen to set up additional pay schedules. The pay frequency options are limited to every week, every other week, twice a month, or monthly.

Vacation and sick leave policies are also set in the **Pay Policies** window. The default settings in QBO for each employee are: 80 hours of vacation and 40 hours of sick leave per year. Click **Edit** to change the policy for vacation or sick leave.

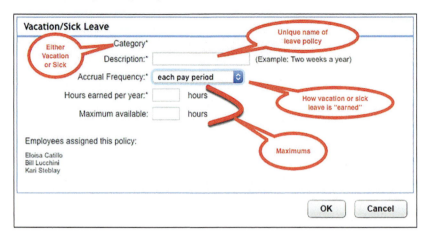

Vacation or sick leave can be accrued (accumulated) (up to the maximum):

- Pro rata over the annual number of pay periods

- Per hour worked

- At the beginning of each year

- On employee's anniversary date (hire date)

BEHIND THE SCENES For companies that allow employees to carry over some but not all unused vacation or sick leave, the **maximum available** hours would represent the total maximum unused hours from prior periods that can be carried over plus the maximum hours accrued for the current year.

Users can have different vacation/sick leave policies for different employees. Click **Create** on the **Edit Pay Policies** screen to set up additional leave policies.

BEHIND THE SCENES Multiple sick and vacation policies would need to be set up if a company provides different levels of benefits. For example, an employee might get two weeks of vacation pay for the first five years. Vacation leave might be increased to three weeks after the five-year anniversary. In other companies, employees in management positions receive more vacation time than non-management employees.

Setting Up Other Deductions and Company Contributions for Payroll

Many companies withhold amounts from employee checks unrelated to payroll taxes. A short list includes

- Employee-paid portion of certain benefits
    - Health insurance
    - Retirement plan contributions
- Deductions to meet legal or contractual agreements

- Union dues
- Repayments of cash advances
- Garnishments

Setting up deductions is done through the **Deductions** tab of the payroll **Preferences** screen.

Setting up a new deduction is fairly straightforward. Click **Add a New Deduction/Contribution**.

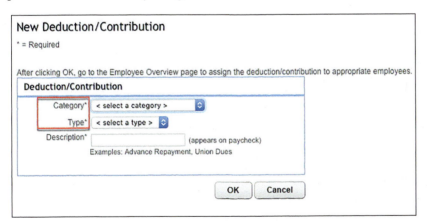

Category options include

- Health Insurance
- Retirement Plans
- Flexible Spending Accounts
    - Tax advantaged savings plan used to cover out-of5pocket medical costs
- HSA Plans
    - Tax advantaged savings plan used to cover out-of-pocket medical costs
- Other Deductions

The **type** options will differ depending on the **category** selected. **Categories** and **types** of payroll deductions will not be covered in detail in this textbook. However, you will have an opportunity to practice setting up a deduction in the next Practice Exercise.

Certain benefits (health insurance, retirement plan contributions) may be paid, in part or in full, by the employer. Details about the employer portion is entered in the employee record. This will be covered in the Managing Employees section of this chapter.

Other Payroll Settings

The **Setup Overview** screen includes links to other payroll related features.

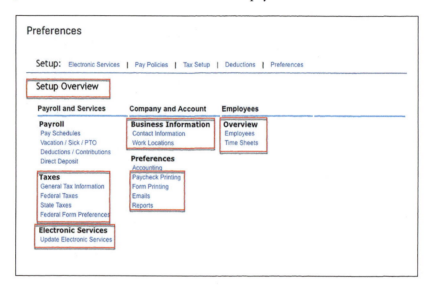

These include:

- Updating general business information

- Entering company tax information

- Setting up preferences for paycheck printing

- Enrolling in electronic filing services (federal and state)

- Links to employee records

- Setting preferences for entering time for hourly employees

PRACTICE EXERCISE

Set up payroll for Collins Paint and Wallpaper Services.

(Collins Paint wants to review the payroll settings for the company. The company doesn't need to track wages in separate accounts. It does need to set up a new vacation policy and a deduction for union dues.)

1. Click **Employees** on the navigation bar. **TIP:** The navigation bar in the Collins Paint test drive includes **Employees**, not **Workers**, as an option.

2. Click **Get Started**.

3. Reread the WARNING in the **Before We Start** section of this chapter if you experience technical difficulties.

4. Click the **gear** icon on the icon bar.

(continued)

5. Click **Payroll Settings**.

6. Click **Accounting Preferences** in the **Preferences** tab to review the accounts associated with payroll.

   a. Click **Customize**.

   b. Click the dropdown arrow next to the **Checking Account** field and select **Checking—Checking**.

   c. Click **I use different accounts for different groups of employees**.

       i. **Make a note** of the number of employees included in the list.

   d. Click **I use different accounts for different wages**.

       i. **Make a note** of the number of wage expense accounts displayed.

   e. Click **OK**.

   f. Click **OK** again to return to the **Setup Overview** screen.

7. Click the **Pay Policies** tab.

8. Click **Create** in the **Vacation and Leave Policies** section to set up a new vacation policy.

   a. Select **Vacation** as the **category**.

   b. Enter "Three Weeks" as the **Description**.

   c. Select **at beginning of year** as the **Accrual Frequency**.

   d. Enter "120" as the **Hours earned per year**.

   e. Enter "240" as the **Maximum available**.

   f. Click **OK**.

9. Click the **Deductions** tab.

   a. **Make a note** of the number of **deductions** set up in the test drive company.

10. Click **Add a New Deduction/Contribution** to set up a deduction for union dues.

    a. Select **Other deductions** in the **Category** dropdown menu.

    b. Select **Other after tax deductions** as the **Type**.

    c. Enter "Union Dues" as the **Description**.

    d. Click **OK**.

    e. Click **Yes** when prompted to assign the deduction to an employee.

    f. Click **Kari Steblay**.

    g. Click **Edit employee**.

    h. Click **Add a new deduction** in group 4.

    i. Select **Deduction/contribution** in the **Deduction/contribution or garnishment** dropdown menu.

    j. Select **Union Dues** in the **Deduction/contribution** dropdown menu.

    k. Select **$ amount** under **Amount per pay period** and enter "15" in the $ field.

    l. Leave the **Annual maximum** field blank.

    m. Click **OK**.

11. Click **Done**.

12. Click **Finish this later** when prompted about finishing the setup for **Kari Steblay**.

13. Click **Dashboard** to exit the Employee Center.

MANAGING EMPLOYEES

You know that payroll is complex. There are multiple payroll taxes and various other deduction types; there are a variety of different compensation plans; there are different payroll schedules (weekly, semi-monthly, monthly, etc.). You might guess that employee records will need to include considerable information as well. You would be correct!

Employee master records are maintained in the Employee Center accessed by clicking **Workers** in the navigation bar.

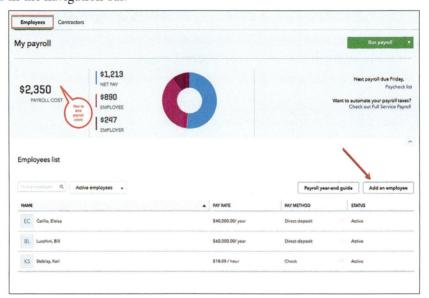

The main page of the Employee Center (**Employees** tab) lists basic payroll information about current employees and gives a snapshot of year-to-date payroll costs.

New Employee Setup

Employees can be added by clicking **Add an employee**.

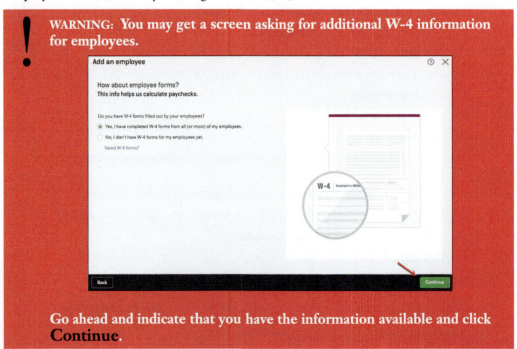

The setup screen looks like this:

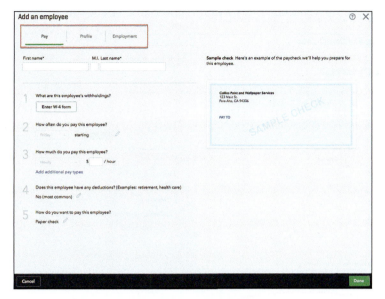

There are three tabs in the **Add an employee** screen.

- **Pay**
    - This is the initial window seen above.
    - Used for entering compensation and withholding information about the employee.

- **Profile**
    - Used for entering employee contact information, gender, and birth date.

- **Employment**
    - Used for entering hire date, work location, and status (active, terminated, etc.).
    - Used to enter an employee identification number (if used) and to set up custom fields.

Pay Tab

The **Pay** tab screen looks like this:

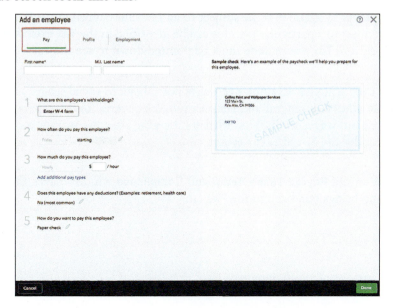

The employee's name is entered first.

The employee's payroll tax information is entered after clicking **Enter W-4 form**.

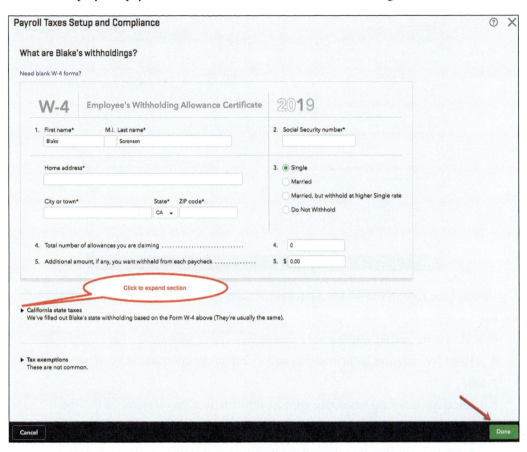

The **Social Security number** field is required. The filing status and number of withholding allowances claimed by the employee are also entered here.

QBO automatically sets up state taxes. The filing default status and number of allowances are based on the information provided by the employee for federal taxes. If necessary, the state information for the employee can be edited by clicking the triangle next to **state taxes** so that options are visible.

Every employee is assumed to be subject to all relevant payroll taxes. If a specific employee is not subject to a particular tax, this can be identified in the **Tax exemptions** section. (The triangle next to **Tax exemptions** must be pointed down to see the various options.)

> **BEHIND THE SCENES** Examples of wages not subject to social security would be wages paid to certain federal and state employees covered under separate retirement plans, and wages to disabled workers the year after the worker qualifies for disability under the Social Security Act.

Clicking **Done** in the **Payroll Taxes Setup and Compliance** window saves the payroll tax information and brings you back to the **Pay** tab.

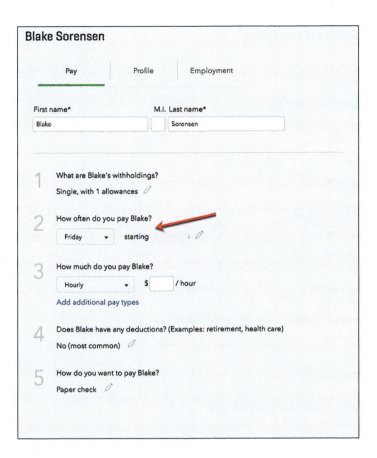

In the second section of the **Pay** tab, the employee pay schedule is identified. The default in the test drive company is weekly (on Fridays).

 HINT: The pay schedule and dates are automatically entered using the information included in the payroll settings. (Payroll settings were covered in the previous section of this chapter.)

Once a pay schedule is set, QBO automatically determines payroll processing dates, taking into account bank holidays and weekends, so that the company has employee paychecks ready on time.

   Pay types and compensation amounts are entered in the third section of the **Pay** tab.

Three default **pay types** are available (**Hourly, Salary**, and **Commission only**). Every employee must be assigned one of those **pay types**.

   If **Hourly** is selected, an hourly rate must be entered. If **Salary** is selected an annual, monthly, or weekly salary must be entered. No rate is necessary if **Commission only** is selected.

   Additional hourly **pay types** can be created for hourly employees but every hourly employee's record must include the basic **pay type** "Hourly."

Click **Add additional pay types**.

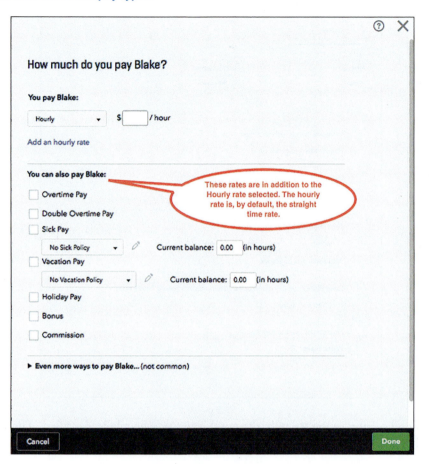

BEHIND THE SCENES Companies might want separate hourly rate **pay types** set up for night shift workers or workers in specific departments. Setting up separate **pay types** gives the company the ability to record wages paid to hourly workers in separate general ledger accounts.

Part-time salaried workers can be accommodated in QBO. If **Salary** is selected as the default **pay type**, the section expands to allow for identifying part-time workers. Checking the box for part-time workers brings up additional fields. For example, the employee setup screen for a half-time salaried worker might look something like this:

Additional **pay types** can be added to salaried employees.

For review purposes, a sample check is displayed on the right side of the screen when compensation data is entered.

The fourth section of the **Pay** tab is used to enter any additional deductions. Clicking the **pencil** icon next to the deductions question opens the following screen:

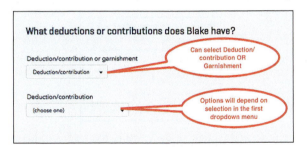

Deduction/contribution would be selected in the first dropdown menu to enter 401(k) contributions, medical/dental insurance contributions, union dues, etc. Additional fields will appear depending on the type of deduction selected. If the employer contributes to any of the employee benefits that information is entered here as well. For example, the final screen to enter a 401(k) contribution might look something like this:

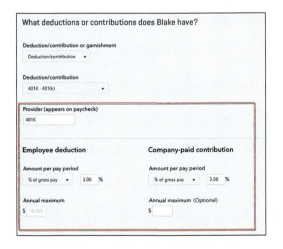

Garnishment would be selected in the top dropdown menu (under **Deduction/contribution or garnishment**) to enter deductions for legally mandated deductions such as child support or tax levies. The final screen for an employee subject to garnishment for child support payments would look something like this:

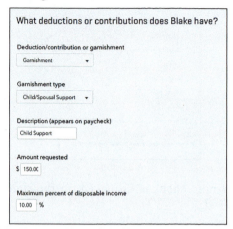

 HINT: More details on setting up deductions are included in the "Managing Payroll Settings" section of this chapter.

The fifth and final section of the **Pay** tab is used to identify the payment method. The following options are available.

A **Sample check**, based on the information provided in the employee set up, is displayed on the **Pay** screen. The check amounts are automatically updated as changes are made to employee compensation information. It would look something like this:

The **Profile** tab of the employee record is used primarily to enter contact information. The screen looks something like this:

The **Employment** tab of the employee record is used to enter information about the **status** of the employee.

> **BEHIND THE SCENES** Status here refers to current employment status and legal status. Form I-9 is the federal form used to verify the identity and employment authorization of individuals.

The initial screen looks something like this:

The **status** selected will change the fields available on the screen. For example, the screenshot above shows the fields available for an employee currently employed. Their hire date, birth date, work location, etc. should be entered. **Employee ID** numbers are not required but larger companies often assign ID numbers to all employees.

If the **status** is changed to **Terminated**, the screen looks something like this:

Clicking **Done** saves the information and closes the employee setup window.

PRACTICE

EXERCISE

Add an employee for Collins Paint and Wallpaper Services.
(Collins Paint hires Blake Sorensen to work half-time as an administrative assistant. Blake is paid twice a month.)

1. If you've logged or timed out since completing the last Practice Exercise, you'll need to set up payroll again before proceeding. Payroll can be set up by repeating the last Practice Exercise. (The Practice Exercise starts on page 9-14.)

2. Click **Employees** on the navigation bar.

3. Click **Add an employee**.

4. Enter the following information on the **Pay** tab.
   a.   First name: "Blake"
   b.   Last name: "Sorensen"

5. Click **Enter W-4 form** and enter the following information
   a.   **Social Security number**: "111-22-3333"
   b.   **Home address**: "212 Los Rios Drive"
   c.   **City or town**: "Sacramento"
   d.   **State:** "CA"
   e.   **ZIP code**: "95822"
   f.   **Marital status**: "Single"
   g.   **Total number of allowances you are claiming**: "1"
   h.   Leave the remaining fields as is.

6. Click **Done**.

7. In the dropdown menu, next to **How often do you pay Blake?**, select **Add new**.
   a.   Select **Twice a Month**.

(continued)

   b.   Click **Custom Schedule**.

       i.   **First payday of the month**: select 2nd

         1.   **Day:** End of Month

         2.   **Month:** previous

       ii.   **Second payday of the month**: select 17th

         1.   **Day**: 15th

         2.   **Month:** same

   c.   Enter "Semi-monthly" as the **name** of the pay schedule.

   d.   Click **Done**.

8. In the dropdown menu, next to **How much do you pay Blake?**, select **Salary**.

   a.   Enter "30,000" as the amount.

   b.   Select **per year** in the dropdown menu next to the amount.

   c.   Check **Blake works part-time**.

   d.   Enter "4" as the **hours per day** and "5" as the **days per week**.

9. Click the **pencil** icon under **Does Blake have any deductions?**

   a.   Select **Deduction/contribution** in the first dropdown menu.

   b.   Select **Good Health Insurance—Medical** in the second dropdown menu.

       i.   **Make a note** of the name of the dental insurance company in the dropdown menu.

   c.   In the **Employee deduction** section, select **$ amount** and enter "10."

   d.   In the **Company-paid contribution** section, select **$ amount** and enter "40."

   e.   Leave the other fields blank.

   f.   Click **OK**.

10. Leave **Paper check** as the payment method in the fifth section of the **Pay** tab.

11. **Make a note** of the **Net pay** on the **Sample check** displayed on the **Pay** tab.

12. Click **Done**.

13. Click the pencil icon to open the **Profile** tab.

   a.   Make sure the address is listed as 212 Los Rios Drive.

   b.   Click **Male** as the **Gender**.

14. Click to open the **Employment** tab.

15. Leave the **status** as **Active**.

16. Enter the current date as the **Hire date**. **TIP:** Formatting for dates must be: XX/XX/XXXX

17. Enter "6/12/1990" as the **Birth date**.

18. Leave the remaining fields as is.

19. Click **Done**.

Editing Employees

Changes can easily be made to employee records.

HINT: Changes to compensation and taxes would be effective for the first pay period **after** the change is made.

Editing employees is done through the Employee Center. Click **Workers** on the navigation bar to open the center.

The initial screen looks something like this:

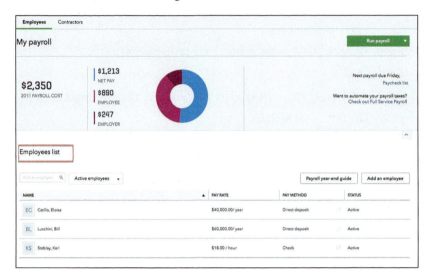

To edit an employee, click the employee name.

The employee record screen looks like this:

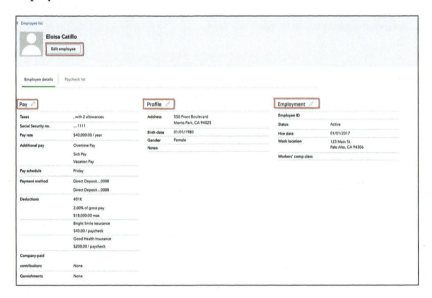

A specific tab can be edited by clicking the **pencil** icon next to the title (**Pay, Profile,** or **Employment**). Clicking **Edit employee** at the top of the screen allows you to edit all sections.

PRACTICE
EXERCISE

Edit employee records for Collins Paint and Wallpaper Services.

(Collins Paint changes payroll information for Eloisa Catillo and Bill Lucchini.)

1. If you've logged or timed out since completing the last Practice Exercise, you'll need to set up payroll again before proceeding. Payroll can be set up by repeating the Practice Exercise that starts on page 9-14.

2. Click Employees on the navigation bar.

3. Click Catillo, Eloisa.

   a. Click the pencil icon next to Pay.

   b. Click Enter W-4 form.

   c. Select Single in box 3.

   d. Click Done.

   e. Click Done again.

4. Click Employee list at the top left of the screen (right above Eloisa Catillo).

5. Click Bill Lucchini.

   a. Click Edit employee.

   b. Click the pencil icon next to Profile.

   c. Change the address to "475 North Ave."

   d. Click the Pay tab.

   e. Click the pencil icon next to Additional pay types in the third section "How much do you pay Bill?".

   f. Change Bill's salary to "65,000."

   g. Click Done.

   h. Click Done again.

   i. Click Finish this later.

6. Click Dashboard to exit out of the Employee Center.

PROCESSING PAYROLL

Creating Paychecks

The payroll function in QBO uses information from various sources within the company file. The sources are:

- Employee record (for pay rates).

- Timesheets, if applicable (for hours worked).

- Payroll settings (for underlying journal entry accounts).

> **! WARNING:** One piece of advice before we continue: Paychecks and payroll tax payments are two transaction types that can be difficult to correct in QBO. This is because the posting of a paycheck affects not only general ledger account balances but also employee payroll subsidiary records. (QBO maintains gross wages and employee tax withholding totals for each employee to facilitate preparation of payroll reports including year-end W-2s.)

Using Timesheets to Process Payroll

For hourly employees, time can be directly entered when paychecks are created in QBO or time can be entered using time sheets. Time sheet hours are then copied to the paychecks when payroll is processed.

To make the election, click the **gear** icon on the icon bar and select **Payroll Settings**.

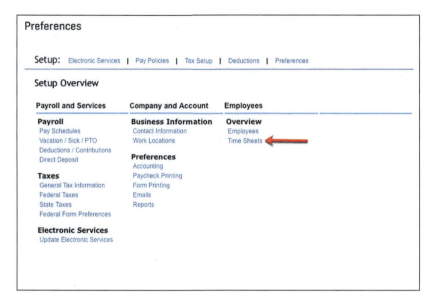

Click **Time Sheets**.

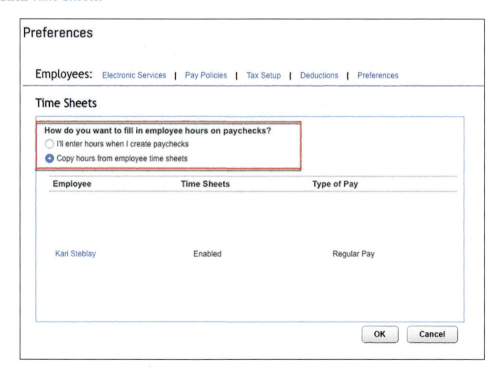

Copying hours from time sheets is the default in the test drive company.

Setting Up Time Tracking

Time can be tracked by type of work performed and customer (project), if necessary. Time included on timesheets can also be used for billing purposes. (Billing time will be covered in Chapter 10.) To turn on time tracking, click the **gear** icon on the icon bar and select **Account and Settings**.

Click the **Advanced** tab.

One or both options in the **Time tracking** section can be activated. Both are activated in the test drive company.

Service fields are used to enter the type of work performed.

Entering Timesheets

Timesheets can be used for salaried or hourly employees. They can also be used for independent contractors. If time is tracked for a salaried employee or an independent contractor, it would most likely be for tracking and/or billing purposes. Timesheets for hourly employees are used to create paychecks. Hourly employee timesheets can also be used for tracking and/or billing purposes.

> **HINT**: Time for hourly employees can also be entered directly into the paycheck without the use of timesheets.

Click the ➕ icon in the icon bar to access the appropriate form.

Although time can be entered as single activities, most companies would opt to use the **Weekly Timesheet** option.

The screen looks something like this:

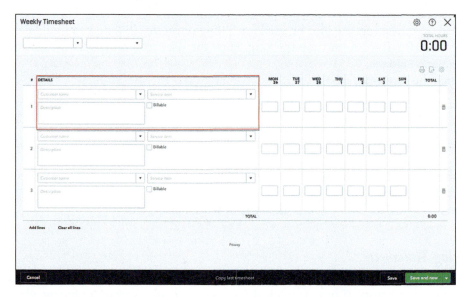

The **DETAILS** section of the timesheet must be filled in if employee time will be billed to a customer or if the company simply wishes to track time by customer or project. The **DETAILS** section includes the customer/project name, the type of service performed (**service item**) and whether the time is **billable** or not. The description is automatically updated when the **service item** is selected.

If employee time is not being tracked by customer, only the hours need to be entered.

A timesheet for an employee who worked 42 hours during a week (26 hours were billable to a client; 16 hours were not related to a specific customer) might look something like this:

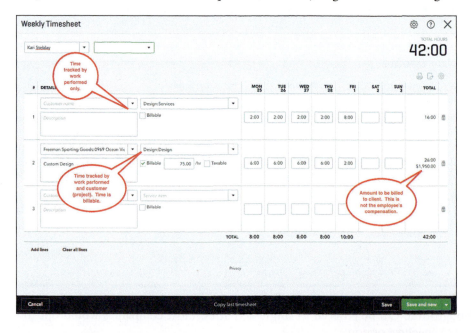

!   **WARNING: QBO currently does not have the ability to track overtime hours on timesheets. If an employee were eligible for overtime, the hours would need to be changed when the paycheck was created.**

If the hours are billable to a client, QBO will automatically display the billing rate identified in the **item** setup. The billing rate can be changed in the timesheet. The total amount of billable revenue is displayed in the **TOTAL** column for that row.

Click **Save and close** to save the timesheet.

Processing Payroll

To create paychecks, click the ✚ icon in the icon bar.

Click **Payroll**.

 HINT: You can also click **Workers** (or **Employees**) on the navigation bar and click **Run Payroll**.

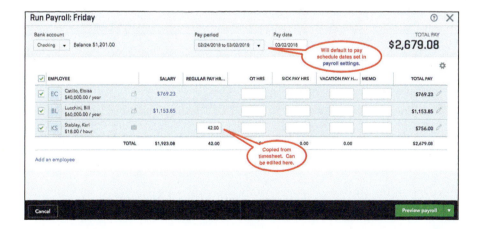

The hours from the timesheet will be automatically transferred to the pay screen for hourly employees. If the employee worked overtime, the hours should be changed before payroll is processed. The changed row would look like this:

Click **Preview payroll** for a final review of the data before paychecks are created.

The preview screen displays the net pay amount for each employee. If necessary, paychecks can be edited by clicking the **pencil** icon at the far right of each row.

The preview screen also displays the amount of employer payroll expense for the pay period.

Clicking **Submit payroll** saves the transactions.

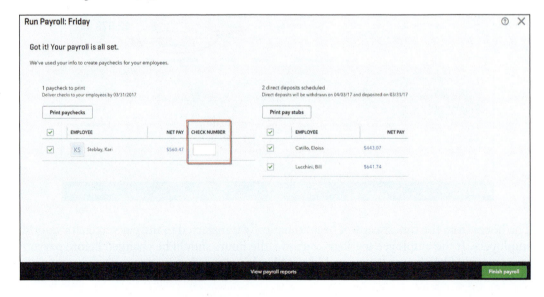

For employees receiving checks, the **check number** field should be completed.

Paychecks are recorded by clicking **Finish payroll**.

QBO will display the above message if any tax related information is missing for employees (employment dates, withholding information, etc.).

What is the underlying journal entry for a paycheck transaction?

QuickCheck
9-1

PRACTICE
EXERCISE

Prepare paychecks for Collins Paint and Wallpaper Services.
(Collins Paint pays employees on the last day of the pay period.)

1. If you've logged or timed out since completing the last Practice Exercise, you'll need to set up payroll again before proceeding. Payroll can be set up by repeating the Practice Exercise that starts on page 9-14.

2. Click the ➕ icon on the icon bar.

3. Click **Weekly Timesheet** to enter time for an hourly employee.

   a. Select **Kari Steblay** in the first dropdown menu.

   b. Select the first **full** week of next month in the date dropdown menu.

      i. A **full** week would include Monday through Sunday, all in the same month.

   c. On the first row in the **DETAILS** section:

      i. Select **Diego Rodriguez** as the **Customer name**.

      ii. Select **Design** as the **Service item**.

      iii. Check the **Billable** box. (Leave the rate at 75.00.)

      iv. Enter "8" in the fields for **MON**, **TUE**, and **WED**.

   d. On the second row in the **DETAILS** section:

      i. Uncheck the **Billable** box, if necessary.

      ii. Enter "8" in the fields for **THU** and **FRI**.

      iii. **TIP:** Kari was not working on customer projects on Thursday and Friday, so customer names and service items aren't necessary.

   e. Click **Save and close**.

4. Click the ➕ icon on the icon bar.

5. Click **Payroll** to process the payroll for the pay period.

6. Toggle **Friday**.

7. Click **Continue**.

8. Select the appropriate pay period (the pay period selected in Step 3b.).

   a. Check to make sure the 40 hours for **Steblay, Kari** appear in the **REGULAR PAY HRS** column.

(continued)

        i. You may have to enter the timesheet multiple times. Payroll in the test drive company can be inconsistent. If you're having trouble, try:

           1. Clicking **Save** and then **Save and close** after completing the timesheet.

           2. Making sure that the default payroll setting is set properly.

               a. Click the **gear** icon on the icon bar.

               b. Click **Payroll Settings**.

               c. Click **Time Sheets**.

               d. Make sure the option **Copy hours from employee timesheets** is selected.

        ii. Go back to the beginning of Step 5 if you need to re-enter timesheets.

    b. Click **Preview payroll**.

    c. **Make a note** of the **net pay** amount for **Bill Lucchini**.

    d. Click **Submit payroll**.

    e. Enter "5113" as the **CHECK NUMBER** for **Steblay, Kari**.

    f. Click **Finish payroll**.

9. Click **I'll do it later** if prompted to set up taxes.

Editing Paychecks

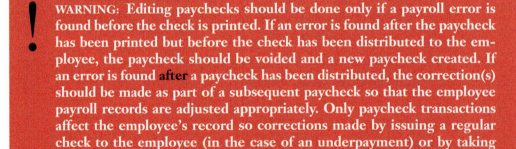

> **WARNING:** Editing paychecks should be done only if a payroll error is found before the check is printed. If an error is found after the paycheck has been printed but before the check has been distributed to the employee, the paycheck should be voided and a new paycheck created. If an error is found **after** a paycheck has been distributed, the correction(s) should be made as part of a subsequent paycheck so that the employee payroll records are adjusted appropriately. Only paycheck transactions affect the employee's record so corrections made by issuing a regular check to the employee (in the case of an underpayment) or by taking cash from an employee (in the case of an overpayment) would not adjust the employee records and should not be used.

To edit a paycheck, you must first open the paycheck form. Paycheck transactions can be found in the employee's record.

    Click **Employees** on the navigation bar.

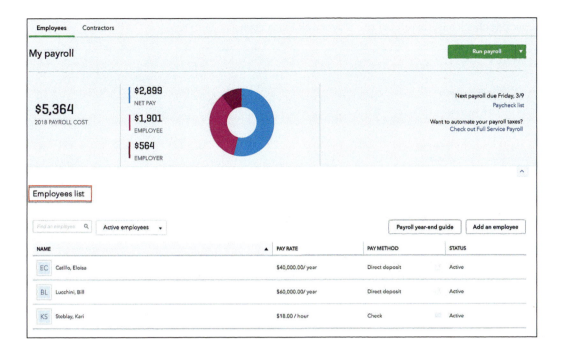

Click the name of the appropriate employee to open the employee record.

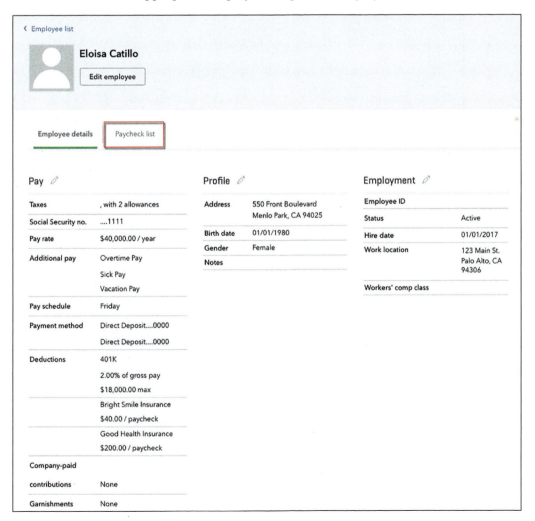

Past paychecks are listed on the **Paycheck list** screen.

The paychecks displayed can be filtered as needed. Open the check to be edited by clicking anywhere in the appropriate row.

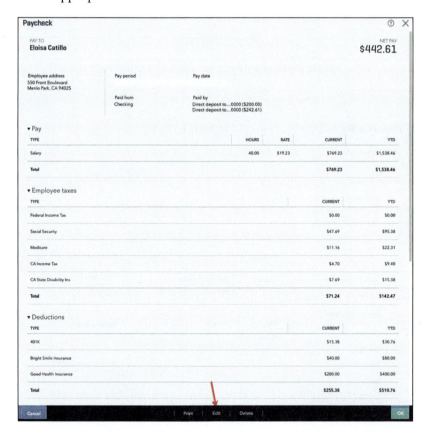

Click **Edit** to display all the components of the paycheck.

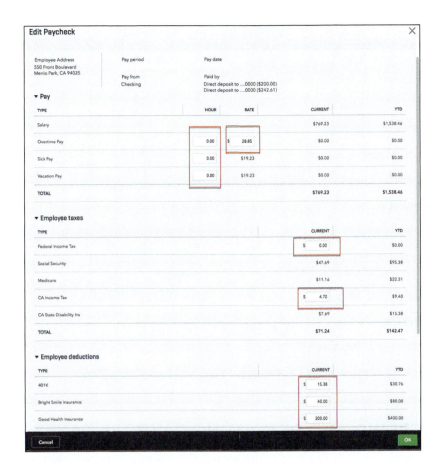

The items in the paycheck that can be changed in QBO will appear in boxes. There are restrictions on which items can be changed. QBO will allow you to change the following:

- All hours for hourly employees; only overtime, sick, or vacation hours for salaried employees.

- Overtime rates. (Salaries and straight-time rates cannot be changed once a paycheck has been recorded. Compensation changes can only be made in the employee's record.)

- Federal and state income tax withholding amounts.

- Employee deduction amounts (other than payroll tax withholdings).

No employer tax amounts can be changed by a user. Employer and employee payroll taxes (other than employee federal or state income tax withholdings) are changed automatically by QBO if hours or rates are changed.

 WARNING: Editing a paycheck should be done only if the check hasn't been issued OR if you're taking this class and made an error the first time through!

Edit a paycheck for Collins Paint and Wallpaper Services.
(The dental insurance premium was calculated incorrectly for Eloisa Catillo. The amount should have been $16. The paycheck has NOT been printed yet.)

PRACTICE
EXERCISE

(continued)

1. If you've logged or timed out since completing the last Practice Exercise, you'll need to set up payroll again before proceeding. Payroll can be set up by repeating the Practice Exercise that starts on page 9-14.

2. Click **Employees** on the navigation bar.

3. Click **Catillo, Eloisa**.

4. Click **Paycheck list**.

5. Check the box next to the most recent paycheck.

6. Click **Edit**.

7. Open the section to be changed by clicking the triangle next to **Employee deductions**.

8. Enter "80" as the amount for **Bright Smile Insurance**.

9. **Make a note** of the **net pay** amount for Eloisa at the top of the window.

10. Click **OK**.

11. Exit out of the window.

12. Click **Dashboard** on the navigation bar to close the Employee Center.

PROCESSING AND REPORTING PAYROLL TAXES

Payroll taxes are generally remitted to the appropriate taxing authorities quarterly, monthly, or semiweekly, depending on the particular tax and the size of the payroll. (Companies with large payrolls remit certain taxes more frequently.)

Here's a brief summary of some of the reporting and remittance requirements of the various types of payroll taxes:

- Federal income tax withholding and FICA taxes:
  - Employee taxes withheld and employer taxes are remitted together.
  - Taxes are deposited quarterly, monthly, or semiweekly, depending on the size of the payroll.
  - Form 941 is used to report wages and taxes and is filed quarterly.

- Federal unemployment taxes:
  - Taxes must be deposited periodically, depending on the size of the payroll.
  - Form 940, filed annually, is used to report wages and taxes.

- State taxes:
  - Each state sets the filing requirements for state payroll taxes.
  - Generally, states with a personal income tax match the state deposit requirements to the federal deposit requirements for federal income taxes and FICA.
  - Quarterly filings are common for other types of state payroll taxes.

Remitting (Depositing) Payroll Taxes

The process for remitting payroll taxes is similar to the process for remitting sales taxes collected from customers (covered in Chapter 8). QBO accumulates the payroll tax liabilities throughout the reporting period in the liability account designated in **payroll settings**.

Payroll tax liability checks are created through the **Payroll Tax Center**. The center is accessed by clicking **Payroll Tax** under **Taxes** in the navigation bar.

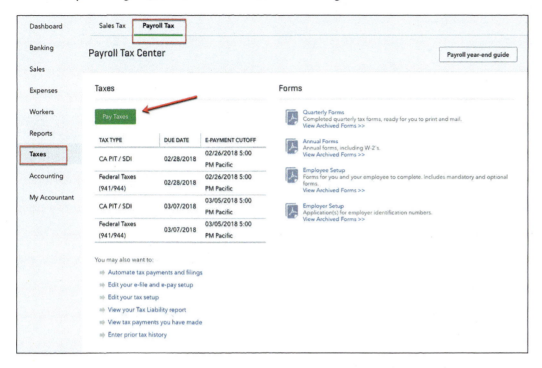

You may need to update some of the information in the test drive company. (If updating is not required, you'll go directly to the **Payroll Tax Center**.)

If you do need to update information, the following screen will appear.

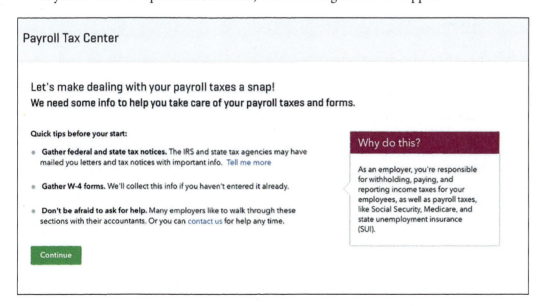

Click **Continue** and follow the prompts displayed.

In the **Payroll Tax Center**, users can remit current payroll taxes and review prior tax payments, view tax liability reports, and edit payroll tax settings. Links to various payroll tax forms are also included.

To remit taxes, click **Pay Taxes**.

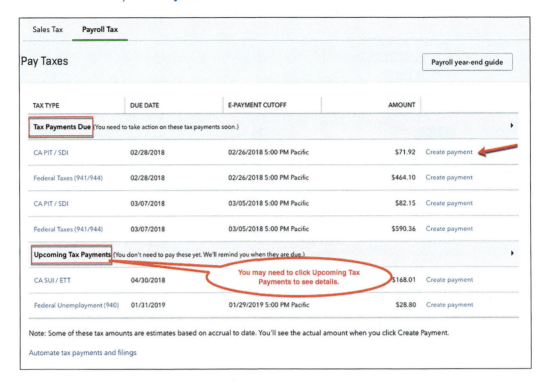

There are two sections on the screen **Tax Payments Due** and **Upcoming Tax Payments**. Due dates are automatically displayed by QBO.

To remit the taxes, click **Create payment** next to the tax type to be paid.

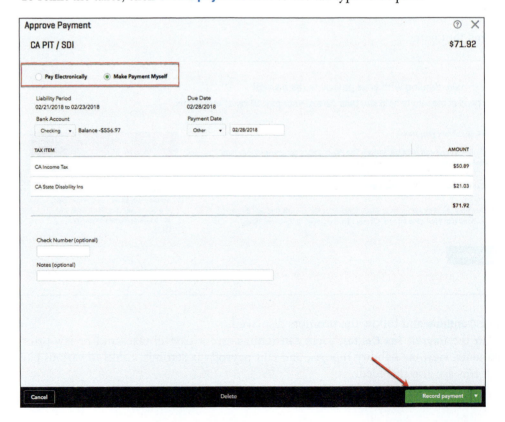

The next screen is the final chance to review the transaction. Although QBO allows you to change the bank account to be credited, any taxes that are remitted electronically will be drawn from the account set up in **Payroll Settings**, not the account selected here.

The payment date can also be changed. The default payment method is electronic. If a company manually remits payroll taxes, **Make Payment Myself** should be clicked.

Click **Record Payment** to save the transaction. (**E-pay** would be selected if payroll taxes are remitted electronically.) A confirmation message will be displayed.

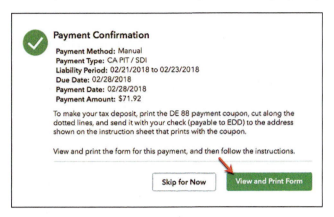

A coupon to attach to the check and instructions for remitting the tax are displayed if **View and Print Form** is selected.

 WARNING: Like sales tax payments, payroll liability checks cannot be edited. They must be voided (or deleted) and reissued if an error is made.

Remit payroll taxes for Collins Paint and Wallpaper Services.
(Collins Paint decides to deposit federal income taxes, FICA taxes, and state employee taxes early.)

1. If you've logged or timed out since completing the last Practice Exercise, you'll need to set up payroll again before proceeding. Payroll can be set up by repeating the Practice Exercise that starts on page 9-14.

2. Click **Taxes** on the navigation bar.

3. Click **Payroll Tax**.

4. Click **Pay Taxes**.
    a.   Click **Create payment** at the end of the **CA PIT/SDI** line.
        i.   This tax type will be in either the **Tax Payments Due** or **Upcoming Tax Payments** section, depending on **when** you are working the Practice Exercise.
    b.   Select **Make Payment Myself**.
    c.   Enter the current date as the **Payment Date**.
    d.   Click **Record payment**.
    e.   Click **View and Print Form** to see the coupon and instructions.

5. Click **Dashboard** to exit out of the **Payroll Center**.

PRACTICE EXERCISE

Editing Payroll Tax Liabilities

There is currently no feature available in QBO that allows users to adjust payroll tax liabilities. Technical support at Intuit should be contacted if changes need to be made.

Preparing Payroll Tax Forms

Federal and state payroll tax forms can be filed directly from QBO if the user has subscribed to a payroll tax plan. The forms are automatically completed by QBO at the end of the appropriate tax period.

The forms are accessed in the **Payroll Tax Center** accessed by clicking **Payroll Tax** under **Taxes** on the navigation bar.

Forms from the test drive company are not available to view.

Preparing Payroll Reports

There are a variety of payroll reports that summarize compensation and payroll tax transactions. Some of the most commonly used reports include:

- **Payroll Summary**
  - Summary by employee of components of gross pay, net pay, and employer taxes for the selected period.

- **Payroll Tax Liability**
  - Shows paid and unpaid payroll liability balances by type.

- **Employee Details**
  - Shows basic details about active employees (salary, deductions, contact information, etc.).

All payroll reports can be accessed through the **Payroll** section of **Reports**.

PRACTICE EXERCISE

Prepare the Payroll Summary report for Collins Paint and Wallpaper Services.

1. If you've logged or timed out since completing the last Practice Exercise, you'll need to set up payroll again before proceeding. Payroll can be set up by repeating the Practice Exercise that starts on page 9-14.

(continued)

2. Click **Reports** on the navigation bar.

4. Click **Payroll Summary** in the **Payroll** section.

 a. You may not be able to access any of the payroll reports in the test drive company. If you get an error message, ignore this Practice Exercise. You will not need to be able to access reports for your assignment.

5. Click **Dashboard** to exit out of the window.

Wage expense (gross payroll)	XXX	
Payroll tax expense (employer taxes)	XXX	
Cash (net pay)		XXX
Payroll taxes payable (employee + employer taxes)		XXX

ANSWER TO
QuickCheck
9-1

CHAPTER SHORTCUTS

Turn on payroll
1. Click **Workers**
2. Click **Turn on Payroll** (or **Choose your plan**)

Add an employee
1. Click **Employees**
2. Click **Add an employee**

Edit an employee
1. Click **Employees**
2. Click the name of the employee to change
3. Click **Edit Employee**

Pay an employee
1. Click the ➕ icon on the icon bar
2. Click **Payroll**

Edit a paycheck
1. Click **Employees**
2. Click employee to open employee record
3. Click **Paycheck list**
4. Click paycheck to be changed
5. Click **Edit**

Pay payroll liabilities
1. Click **Taxes**
2. Click **Payroll Taxes**
3. Click **Pay Taxes**

CHAPTER REVIEW (Answers available on the publisher's website.)

Matching
Match the term or phrase (as used in QuickBooks Online) to its definition.

1. employee status
2. payroll settings
3. pay type
4. pay frequency
5. paycheck
6. pay policies
7. pay schedule
8. profile

_____ a category of compensation

_____ transaction type used to record wage payments to employees

_____ tool available to pay employees in specific cycles

_____ how often employee wages are paid

_____ section in employee record where contact information and birth date are recorded

_____   place where preferences for tax, pay policies, and payroll accounts are identified

_____   indicator of employee's current standing as an employee

_____   available paid time off benefits offered by a company

Multiple Choice

1. W-4 information for new employees is entered in the _____ tab of the new employee record.
   a. Pay
   b. Profile
   c. Employment

2. Which of the following statements is true?
   a. Employees are limited to one **pay type**.
   b. An employee must be identified as either a salaried, hourly, or commission only employee.
   c. Salaried employees would never be eligible for overtime pay.
   d. Hourly employees can be assigned only one hourly pay rate.

3. Which of the following taxes are paid by both the employee and the employer?
   a. Federal withholding
   b. Federal unemployment
   c. FICA
   d. State withholding (if applicable)

4. Taxes withheld from employees are:
   a. remitted on or before the tax report due date, depending on the size of the employer.
   b. always remitted monthly.
   c. always remitted within three days of issuing paychecks.
   d. always remitted with the tax report.

5. Which of the following is not an expense of the employer?
   a. State unemployment
   b. Federal unemployment
   c. FICA
   d. All of the above are expenses of the employer.

ASSIGNMENT

Assignment 9

Collins Paint and Wallpaper Service

Academic licenses do not include access to payroll processing in QBO so you will not be working in your company file for this assignment. Instead, you will be recording some payroll transactions in the payroll practice exercise company (Collins Paint and Wallpaper Services).

> **WARNING:**
> - In order to avoid having to redo setup work make sure you complete each task before logging or timing out.
> - Payroll reports (the payroll summary report for example) are often unavailable in QBO. Make sure you keep notes of the amounts identified in each task.

Task 1: Working with payroll settings

- You turn on payroll in the test drive company.

- You change the **payroll settings** for the following:
    - Under **Preferences** (**Accounting Preferences**),
        - you select **Checking** as the **Bank Account**.
        - you accept the other default payroll accounts.
    - Under **Pay Policies**,
        - You edit the **Pay Schedule** so that the **Pay Period** is **Twice a Month**. **TIP:** Click **Edit** next to the existing **Friday** schedule.
        - You enter the next payday as the 15th of the **current** month. **TIP:** If you are doing your homework on October 10th, you would enter 10/15 as the **Pay Date**. You would also enter 10/15 if you are doing your homework on October 25th.
        - You enter the same date as the **pay period ending** date.
        - You check **Use this schedule as the default for employees I add**.
        - You enter "Semi-monthly" as the **Pay Schedule** description.
    - Under **Deductions**,
        - You add a new deduction for union dues. **TIP:** Union dues are an **after tax deduction** type.
        - You assign the new deduction to **Kari Steblay** when prompted.
            - Kari's dues are $25 per pay period. There is no annual maximum.
            - **TIP:** The new deduction can be added by clicking **Edit employee** in Kari's employee record. Click **Add a new deduction** on the **Pay** tab.
    - You edit Kari's W-4 information to include 254-55-7777 as her **Social Security number**.

REQUIRED: With the **Pay** tab open, change the **Sample check** hours to 50. Hours can be changed directly above the image of Kari's paycheck. Gross pay should be $900. Make a note of:

- Net pay
- Taxes withheld
- Total deductions

Sign out of QBO before continuing with Task 2.

Task 2: Editing employees and processing payroll

- You turn on payroll in the test drive company.

- You change the **payroll settings** for the following:
    - Under **Preferences** (**Accounting Preferences**),
        - you select **Checking** as the **Bank Account**.
        - you accept the other default payroll accounts.

- You edit employees as follows:
  - Eloisa Catillo—You change her employee status to terminated.
    - You enter 8/1/18 as her termination date.
  - Bill Lucchini—You change his W-4 information.
    - Social Security number is 252-55-6666.
    - He is married and claims 4 allowances for federal income taxes. His filing status for California is Married (one income); 4 allowances.
  - Kari Steblay—You change her W-4 information.
    - Social Security number is 254-55-7777.
    - She withholds at the single rate. 0 withholding allowance (federal and state)
- You process payroll for the next payroll period. **TIP:** QBO will default to the next period. The payroll period should cover one week and end on a Friday.
  - You enter 42 hours for Kari. Two of the hours should be paid at the overtime rate.
- **REQUIRED:** On the **Review and submit** screen, make a note of:
  - Gross pay (total compensation)
  - Net pay
  - Employee withholdings
  - Employer payroll taxes
  - Total labor cost
  - Total hours
- You submit payroll. (Use 1995 as the check number for Kari.)
- Click **I'll do it later** if prompted to remit payroll taxes.

You can continue on to Task 3 without logging off.

Task 3: Adding employees

- You turn on payroll in the test drive company.
- You set up a new employee.
  - His name is Armond Franz
    2155 Fortress Blvd
    Sacramento, CA 95822
    His birth date is 7/6/1986
  - Armond is single and claims 1 allowance (federal and state).
    - His Social Security number is 456-22-7748.
  - His salary is $55,000 per year.
    - He will be paid, by check, every two weeks on Friday. His first paycheck will be next Friday. That will also be the last day of work for that payday. He's the only employee using this pay schedule.
  - Armond has enrolled in the company's 401k plan. He will contribute 2% of his salary to the plan. Collins will match that contribution amount up to a maximum of $1,000.
  - He started working at Collins on the first Monday of the current pay period.
  - All required forms (new hire report and I-9) have been completed.

REQUIRED:

- After the employee setup is complete, take a screenshot of the **Employee details** screen. **TIP:** Details from all three tabs (**Pay**, **Profile**, **Employment**) should be visible.

- Make a note of the following information included on the **Sample check** displayed on the **Pay** tab. (**TIP:** Click the pencil icon next to **Pay** to see the sample check.)
  - Gross Pay
  - Net pay
  - Taxes withheld
  - Total deductions

Sign out of QBO before continuing with Task 4.

Task 4: Remitting payroll taxes

- You turn on payroll in the test drive company.

- You change the **payroll settings** for the following:
  - Under **Preferences** (**Accounting Preferences**),
    - you select **Checking** as the **Bank Account**.
    - you accept the other default payroll accounts.

- You record payment of Federal and State taxes currently due, by check. You use check number 1445 for the state tax payment and 1446 for the federal (941) tax payment.

REQUIRED:

- After recording tax payment, view the forms.
  - For the California tax deposit, make a note of amounts remitted for:
    - DI (State disability insurance)
    - PIT (Personal income tax)
  - For the federal tax deposit, make a note of the amounts remitted for:
    - Social Security
    - Medicare
    - Tax Withholding

Billing for Time and Expenses

Objectives

After completing Chapter 10, you should be able to:

1. Set up project tracking.

2. Set up independent contractors.

3. Track time by customer and by service using timesheets.

4. Create invoices from tracked time.

5. Add billable expenses to invoices.

In this chapter, we're going to cover billing for time and expenses.

Most of the time, companies don't need to track employee time by customer or by project. In a retail store, for example, management generally doesn't track how much profit the store makes on a specific customer during the month. Instead, management might track how much gross profit the store makes on sales of a specific product or how much profit it makes in a specific store. Management may need to track which store an employee works in but it doesn't generally need to track how much time a specific employee spent helping a specific customer. Restaurants, banks, manufacturing companies, and gas stations are examples of other companies that don't need to track time by customer. This chapter will not apply to those types of companies. (We'll talk about tracking profit by department or location in Chapter 11.)

However, there are many companies that **do** need to track time by customer and/or project.

For example, let's look at two construction companies. One bills its customers under "time and materials" contracts. The other bills its customers under "fixed fee" contracts. The time and materials contractor is billing for labor and materials plus some kind of markup. Payroll records **must** include the hours for each customer, by project **and** by type of work if billing rates differ, because those hours will be used to invoice customers. If those hours are tracked in QBO (which they can be), the invoicing process is more efficient.

The fixed fee contractor generally bills a percentage of the agreed upon price (the fixed fee) as the work progresses. The number of hours worked aren't needed to prepare the invoice. However, in order to evaluate project profitability, fixed fee contractors need to be able to compare the revenue earned on a specific project to the specific costs of that project. That information helps them evaluate the company's overall performance and the specific performance of project managers and improves their ability to bid on future projects.

Tracking revenues and costs by job is commonly known as project costing (or job costing).

BEFORE WE BEGIN

QBO does not currently have a full project costing feature. Hours can be tracked by project using timesheets for billing purposes and certain outside costs can be tracked by project for both billing and costing purposes but there is currently no way to automatically allocate labor dollars to projects based on timesheet data.

SETTING UP PROJECTS

Understanding a few basic concepts will help when working with projects in QBO:

- Multiple projects can be tracked for a single customer.
  - Time and expenses can be charged to **customers** as well so be careful to identify the specific **project** when recording transactions.

- Multiple **projects** for a **customer** cannot be billed on the same invoice. A separate invoice should be created for each project.

- All hours and any external costs incurred on a project must be defined as billable if you intend to later charge the customer for those hours or costs. A **billable** field is included on all appropriate forms (**timesheets**, **bills**, **checks**, etc.).
  - External costs that are not defined as **billable** will be included in all project reports but will not be accessible when preparing invoices or sales receipts.

Before you can start using **Projects**, the feature must be turned on.

Click the **gear** icon on the icon bar and select **Account and Settings**.

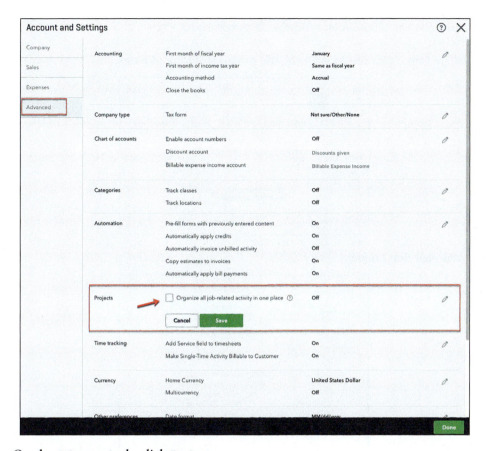

On the **Advanced** tab, click **Projects**.

 HINT: **Projects** are a relatively new feature in QBO. If the **Projects** feature is not available in your homework company file, you can use sub-customers as an alternative. See Appendix 10A for further information.

Check the box next to **Organize all job-related activity in one place**.
Click **Save** to activate **projects** and **Done** to exit the **Account and Settings** window.
Once **project** tracking is activated a new link will appear in the navigation bar.

To set up a project, click **Projects** on the navigation bar.

The first time you access **projects**, the screen will look like this:

Click **Add your first project**.

On the sidebar, enter a **project name** and select the **customer**. You can also enter notes here. Some companies might want to add information about the scope of the project or the names of customer personnel in charge of the project.

Click **Save**.

PRACTICE
EXERCISE

Add jobs for Craig's Design and Landscaping.
(Craig's Design has just gotten a request from Jeff's Jalopies for some landscaping work. Jeff has other projects in mind for the future so Craig's Design wants to set up a project for tracking hours spent on the landscaping job.)

1. Turn on project tracking.
   a. Click the **gear** icon on the icon bar.
   b. Click **Account and Settings**.
   c. Click **Advanced**.
   d. Click **Projects**.
   e. Check the box next to **Organize all job-related activity in one place**.
   f. Click **Done**.

(continued)

2. Set up job.

    a.   Click **Projects** on the navigation bar.

    b.   Click **Add your first project**.

    c.   Enter **Jalopies' Landscaping** as the **project name**.

    d.   Select **Jeff's Jalopies** as the **Customer**.

    e.   Click **Save**.

    f.   Click **OK**.

    g.   lick **Dashboard**.

SETTING UP INDEPENDENT CONTRACTORS

In Chapter 4, we covered setting up 1099 vendors (landlords, attorneys, independent contractors, etc.) in QBO. In this chapter, we're going to look specifically at independent contractors.

Independent contractors are often used by companies to work on projects. This works especially well when a company is growing. As new customers come in, there might be too much work for existing employees to manage but not quite enough new work to justify hiring another permanent employee.

QBO has improved the process for setting up independent contractors.

Click **Workers** on the navigation bar.

> **!** **WARNING: After project tracking is turned on in QBO, the navigation bar may change slightly. The Workers link may change to Employees. This will not cause any problems as you move forward.**

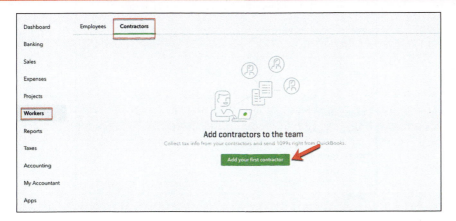

Click **Add your first contractor**.

The contractor's name is entered here. If the user elects to have the contractor enter the tax information online, an email address must be entered as well.

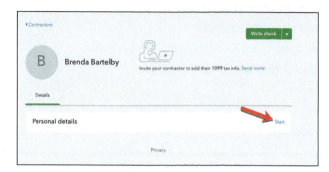

If the user does not invite the contractor to enter personal information online, the user must click **Start** to complete the setup.

In this next window, the user must indicate whether the contractor is an individual or a business.

    If **Individual** is selected, the final screen will look like this:

A tax ID number and address information is required. The screen for **Business** has similar fields.

    Click **Save** to complete the setup.

Once a contractor has been set up, the information will be included in the **Vendor** list. Additional information about the vendor (terms, billing rates, phone number, etc.) can be entered there. Similarly, independent contractors that are initially set up through the **Vendors** tab of **Expenses** (and identified as 1099 vendors) will be added to the **Contractor** list.

PRACTICE
EXERCISE

Add an independent contractor for Craig's Design and Landscaping.
(Craig has a large installation project coming up soon and expects to need some additional help. One of Craig's employees has a friend (Sue Stevens) who has landscaping experience and is looking for work. Craig brings her on as an independent contractor.)

1. Set up Sue Stevens as a **Contractor**.
    a. Click **Workers** (or **Employees**) on the navigation bar.
    b. Click **Contractors**.
    c. Click **Add a contractor**.
    d. Enter "Sue Stevens" as the **Name**.
    e. Remove the checkmark in the box next to **invite them to fill out the rest**.
    f. Click **Add contractor**.
    g. Click **Start**.
    h. Check **Individual**.
    i. Enter the following information:
        i. Sue Stevens
        ii. 444-54-4474 as the social security number.
        iii. 2111 Riversedge Drive
             Sacramento, CA 95822
    j. Click **Save**.

2. Edit Sue's vendor record.
    a. Click **Expenses** on the navigation bar.
    b. Click **Vendors**.
    c. Click **Sue Stevens**.
    d. Click **Edit**.
    e. Enter "50" as the **Billing rate**. **TIP:** This is the amount per hour that Sue bills Craig's. This is not the amount that Craig's bills customers for Sue's time.
    f. Select **Due on receipt** as the **Terms**.
    g. Click **Save**.
    h. Click **Dashboard**.

USING TIMESHEETS TO TRACK HOURS

The timesheet feature in QBO is available to track hours worked by both hourly and salaried employees in a company. You can also use timesheets to track hours worked by nonemployees (independent contractors, for example). Timesheet data can be used to do one or more of the following:

- Create a paycheck based on hours worked for hourly employees if the user subscribes to a payroll plan in QBO.

- Track paid time off for all employees if the user subscribes to a payroll plan in QBO.
- Track billable hours for invoicing customers.
- Track billable and non-billable hours for management purposes.

In Chapter 9, creating paychecks from timesheets was covered. In this chapter, timesheets will only be used to track hours for billing purposes.

Entering Timesheet Data

The process for entering timesheet data was covered in Chapter 9. A brief summary is included here.

Click the ➕ icon in the icon bar to access the **Single Time Activity** or **Weekly Timesheet** form. The **Weekly Timesheet** form is the more commonly used of the two.

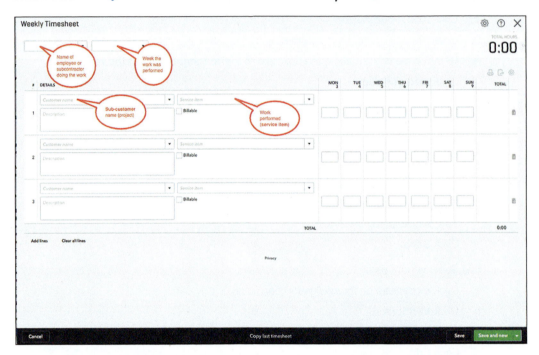

The timesheet must include information about the person doing the work, the dates of the work, **project** (or **customer**) name, and work performed (**service item**) as highlighted above. **Billable** must be checked if the hours will be billed to the customer.

A timesheet for work performed on various projects might look something like this:

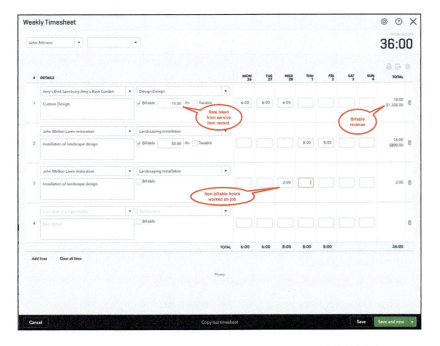

The billing rate field and the tax status checkbox are automatically updated by QBO from the **item** record when the **Billable** option is checked. The rate and taxability of the **item** can be changed if necessary. If the user is only tracking hours for management purposes (not for billing purposes), the **Billable** option should not be checked.

The total amount to be charged to the customer for the service is included in the **Total** column for each row. The amount would not include any possible sales tax to be collected.

> **BEHIND THE SCENES** In states with a sales tax, most sales of tangible items are subject to sales tax. Some charges for services performed are also subject to sales tax. The taxability of **service items** is usually determined by the nature of the service performed. For example, in many states landscaping (because it creates a "product") would be taxable; consulting services would not be taxable. In QBO, users are responsible for identifying which **items** and which **customers** are taxable.

Timesheets automatically display four rows. If more are needed, clicking **Add lines** (bottom left corner of the form) will add another four to the form. Any empty rows are automatically deleted when the form is saved.

Entering time for projects in Craig's Design and Landscaping.

(Craig needs someone to help with several projects. He hires John Wetzel as an independent contractor. He agrees to pay him $30 per hour for his time.)

PRACTICE EXERCISE

1. Turn on **project** tracking. (NOTE: If have not logged off since you completed the Practice Exercise starting on page 10-4, you can skip this step.)

   a. Click the **gear** icon on the icon bar.

   b. Click **Account and Settings**.

(continued)

(continued from previous page)

    c. Click **Advanced**.

    d. Click **Projects**.

    e. Check the box next to **Organize all job-related activity in one place**.

    f. Click **Save**.

    g. Click **Done**.

2. Set up two **projects**.

    a. Click **Projects** on the navigation bar.

    b. Click **Add your first project** (or **New project**).

    c. Enter "Paulsen Courtyard" as the **Project name**.

    d. Select Paulsen Medical Supplies as the **Customer**.

    e. Click **Save**.

    f. Click **Projects** on the navigation bar.

    g. Click **New project**.

    h. Enter "Fountain Installation" as the **Project name**.

    i. Select Gevelber Photography as the **Customer**.

    j. Click **Save**.

    k. Click **Dashboard**.

3. Add John Wetzel as a contractor.

    a. Click **Workers** (or **Employees**) on the navigation bar.

    b. Click **Contractors**.

    c. Click **Add a contractor**.

    d. Enter "John Wetzel" as the **Name**.

    e. Remove the checkmark in the box next to **invite them to fill out the rest**.

    f. Click **Add contractor**.

    g. Click **Start**.

    h. Select **Individual**.

    i. Enter the following information:

        i.   Social security number: 444-44-5556

        ii. Address: 21 Houston St, Sacramento, CA 95822

    j. Click **Save**.

    k. Click **Expenses** on the navigation bar.

    l. Click John Wetzel.

    m. Click **Edit**.

    n. Enter 30 as the **Billing rate (/hr)**.

    o. Click **Save**.

4. Enter John's time for the week.

    a. Click the ➕ icon.

    b. Click **Weekly Timesheet**.

    c. Select John Wetzel in the name field.

    d. Select the current week in the date field.

(continued)

   e. In the first row of the **Details** section:

      i. Select Paulsen Courtyard as the **project name**.

      ii. Select **installation** as the **service item**

      iii. Check the box next to **Billable**.

      iv. Enter 7 hours for Monday, Tuesday, and Wednesday. (7 hours each day.)

      v. Make a note of the total amount billable to Paulsen Medical Supplies for the work.

   f. In the second row of the **Details** section:

      i. Select Installation (Gevelber Photograph) as the **project name**.

      ii. Select **Design** as the **service item**.

      iii. Enter 4 hours for Thursday and Friday (4 hours each day)

      iv. Make a note of the default billing rate for design work

   g. In the third row of the **Details** section.

   i. Select **Design** as the **service item**.

   ii. Enter 3 hours for Friday.

      1. John took 3 hours putting together some new design ideas for Craig. This isn't billable and doesn't relate to a specific customer.

   h. Total hours should be 32.

   i. Click **Save and close.**

TRACKING COSTS OTHER THAN LABOR BY PROJECT

Many companies that work with projects (jobs) bill some or even all direct expenses to their customers in addition to labor hours.

    For example, construction companies would likely bill their customers for appliances purchased for their home. Law firms would likely bill their clients for work performed by outside investigators.

    If certain features are turned on in QBO, users can flag purchases as billable to specific customers when **bills**, **checks**, and **expenses** are entered. Those charges are then available when **invoices** are created.

Turning on Features for Tracking and Billing Direct Expenses

Features needed to track and bill expenses are activated by clicking the **gear** icon on the icon bar and selecting **Account and Settings**.

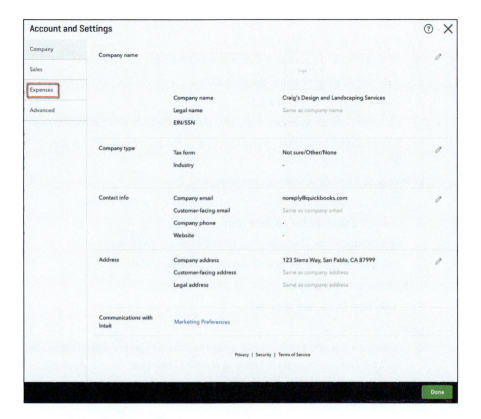

Click **Expenses** to display the options available.

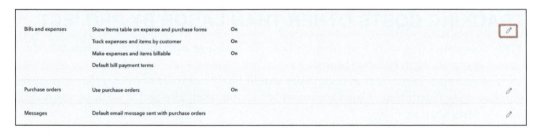

Click the **pencil** icon in the **Bills and expenses** section.

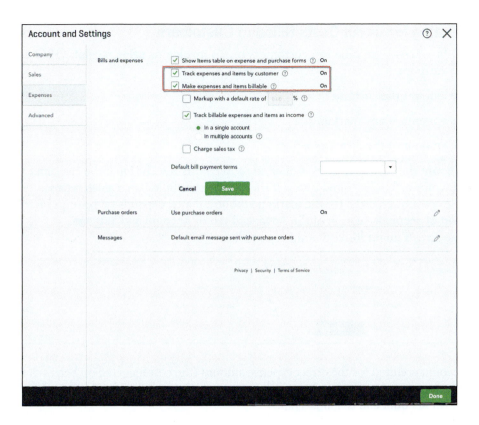

Both **Track expenses and items by customer** and **Make expenses and items billable** should be turned **On**.

There are three questions that must be answered if a company bills customers for direct expenses.

- Does the company expect to earn a profit on costs it incurs on behalf of customers?

- Are billable direct expenses subject to sales tax?

- In which general ledger account should billable costs and any markups be recorded?

Profits are earned on direct expenses by "marking up" the cost on the customer invoice. This is normally done using a percentage. For example, an accounting firm might incur a cost of $500 on software purchased for a client's use. The accounting firm might decide to add 10% to the cost when billing it to the customer. The client would be billed $550. (The $500 cost plus the 10% ($50) markup.) Adding a markup gives the company a profit on the direct expenses. In the example given, the firm's profit would be $50.

If the company has a standard markup rate that is applied to all billable direct expenses, the rate can be entered in this screen.

Taxability of customer charges is dictated by state laws. However, in general, direct costs (plus markup) billed to customers are subject to sales tax unless the company paid tax as part of the original purchase or the direct cost isn't taxable.

> **BEHIND THE SCENES** If taxes are paid by the company on the original purchase, the full amount (tax included) should be billed to the customer. No additional tax would, of course, be added to that amount.

Accounting for Direct Costs Billed to Customers

When direct costs are billed to customers on an **invoice** or **sales receipt**, QBO creates a journal entry for:

- the amount the customer owes

- the amount of any markup

- the amount of the direct expense

The amount the customer owes is debited to Accounts Receivable if the customer is billed on an invoice or Undeposited Funds if the customer is billed on a **sales receipt**.

The account credited for the markup amount, if any, depends on settings identified in the **Chart of accounts** section of the **Advanced** tab of **Account and Settings**.

The screen might look something like this:

The account credited for the direct expense amount (the cost incurred on behalf of the customer, not the markup amount) is a little more complicated. Let's go back to the **Expense** window in **Account and Settings** again.

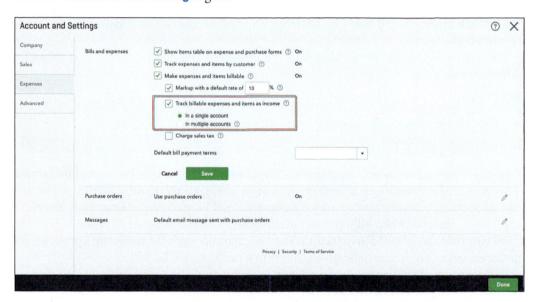

If **Track billable expenses and items as income** is NOT checked, then the amount charged to the customer for the direct cost will be credited to the account that was debited when the original cost was entered. For example, let's say a company incurred $320 in travel costs billable to a customer. When the bill for the travel costs is entered, the company might debit a Travel and Entertainment expense account and flag the cost as billable. The company adds a 10% markup to all direct costs. When the invoice is later created to bill the customer for the travel, QBO would automatically debit the $352 to Accounts receivable and credit $320 to the Travel and Entertainment account and $32 to the markup account identified in the **Advanced** tab of **Account and Settings**. The balance in the Travel and Entertainment account, related to this transaction, would be zero. The journal entry underlying the **invoice** would be:

	Accounts receivable	352	
	Travel and Entertainment expense		320
	Markup on billable direct costs		32

If **Track billable expenses and items as income** IS checked, the company must decide whether to track the transactions in a single account or in multiple accounts. If the transactions are tracked in a single account, then the account to be credited must be identified in the **Advanced** tab of **Account and Settings**.

The screen would look something like this if an income account called Job Costs was set up.

Using the travel cost example again, the journal entry underlying the **invoice** would now look like this:

	Accounts receivable	352	
	Job costs		320
	Markup on billable direct costs		32

If **Track billable expenses and items as income** is checked and **in multiple accounts** is also selected, any **expense** or **cost of goods sold** account that might include billable costs must be associated with an income account. QBO will automatically add a field to the account record just for this purpose. The screen looks like this

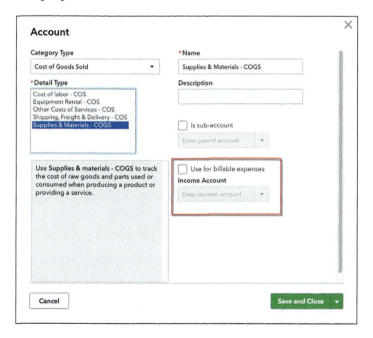

This can be done when the account is originally set up or by editing the account. It cannot be done through **Account and Settings**.

Going back once more to the example we were using, let's say that in addition to travel costs, the company purchased $700 in job materials billable to the customer. If the **income** associated with billable materials was **Landscaping Services**, the journal entry underlying the **invoice** would now look like this:

Accounts receivable	1,152	
Landscaping Services		700
Job costs		320
Markup on billable direct costs		102

Identifying Costs as Billable

Any costs (including costs of **items**) can be identified as **billable** on **Expense**, **Check**, or **Bill** forms. Although customers can be identified on **Purchase Orders**, costs cannot be marked as billable until the related **bill** is entered.

The necessary fields are automatically added to the forms when the option of tracking and billing customers for direct costs is turned on in **Account and Settings**.

For example, the form for entering a **Check** looks something like this after the tracking feature is turned on.

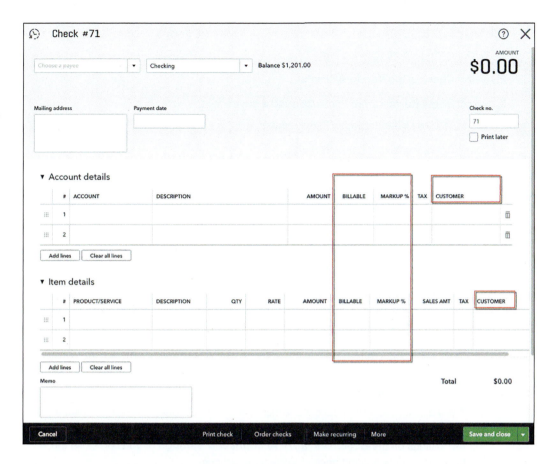

The **BILLABLE** field must be checked. The **CUSTOMER** must also be selected. This would be the **project** name if multiple projects existed for the customer.

In the **Account Details** section, any default markup % already set up will automatically display in the **MARKUP %** field. The percent can be changed.

In the **Item details** section, the percent displayed in the **MARKUP %** field will correspond to the difference between the default cost displayed in the **AMOUNT** field and the **SALES AMT** identified in the **item** record. If the **AMOUNT** field is changed (a new cost amount entered), QBO will recalculate the **SALES AMT** using the default **MARKUP %**. The **AMOUNT** and **MARKUP %** fields can be changed by the user; the **SALES AMT** cannot be changed in the form. (The sales amount can be changed in the **item** record however.)

For example, let's say wheelbarrows were sold by Craig's. In the **item** record the default cost is set at $50 and the default sales price is set at $75. (That represents a 50% markup. The cost of $50 times 1.5 (150%) is $75.)

Now let's say Craig's purchases a wheelbarrow for a customer. The cost of this wheelbarrow is $55. When the **check** or **bill** for the wheelbarrow purchase is entered, the **Sales AMT** field will automatically change to $82.50. ($55 times 1.50 (150%) equals $82.50). When the **invoice** for the customer is later created, the sales price will show as $82.50. The sales price could be edited back to $75 at that point if appropriate.

Enter a billable cost for Craig's Design and Landscaping.

(Craig's Design staff work overtime on the Cool Cars job at the client's request. Craig stops at Bob's Burger Joint to pick up dinner for the crew and pays with a check. He decides to bill the client for the meal but not charge them a markup.)

PRACTICE
EXERCISE

(continued)

1. Click the ⊕ icon on the icon bar.

2. Select **Check** in the **Vendors** column.

3. Select **Bob's Burger Joint** in the **Choose a payee** field.

   a. Ignore any **Bills** displayed in the sidebar.

4. Leave **Checking** as the bank account.

5. **Make a note** of the balance (dollar balance) displayed next to Checking.

6. Use the current date as the **Bill date**.

7. Enter "83" as the **Check no.**

8. Select **Meals and Entertainment** as the **ACCOUNT** in the **Account details** section.

9. Enter "43" as the **AMOUNT**.

10. Check the **BILLABLE** box.

11. Delete any **MARKUP %**. **TIP:** A markup field would only appear if you didn't log out after the last practice exercise.

12. Select **Cool Cars** as the **CUSTOMER**.

13. Click **Save and close**.

   a. If you are not allowed to save the transaction in the test drive company because no income account has been associated with the account, you can either change the settings on the **Expenses** tab of **Account and Settings** or you can close the browser window and log back in to clear all settings.

BILLING FOR TIME AND COSTS

If there are pending billable costs for a specific customer, the details will appear in a sidebar when an **invoice** is opened. At the time this book was written, billable hours and direct costs were not available when entering a **sales receipt**.

The sidebar will look something like this for customers with billable labor hours:

Some or all billable time or costs can easily be **added** to the **invoice**. If **Add all** was selected in the screen shown above, the **invoice** would look like this:

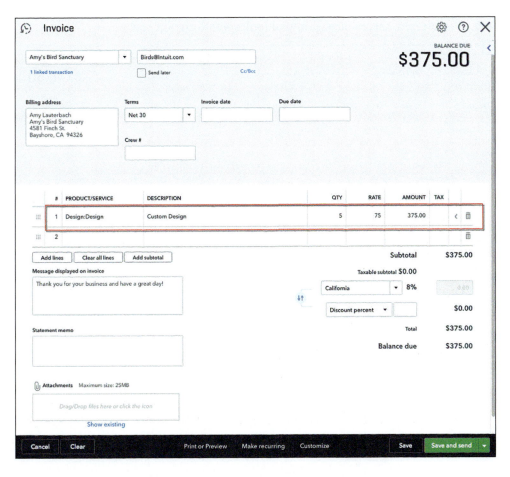

All fields (**RATES, QTY, DESCRIPTION**, etc.) can be changed before the form is saved.

> **BEHIND THE SCENES** Remember, the **rate** used on the **invoice** or **sales receipt** for labor hours will be the rate specified in the **service item** record **not** the wage rate.

The sidebar will look something like this for a customer with billable direct costs, assuming a markup rate of 10%:

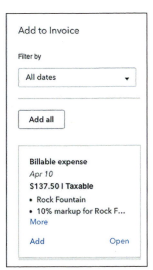

If **Add all** is selected, the **Invoice** form will look something like this:

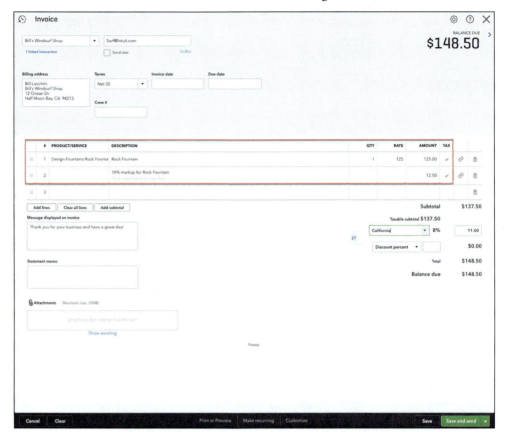

The markup is shown on a separate line for internal purposes only. This allows the user to change the tax status for either the item or the markup if necessary. In some states, markup amounts are subject to sales tax even if the cost itself is not.

The final **invoice** might look something like this:

BEHIND THE SCENES If an **invoice** is later deleted, the status of any included billable hours or costs automatically changes back to "billable."

PRACTICE EXERCISE

Charge a Craig's Design and Landscaping client for time.
(Craig's Design is worried about getting low on cash. It decides to bill Video Games by Dan for some work originally set up as a **delayed charge**.)

1. Click the ➕ icon on the icon bar.

2. Select **Invoice** in the **Customers** column.

3. Select **Video Games by Dan** in the **Choose a customer** field.

4. Click **Add all** in the sidebar.

5. Use the current date as the **Invoice date**.

6. Leave the **Terms** at **Net 30**.

7. **Make a note** of the total amount billed.

8. Click **Save and close**.

QuickCheck
10-1

Employees at Davis Industries work for four hours on the Selma project. Their billing rate is $100 per hour. Their wage rate is $40 per hour. A special tool costing $35 was needed for the job. This cost of the tool plus a markup of 10% was charged to the client. How much profit did Davis make on the Selma project?

PREPARING PROJECT REPORTS

There are a variety of reports that can be used to review and evaluate projects. Four of the most commonly used reports are:

- Profit and Loss by Customer
  - Shows revenues and direct costs for each **customer**, **project**, or **sub-customer**, by general ledger account, for a specified accounting period.
  - Accessed in the **Business Overview** section of **Reports**.

- Project Profitability
  - Shows revenues and costs for a specific **project**.
  - Accessed by clicking **Projects** on the navigation bar and clicking the **project** name.

- Unbilled Time and Expenses
  - Shows all unbilled direct costs and hours for a specific **project**.
  - Accessed by clicking **Projects** on the navigation bar and clicking the **project** name.

- Nonbillable Time
  - Shows all hours charged to a **project** but not identified as billable.
  - Accessed by clicking **Projects** on the navigation bar and clicking the **project** name.

PRACTICE EXERCISE

Prepare project reports for Craig's Design and Landscaping.
NOTE: Make sure you log out of QBO before beginning this Practice Exercise. Since **projects** aren't automatically activated in the test drive company, reports available when **sub-customers** are used are demonstrated in this Practice Exercise. The same report could be used for **projects**.

(continued)

1. Click **Reports**.

2. Click **Profit and Loss by Customer** in the **Business Overview** section.

   a. In the **Report period** dropdown menu, select **All Dates**.

   b. In the **Display columns** by dropdown menu, select **Customers**.

   c. Click **Customize**.

   d. Click **Filter**.

   e. Check the **Customer** box.

   f. Select **0969 Ocean View Road** and **55 Twin Lane** in the dropdown menu for **Customer**. (Both are sub-customers of **Freeman Sporting Goods**.)

   g. Click **Run Report**.

   h. **Make a note** of the net income amount for each customer.

3. Click **Dashboard** to close the report window.

ANSWER TO
QuickCheck
10-1

Davis earned a profit of $243.50. Total revenue related to hours was $400 (4 × $100 per hour). Total billed to Selma for the tool was $38.50 ($35 plus a 10% ($3.50) markup). Total cost to Davis was $160 for labor (4 × $40 per hour) and $35 for the tool.

CHAPTER SHORTCUTS

Add a project

1. Click **Projects** on the navigation bar

2. Click **New project**

Enter a timesheet

1. Click the ➕ icon on the icon bar

2. Click **Weekly Timesheet**

Charge customers for billable time and expenses

1. Click the ➕ icon on the icon bar

2. Click **Invoice**

3. Choose the **customer**

4. Add billable hours or costs appearing in the sidebar

CHAPTER REVIEW (Answers available on the publisher's website.)

Matching

Match the term or phrase (as used in QuickBooks Online) to its definition.

1. project
2. unbilled charges report
3. account and settings
4. Project Profitability Report
5. billable
6. add all
7. parent customer
8. markup %

_____   customer with multiple separately tracked projects

_____   command included in the sidebar of an invoice form

_____   name of window used to select features and set preferences

_____   identifiable job tracked for a specific customer

_____   report that summarizes revenues and expenses by job

_____   status of hours or direct costs to be charged to customers

_____   list of all pending employee hours and direct costs identified as billable

_____   default rate used to increase direct cost billable to customer

Multiple Choice

1. An engineering company enters into "fixed fee" and "time and materials" contracts with their clients. The company _____.
    a. would have no reason for tracking labor hours for "fixed fee" jobs
    b. would have no reason for tracking labor hours for "time and materials" jobs
    c. would normally track labor hours for both "fixed fee" and "time and materials" jobs
    d. must track hours for "time and materials jobs" but should never track hours for "fixed fee" jobs

2. A **service item** must be selected for timesheet entries _____.
    a. only if time will be billed to a client
    b. only if the user tracks time by job but doesn't bill time to clients
    c. if user tracks time by client (whether time is billed or not)
    d. None of the above. **Service items** must be identified for all timesheet entries.

3. The rates used to bill clients for employee or independent contractor hours are _____.
    a. found in the **item** list
    b. found in the employee record
    c. always set when the **invoice** or **sales receipt** is created
    d. found in either the **item** list or employee record, depending on preferences selected

4. Which of the following statements is not true?
    a. Both **expenses** and **items** can be identified as **billable** as part of the entry of a vendor bill.
    b. Changes to billable hours and rates can be made in the **invoice** form.
    c. If **Bill with parent** is selected in a **sub-customer** record, payments received from the **parent customer** can be applied to open **invoices** charged to the **sub-customer**.
    d. If **Bill this customer** is selected in a **sub-customer** record, payments received from the **parent customer** can be applied to open **invoices** charged to the **sub-customer**.

5. The **Profit and Loss by Customer** report is found in the _____ section of **Reports**.
    a. **Sales and Customers**
    b. **Projects**
    c. **Business Overview**
    d. **For my accountant**

ASSIGNMENTS

Background information: Martin Smith, a college student and good friend of yours, had always wanted to be an entrepreneur. He is very good in math so, to test his entrepreneurship skills, he decided to set up a small math tutoring company serving local high school students who struggle in their math courses. He set up the company, Math Revealed!, as a corporation in 2018. Martin is the only owner. He has not taken any distributions from the company since it opened.

The business has been successful so far. In fact, it's been so successful he has decided to work in his business full time now that he's graduated from college with a degree in mathematics.

He has decided to start using QuickBooks Online to keep track of his business transactions. He likes the convenience of being able to access his information over the Internet. You have agreed to act as his accountant while you're finishing your own academic program.

He currently has a number of regular customers that he tutors in Pre-Algebra, Algebra, and Geometry. His customers pay his fees by cash or check after each tutoring session but he does give terms of Net 15 to some of his customers. He has developed the following fee schedule:

Name	Description	Rate
Refresher	One-hour session	$40 per hour
Persistence program	Two one-hour sessions per week	$75 per week
Crisis program	Five one-hour sessions per week	$150 per week

The tutoring sessions usually take place at his students' homes but he recently signed a two-year lease on a small office above a local coffee shop. The rent is only $200 per month starting in January 2019. A security deposit of $400 was paid in December 2018.

The following equipment is owned by the company:

Description	Date placed in service	Cost	Life	Salvage Value
Computer	7/1/18	$3,000	36 months	$300
Printer	7/1/18	$ 240	24 months	$ 0
Graphing Calculators (2)	7/1/18	$ 294	36 months	$ 60

All equipment is depreciated using the straight-line method.

As of 12/31/18, he owed $2,000 to his parents who initially helped him get started. They are charging him interest at a 6% annual rate. He has been paying interest only on a monthly basis. His last payment was 12/31/18.

Over the next month or so, he plans to expand his business by selling a few products he believes will help his students. He has already purchased a few items:

Category	Description	Vendor	Quantity On Hand	Cost per unit	Sales Price
Books and Tools					
	Geometry in Sports	Books Galore	20	12	16
	Solving Puzzles: Fun with Algebra	Books Galore	20	14	18
	Getting Ready for Calculus	Books Galore	20	15	20
	Protractor/Compass Set	Math Shack	10	10	14
	Handheld Dry-Erase Boards	Math Shack	25	5	9
	Notebooks (pack of 3)	Paper Bag Depot	10	15	20

HINT: If you didn't turn off Automation in Chapter 2, you might want to consider doing that now. It's easy to get confused when QBO automatically adds accounts to your transactions. Click the **gear** icon on the icon bar and select **Account and Settings**. In the **Automation** section of the **Advanced** tab, turn **Prefill forms with previously entered content** to **Off**.

3/1/19

✓ Martin is confident that his new business is going to grow significantly over the next several months. He has agreed to provide tutoring services and math games to several Sacramento middle schools. He's also been asked to present a number of workshops in March. He knows he's going to need some help.

✓ Martin talks with two of his former classmates (Shaniya Montero and Kenny Chen). Shaniya is interested in tutoring at the schools and Kenny is interested in doing training for the new math game product for Math Revealed!. Martin will focus on developing and delivering workshops and continuing his tutoring of existing customers.

- Both Shaniya and Kenny will submit timesheets to you every two weeks.
- Martin agrees to pay them $30 per hour

✓ He's not sure how much work he'll have for them and both will continue to offer their services to other companies, so you plan to treat both Shaniya and Kenny as **contractors** in QBO using the following information.

Name	Kenny Chen	Shaniya Montero
Street address	259 Rosa Court	3 Pocket Dr
City, State	Sacramento, CA	Sacramento, CA
Zip code	95822	95822
SSN	999-88-7777	888-77-6666
Billing rate	$30	$30
Terms	Net 15	Net 15

TIP: You'll need to enter the **billing rate** and **terms** in the vendor record after you set them up as **contractors**.

✓ You turn on **Time tracking** in the **Advanced** tab of **Account and Settings**.

- You add **service field** to timesheets and make activity billable to customers.
- You check **Show billing rate to users entering time**.
- You set Monday as the **first day of work week**.

✓ You set up Sacramento Public Schools as a new customer.

- 2566 Central Avenue
  Sacramento, CA 95822
  Terms are Net 30.
  Sales of products to public schools are taxable in California.

✓ Although all **invoices** will be paid by Sacramento Public Schools, school administrators do want information about the tutoring hours by school so you turn on **project** tracking and add the three schools as **projects**. All of them have Sacramento Public Schools as the **parent customer**.

- Northside
- Central
- Southside

✓ You also decide to set up two new **service items**. **TIP:** Neither **service item** is taxable.

■ One for tutoring at the schools.

- ○ Item name: School

- ○ Description: In school group tutoring

- ○ Category: Tutoring

- ○ Sales price/rate: $50 (per hour)

- ○ Income accounting: 400 Tutoring

- ○ Cost: $30

- ○ Expense account: 605 Contract labor

- One for math game training. **TIP:** You'll need to set up the new income account first.

- ○ Item name: Game training

- ○ Description: Math Games Training

- ○ Category: Training (This is a new category.)

- ○ Sales price/rate: $50 (per hour)

- ○ Income accounting: 408 Training (This is a new income account. Use **Service/Fee** Income as the **Detail Type**.)

- ○ Cost: $30

- ○ Expense account: 605 Contract labor

3/4/19

✓ Martin is putting together several workshops. For the first one at the Teacher's College, he needs to have a projector and screen. The College agrees to cover the cost.

- You turn on the features related to tracking and billing expense and items by customer in the **Expenses** tab of **Account and Settings**.

- ○ You make sure **Track expenses and items by customer** and **Make expenses and items billable** are both turned on.

- ○ Martin has agreed on a markup of 5% with the Center. He thinks he'll use the same markup on other costs incurred for customers.

- ○ You decide not to track the billable expenses and items as income.

- ○ On the **Advanced** tab of **Account and Settings**, you click **Add new** in the **Markup income account** field. You set up a new account (480 Markup Income) as the **markup income account**. You use **Service/Fee Income** as the **detail type**.

- You decide to track reimbursable costs in a separate account. You set up a "Reimbursable Costs" account as an **Expense** and an **Other Miscellaneous Service Costs detail type**. You make it a **sub-account** of **Other Costs** and use "698" as the account number.

✓ Martin goes to Paper Bag Depot and picks up a projector and a screen. The total, including tax, is $394.20. He uses the credit card to make the purchase. You make it billable to Teacher's College. **TIP:** You don't need to check the **Taxable** box since the $394.20 won't be taxable to the customer.

3/5/19

✓ You write yourself a check (#1125) for the $300 owed to you for February's bookkeeping services. **TIP:** You accrued that cost at the end of February.

✓ You look at the collections report and notice that you have quite a few past due bills. You make calls to Debbie Han, Paul Richard, and Annie Wang.

- Debbie and Annie apologize and agree to send their checks by next Friday.

- Paul explains that he's been waiting to receive a credit for the two missed sessions in February. You tell him that you'll talk to Martin and get that credit memo to him as soon as possible.

✓ You ask Martin about Paul's missed sessions. He explains that he forgot to tell you about that. You create the credit memo (CM1115) in QBO and send it off to Paul. You charge the $60 to the **Crisis item** since that was the package Paul had purchased. You enter "Credit for missed sessions. Sorry for the delay!" in the **Message displayed on credit memo** box.

3/6/19

✓ You receive two checks in the mail and record them in QBO:

- $300 from Annie Wang for Invoice #1009. Check #1025, dated 3/6.
- $600 from Debbie Han for Invoice #1116. Check #4555, dated 3/6.

✓ You deposit both checks in the bank. The total deposit is $900.

✓ You receive the remaining products ordered from Books Galore on PO 100 and PO 104. The total amount on the invoice (#2244) is $518.60. (The terms are Net 30.) In addition to the books, Books Galore charged $48.60 (including tax) for some office supplies Martin had called them about. You don't think you'll use all the supplies in March so you charge them to the Supplies on Hand account.

✓ Martin lets you know that the workshop for the Teacher's College went great. You create an invoice (#1021) for the agreed-upon fee of $1,750 for the **Educator Workshop** plus the charge for the projector/screen setup on the invoice. The workshop fee was a little higher than last time because Martin added some additional training sessions. The total invoice amount is $2,163.91. The terms are Net 30.

3/7/19

✓ Kenny ships out two orders today to Sacramento Public Schools. Martin has agreed to give the schools a 5% sales discount as an introductory offer. The terms are Net 15. (**TIP**: Don't forget to charge tax on these items. The discount should be taken before tax.)

- Sale to Southside Middle School (Invoice #1022, for $1,336.89)
  - ○ 3 **Consoles**
  - ○ 2 **Fractions**
  - ○ 2 **Equations**
  - ○ 1 **Ratios**
- Sale to Central Middle School (1023, for $1,079.79)
  - ○ 2 **Consoles**
  - ○ 2 **Fractions**
  - ○ 2 **Equations**
  - ○ 3 **Ratios**

✓ He asks you to put a rush order through for more Math Games. You create PO #105 and email it to Cartables. The purchase order total is $3,300.

- 10 **Consoles**
- 10 **Fractions**
- 10 **Equations**
- 10 **Ratios**

3/11/19

✓ Cartables was quick! All items on PO # 105 are received today. The invoice (#949450-22) for $3,300 is dated 3/11. Cartables' payment terms are 2%10, Net 30.

3/12/19

✓ You pay all bills due on or before 3/20.

- There are four bills. Total amount paid is $1,110.93. The first check number is #1126.

✓ You receive two utility bills in the mail. Both are dated 3/12.

- Sacramento Utilities for March services, #10112, $128.92. The terms are Net 30.

- Horizon Phone for March service, #121-1000, $50.90. The terms are Net 30.

✓ You receive a check from Sacramento Public Schools in payment of Invoices #1022 and #1023. You're relieved to get the check so quickly. You were worried about having enough cash to pay Shaniya and Kenny. The check (#3333) was for $2,416.68.

✓ You deposit the check in the bank.

3/13/19

✓ Martin decides to bring along a math instructor to help with this weekend's workshop. Dynamic Teaching has agreed to pay a fee of $1,200 for Martin's services and agrees to pay for the additional help including Martin's customary 5% markup. The instructor is charging $300.

- The instructor is:

  Olen Petrov

  2 Granite Way

  Sacramento, CA 95822

- You set him up as a **contractor**. Olen is an individual so you enter his social security number (191-99-9911).

✓ You enter a bill for the $300 service (#03-16 with terms of Net 15) and make it billable to Dynamic Teaching. Since Dynamic Teaching had agreed to cover Olen's fee, you charge it to the Reimbursable costs account. The instructor's fee is not taxable.

3/15/19

✓ Shaniya turns in her timesheet for the first two weeks.

Date	Day of the Week	Project	# of hours	Billable?
3/1	Friday			
3/4	Monday	Southside	4	Y
3/5	Tuesday			
3/6	Wednesday	Central	4	Y
3/7	Thursday	Northside	6	Y
3/8	Friday			
3/11	Monday	Southside	6	Y
3/12	Tuesday			
3/13	Wednesday	Central	5	Y
3/14	Thursday	Northside	5	Y
3/15	Friday	Southside	4	Y
		Total Hours	34	

- You enter Shaniya's timesheet data using **School** as the **service item** and the **project** as the **customer**. All hours are billable. **TIP:** You should show 14 hours for the first week and 20 hours for the second week.

- You also enter a bill for the amount Sally owes Shaniya ($1,020—SM315). You use **School** for the **service item**. Since you will be creating the invoice for Sacramento Public Schools using the timesheet hours, you don't make the charges billable here. **TIP:** Don't forget to charge the hours to the correct **project** though. Sally spent 14 hours at Southside, 11 hours at Northside, and 9 hours at Central.

✓ Kenny turns in his timesheet for the first two weeks.

Date	Day of the Week	Project	# of hours	Billable?
3/1	Friday			
3/4	Monday	Northside	4	Y
3/5	Tuesday			
3/6	Wednesday			
3/7	Thursday	Central	3	Y
3/8	Friday			
3/11	Monday			
3/12	Tuesday	Southside	3	Y
3/13	Wednesday			
3/14	Thursday			
3/15	Friday			
		Total Hours	10	

- You enter Kenny's timesheet data using **Game Training** as the **service item** and the **project** as the **customer**. All hours are billable. **TIP:** You should show 7 hours for the first week and 3 hours for the second week.

- You also enter a **bill** for the amount Sally owes Kenny ($300—KC315). You use **Game Training** for the **service item**. Since you will be creating the invoice for Sacramento Public Schools using the timesheet hours, you don't make the charges billable here. **TIP:** Don't forget to charge the hours to the correct **project** though. Kenny spent 3 hours at Southside, 4 hours at Northside, and 3 hours at Central.

✓ You pay Kenny ($300—check #1130) and Shaniya ($1,020—check #1131).

✓ You create invoices for Shaniya's and Kenny's work. The invoices are dated 3/15 with terms of Net 30.

- Southside (Invoice #1024) $850
- Central (Invoice #1025) $600
- Northside (Invoice #1026) $750

3/18/19

✓ Martin gives you the information on his tutoring sessions for the last two weeks. You record them using 3/18 as the sales date. Everyone paid with credit cards.

- Alonso Luna—8 **Refresher** sessions $320 (#111)
- Navi Patel—2 **Persistence** $150 (#112)
- Marley Roberts—2 **Persistence** $150 (#113)
- Jon Savidge—1 **Crisis** $150 (#114)

✓ You prepare a deposit for the credit card receipts. The total (after the 2% merchant fee) is $754.60.

3/19/19

✓ The workshop at Dynamic Teaching last weekend went well. Martin wants to encourage Dynamic Teaching to continue to use his services so he gives them a 5% discount on the bill. You create an invoice (#1027) for $1,439.25. **TIP:** The **Educator Workshop** fee was $1,200 before the discount.

✓ Martin gets a phone call that the March 22nd–23rd workshop has been cancelled. He's a bit relieved. He doesn't want to miss the Mathmagic Clinic on Saturday.

✓ You receive the following checks in the mail.

- • $390 from Paul Richard for Invoice #1015. Check # 45777, dated 3/19 **TIP:** Check the invoice and credit memo first. The payment field will automatically change to $390.
- • $300 from Navi Patel for Invoice #1019. Check #4555, dated 3/19

✓ Martin wants to have plenty of books and tools on hand for the Mathmagic Clinic coming up this Saturday. There aren't many notebooks in stock so he goes down to Paper Bag Depot and uses his credit card to purchase 15 packages of them. The total charge is $225.00.

3/22/19

✓ Kenny ships out another two orders today to Sacramento Public Schools. Kenny agreed to give the schools a 5% sales discount as an introductory offer. He already gave discounts to Southside and Central so you only record the discount on the shipment to Northside. (**TIP:** The discount is given before tax.)

- • Sale to Northside Middle School (Invoice #1028, for $1,542.56)
  - ○ 3 **Consoles**
  - ○ 3 **Fractions**
  - ○ 3 **Equations**
  - ○ 3 **Ratios**
- • Sale to Southside Middle School (Invoice #1029, for $866.00)
  - ○ 2 **Consoles**
  - ○ 2 **Ratios**
- • Sale to Central Middle School (Invoice #1030, for $541.25)
  - ○ 1 **Console**
  - ○ 1 **Equation**
  - ○ 1 **Fraction**
  - ○ 1 **Ratio**

3/23/19

✓ Mathmagic was almost standing room only today. 55 students attended. You record the cash sale (#115) of $1,342.48. **TIP:** Use Drop-in as the customer.

- • Total tutoring income collected was $1,100.
- • Product sales (all taxable):
  - ○ 5 **Notebooks**
  - ○ 4 **Dry Erase**
  - ○ 2 **Ready**
  - ○ 3 **Sports**

3/26/19

✓ You talk to Martin about your increasing workload. He is very appreciative of your work and agrees to pay you $500 for March. You agree to talk again in a few months about maybe coming on as a permanent employee. You write yourself a check (#1132).

✓ Gus Ranting is back again! He's sure that his son is wasting his time at the Mathmagic Clinic. Martin lets him know that his son is a great kid who obviously believes the tutoring is helping him. He shows Gus his son's work and encourages him to follow up with the math teachers at the school. He gives Gus a partial refund of $10 (Check #1133) but says this will be the last time for any refunds (RR102).

✓ You deposit the checks from 3/19 and the cash from 3/23 in the bank. The deposit totals $2,032.48.

✓   Martin hands you two gas receipts for March. One, dated 3/14 for $19 and one dated 3/25 for $26. He used the credit card each time to pay for the gas he purchased at Cardinal Gas & Snacks. You enter the charges in QBO using the credit card receipt dates.

3/27/19

✓   Math Shack calls and says there's a shipping delay with the **Kits** ordered on PO #104. You decide to cancel the order since none of the **Kits** have been sold this month. You change the status of PO #104 to **Closed**. **TIP:** Consider using the search feature to find the purchase order.

✓   You receive the following checks in the mail.

- Teacher's College $2,163.91(Check # 7788156)
- Eliot Williams $75.00 (Check #8126)

✓   You deposit the checks in the bank. The deposit total is $2,238.91.

✓   Martin's final workshop for March was given at the Center of High Academic Achievement this week. This was a new workshop called "Creating Math Magic in the Classroom." You create a new **service item** for the new presentation using "Magic" as the **name**. You can leave the **sales price/rate** blank since the amount will change depending on the audience size.

- Martin is getting quite a good reputation as a presenter and the audience was full. You create Invoice #1031 for $2,500 for the Center.

3/29/19

✓   Martin gives you the information on his tutoring sessions for the last two weeks. You record them using 3/29 as the sales date. This time everyone paid with cash! All sessions were completed by 3/29.

- Eliot Williams—3 **Refresher** sessions $120 (#116)
- Annie Wang—2 **Crisis** $300 (#117)
- Marley Roberts—2 **Persistence** $150 (#118)
- Kim Kowalski—2 **Crisis** $300 (#119)

✓   You don't have time to make the bank deposit today. You make a note to yourself to bring the cash down to the bank when you come to work next Monday.

✓   Shaniya turns in her timesheet for the last two weeks.

Date	Day of the Week	Activity	# of hours	Billable?
3/18	Monday	Southside	4	Y
3/19	Tuesday			
3/20	Wednesday	Central	6	Y
3/21	Thursday	Northside	6	Y
3/22	Friday			
3/25	Monday	Meeting with Martin	3	N
3/26	Tuesday	Southside	3	Y
3/27	Wednesday	Central	5	Y
3/28	Thursday	Northside	5	Y
3/29	Friday	Southside	4	Y
		Total Hours	36	

- You enter Shaniya's timesheet data using **School** as the **service item** and the **project** as the **customer** for all billable hours. Only hours need to be included for the time spent meeting with Martin. **TIP:** You should show 16 hours for the first week and 20 hours for the second week.

- You also enter a **bill** for the amount Sally owes Shaniya ($1,080—SM331). You charge the meeting hours ($90) to **608 Staff Relations**. For the tutoring time, you use **School** for the **service item**. Since you will be creating the invoice for Sacramento Public Schools using the timesheet hours, you don't make the charges billable here. **TIP:** Don't forget to charge the hours to the correct **project** though. Sally spent 11 hours at Southside, 11 hours at Northside, and 11 hours at Central.

✓ Kenny turns in his timesheet for the last two weeks.

Date	Day of the Week	Activity	# of hours	Billable?
3/18	Monday	Northside	4	Y
3/19	Tuesday			
3/20	Wednesday			
3/21	Thursday	Central	4	Y
3/22	Friday			
3/25	Monday	Meeting with Martin	3	N
3/26	Tuesday	Southside	4	Y
3/27	Wednesday			
3/28	Thursday			
3/29	Friday			
		Total Hours	15	

- You enter Kenny's timesheet data using **Game Training** as the **service item** and the **project** as the **customer** for all billable hours. Only hours need to be included for the time spent meeting with Martin. **TIP:** You should show 8 hours for the first week and 7 hours for the second week.

- You also enter a **bill** for the amount Sally owes Kenny ($450—KC331). You charge the meeting hours ($90) to **608 Staff Relations**. For the training time, you use **Game Training** for the **service item**. Since you will be creating the invoice for Sacramento Public Schools using the timesheet hours, you don't make the charges billable here. **TIP:** Don't forget to charge the hours to the correct **project** though. Kenny spent 4 hours at Southside, 4 hours at Northside, and 4 hours at Central.

✓ You pay Kenny ($ 450—check #1134) and Shaniya ($1,080—check #1135).

✓ You create invoices for Shaniya's and Kenny's work. The invoices are dated 3/31 with terms of Net 30.

- Southside (Invoice #1032) $750.00
- Central (Invoice #1033) $750.00
- Northside (Invoice #1034) $750.00

✓ You write Martin a dividend check for $2,500. (Check #1136)

3/30/19

✓ You spend Saturday making the final adjustments for March. You want to be able to give Martin some good management reports next week.

✓ You don't have your bank statement yet but you go online and see that the balance is $8,418.20 at 3/30. All deposits for March and all checks written prior to 3/20/19 cleared the bank. There were no services charges during March. You reconcile the books to the $8,418.20 balance.

✓ You also reconcile the credit card statement as of 3/30. The balance is $664.20. All recorded charges and payments are included on the statement. You enter the bill for payment later. You use MARCC as the **bill no**.

✓ You compare the inventory on hand to the inventory report in QBO. All amounts agree.

✓ You make the necessary adjustments, dated 3/31, after considering the following:

- Supplies on Hand at 3/31 equal $43.85.

- You look carefully at the profit and loss statement and make sure that all March expenses are properly recorded. (**TIP:** Include the YTD column on your profit and loss report. Compare the March expenses with the year-to-date expenses. Are there any of the common operating expenses missing? Do any of the expenses appear unusually high?)

- You look carefully at the balance sheet paying particular attention to Other Current Assets and Other Current Liabilities. Many of the common month-end adjustments affect accounts in those categories. **TIP:** Look at the journal entries you made at February 28th.

- **HINT:** Interest on both loans is 6% (annual rate). No payments were made on either of the loans in March.

Check numbers 3/31

Checking account balance:. . . . .$ 3,878.20
Other Current Assets: . . . .$ 4,373.85
Total assets: $25,635.36
Total liabilities: $10,262.09
Gross profit (March). $14,164.46
Net income for March:. $10,097.45

Reports to create for Chapter 10:

All reports should be in portrait orientation.

- Balance Sheet as of 3/31

- Profit and Loss (March)

- Sales by Product/Service Summary (March)

- Inventory Valuation Summary (March 31)

- Profit and Loss by Customer (March)

Background information: Sally Hanson, a good friend of yours, double majored in Computer Science and Accounting in college. She worked for several years for a software company in Silicon Valley but the long hours started to take a toll on her personal life.

Last year she decided to open up her own company, Salish Software Solutions (a corporation). Sally currently advises clients looking for new accounting software and assists them with software installation. She also provides training to client employees and occasionally troubleshoots software issues.

She has decided to start using QuickBooks Online to keep track of her business transactions. She likes the convenience of being able to access financial information over the Internet. You have agreed to act as her accountant while you're working on your accounting degree.

Sally has a number of clients that she is currently working with. She gives 15-day payment terms to her corporate clients but she asks for cash at time of service if she does work for individuals. She has developed the following fee schedule:

Assignment 10B

Salish Software Solutions

Name	Description	Rate
Select	Software Selections	$500 flat fee
Set Up	Software Installation	$ 50 per hour
Train	Software training	$ 40 per hour
Fix	File repair	$ 60 per hour

Sally rents office space from Alki Property Management for $800 per month.

The following furniture and equipment is owned by Salish:

Description	Date placed in service	Cost	Life	Salvage Value
Office Furniture.	6/1/18	$1,400	60 months	$200
Computer	7/1/18	$4,620	36 months	$300
Printer.	5/1/18	$ 900	36 months	$ 0

All equipment is depreciated using the straight-line method.

As of 12/31/18, she owed $3,500 to Dell Finance. The monthly payment on that loan is $150 including interest at 5%. Sally's last payment to Dell was 12/31/18.

Over the next month or so, Sally plans to expand her business by selling some of her favorite accounting and personal software products directly to her clients. She has already purchased the following items.

Item Name	Description	Vendor	Quantity On Hand	Cost per unit	Sales Price
Easy1	Easy Does it	Abacus Shop	15	$100	$175
Retailer.	Simply Retail	Simply Accounting	2	$400	$700
Contractor.	Simply Construction	Simply Accounting	2	$500	$800
Organizer	Organizer	Personal Solutions	25	$ 25	$ 50
Tracker	Investment Tracker	Personal Solutions	25	$ 20	$ 40

> **HINT:** If you didn't turn off Automation in Chapter 2, you might want to consider doing that now. It's easy to get confused when QBO automatically adds accounts to your transactions. Click the **gear** icon on the icon bar and select **Account and Settings**. In the **Automation** section of the **Advanced** tab, turn **Prefill forms with previously entered content** to **Off**.

3/1/19

✓ Sally just got a call from Hiroshi Tanaka, the IT director at Delucca Deli, a Northern California deli chain. He had gotten Sally's name from the IT Director at Metro Market. They've decided to start expanding their operations and would like to hire Sally to make sure all their new stores are properly set up with **Simply Retail**. They also want her to train all the new store managers. She is excited about the opportunity but explains that she wouldn't be able to do all the work herself. Hiroshi is fine with using assistants as long as Sally oversees their work. They agree on a rate of $75 per hour for installation and training.

✓ Sally talks first with Oscar Torres. He helped her at one of the workshops and she was impressed with his work. She also gives Olivia Patel a call. Sally successfully worked with Olivia a few years ago on a large project and they've stayed in touch ever since. They both agree to work with Sally on the Delucca project. Olivia will take over the installation work and Oscar will do the training.

- Sally agrees to pay them both $50 per hour.
- Both Olivia and Oscar will submit timesheets to you every two weeks.

✓ Sally's not sure how much work she'll have for them and both will continue to offer their services to other companies, so you plan to treat both Oscar and Olivia as **contractors**. You set Olivia and Oscar up in QBO using the following information. (Oscar is already set up as a contractor. You just add the rate and payment terms to his vendor record.)

Name	Oscar Torres	Olivia Patel
Street address		3667 Admiral Avenue
City, State		Sacramento, CA
Zip code		95822
SSN		455-22-9874
Billing rate	$50	$50
Terms	Net 15	Net 15

TIP: You'll need to enter the **billing rate** and **terms** in the vendor record.

✓ You turn some features on in the **Time tracking** section of the **Advanced** tab of **Account and Settings**.

- You **Add service field to timesheets** and **Make Single-Time Activity Billable to Customer**.

- You check **Show billing rate to users entering time**.

- You set Monday as the **first day of work week**.

✓ You set up Delucca Deli as a new customer.

- 3582 Expansion Drive
  Sacramento, CA 95822
  Terms are Net 15.

✓ Since the rates are higher for this type of work, you decide to set up two new **service items**. Neither item is taxable.

- One for the initial setup

  ○ Item name: Corporate

  ○ Description: Set up of software system at corporate location

  ○ Category: Consulting and Installation

  ○ Sales price/rate: $75 (per hour)

  ○ Income accounting: 400 Software Selection and Installation

  ○ Cost: $50

  ○ Expense account: 609 Contract labor

- One for the training

  ○ Item name: Group Train

  ○ Description: Group software training at corporate location

  ○ Category: Consulting and Installation

  ○ Sales price/rate: $75 (per hour)

  ○ Income accounting: 400 Software and Installation

  ○ Cost: $50

  ○ Expense account: 609 Contract labor

✓ Although all **invoices** will be paid by Delucca Deli, management does want information about the hours by location so you turn on project tracking in the **Advanced** tab of **Account and Settings** and add the first 4 locations as **projects**. All of them have Delucca Deli as the **parent customer**.

- Mendocino

- Sausalito

- Half Moon Bay

- Palo Alto

✓ Sally continues to put on workshops. This first one in March will be for Metro Market. They are bringing in some of their IT staff for the **Effective Troubleshooting** workshop. They've agreed to pay the facility costs (plus a markup of 10%) but have asked Sally to find a suitable location. She has secured space at Hacker Spaces.

✓ You realize you're going to have to activate some features in QBO to handle billable costs.

- You decide to track reimbursable costs in a separate account. You set up a "Reimburs-able costs" account as an **Expense account type** and an **Other Miscellaneous Ser-vice Costs detail type**. You make it a sub-account of **Other Costs** and use "698" as the account number.

- You turn on the features related to tracking and billing expenses and items by cus-tomer in the **Expenses** tab of **Account and Settings**. **TIP:** You may need to open **Make expenses and items billable** to see the options.
  - ○ You decide not to track the billable expense as income.
  - ○ Sally will be charging a 10% markup on Delucca. She expects to use the same rate for other customers.

- You do want to track the markup amounts separately. You set up a new account (480 Markup Income). You use **Service/Fee income** as the **detail type**. You make the ap-propriate change on the **Advanced** tab of **Account and Settings**.

3/4/19

✓ You write yourself a check (#1124) for the $350 owed to you for February's bookkeeping services. **TIP:** You accrued that cost at the end of February.

✓ You also make the $150 monthly debt payment to Dell Finance. (Check #1125.) **TIP:** You're paying interest through 2/28 plus some principal.

✓ Sally places an order for 4 copies of **Retailer** from Simply Accounting. You record the $1,600 order on PO #104.

✓ Sally brings you a credit card receipt for her $1,200 purchase of an **annual** subscription to Advances in Software Design, a well-respected magazine. The magazine is published monthly. She received the March issue already. This is a professional development type of cost (technical reading materials).

3/5/19

✓ You receive three checks in the mail and record them in QBO. All were dated 3/5.
- $710 from Fabulous Fifties for Invoice 1021. Check # 987744.
- $480 from Butter and Beans for Invoice 1020. Check # 722258
- $270 from Reyelle Consulting for Invoice 1014. Check # 433352

✓ You deposit the checks in the bank. The total deposit is $1,460.

✓ You receive 4 of the 5 **Easy1** products ordered from Abacus Shop on PO 103. The total amount on the invoice (#5277-99) is $1,600. In addition to the books, Abacus shipped two laptops Sally had ordered for Oscar and Olivia to use in the field. The total cost of the laptops was $1,200 (including tax).

✓ You write a $400 check to Hacker Spaces to pay for the rental space for the Metro Market workshop this week. You record the payment (Check #1126) and make it billable with a 10% markup.

3/6/19

✓ Sally decides to do some advertising of her new management products. She places an ad in the Sacramento Journal. The ad will run in the March online issue, out 3/11. She uses the credit card to pay the $250 fee.

✓ The software arrives from Simply Accounting. All 4 copies ordered on PO 104 are in-cluded along with a bill for $1,600 (#WE-4477) dated 3/6. Simply Accounting's payment terms are 2%10, Net 30.

✓ You let Sally know about the early payment discount available from Simply Accounting. You encourage her to pay the bill by the 16th to take advantage of the 2%. You are a bit concerned about having enough cash though. Sally says she'll draw on the line of credit if necessary.

3/8/19

✓ You receive two bills in the mail. Both are dated 3/8.
  - Sacramento Light and Power's March bill (for heat and light) #01-94442—$90.18. The terms are Net 30.
  - Western Phone March bill #9144-64 for $122.45. The terms are Net 30.

✓ You receive 2 checks in the mail, both dated 3/8.
  - Check #77066 from Alki Deli for $200, in payment of Invoice 1019.
  - Check #989899 from Metro Market for $500, in payment of Invoice 1018.

✓ You deposit the checks in the bank. ($700 total).

3/13/19

✓ You get ready to pay bills. You know you're going to take the early payment discount on the Simply Accounting $1,600 bill so you create a **vendor credit** for $32. You use WE4477D as the **ref no**. You charge the amount to **Purchase discounts**.

✓ You realize that you've missed the due dates on some of the bills. You apologize to Sally. You've been really busy this month and completely forgot. You also let her know that the cash balance will be low after the bills are paid. Sally agrees to call the bank on Friday if there's not enough cash to pay Oscar and Olivia.

✓ You pay all bills due on or before 3/20. **TIP:** This includes the bill from Simply Accounting. This discount expires on 3/16.
  - There are six bills. Total amount paid is $6,017.61. The first check number is #1127.

3/14/19

✓ Sally can't believe the response she's getting from her ad in the Sacramento Journal. She has already gotten calls from 5 different companies. Two of them stopped by to pick up the software. Both paid with a credit card. You use the office address as the **billing address** so that the appropriate amount of tax is charged. (3835 Freeport Blvd., Sacramento, CA 95822)
  - Delightful Dental purchased Managing Your Medical Practice (**Medical**) for $541.25 (#108).
  - Westside Engineers purchased Managing Your Engineering Firm (**Engineering**) for $541.25 (#109).

✓ Sally places an order with Abacus Shop. You record the order on PO 105. The total is $1,750.
  - 2 **Medical**
  - 2 **Engineering**
  - 1 **Legal**

3/15/19

✓ You receive a check in the mail from Reyelle Consulting in full payment of Invoice #1017. You're relieved to get the check so quickly. The check (#3333) was for $1,400.

✓ You get the credit card receipts from yesterday and the check from today deposited right away. The credit card deposit totals $ 1,060.85 (after the 2% fee). The check deposit totals $1,400.

✓ Although it looks like there will be enough cash to pay Oscar and Olivia, Sally decides to draw the full $5,000 on the line. She wants to have a bit of a cushion in case a really good deal comes along. You record the deposit into your account by Sacramento City Bank. **TIP:** You already have an account set up for the credit line (account #275).

✓ Olivia turns in her timesheet for the first two weeks.

Date	Day of the Week	Project	# of hours	Billable?
3/1	Friday			
3/4	Monday			
3/5	Tuesday	Sausalito	2	Y
3/6	Wednesday	Mendocino	2	Y
3/7	Thursday			
3/8	Friday			
3/11	Monday	Sausalito	8	Y
3/12	Tuesday			
3/13	Wednesday	Mendocino	8	Y
3/14	Thursday			
3/15	Friday			
		Total Hours	20	

- You enter Olivia's timesheet data using **Corporate** as the **service item** and the **project** as the **customer**. All hours are billable. **TIP:** You should show 4 hours for the first week and 16 hours for the second week.

- You also enter a bill for the amount Sally owes Olivia ($1,000—OP315). You use **Corporate** for the **service item**. Since you will be creating the invoice for Delucca using the timesheet hours, you don't make the charges billable here. **TIP:** Don't forget to charge the hours to the correct **project** though. Olivia spent 10 hours at Mendocino and 10 hours at Sausalito.

✓ Oscar turns in his timesheet for the first two weeks.

Date	Day of the Week	Project	# of hours	Billable?
3/1	Friday			
3/4	Monday			
3/5	Tuesday			
3/6	Wednesday			
3/7	Thursday	Sausalito	4	Y
3/8	Friday	Mendocino	4	Y
3/11	Monday			
3/12	Tuesday	Sausalito	8	Y
3/13	Wednesday			
3/14	Thursday	Mendocino	8	Y
3/15	Friday			
		Total Hours	24	

- You enter Oscar's timesheet data using **Group Train** as the **service item** and the **project** as the **customer**. All hours are billable. **TIP:** You should show 8 hours for the first week and 16 hours for the second week.

- You also enter a **bill** for the amount Sally owes Oscar ($1,200—OT315). You use **Group Train** for the **service item**. Since you will be creating the invoice for Delucca using the timesheet hours, you don't make the charges billable here. **TIP:** Don't forget to charge the hours to the correct **project** though. Oscar spent 12 hours at Sausalito and 12 hours at Mendocino.

✓ You pay Olivia ($1,000—check #1132) and Oscar ($1,200—check #1133).

✓ You create invoices for Olivia and Oscar's work for Delucca Deli. You also add the charges for the software (**Retailer**) to the invoices. One package per store. The invoices are dated 3/15 with terms of Net 15.

- Sausalito $2,516 (#1023)
- Mendocino $2,516 (#1024)

3/18/19

✓ The Effective Troubleshooting workshop for Metro Markets was a success. Sally says she even got some leads on other companies that might be interested in her services. You record the invoice (#1025) to Metro with terms of Net 15. The total amount billed (including the space rental cost and the $2,500 workshop fee) is $2,940.

✓ Sally gives you the information on her client work for the last two weeks. You invoice the customers using 3/18 as the sales date.

- Fabulous Fifties—20 **Train** hours $800 (#1026)
- mSquared Enterprises—12 **Set Up** hours $600 (#1027)

3/19/19

✓ Sally continues to receive calls about the management products so she decides to put on a workshop, highlighting the new management products, in the office on Friday. She decides to charge $75 per attendee. She sends out an email to all the people who have contacted her for information.

✓ Cezar Software pays invoice 1022 with a $1,875 check (#740062) dated 3/19.

3/21/19

✓ All products ordered from Abacus Shop (PO 105) are received today. You record the bill (#6011-11) for $1,750. Terms are Net 30.

✓ You notice that the 5th copy of **Easy1** you ordered from Abacus on PO 103 still hasn't arrived. Sally gives them a call. They explain that they're having trouble getting that product from their supplier. She decides to go ahead and cancel the PO for now. You change the PO status to **closed** in QBO. **TIP:** Consider using the search feature to find the purchase order.

3/22/19

✓ Only five people showed up for the demonstration today. Definitely not as many as Sally had hoped for. Only one product was sold. She's disappointed but she realizes that she should have done more marketing. She thinks the $75 fee was probably too high as well. Everyone paid with a credit card.

- You record the income using a **sales receipt** (#110), and Cash Customer as the **customer**. You use **Picks** as the **service item**. The Cash Customer address should be 3835 Freeport Blvd, Sacramento, CA 95822
- The total Including the sale of one **Legal** was $916.25. **TIP:** Tax would only be charged on the product sale.

3/26/19

✓ Reyelle Consulting returned another **Organizer**. Sally asks you to refund them the $50 with a check. You enter the refund receipt (RR101) and use Check #1134. **TIP:** There should be no tax on this transaction. Reyelle is a reseller.

✓ Sally calls Personal Software to complain. They apologize and send over a credit for $25 for the returned **Organizer**. (#4494CM)

✓ You receive a check for $5,032 from Delucca Deli in the mail. The check (#3131888) is payment in full of invoices 1023 and 1024.

✓ You deposit the Delucca check, the check from 3/19, and the credit card sales from 3/22 in the bank. **TIP:** You create two **deposits**. One for the checks and one for the credit card payments.

- The check deposit totals $6,907.00
- The credit card deposit totals $897.92

3/27/19

✓   Sally meets with Oscar and Olivia at The Blue Door to discuss progress on Delucca Deli. Both Oscar and Olivia think everything's going well so far and are wondering if more projects will be coming in April. Sally agrees to check with Hiroshi and Delucca and let them know. Sally uses the credit card to pay for the $105.82 lunch. She doesn't want to charge Delucca so you expense the amount to **608 Staff meetings expense**. You don't charge the cost to any of the projects.

3/28/19

✓   You pay the Dovalina & Diamond and Abacus Shop bills. The total is $2,300. The first check is 1135.

3/29/19

✓   Sally gives you the information on her client work for the last two weeks. You record the invoices using 3/29 as the sales date.

- Fabulous Fifties—5 **Train** hours $200. #1028
- Lou's Barber Shop—4 **Fix** hours $240. #1029
- mSquared Enterprises—6 **Set Up** hours and 10 **Train** hours $700. #1030

✓   Olivia turns in her timesheet for the last two weeks.

Date	Day of the Week	Project	# of hours	Billable?
3/18	Monday	Palo Alto	2	Y
3/19	Tuesday			
3/20	Wednesday	Half Moon Bay	2	Y
3/21	Thursday			
3/22	Friday			
3/25	Monday	Palo Alto	8	Y
3/26	Tuesday			
3/27	Wednesday	Meeting with Sally	3	
3/28	Thursday	Half Moon Bay	8	Y
3/29	Friday			
		Total Hours	23	

- You enter Olivia's timesheet data using **Corporate** as the **service item** and the **project** as the **customer**. All hours are billable. **TIP:** You should show 4 hours for the first week and 19 hours for the second week.
- You also enter a **bill** for the amount Sally owes Olivia ($1,150 OP331). You charge the meeting hours ($150) to **608 Staff meetings expense**. You use **Corporate** for the **service item** on the billable hours. Since you will be creating the invoice for Delucca using the timesheet hours, you don't make the charges billable here. **TIP:** Don't forget to charge the hours to the correct **project** though. Olivia spent 10 hours at Palo Alto and 10 hours at Half Moon Bay

✓   Oscar turns in his timesheet for the last two weeks.

Date	Day of the Week	Project	# of hours	Billable?
3/18	Monday	Mendocino	4	Y
3/19	Tuesday			
3/20	Wednesday			
3/21	Thursday	Palo Alto	4	Y
3/22	Friday	Half Moon Bay	4	Y
3/25	Monday			
3/26	Tuesday	Palo Alto	8	Y
3/27	Wednesday	Meeting with Sally	3	
3/28	Thursday	Sausalito	5	Y
3/29	Friday			
		Total Hours	28	

- You enter Oscar's timesheet data using **Group Train** as the **service item** and the **project** as the **customer**. All hours are billable. **TIP:** You should show 12 hours for the first week and 16 hours for the second week.

- You also enter a **bill** for the amount Sally owes Oscar ($1,400—OT331). You charge the meeting hours ($150) to **608 Staff meetings expense**. You use **Group Train** for the **service item**. Since you will be creating the invoice for Delucca using the timesheet hours, you don't make the charges billable here. **TIP:** Don't forget to charge the hours to the correct **project** though. Oscar spent 4 hours at Mendocino, 4 hours at Half Moon Bay, 12 hours at Palo Alto, and 5 hours at Sausalito

✓ You pay Olivia ($1,150—check #1137) and Oscar ($1,400—check #1138).

✓ You create invoices for Olivia and Oscar's work for Delucca Deli. You also add the charges for the software (**Retailer**) to the invoices for Half Moon Bay and Palo Alto. The invoices are dated 3/31 with terms of Net 15.

  - Sausalito $375 (#1031)
  - Mendocino $300 (#1032)
  - Half Moon Bay $1,916 (#1033)
  - Palo Alto $2,516 (#1034)

✓ You write yourself a check (#1139 for $350) for March accounting work.

✓ You also write a check (#1140) for $2,500 to Sally for March dividends.

✓ Before you leave for the day, you talk to Sally about the credit line. You have a healthy cash balance now and you suggest that Sally pay down the line a bit. She can always borrow again if needed. Sally agrees. You pay Sacramento City Bank $2,500 plus interest with check #1141. **TIP:** The simple annual interest rate charged by the bank is 6%. Sally borrowed $5,000 on 3/15. Use ½ month for the interest payment.)

3/30/19

✓ You spend Saturday making the final adjustments for March. You want to be able to give Sally some good management reports next week.

✓ You don't have your bank statement yet but you go online and see that the balance is $14,837.46 at 3/30. All deposits for March and all checks written prior to 3/20 cleared the bank. There were no services charges in March. You reconcile to the $14,837.46 balance.

✓ You also reconcile the credit card statement dated 3/31. The balance is $1,555.82. All recorded charges and payments are included on the statement. You enter the bill for payment later. You use MARCC as the **bill no**.

✓ You compare the inventory on hand to the inventory report in QBO. All amounts agree.

✓ You make the necessary adjustments, dated 3/31, after considering the following:

- Supplies on Hand at 3/31 equal $185.

- You purchased laptops for Oscar and Olivia on 3/5 for $1,200. They were placed in service right away. You go ahead and take a full month's depreciation on the computers. Sally thinks they'll last 2 years, with no salvage value. **TIP:** There's no change on depreciation expense for the other assets purchased prior to March 1.

- You look carefully at the profit and loss statement and make sure that all March expenses are properly recorded. (**TIP:** Include the **Prior Period** column on your profit and loss report. Compare the March expenses with the February expenses. Are there any of the common operating expenses missing? Do any of the expenses appear unusually high?)

- You look carefully at the balance sheet paying particular attention to Other Current Assets and Other Current Liabilities. Many of the common month-end adjustments affect accounts in those categories. **TIP:** Look at the journal entries you made at February 28th. There will likely be similar entries for March.

- **HINT:** Interest on the Dell Finance loan is 5% (simple, annual rate). The last payment to Dell was 3/1.

Check numbers 3/31

Checking account balance:. . . . .$ 4,574.96
Other Current Assets: $10,621.50
Total assets: $35,509.71
Total liabilities:. . . . .$ 7,873.25
Gross Profit (March):. $14,187.00
Net income for March:. . . . .$ 7,096.37

Reports to create for Chapter 10:

- Balance Sheet as of March 31

- Profit and Loss (March)

- Sales by Product/Service Summary (March)

- Inventory Valuation Summary (March 31)

- Profit and Loss by Customer (March)

APPENDIX 10A TRACKING PROJECTS USING SUB-CUSTOMERS

Projects is a relatively new feature in QBO. If companies don't have the feature available, **sub-customers** can be used for tracking jobs.

BEHIND THE SCENES In Chapter 3, **sub-customers** were used for tracking company branches. Whether a user is tracking branches or projects, **sub-customers** is a tool for maintaining detailed records for related entities.

Some rules apply when using **sub-customers** to track projects.

- Multiple projects (**sub-customers**) can be tracked for a single customer.

- Multiple projects (**sub-customers**) cannot be billed on the same invoice or sales receipt.

- A **sub-customer** can also be a **parent customer**.

- All hours and any external costs incurred on a project (**sub-customers**) must be defined as billable if you intend to later charge the customer for those hours or costs.

    - A **billable** field is included on all appropriate forms (**timesheets**, **bills**, **checks**, etc.).

    - Costs that are not defined as **billable** will be included in all reports but will not be accessible when preparing **invoices** or **sales receipts**.

Sub-customers are set up in the Customer Center.

Click **Sales** on the navigation bar and select the **Customers** tab.

Click **New customer**.

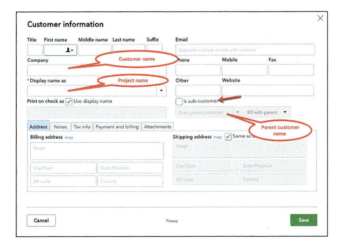

The **Company** name entered would normally be the name of the **parent customer**. The **Display name as** field would contain the name of the project.

Is sub-customer must be checked and the **parent customer** identified.

The user must also select an option from the dropdown menu next to the **parent customer** name:

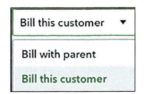

If **Bill with parent** is selected, any **invoices** or **sales receipts** prepared for the **sub-customer** (project) will also be part of the **parent customer** record. Statements can be sent to the **parent customer** including all **sub-customer** activity and payments received from the **parent customer** for multiple projects (**sub-customers**) can be processed as a single transaction.

If **Bill this customer** is selected, access to the **sub-customer** transactions is not shared with the **parent customer**.

APPENDIX 10B WORKING WITH ESTIMATES

Construction contractors and other companies that enter into large, long-term arrangements with their clients often provide up-front estimates of the total expected cost of the project to their clients. The estimates will normally list, in some detail, the various components of the job. As the work is performed, the company bills the actual labor and materials.

An important benefit of estimates is that they define what is being included in the scope of the project. Clients that request changes to the original scope would be given an estimate related to the change. (These are often called "change orders.") In a time and materials job, well-constructed estimates help reduce misunderstandings between the client and the company.

Estimates can be used even when the company is charging a fixed fee for the job. In a fixed fee job, an estimate is used simply to define what work is included in the fee. The fixed fee amount would be changed only if the client requested additional work not specified in the original agreement.

Companies can create estimates in QBO and can use those estimates when billing for work performed.

Creating Estimates

To create an **estimate**, click the ✚ icon on the icon bar.

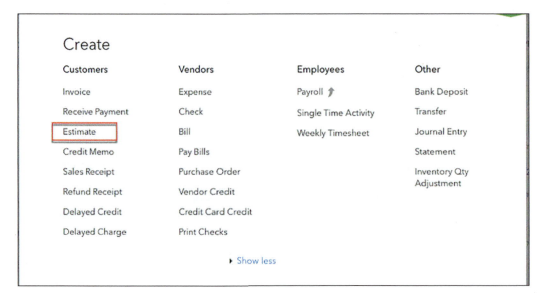

Click **Estimate**. The form will look something like this:

A client would normally be expected to either accept or reject an estimate in a reasonable period of time. If a client waits too long, costs to the company may have changed considerably. The date by which an estimate must be accepted is entered in the **expiration date** field.

A completed **estimate** might look something like this:

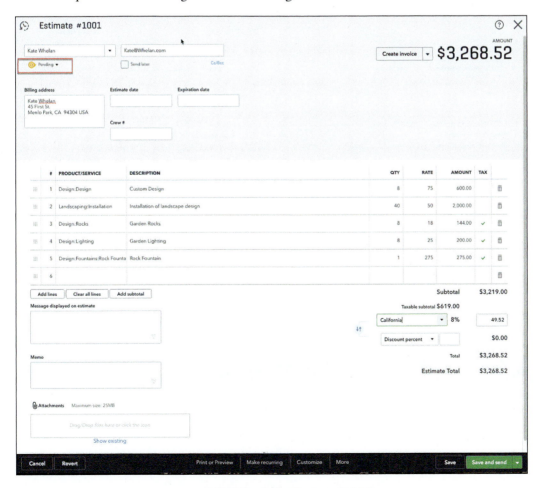

Once the client has reviewed and either accepted or rejected the estimate, the status can be changed by clicking the arrow next to **Pending**. The status options are:

Creating Invoices from Estimates

To bill for some or all of the **estimate**, a company would open an invoice form and enter the **customer name**. (As of now, estimates cannot be billed through **sales receipts** in QBO.)

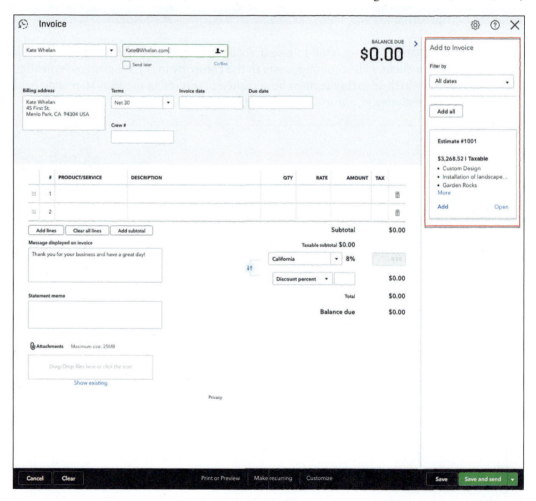

Click **Add** to transfer the information to the **invoice**.

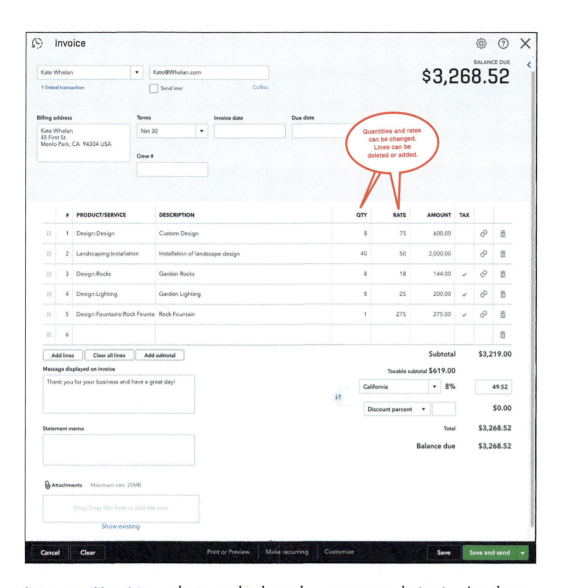

Items, quantities, dates, and rates can be changed as necessary on the invoice. Any changes made will not be reflected on the original estimate. Once an estimate has been used to create an invoice, the status of the estimate will automatically change to closed.

Clicking Closed (upper left corner) opens the following dialog box.

Information about customer acceptance can be entered here.

Copying Estimates

If the project is not completed, the company can create a copy of the original estimate adjusted to reflect the new open items.

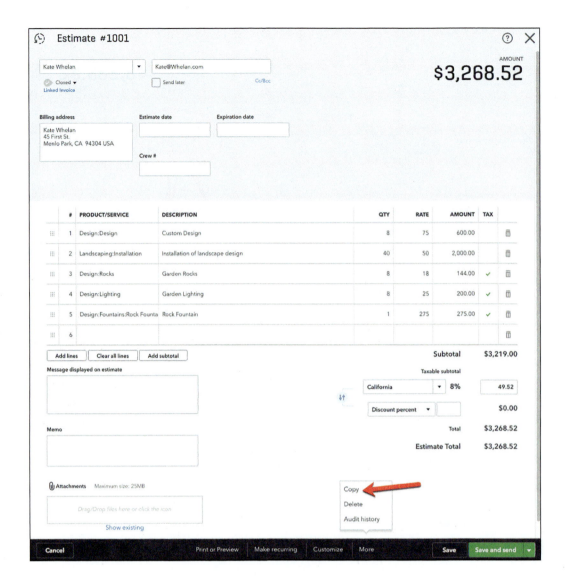

A copy of the original **estimate** can also be used to reflect additional work requested by the client. A change order might look something like this:

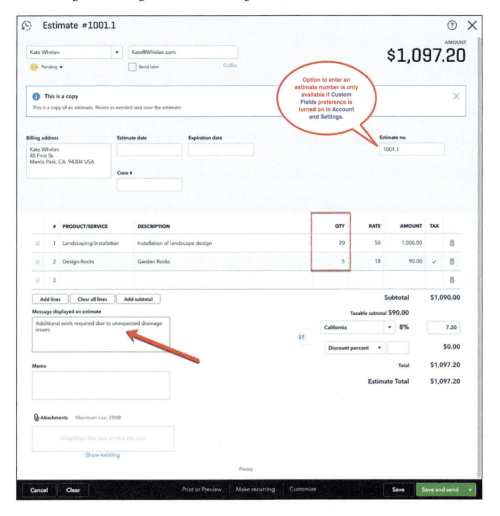

Creating Purchase Orders from Estimates

If **estimates** include **inventory** or **non-inventory part items** that must be purchased specifically for the project, a company can create a purchase order directly from the **estimate**.

The **estimate** might look something like this:

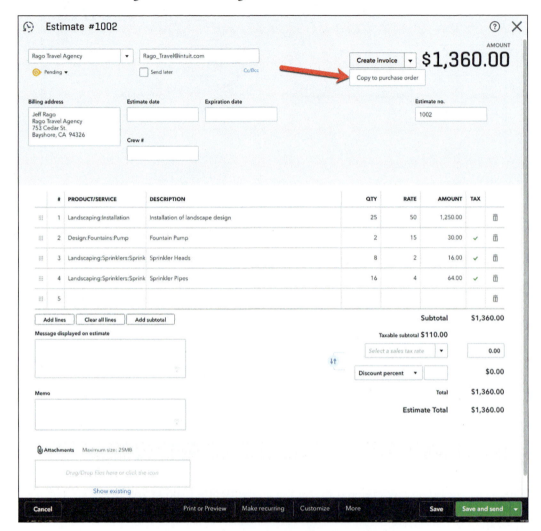

The following message will appear if **Copy to purchase order** is clicked.

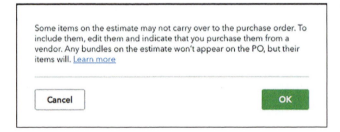

Click **OK**.

A **purchase order** will be created for all **inventory** or **non-inventory part items**.

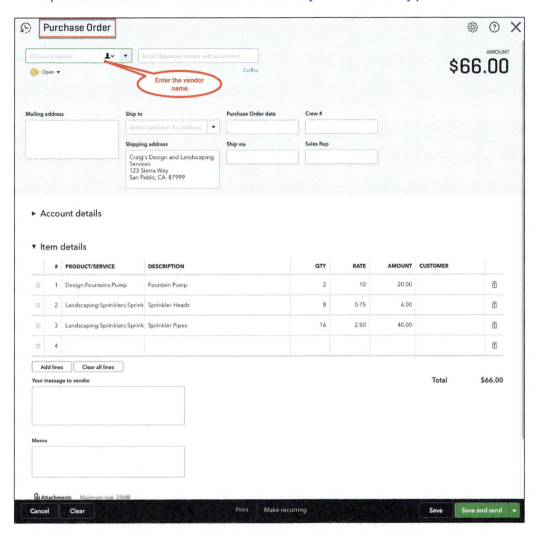

The **purchase order** is completed by adding a **vendor** and making any necessary changes. If the **items** included are purchased from multiple vendors, the **purchase order** would need to be copied.

QuickBooks

Beyond the Basics

Although recording transactions is a very important part of accounting, reporting accounting activity in a way that is useful to management is just as important.

In this section, a number of tools and features that can be very useful in managing a business will be introduced.

- Chapter 11 will cover segment reporting (using **classes** and **locations**) and budgeting, two important management tools in QBO.

- Chapter 12 will cover a variety of other tools including customizing forms and reports, managing attachments, and exporting reports to Excel.

Management Tools

After completing Chapter 11, you should be able to:

1. Use **class** and **location** tracking in QBO.

2. Prepare reports by **class** and **location**.

3. Set up budgets in QBO.

4. Prepare budget and budget variance reports.

Accounting is a system in which an organization's economic events are identified, recorded, summarized, analyzed, and reported. From this system comes financial information that can be used by management, creditors, and investors to plan and evaluate.

In this course, we focus on **recording and reporting** transactions in an electronic environment but it's also important to look at ways accounting software might be helpful in the planning and evaluation functions of an organization.

In this chapter, we're going to cover a few of the tools in QBO that can be used to provide useful information to management. There are a few others that are introduced in Chapter 12 but for now we will cover:

* Tracking operating results by **class** and by **location**

* Preparing budgets

TRACKING BY CLASS AND LOCATION

One of the main advantages of computerized accounting systems is the incredible amount of detail that can effectively AND efficiently be maintained. The use of **inventory part items** in QBO is a good example of that. A company can easily track revenues and costs for every model of every product sold by a company and still have a one-page income statement!

Class and **location** are additional tools in QBO available for tracking detail. Both are used to represent specific reporting **segments**. Examples of business segments include:

Segment A subdivision of an entity for which supplemental financial information is disclosed.

* Departments

* Divisions

* Sales regions

* Product lines

* Service types

* Stores

Users can use **class** tracking or **location** tracking or both.

Users can have up to five levels of tracking for **classes** and **locations**. Levels 2–5 are known as **sub-classes** or **sub-locations**.

Although the two features are similar, there is one important distinction between the two. If **class** tracking is used, a preference can be set allowing users to link each line item within each transaction (each form) to a specific **class**. If **location** tracking is used, the entire transaction is linked to one specific **location** on forms other than timesheets and journal entries. On timesheets and journal entries, it is possible to assign **location** by line item.

Because of that difference, it generally makes the most sense to use **location** tracking for business units like stores or departments or divisions and to use **class** tracking for focus areas, like product lines or service types that cross a number of business units.

Both types are available for filtering in reports. For example, if you had a **class** setup for Consulting Services, you could filter a sales report or a profit and loss report so that only transactions classified as Consulting Services would be included in your report. If you had a **location** setup for Portland, you could filter a report of expenses so that only Portland expenses would be included.

Segment tracking requires additional work so it should only be used if an organization CAN be separated into segments AND there are meaningful differences between the segments that make them worth tracking.

As an example, let's look at three retail companies selling jewelry. Company A has one store and one manager and only sells diamond rings. Company B has five stores and five managers and only sells diamond rings. Company C has three stores and three managers and sells diamond rings and also provides cleaning and repair services related to diamond rings.

Company A **could** set up a **class** for every type of diamond ring sold but that information is already available in **item** reports. The company could also set up a **class** for every day of the week but that probably wouldn't give management much meaningful information and would require a LOT of allocation! Company A has only one store so **location** tracking is unnecessary. Company A doesn't appear to have any meaningful segments.

Company B, on the other hand, might use **locations** to track sales and costs by store. Management could then use that information to evaluate product mix at the various stores, to evaluate the performance of store managers or in planning for new stores. Because the only product is diamond rings, it would be unlikely that using **classes** would be helpful.

Company C, like Company B, might use **locations** to track store operations. **Classes** might be used to track information about sales from rings separate from information about the cleaning and repair services they provide.

Here are two tips for using segment tracking:

- Set up **classes** or **locations** for the segments that provide the most useful information.
    - Segment information is useful if it can help a company evaluate or plan OR if segment detail is necessary for reporting to regulatory authorities.

- Make sure all transactions are assigned to a segment.
    - Most companies set up a separate **class** and **location** to be used to track activities that don't fit in one of the other identified business segments.
        - If, for example, a company sets up a **class** for each product line, owners' salaries or corporate legal fees might be examples of transactions that would be assigned to an "Other" or "Administration" **class**.

Using **class** or **location** tracking is not mandatory in QBO. It is a preference.

Turning on Class Tracking

Setting up **class** tracking is done in **Account and Settings**. (Use the **gear** icon on the icon bar to open **Account and Settings**.)

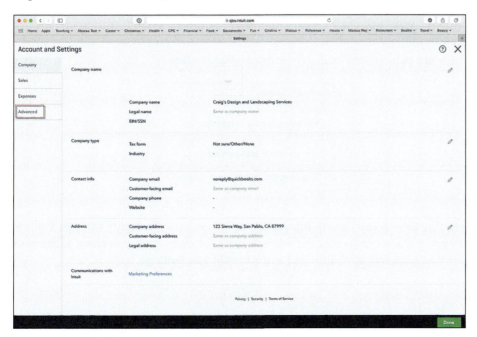

Open the **Advanced** tab and click the **pencil** icon in the **Categories** section to turn **class** tracking on.

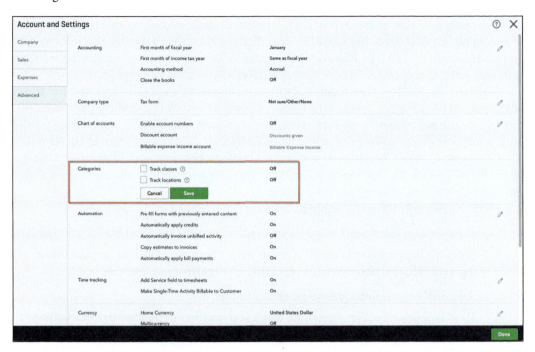

Check the **Track classes** box.

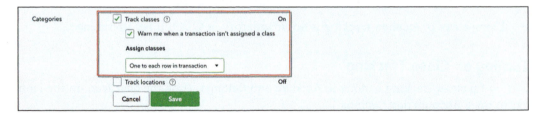

Using the **Warn me when a transaction isn't assigned a class** feature is an optional (but very useful!) tool.

There are two options available under **Assign classes**.

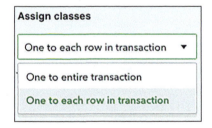

Selecting **One to each row in transaction** provides more flexibility because it allows you to easily enter transactions that include activities for more than one **class**. Click **Save** and then **Done** to complete the setup and exit **Account and Settings**.

Once **class** tracking is turned on, fields will be available on most forms for designating the appropriate classification. Here's an example of an **invoice** form after **class** tracking is activated.

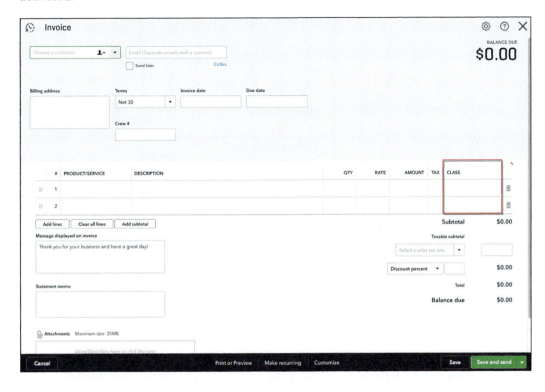

BEHIND THE SCENES: **Transfer** and **Payment transaction types** (forms) do not include boxes for tracking **location** or **class**. The segments would already have been identified on the related **invoice** or **sales receipt** forms so that information would not be necessary on **payment** transactions.

Turning on Location Tracking

Setting up **location** tracking is also done on the **Advanced** tab of **Account and Settings**. Click the **pencil** icon in the **Categories** section to turn **location** tracking on.

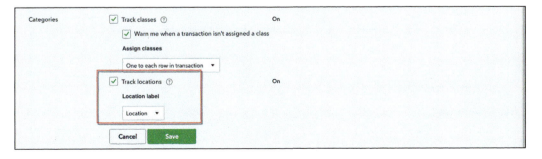

QBO uses "location" as the default title for this type of segment but users can change the title to one of the following:

Click **Save** and then **Done** to complete the setup and exit **Account and Settings**.

Once **location** tracking is turned on, fields will be available on most forms for designating the appropriate classification. Here's an example of a **bill** form after both **class** tracking and **location** tracking have been activated.

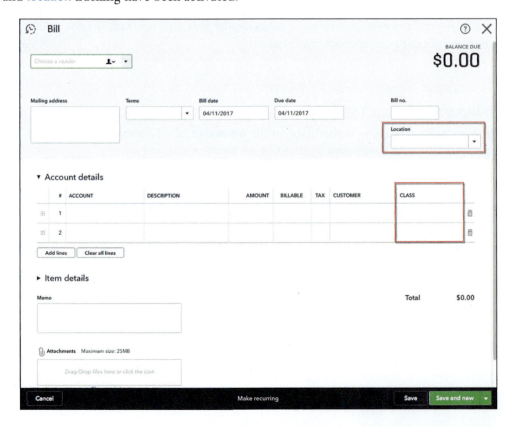

PRACTICE
EXERCISE

Turn on class tracking for Craig's Design and Landscaping.
(Craig's Design decides to track revenues and costs related to their primary sources of revenue.)

1. Click the **gear** icon on the icon bar.

2. Click **Account and Settings**.

3. Click **Advanced**.

4. Click the **pencil** icon in the **Categories** section.

5. Place a checkmark in the boxes next to **Track Classes** and **Warn me when a transaction isn't assigned a class**.

6. Select **one to each row in transaction** in the **Assign classes** dropdown menu.

7. Place a checkmark in the box next to **Track Locations**.

8. Select **Territory** in the **Location label** dropdown menu.

9. Click **Save**.

10. Click **Done**.

Setting Up Classes and Locations

Once you've activated segment reporting in QBO and identified the segments you want to track, setting up the categories is a simple process.

Click the **gear** icon on the icon bar to open the following window.

Craig's Design and Landscaping Services			
Your Company	**Lists**	**Tools**	**Profile**
Account and Settings	All Lists	Import Data	User Profile
Manage Users	Products and Services	Export Data	Feedback
Custom Form Styles	Recurring Transactions	Reconcile	Privacy
Chart of Accounts	Attachments	Budgeting	
QuickBooks Labs		Audit Log	🔒 Sign Out
		Order Checks ↗	

Click **All Lists** under the **Lists** column.

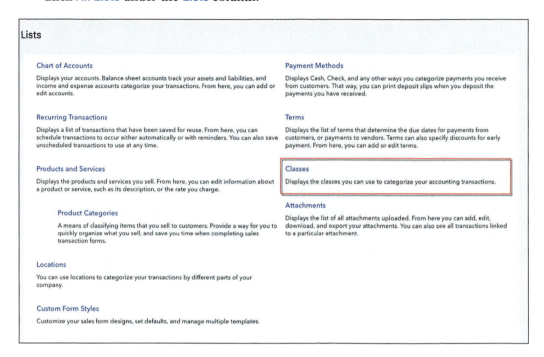

Click **Classes**.

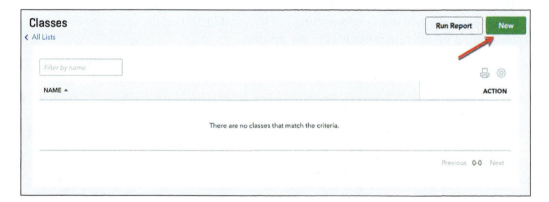

Click **New**.

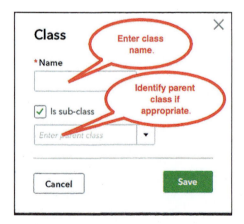

Enter a **Name** for the **class**. Check **Is sub-class** and select the appropriate **parent class** if multiple **class** levels are used.

 HINT: You can't rearrange the order of the **classes** on the **Class List**. The order listed is the order that will be displayed on reports. If it's important to have the **classes** in a particular order, companies might consider using numbers as part of the **class** names. The names could then be edited later to change the order. Reports can also be downloaded into Excel and reordered there. (Exporting to Excel is covered in Chapter 12.)

Clicking **Save** completes the setup of a new **class**.

The process for setting up **locations** is similar to the process for **class** setup.

Click the **gear** icon on the icon bar and select **All Lists** to open the following window.

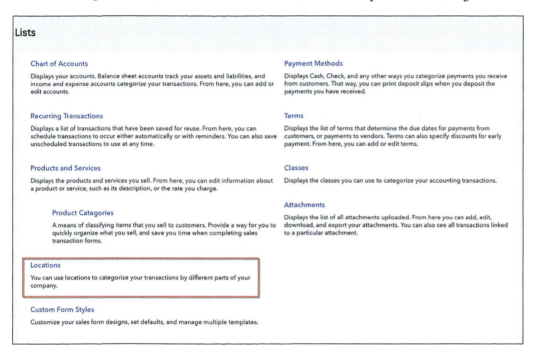

Click **Locations**.

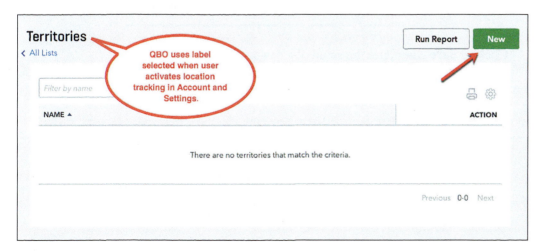

Click **New**.

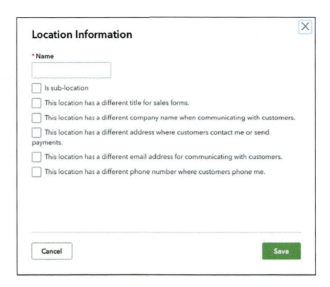

Since **locations** are often used by companies to represent separate stores or subsidiary locations, QBO allows users to customize titles of forms and contact information for various locations in this screen. For example, if a user wanted to use a different company name for each store or subsidiary on **invoices**, **sales receipts**, and other forms sent to customers, the setup might look something like this:

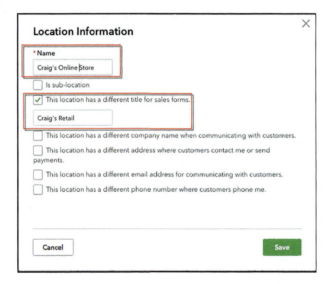

Clicking **Save** completes the setup of a new **location**.

Classes and **locations** can be edited or deleted by selecting **Edit** or **Delete** on the dropdown menu in the **Action** column of the appropriate list.

PRACTICE
EXERCISE

Set up classes and locations for Craig's Design and Landscaping.
(Craig's Design has decided to track operations by type of service and by territory. One class, labeled Design and Installation, will be used to report on landscape design services. A

(continued)

class labeled Gardening will be used to track all gardening services. A class labeled General will be used for all shared costs. Two territories will be used (Midtown and Uptown).)

1. If you have logged out since the last Practice Exercise, you'll need to activate **class** and **location** tracking as follows:

   a. Click the **gear** icon on the icon bar.

   b. Click **Account and Settings**.

   c. Click **Advanced**.

   d. Click the **pencil** icon in the **Categories** section.

   e. Place a checkmark in the box next to **Track Classes** and **Warn me when a transaction isn't assigned a class**.

   f. Select **one to each row in transaction** in the **Assign classes** dropdown menu.

   g. Place a checkmark in the box next to **Track Locations**.

   h. Select **Territory** in the **Location label** dropdown menu.

   i. Click **Save**.

   j. Click **Done**.

2. Click the **gear** icon on the icon bar.

3. Click **All Lists**.

4. Click **Classes**.

   a. Click **New**.

   b. Enter "Design and Installation" as the **Name**.

   c. Click **Save**.

   d. Click **New**.

   e. Enter "Gardening" as the **Name**.

   f. Click **Save**.

   g. Click **New**.

   h. Enter "General" as the **Name**.

   i. Click **Save**.

5. Click the **gear** icon on the icon bar.

6. Click **All Lists**.

7. Click **Territories**.

   a. Click **New**.

   b. Enter "Midtown" as the **Name.**

   c. Leave the other boxes unchecked.

   d. Click **Save**.

   e. Click **New**.

   f. Enter "Uptown" as the **Name.**

   g. Leave the other boxes unchecked.

   h. Click **Save**.

8. Click **Dashboard** to exit out of the window.

Adding Class and Location to Transactions

Assigning **classes** and **locations** is done within forms (**invoices**, **bills**, **journal entries**, **timesheets**, etc.). The assignment can be changed at any time by simply editing the form.

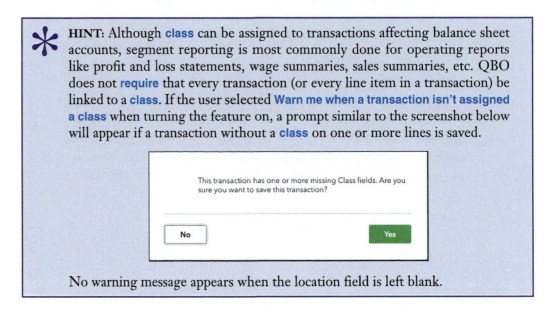

HINT: Although **class** can be assigned to transactions affecting balance sheet accounts, segment reporting is most commonly done for operating reports like profit and loss statements, wage summaries, sales summaries, etc. QBO does not **require** that every transaction (or every line item in a transaction) be linked to a **class**. If the user selected **Warn me when a transaction isn't assigned a class** when turning the feature on, a prompt similar to the screenshot below will appear if a transaction without a **class** on one or more lines is saved.

> This transaction has one or more missing Class fields. Are you sure you want to save this transaction?
>
> **No**   **Yes**

No warning message appears when the location field is left blank.

Since only one **location** can be assigned to a single form in most cases, the **location** field is usually located in the top right section of the form.

If the preference for adding **class** to line items is selected, fields for entering **class** are normally entered in one of the final columns for each row. If the preference is set to one **class** per transaction, the **class** field is normally displayed directly below the **location** field.

Here's an example of a **bill** when both **class** and **location** tracking are turned on and the preference is to assign **class** by line item.

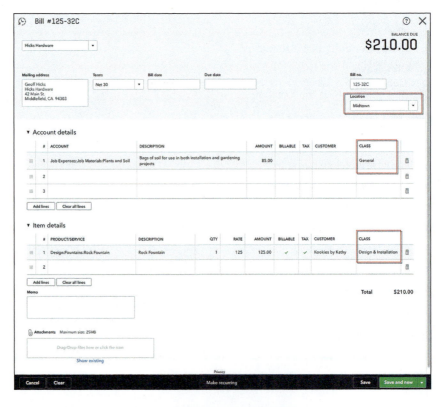

If you take a minute to think about it, you'll realize that there's quite a bit of information included in this bill. In this one form, the user would have:

- Increased inventory
- Expensed some supply costs
- Set up a liability
- Identified an amount to be billed to the client
- Classified the transaction by location and class

PRACTICE EXERCISE

Assign classes to a few transactions for Craig's Design and Landscaping.
(Craig's Design invoices Rondonuwu Fruit and Vegi for some gardening work and records a check for a consultation with an advertising agency about promoting the design services in the Uptown neighborhood.)

1. If you have logged out since the last Practice Exercise, you'll need to activate **class** and **location** tracking and set up some **classes** and **locations**:
   a. Activate segment tracking:
      i. Click the **gear** icon on the icon bar.
      ii. Click **Account and Settings**.
      iii. Click **Advanced**.
      iv. Click the **pencil** icon in the **Categories** section.
      v. Place a checkmark in the box next to **Track Classes** and **Warn me when a transaction isn't assigned a class.**
      vi. Select **one to each row in transaction** in the **Assign classes** dropdown menu.
      vii. Place a checkmark in the box next to **Track Locations**.
      viii. Select **Territory** in the **Location label** dropdown menu.
      ix. Click **Save**.
      x. Click **Done**.
   b. Set up **classes** and **territories**:
      i. Click the **gear** icon on the icon bar.
      ii. Click **All Lists**.
      iii. Click **Classes**.
         1. Click **New**.
         2. Enter "Design and Installation" as the **Name**.
         3. Click **Save**.
         4. Click **New**.
         5. Enter "Gardening" as the **Name**.
         6. Click **Save**.
         7. Click **New**.
         8. Enter "General" as the **Name.**
         9. Click **Save**.
      iv. Click the **gear** icon on the icon bar.

(continued)

     v. Click **All Lists**.

    vi. Click **Territories**.

       1. Click **New**.

       2. Enter "Midtown" as the **Name**.

       3. Leave the other boxes unchecked.

       4. Click **Save**.

       5. Click **New**.

       6. Enter "Uptown" as the **Name**.

       7. Leave the other boxes unchecked.

       8. Click **Save**.

2. Click the ➕ icon on the icon bar.

3. Click **Invoice**.

    a. Select **Rondonuwu Fruit and Vegi** as the customer.

    b. Use the current date as the **Invoice date**.

    c. Select **Midtown** as the **Territory**.

    d. Select **Trimming** as the **PRODUCT/SERVICE**.

    e. Leave the **QTY** and **RATE** as is.

    f. Check the **TAX** box.

    g. Select **Gardening** as the **Class**.

    h. Select **California** in the **select a sales tax rate** dropdown menu.

    i. Make a note of the total amount due.

    j. Click **Save and close**.

4. Click the ➕ icon on the icon bar.

5. Click **Check**.

    a. Select **Lee Advertising** as the vendor.

    b. Use the current date as the **Payment date**.

    c. Leave the check number as is.

    d. Select **Uptown** as the **Territory**.

    e. Select **Advertising** as the **ACCOUNT**.

    f. Enter "Consultation" as the **DESCRIPTION**.

    g. Enter "500" as the **AMOUNT**.

    h. Select **Design and Installation** as the **Class**.

    i. Click **Save and close**.

Reporting by Class or Location

There are several reports that are frequently used to report segment information but most reports can be filtered by **class** or **location**.

The **Profit & Loss by Class** and **Profit & Loss by Location** reports are probably the ones most commonly used. Both reports can be accessed in the **Business Overview** page of

Reports. Each **class** or **location** will be shown in a separate column. Any transactions that have NOT been classified will appear in a **Not Specified** column.

 HINT: Users can drill down on transactions appearing in the **Not Specified** column. The transactions can then be edited so that they are properly classified.

Here's an example of what a **Profit and Loss by Class** might look like:

Classes created and assigned by author.

Craig's Design and Landscaping Services

PROFIT AND LOSS BY CLASS

	ADMINISTRATION	DESIGN AND INSTALLATION	GARDENING	TOTAL
▾ Income				
Design income		937.50		$937.50
Discounts given		-59.00		$ -59.00
▾ Landscaping Services			210.00	$210.00
▾ Job Materials				$0.00
Fountains and Garden Lighting		775.00	129.00	$904.00
Plants and Soil			300.00	$300.00
Total Job Materials		775.00	429.00	$1,204.00
▾ Labor				$0.00
Installation		250.00		$250.00
Total Labor		250.00		$250.00
Total Landscaping Services		1,025.00	639.00	$1,664.00
Pest Control Services			70.00	$70.00
Services			103.55	$103.55
Total Income	$0.00	$1,903.50	$812.55	$2,716.05
GROSS PROFIT	$0.00	$1,903.50	$812.55	$2,716.05
▾ Expenses				
Advertising	74.86			$74.86
▾ Automobile	19.99			$19.99
Fuel			63.15	$63.15
Total Automobile	19.99		63.15	$83.14
Equipment Rental		112.00		$112.00
▾ Job Expenses		46.98		$46.98
▾ Job Materials				$0.00
Decks and Patios		103.55		$103.55
Total Job Materials		103.55		$103.55
Total Job Expenses		150.53		$150.53
▾ Maintenance and Repair				$0.00
Equipment Repairs	755.00			$755.00
Total Maintenance and Repair	755.00			$755.00
Total Expenses	$849.85	$262.53	$63.15	$1,175.53
NET OPERATING INCOME	$ -849.85	$1,640.97	$749.40	$1,540.52
NET INCOME	$ -849.85	$1,640.97	$749.40	$1,540.52

Here's an example of what a **Profit and Loss by Location** might look like:

Locations created and assigned by author.

Craig's Design and Landscaping Services
PROFIT AND LOSS BY LOCATION

	ADMINISTRATION	MENLO PARK	OUT OF STATE	PALO ALTO	TOTAL
▾ Income					
Design income				937.50	$937.50
Discounts given			-8.75	-50.25	$ -59.00
▾ Landscaping Services		100.00	80.00	30.00	$210.00
▾ Job Materials					$0.00
Fountains and Garden Lighting		84.00		820.00	$904.00
Plants and Soil		300.00			$300.00
Total Job Materials		384.00		820.00	**$1,204.00**
▾ Labor					$0.00
Installation				250.00	$250.00
Total Labor				250.00	**$250.00**
Total Landscaping Services		484.00	80.00	1,100.00	**$1,664.00**
Pest Control Services		-17.50	87.50		$70.00
Services		103.55			$103.55
Total Income	**$0.00**	**$570.05**	**$158.75**	**$1,987.25**	**$2,716.05**
GROSS PROFIT	$0.00	$570.05	$158.75	$1,987.25	$2,716.05
▾ Expenses					
Advertising	74.86				$74.86
▾ Automobile	19.99				$19.99
Fuel				63.15	$63.15
Total Automobile	19.99			63.15	**$83.14**
Equipment Rental		112.00			$112.00
▾ Job Expenses				46.98	$46.98
▾ Job Materials					$0.00
Decks and Patios				103.55	$103.55
Total Job Materials				103.55	**$103.55**
Total Job Expenses				150.53	**$150.53**
▾ Maintenance and Repair					$0.00
Equipment Repairs	755.00				$755.00
Total Maintenance and Repair	755.00				**$755.00**
Total Expenses	**$849.85**	**$112.00**	**$0.00**	**$213.68**	**$1,175.53**
NET OPERATING INCOME	$ -849.85	$458.05	$158.75	$1,773.57	$1,540.52
NET INCOME	$ -849.85	$458.05	$158.75	$1,773.57	$1,540.52

The **Sales and Customers** section in **Reports** includes a number of segmented reports preset by QBO.

CREATING AND USING BUDGETS

"The general who wins the battle makes many calculations in his temple before the battle is fought. The general who loses makes but few calculations beforehand."—Sun Tzu

Managing a business is certainly not like going to war but having a plan and being able to evaluate actual results against that plan can definitely help a business succeed.

A financial plan for a business is commonly called a "budget." In a simple budget, revenues and costs are generally estimated by month. Estimates might be based on:

- Past experience

- Projections of sales growth (or contraction)

- Industry statistics

- Combinations of the above

There are a number of tools in QBO for creating and using profit and loss budgets.

Creating Budgets

Companies can create multiple budgets in QBO.

Profit and loss budgets can be prepared for a company overall, by **Customer**, by **Class**, or by **Location**. In this course, we'll cover creating a budget for a company overall.

All of the planning tools in QBO are accessed by first clicking the **gear** icon on the icon bar.

Select **Budgeting** in the **Tools** column.

Click **Add Budget**.

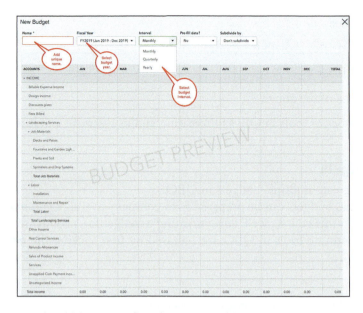

A unique name should be entered in the **Name** field. The appropriate **Fiscal Year** should also be selected.

Users can create monthly, quarterly, or yearly budgets. (The choice is selected in the **Interval** field.) For the most flexibility in reporting, most companies would create monthly budgets. Users have two choices for setting up budgets.

- Budgets can be started from scratch. (**No** selected in **Pre-fill data?** field.)

- Budgets can be filled with actual data from one of the two prior fiscal years. (The appropriate year selected in **Pre-fill data?** field.)

  - Edits can be made to budgets created using prior period data.

All budgets must be set up by account and by period (month, quarter, or year). You can expand the budget by adding **location**, **class**, or **customer**. This is called **subdividing** in QBO.

For each fiscal year then, a company could have an overall budget, budgets for each **class**, budgets for each **location**, AND budgets for each **customer** (project). Each one would be created separately and each would include amounts by account and by period.

Subdivisions are selected in the final field. The dropdown menu looks like this:

Click **Next** after all options are selected.

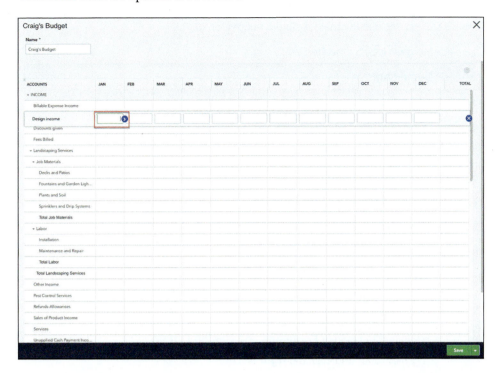

Enter the budget amounts in the appropriate month fields. It is not necessary to enter an amount for every month. There are some income and expense accounts that may have activity only in the first half of the year or only in every other month. Budget amounts should represent the best estimates of the expected activity. If it's expected that an account will have the same activity in successive periods, enter the amount in the first month and click the right arrow next to the amount to copy across the row. You can copy across from any field in the budget form.

Click **Save and close** when all budget amounts have been entered.

To see the final budget, click **Reports** on the navigation bar. Select **Budget Overview** in the **Business overview** section. A final budget might look something like this:

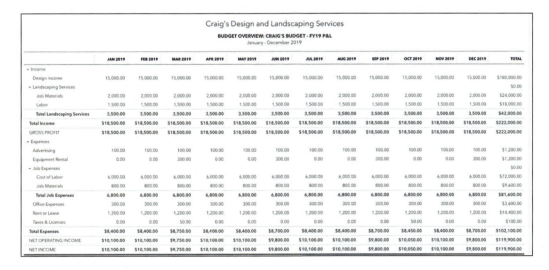

PRACTICE
EXERCISE

Set up a budget for Craig's Design and Landscaping.
(Craig's Design decides to create a simple budget for 2019.)

1. Click the **gear** icon on the icon bar.

2. Click **Budgeting**.

3. Click **Add budget**.

4. Enter "Craig's Budget" as the **Name**.

5. Select **Monthly** as the **Interval**.

6. Select **No** in **Pre-fill data?**.

7. Select **FY2019(Jan 2019–Dec 2019)**.

8. Select **Don't subdivide** in **Subdivide by**.

9. Click **Next**.

10. In the **INCOME** section,
    a. Click in the **Jan** field of **Design income**.
       i. Enter "2,000" and click the **right arrow**.
    b. Click in the **Jan** field of **Fountains and Garden Lighting**
       i. Enter "500" and click the **right arrow**.
    c. Click in the **Jan** field of **Installation**.
       i. Enter "4,000" and click the **right arrow**.

11. In the **COST OF GOODS SOLD** section,
    a. Click in the **Jan** field of **Cost of Goods Sold**.
       i. Enter "200" and click the **right arrow**.

12. In the **EXPENSES** section,
    a. Click in the **Jan** field of **Advertising**.
       i. Enter "200" and click the **right arrow**.
    b. Click in the **Jan** field of **Equipment Rental**.
       i. Enter "300" in the **Mar**, **Jun**, **Sep**, and **Dec** fields.
    c. Click in the **Jan** field of **Job Materials**.
       i. Enter "400" and click the **right arrow**.
    d. Click in the **Jan** field of **Office Expenses**.
       i. Enter "300" and click the **right arrow**.
    e. Click in the **Jan** field of **Rent or Lease**.
       i. Enter "1,200" and click the **right arrow**.
    f. Click in the **Jan** field of **Taxes and Licenses**.
       i. Enter "50" in the **Mar** and **Oct** fields.

13. Click **Save and close**.

14. Click **Dashboard** to exit out of the budget window.

WARNING: The Practice Exercise in the next section depends on the work you just performed. To save yourself time, complete the next Practice Exercise before you log out.

Creating Budget Reports

There are a variety of budget reports in QBO. All of them can be accessed in the **Business overview** section of **Reports**.

- The **Budget Overview** report presents budget figures only.

- The **Budget vs. Actuals** report presents actual and budget figures by month. The dollar difference (actual less budget) and the percentage relationship of actual to budget (actual divided by budget) are also displayed for each account.

 HINT: There are many options for customizing this report. In the **Rows/Columns** section of the **Customize Report** sidebar, users can elect to summarize data by quarter instead of by month. Comparison fields can be added or deleted as well. For example, if the report is being created for a manager during the budget period, **$ Remaining** or **% Remaining** columns can be very helpful.

Prepare budget report for Craig's Design and Landscaping.
(Craig's Design wants to review the budget just created.)

1. Click **Reports** on the navigation bar.

2. Click **Budget Overview** in the **Business overview** section.

3. **Make a note** of the budgeted **GROSS PROFIT** for 2019.

4. Click **Dashboard** to close the window.

PRACTICE EXERCISE

CHAPTER SHORTCUTS

Set up class and location tracking
1. Click the **gear** icon on the icon bar
2. Click **Account and Settings**
3. Click **Advanced**
4. Click the **pencil** icon in **Categories** section
5. Check the boxes next to **Track classes** and **Track locations**

Set up classes or location
1. Click the **gear** icon on the icon bar
2. Click **All Lists**
3. Click **Classes** or **Locations**
4. Click **New**

Create a budget
1. Click the **gear** icon on the icon bar
2. Click **Budgeting**

CHAPTER REVIEW (Answers available on the publisher's website.)

Matching

Match the term or phrase (as used in QBO) to its definition.

1. budget subdividing
2. class tracking
3. budget v actuals report
4. copy across
5. budget
6. budget overview
7. location tracking
8. profit and loss by class report

_____   report that displays revenue and expenses by class for a specified period of time

_____   tool most likely to be used to classify revenues and expenses by product line

_____   report that shows variances between actual and budgeted results for a period of time

_____   tool most likely to be used to classify revenues and expenses by store

_____   estimate of future operating results

_____   tool used to add class, location, or customer when creating a budget

_____   copies amounts entered in a budget line item for a specific month to all subsequent months for that line item

_____   report that shows budgeted account balances for a period of time

Multiple Choice

1. In QBO, a **class** might represent a specific _____.
   a. department in a company
   b. customer type
   c. product line
   d. any of the above could be used

2. Which of the following statements is true?
   a. **Class** tracking is done automatically by QBO.
   b. A **class** must be designated for every entry in a transaction.
   c. Users can track by **class** or **location** but not both.
   d. Only one **location** can be set per vendor bill.

3. Budgets can be created for:
   a. the company overall.
   b. a specific customer (project).
   c. a specific **class**.
   d. a specific **location**.
   e. any of the above.

4. When creating a budget for a company with a 12/31 year end, you enter $300 in March for one of the rows and click **Copy Across**. The amount that will appear as the total for that row will be:
   a. $3,000.
   b. $2,700.

c. $600.

d. $300.

5. Which of the following QBO reports compares actual amounts to budgeted amounts by month (in dollars and percent)?

a. Budget Overview

b. Budget vs Actuals

c. Profit & Loss Budget Performance

d. Budget Variance Report

ASSIGNMENTS

Assignment 11A

Math Revealed!

MBC

Assignments with the MBC are available in myBusinessCourse.

Background information: Martin Smith, a college student and good friend of yours, had always wanted to be an entrepreneur. He is very good in math so, to test his entrepreneurship skills, he decided to set up a small math tutoring company serving local high school students who struggle in their math courses. He set up the company, Math Revealed!, as a corporation in 2018. Martin is the only owner. He has not taken any distributions from the company since it opened.

The business has been successful so far. In fact, it's been so successful he has decided to work in his business full time now that he's graduated from college with a degree in mathematics.

He has decided to start using QuickBooks Online to keep track of his business transactions. He likes the convenience of being able to access his information over the Internet. You have agreed to act as his accountant while you're finishing your own academic program.

He currently has a number of regular customers that he tutors in Pre-Algebra, Algebra, and Geometry. His customers pay his fees by cash or check after each tutoring session but he does give terms of Net 15 to some of his customers. He has developed the following fee schedule:

Name	Description	Rate
Refresher	One-hour session	$40 per hour
Persistence program	Two one-hour sessions per week	$75 per week
Crisis program	Five one-hour sessions per week	$150 per week

The tutoring sessions usually take place at his students' homes but he recently signed a two-year lease on a small office above a local coffee shop. The rent is only $200 per month starting in January 2019. A security deposit of $400 was paid in December 2018.

The following equipment is owned by the company:

Description	Date placed in service	Cost	Life	Salvage Value
Computer	7/1/18	$3,000	36 months	$300
Printer	7/1/18	$ 240	24 months	$ 0
Graphing Calculators (2)	7/1/18	$ 294	36 months	$ 60

All equipment is depreciated using the straight-line method.

As of 12/31/18, he owed $2,000 to his parents who initially helped him get started. They are charging him interest at a 6% annual rate. He has been paying interest only on a monthly basis. His last payment was 12/31/18.

Over the next month or so, he plans to expand his business by selling a few products he believes will help his students. He has already purchased a few items:

Category	Description	Vendor	Quantity On Hand	Cost per unit	Sales Price
Books and Tools					
	Geometry in Sports	Books Galore	20	12	16
	Solving Puzzles: Fun with Algebra	Books Galore	20	14	18
	Getting Ready for Calculus	Books Galore	20	15	20
	Protractor/Compass Set	Math Shack	10	10	14
	Handheld Dry-Erase Boards	Math Shack	25	5	9
	Notebooks (pack of 3)	Paper Bag Depot	10	15	20

4/1/19

✓ You talk to Martin today about the need for more management tools to help him run his business effectively. You both decide that using **class** and **location** tracking would be helpful.

✓ You turn on **class** tracking in the **Advanced** tab of **Account and Settings**.

- You want to be able to assign a class to individual line items in transaction forms.

- You also turn on the "warning" feature. You don't want to have to go back and fix issues later.

✓ You also turn on **location** tracking. You decide to keep **location** as the **label**.

✓ You decide to set up four **classes**.

- Products

  ○ To be used for tracking revenues and costs related to sales of products and product training revenues.

- Workshops

  ○ To be used for tracking revenues and costs related to Workshop presentations.

- Tutoring

  ○ To be used for tracking revenues and costs related to all tutoring services.

- Administrative

  ○ To be used for tracking general business costs.

✓ You set up four **locations**. **TIP:** You don't need to check any of the options available.

- Sacramento Public Schools

  ○ To be used for tracking transactions related to business with Sacramento Public Schools.

- Groups—Education

  ○ To be used for tracking transactions related to business with other educational groups.

  ○ Dynamic Teaching, Teacher's College, and Center for High Academic Achievement would be included in Groups-Education.

- In-Office

  ○ To be used for tracking transactions related to tutoring services conducted in the office.

    ❑ Martin's tutoring and Mathmagic Clinic would be an In-Office location.

- General

  ○ To be used for tracking any general business transactions.

✓ You also decide you want to use the budgeting tool in QBO.

✓ You create a monthly profit and loss budget for 2019 from scratch (no subdividing). (You use "2019 Budget" for the name.) You use the following estimates:

- Tutoring ($2,000 for January and February: $4,000 for March through December)

- Workshops ($1,500 for February; $2,200 for March through August; $3,000 for September through December)
- Sales of Product Income ($1,000 for January and February; $3,000 from March through December)
- Cost of Goods Sold ($500 for January and February; $1,500 from March through December)
- Vehicle costs
  - Gasoline Expense ($50 every month)
- Facility Costs
  - Rent Expense ($200 every month)
  - Utilities Expense ($120 every month)
- Marketing Costs
  - Advertising ($400 every other month, starting in February)
- Office Costs
  - Office Supplies ($75 every month)
  - Teaching Supplies ($25 every month)
  - Office Equipment Depreciation ($125 every month)
- Taxes, Insurance, and Professional Services
  - Professional Fees ($300 for January and February, $500 for March through December)
  - Insurance Expense ($40 every month)
  - Business Taxes ($25 March, June, September, and December)
- Other Costs
  - Bank Service Charges ($10 every month)
- Interest Expense ($10 every month)

✓ You let Martin know that the budget shows $70,740 in profit for the year. **TIP:** You might need to click **Save** to see the totals.

4/2/19

✓ You spent a lot of time working on the budget yesterday and you got a bit behind in your work.

✓ You write checks for the following: [**TIP:** Don't forget to add **class** and **location**. Remember, if it's not related to a specific segment of the business, it's most likely Administrative (**Class**) and General (**Location**).]

- Rent $200 (Check #1137)
- Interest payment to Martin's parents (Richard Sorensen) for March plus $100 principal payment. (Check #1138)
- Monthly loan payment to the City Bank of Sacramento ($215.92—Check #1139)
  - **TIP:** Don't forget that some of that payment covers the March interest.

✓ You receive the following checks in the mail:

- Center for High Academic Achievement $2,500, Check #9760005
- Sacramento Public Schools $2,200 in payment of invoices #1024–1026, Check #1122777

✓ You deposit the checks received today and the cash received last week into the bank account. The deposit totals $5,570.

✓ Martin brings back some supplies he purchased from Paper Bag Depot. These are supplies he only uses for his in-office tutoring sessions. He thinks he'll use them all in the next few weeks. He bought them on account. (Invoice #8009, $21.88, Terms of Net 30)

4/3/19

✓   Martin is putting on a workshop this Friday/Saturday for Dynamic Teaching. It's the newly developed workshop he's calling "Creating Math Magic in the Classroom (**Magic**)." He needs some poster boards and other supplies for his presentation. He heads down to Math Shack and charges $50.92 on the credit card. He will not be charging any of the supplies to Dynamic Teaching so you don't make the transaction **billable** but you do identify Dynamic Teaching as the **Customer**. You set up two new accounts. One account (680 Workshop Costs) will be used as the parent account. The second account (683 Workshop supplies) will be a sub-account of Workshop Costs. You use **Other Miscellaneous Service Cost** as the **detail type** for both. You charge the presentation materials to account 653.

4/4/19

✓   The Center for High Academic Achievement (Elk Grove) places an order for books. They let you know that they'll be using the books in their tutoring center. They will not be selling them so you remove the check in the **This customer is tax exempt** box on the **invoice**. You ship them out and bill the Center for the following:

- 4 **Modeling**
- 10 **Puzzles**
- 10 **Ready**
- 5 **Sports**
- The invoice (#1035) totals $606.20. The terms are Net 15.

TIP: Although the Center is supported by local high schools, it is not part of the Sacramento Public School system.

4/8/19

✓   You create an invoice (#1036) for last week's **Magic** workshop at Dynamic Teaching. The total fee was $1,800. The terms are Net 30.

✓   Martin ships out three orders today to Sacramento Public Schools. You create invoices with terms of Net 30.

- Sale to Southside Middle School (Invoice #1037, for $324.75)
    - 2 **Fractions**
    - 2 **Equations**
    - 2 **Ratios**
- Sale to Central Middle School (Invoice #1038, for $270.63)
    - 2 **Fractions**
    - 2 **Equations**
    - 1 **Ratios**
- Sale to Northside Middle School (Invoice #1039, for $324.75)
    - 2 **Fractions**
    - 2 **Equations**
    - 2 **Ratios**

4/9/19

✓   Martin has been contacting some of the middle schools in neighboring towns. The schools are very interested in the math games product. Inventory is very low so he calls Cartables and places an order. You create a purchase order (#106, $3,825) for:

- 10 **Consoles**
- 15 **Fractions**
- 15 **Equations**

- 15 **Ratios**

TIP: Go ahead and use **In-Office** as the location. The location could be adjusted when the products were sold.

✓ You receive two bills in the mail. Both are dated 4/9.

- Sacramento Utilities for April services, #10222, $119.20. The terms are Net 30.
- Horizon Phone for April service, #121-1180, $49.35. The terms are Net 30.

✓ You receive the following checks in the mail:

- Dynamic Teaching—$2,339.25 in payment of invoices #1118 and #1127, check #743255
- Sacramento Public Schools—$2,949.81 in payment of invoices #1128–#1130, check #1132888
- Center for High Academic Achievement—$603.40 in payment of invoice #1135, check #9760432

✓ You deposit the checks in the bank. The deposit totals $5,892.46.

4/10/19

✓ Martin was asked to put on a **Magic** workshop at Central Middle School this week. He decided to bring Olen along to help out. You enter Olen's $250 bill for the service (#04-12 with terms of Net 15). You charge Olen's fee to Central but you don't make it billable. You use a new account (682 Workshop helpers) for the **bill**. **TIP:** Workshop helpers should be a sub-account of Workshop Costs. Use **Other Miscellaneous Service Cost** as the **Detail Type**.

✓ Shaniya needs some handheld calculators for her school tutoring. You purchase 5 of them at Math Shack for $25, using the credit card. The dollar amount is small; you decide to expense the cost to **Teaching Supplies** instead of capitalizing it.

4/12/19

✓ You pay all bills due on or before 4/20.

- There are seven bills. Total amount paid is $5,412.62. The first check number is #1140.
  - You realize you missed the 2% discount on the Cartables bill because cash is tight. You think you may need to go back and get an increase in the bank loan.

✓ The Central Middle School **Magic** workshop was held on Monday and Tuesday of this week. You prepare an invoice (#1040 dated 4/12) for the $1,650 fee.

✓ Martin gives you the information on his tutoring sessions for the last two weeks. All sessions were completed as of 4/12. You prepare invoices, dated 4/12, for the following.

- Alonso Luna—2 **Persistence** $150 (#1041, Net 15)
- Navi Patel—2 **Persistence** $150 (#1042, Net 15)
- Paul Richard—1 **Crisis** $150 (#1043, Net 15)
- Jon Savidge – 1 **Crisis** $150 (#1044, Net 15)

4/15/19

✓ You received the math games ordered from Cartables today. All the ordered items were included. The bill (#949115-6) totaled $3,825.00. The terms were 2%/10, net 30.

✓ Shaniya turns in her timesheet for the first two weeks of April. Because the first week of April was Spring Break, she increased her hours during the second week.

Date	Day of the Week	Project	# of hours	Billable?
4/8	Monday	Northside	8	Y
4/9	Tuesday	Southside	8	Y
4/10	Wednesday	Central	8	Y
4/11	Thursday	Central	8	Y
4/12	Friday	Northside	8	Y
		Total Hours	40	

- You talk to Martin about the number of hours Shaniya is working. You suggest he consider hiring her as an employee if he thinks this will continue. Martin understands and says he plans to talk to Shaniya at the end of April.

- You enter Shaniya's timesheet data using **School** as the **service item** and the **project** as the **customer** for all billable hours. The **class** is **Tutoring** and the **location** is **Sacramento Public Schools** for all hours.

- You also enter a **bill** for the amount Sally owes Shaniya ($1,200—SM415). You use **School** for the service item. Since you will be creating the invoice for Sacramento Public Schools using the timesheet hours, you don't make the charges billable here. **TIP:** Don't forget to charge the hours to the correct **project** and don't forget to add **class** and **location**. Shaniya worked 16 hours at Northside, 8 hours at Southside, and 16 hours at Central.

✓ Kenny turns in his timesheet for the first two weeks of April. Kenny didn't have much training to do for the first two weeks. Martin expects that training will pick up again in the fall as new teachers arrive.

Date	Day of the Week	Project	# of hours	Billable?
4/8	Monday	Northside	2	Y
4/9	Tuesday	Central	2	Y
4/10	Wednesday	Southside	2	Y
4/11	Thursday			
4/12	Friday			
4/15	Monday			
		Total Hours	6	

- You enter Kenny's timesheet data using **Game Training** as the **service item** and the **project** as the **customer** for all billable hours. The **location** is **Sacramento Public Schools** for all hours. You decide to use **Products** as the **class**. Martin may be doing training for other customers who purchase the game products and he considers this additional revenue a part of the product sales.

- You also enter a **bill** for the amount Sally owes Kenny ($180—KC415). You use **Game Training** for the **service item**. Since you will be creating the invoice for Sacramento Public Schools using the timesheet hours, you don't make the charges billable here. **TIP:** Don't forget to charge the hours to the correct project though and don't forget to add **class** and **location**. Kenny worked 2 hours at each of the three locations.

✓ You pay Kenny ($180—check #1147) and Shaniya ($1,200—check #1148).

✓ You also pay yourself $250 for the work you've done so far in April. (Check #1149)

✓ You remember that the sales taxes are due. You write a check (#1150) to remit sales taxes of $427.47. **TIP:** Use a **check** form if you can't pay the tax through the Sales Tax Center.

✓ You create invoices for Shaniya and Kenny's work. The invoices are dated 4/15 with terms of Net 30.

- Southside (Invoice #1045) $500
- Central (Invoice #1046) $900

- Northside (Invoice #1047) $900

✓ You and Martin are going to meet soon to go over the first 3 ½ months of the year. You want to give Martin a clear picture of operations so you make some adjusting journal entries, dated 4/15, related to activity in the first half of the month:

- You check the inventory. All counts agree to the quantities in QBO.
- Supplies on Hand at 4/15 equal $25.20. There were no teaching supplies on hand. Martin is planning to restock tomorrow.
- You adjust the following expense accounts so that they represent one-half of April's expenses.
  - Rent should be $100
  - Utilities should be $83.55
  - Insurance should be $20
  - Office Depreciation should be $79
  - Interest should be $10
  - **TIP:** In some of the above entries you'll be debiting expenses; in some you'll be crediting expenses. Costs not directly attributable to a particular type of service or customer would be included in the **Administrative** class and **General** location.
- You ask Martin whether he has used the credit card to purchase gasoline in April. He says he hasn't needed to fill the tank.

Check numbers 4/15

Checking account balance:	**$ 7,345.15**
Other Current Assets:	**$ 6,462.20**
Total assets:	**$28,392.73**
Total liabilities:	**$ 8,561.46**
Net income for April 1–15:	**$ 4,458.00**

Reports to create for Chapter 11:

All reports should be in portrait orientation.

- Balance Sheet as of 4/15
- Profit and Loss (April 1–15)
- Budget Overview Report 2019 (by Quarter)
  - To display quarters, click Customize, click Rows/Columns, select Accounts vs Qtrs on Show Grid dropdown menu.
- Budget vs Actual report (January 1 through March 31)
- Profit and Loss by Class (April 1–15)
- Profit and Loss by Location (April 1–15)

Assignment 11B

Salish Software Solutions

Background information: Sally Hanson, a good friend of yours, double majored in Computer Science and Accounting in college. She worked for several years for a software company in Silicon Valley but the long hours started to take a toll on her personal life.

Last year she decided to open up her own company, Salish Software Solutions (a corporation). Sally currently advises clients looking for new accounting software and assists them with software installation. She also provides training to client employees and occasionally troubleshoots software issues.

She has decided to start using QuickBooks Online to keep track of her business transactions. She likes the convenience of being able to access financial information over the Internet. You have agreed to act as her accountant while you're working on your accounting degree.

Sally has a number of clients that she is currently working with. She gives 15-day payment terms to her corporate clients but she asks for cash at time of service if she does work for individuals. She has developed the following fee schedule:

Name	Description	Rate
Select	Software Selections	$500 flat fee
Set Up	Software Installation	$ 50 per hour
Train	Software training	$ 40 per hour
Fix	File repair	$ 60 per hour

Sally rents office space from Alki Property Management for $800 per month.

The following furniture and equipment is owned by Salish:

Description	Date placed in service	Cost	Life	Salvage Value
Office Furniture...........	6/1/18	$1,400	60 months	$200
Computer	7/1/18	$4,620	36 months	$300
Printer..................	5/1/18	$ 900	36 months	$ 0

All equipment is depreciated using the straight-line method.

As of 12/31/18, she owed $3,500 to Dell Finance. The monthly payment on that loan is $150 including interest at 5%. Sally's last payment to Dell was 12/31/18.

Over the next month or so, Sally plans to expand her business by selling some of her favorite accounting and personal software products directly to her clients. She has already purchased the following items.

Item Name	Description	Vendor	Quantity On Hand	Cost per unit	Sales Price
Easy1	Easy Does it	Abacus Shop	15	$100	$175
Retailer...........	Simply Retail	Simply Accounting	2	$400	$700
Contractor........	Simply Construction	Simply Accounting	2	$500	$800
Organizer	Organizer	Personal Solutions	25	$ 25	$ 50
Tracker	Investment Tracker	Personal Solutions	25	$ 20	$ 40

4/1/19

✓ Business is going well for Sally. She has a number of different revenue streams and new opportunities keep coming her way. You talk to her about the need to understand how each segment of her company is doing. She's open to your suggestions.

✓ You turn on **class** tracking in the **Advanced** tab of **Account and Settings**.

- You want to be able to assign a **class** to individual line items in transaction forms.

- You also turn on the "warning" feature. You don't want to have to go back and fix issues later.

✓ You also turn on **location** tracking. You decide to use **Division** as the **label**.

✓ You decide to set up four **classes**.

- Products

  ○ To be used for tracking revenues and costs related to sales of products.

- Workshops

  ○ To be used for tracking revenues and costs related to Workshop presentations.

- Consulting

  ○ To be used for tracking revenues and costs related to all software consulting services.

- ❏ e.g., Installation, Setup, Training
- Administrative
  - ○ To be used for tracking general business costs.
- ✓ You set up four **divisions**. **TIP:** You don't need to check any of the options available.
  - Corporate
    - ○ To be used for tracking transactions with larger clients.
      - ❏ e.g., Butter and Beans, Delucca Deli, and Metro Market
  - Small business
    - ○ To be used for tracking transactions with smaller businesses including sole proprietorships
      - ❏ e.g., Fabulous Fifties, Lou's Barber Shop, Alki Deli
  - Industry
    - ○ To be used for tracking transactions with companies in the software industry
      - ❏ e.g., Cezar Software and Albus Software
  - Administration
    - ○ To be used for tracking any general business transactions.
- ✓ You also decide you want to use the budgeting tool in QBO.
- ✓ You create a monthly profit and loss budget for 2019 from scratch (no subdividing). (You use "2019 Budget" for the name.) Sally gives you some projections that she put together when she was first starting out. You use her numbers as a starting place:
  - Software Selection and Installation—$3,000 January through March: $5,000 April through December
  - Workshop Fees—$2,000 every month
  - Sales of Product Income—$2,500 February to June; $4,000 July to December
  - Cost of Goods Sold—$1,250 February through June; $2,000 July through December
  - Facility Costs
    - ○ Rent expense—$800 every month
    - ○ Telephone expense—$100 every month
    - ○ Utilities expense—$100 every month
  - Marketing Costs
    - ○ Advertising expense—$200 every other month, starting in January
  - Office Costs
    - ○ Office supplies expense—$50 every month
    - ○ Depreciation expense—$200 every month
  - Taxes, Insurance, and Professional Services
    - ○ Professional fees—$300 January through March; $500 April through December
    - ○ Insurance Expense—$100 every month
  - Other Costs
    - ○ Bank Service Charges—$15 every month
  - Interest Expense—$15 every month
  - You let Sally know that the budget shows $73,090 in profit for the year. **TIP:** You might need to click **Save** to see the totals.

4/2/19

- ✓ You spent a lot of time working on the budget yesterday and you got a bit behind in your work.

✓ You write checks for the following: [**TIP:** Don't forget to add **class** and **division**. Remember, if it's not related to a specific segment of the business, it's most likely Administrative (**Class**) and Administration (**Division**).]

- Rent $800 (#1142)
- Monthly Dell Finance payment $150 (#1143)

✓ You receive the following checks in the mail, all dated 4/2:

- mSquared Enterprises $600 in payment of invoice 1027, Check #8755
- Fabulous Fifties $800 in payment of invoice 1026, Check #9775
- Metro Market $2,940 in payment of invoice 1025, Check #87799

✓ You deposit the checks received today into the bank account. The deposit totals $4,340.

4/4/19

✓ Sally is putting on a workshop on April 12 for Albus Software. It's a newly developed workshop she's calling "Getting to the Source of the Problem." You set up a new **service item**. You name it "Source." You leave the **Sales price** blank for now. Workshops aren't taxable. In case you need some help with the workshop, you select account 665 (Workshop helpers) as the **Expense** account.

4/5/19

✓ Reyelle Consulting places an order for more **trackers** and for some of the management software products. They have quite a few professional services clients and they think they might be able to sell the product to them. They're going to start with a small order and see how it goes.

- 10 **Tracker**
- 1 **Engineering**
- 1 **Legal**
- 1 **Medical**
- The invoice (#1035) totals $1,900. The terms are Net 30. Sally ships the order to Reyelle.
- Sally considers Reyelle a small business client.

✓ Sally places an order with Personal Software for 20 **Trackers**. You record the order on PO 106 ($400). **TIP:** Go ahead and enter **Small business** as the **division** and **Product** as the **class**. This can be adjusted when the products are sold.

✓ You receive the following bills in the mail today. Both are dated 4/5.

- Sacramento Light and Power's April bill (for heat and light) #01-988811—$98.45. The terms are Net 30.
- Western Phone Company's April bill #9299-64 for $182.45. The terms are Net 30.

4/8/19

✓ mSquared Enterprises has referred a new customer to Sally. After talking with Sally, they decide to purchase **Contractor** and they hire Sally to set the system up. You set up the new customer:

- Green Design
  254 Indiana St
  Sacramento, CA 95822
  Terms are Net 15.

✓ Green Design pays for the software with a check (#74882). You enter the sale, which totals $1,082.5. (#111)

- Green Design is a small business.

4/9/19

✓   You receive the following checks in the mail:

- mSquared Enterprises—$700 in payment of invoice 1030. Check # 8811
- Lou's Barber Shop—$240 in payment of invoice 1029. Check #6522

✓   You deposit the checks received yesterday and today in the bank. The deposit totals $2,022.50

4/11/19

✓   Sally called in very sick. She's got a terrible case of the flu and won't be able to be at the **Source** workshop tomorrow. She has already called Olivia who is more than willing to help out.

4/12/19

✓   The workshop went very well. Olivia did a great job. You enter her bill for $500 (#OP412). You select **Source** as the **item**. You identify Albus Software as the **customer** but you don't make the amount billable. This is not a reimbursable cost. You use **Industry** as the **division** and **Workshop** as the **class**.

✓   You also prepare the **invoice** for Albus (#1036). The total fee set by Sally was $2,500 for the **Source** workshop.

✓   Sally emails you details of her client work for the last two weeks. Both of these clients are small businesses. All sessions were completed as of 4/12. You prepare invoices, dated 4/12, for the following.

- Green Design 7 hours of **Set Up** ($350—#1037)
- mSquared Enterprises—5 hours of **Train** ($200—#1038)

✓   You received the products ordered from Personal Software on PO 106 today. All the ordered items were included. The bill (#778922) totaled $400. Leave **Small Business** as the **division** and **Products** as the **class**.

✓   You pay all bills due on or before 4/15 and the $500 due to Olivia (#OP412).

- There are four checks, starting with check #1144. The amount paid totaled $2,268.45.

4/15/19

✓   You open a letter from the Board of Equalization notifying you that you have not remitted sales taxes collected in March. They assessed you a $15 penalty. You pay the total $402.75 due, including the penalty, with check #1148. You charge the penalty to the Business tax expense account and use **administration** for the **division** and **administrative** for the **class**. **TIP:** If you are completing this assignment prior to April 2019, you will most likely be unable to pay the tax through the Tax Center. Use the **check** form instead and make the check out to the Board of Equalization.

✓   Olivia turns in her timesheet for the first two weeks of April. There were no new installations at Delucca's but she did stop by each location to make sure the systems were working well.

Date	Day of the Week	Project	# of hours	Billable?
4/1	Monday			
4/2	Tuesday	Sausalito	2	Y
4/3	Wednesday			
4/4	Thursday	Mendocino	2	Y
4/5	Friday			
4/8	Monday			
4/9	Tuesday	Half Moon Bay	2	Y
4/10	Wednesday			
4/11	Thursday	Palo Alto	2	Y
4/12	Friday			
4/15	Monday			
		Total Hours	8	

- You enter Olivia's timesheet data using **Corporate** as the **service item** and the **project** as the **customer**. The **class** is **Consulting** and the **division** is **Corporate**. All hours are billable.

- You also enter a **bill** for the amount Sally owes Olivia ($400—OP415). You use **Corporate** for the **service item**. Since you will be creating the invoice for Delucca using the timesheet hours, you don't make the charges billable here. **TIP:** Don't forget to charge the hours to the correct **project** though. Delucca is a large company. The **class** is **Consulting**. Olivia worked 2 hours at each of the four locations..

✓ Oscar turns in his timesheet for the first two weeks.

Date	Day of the Week	Project	# of hours	Billable?
4/1	Monday			
4/2	Tuesday	Half Moon Bay	8	Y
4/4	Wednesday	Half Moon Bay	4	Y
4/5	Thursday	Palo Alto	4	Y
4/5	Friday			
4/8	Monday			
4/9	Tuesday	Mendocino	3	Y
4/10	Wednesday	Sausalito	3	Y
4/11	Thursday			
4/12	Friday			
4/15	Monday			
		Total Hours	22	

- You enter Oscar's timesheet data using **Group Train** as the **service item** and the **project** as the **customer**. The **class** is **consulting** and the **division** is **corporate**. All hours are billable. **TIP:** Oscar worked 16 hours the first week and 6 hours the second week

- You also enter a **bill** for the amount Sally owes Oscar ($1,100—OT415). You use **Group Train** for the **service item**. Since you will be creating the invoice for Delucca using the timesheet hours, you don't make the charges billable here. **TIP:** Don't forget to charge the hours to the correct **project** though. Delucca is a large company. The **class** is **Consulting**. Oscar worked 12 hours at Half Moon Bay, 4 hours at Palo Alto, and 3 hours each at Mendocino and Sausalito.

✓ You pay Olivia ($400—check #1149) and Oscar ($1,100—check #1150).

✓ You create invoices for Olivia and Oscar's work for Delucca Deli. The invoices are dated 4/15 with terms of Net 15.

- Sausalito $375 (#1039)
- Mendocino $375 (#1040)
- Palo Alto $450 (#1041)
- Half Moon Bay $1,050 (#1042)

✓ You and Sally are going to meet and go over the first 3 ½ months of the year. You want to give her a clear picture of operations so you make some adjusting journal entries related to activity in the first half of the month:

- Supplies on Hand at 4/15 equal $170.
- You adjust the following expense accounts so that they represent one-half of April's expenses.
  - ○ Rent should be $400.
  - ○ Utilities should be $48.45
  - ○ Telephone should be $92.45
  - ○ Insurance should be $75
  - ○ Depreciation should be $134
  - ○ Interest should be $14
  - ○ Professional fees—you estimate $175 for the first two weeks of your time.
  - ○ Technical reading materials should be $50 (half month of the subscription to Advances in Software Design)
- **TIP:** In some of the above entries you'll be debiting expenses; in some you'll be crediting expenses. Costs not attributable to a specific type of service or customer would be included in the **Administrative class** and the **Administrative division**.

Check numbers 4/15

Checking account balance:. . . . .$ 5,816.26
Other Current Assets: . . . .$ 9,669.50
Total assets: $37,585.01
Total liabilities: . . . .$ 6,519.45
Net income for April 1–15:. . . . .$ 3,429.10

Reports to create for Chapter 11:

- Balance Sheet as of 4/15
- Profit and Loss (April 1–15)
- Budget Overview Report 2019 (by Quarter)
  - ▪ To display quarters, click **Customize**, click **Rows/Columns**, select **Accounts vs Qtrs** on **Show Grid** dropdown menu.
- Budget vs Actual report (Jan 1–March 31)
- Profit and Loss by Class (April 1–15)
- Profit and Loss by **Division** (April 1–15)

Additional Tools

After completing Chapter 12, you should be able to:

1. Create reversing entries.

2. Create recurring transactions.

3. Save a customized report.

4. Create a management report.

5. Create custom fields.

6. Customize forms.

7. Export reports to Excel.

8. Manage attachments.

In this chapter, we will cover a few additional tools in QBO that can be very useful in practice.

REVERSING ENTRIES

I'm sure it's clear by now that accountants typically make a lot of adjusting journal entries when financial statements are prepared!

Many (if not most) of the adjusting entries are made to properly recognize (or defer) revenues or expenses for the reporting period. These adjusting entries must be made because physical transactions (sending out invoices to customers, receiving bills from vendors, preparing paychecks for employees) don't always occur in the same month that the related activities should be recognized in the financial statements.

To use QBO effectively and efficiently, however, the accountant should normally enter transactions using the appropriate QBO forms (**invoices**, **bills**, **paychecks**, etc.). If the accountant isn't careful, the same transaction can inadvertently be recorded twice—once through an adjusting entry and once through a standard entry (a form).

For example, many companies receive bills from vendors in the month **after** costs were incurred. The bill from the company's attorney for work performed in January might be received (and dated) in February. The accountant would need to accrue those expenses in January using an adjusting journal entry so that the profit and loss statement for January includes all expenses incurred in January. The accountant would also want to enter the vendor invoice (through the **enter bill** form) using the date on the attorney's bill so that the accounts payable subsidiary ledger agrees to the attorney's records and so that the bill can be easily paid through QBO. If the accountant records the **bill** in February and distributes the amount to the same expense that was used in January, the attorney fees are now reported in TWO months. (They were recorded in January through the adjusting **journal entry** and in February through the **bill**.) The accountant would now need to remember to make an additional journal entry in February to offset the February charge. Depending on the number of transactions in a company, remembering to adjust for those duplications can be difficult.

Reversing entries in QBO are a tool for minimizing the possibility of duplicate transactions not being cleared. When an adjusting entry is dated the month **before** the standard entry (form) is recorded, the accountant can flag the journal entry as a reversing entry. QBO will then automatically create a new entry (dated the first day of the subsequent month) to completely reverse the original entry. That way, when the appropriate form is created, it will not result in a double recognition of the same transaction. Reversing entries are very easy to create.

As an example, let's say a company hired an attorney to look over some employment contracts. The attorney estimated the fee would be about $1,000. The attorney did the work in November and sent a bill, dated December 15, to the company for the $1,000. The expense needs to be recognized in November (since the work was performed in November) so the company would make an adjusting entry dated November 30.

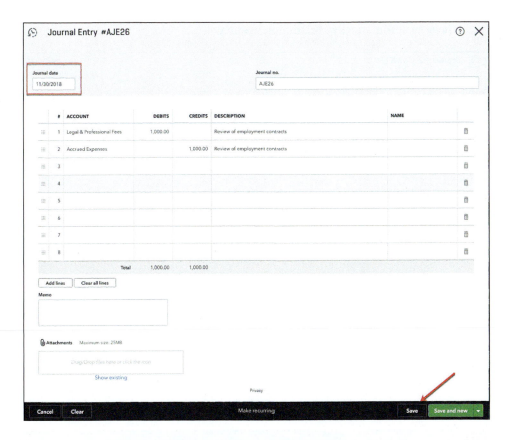

Once the entry is saved (click **Save**, not **Save and new**), the option to reverse the entry becomes available.

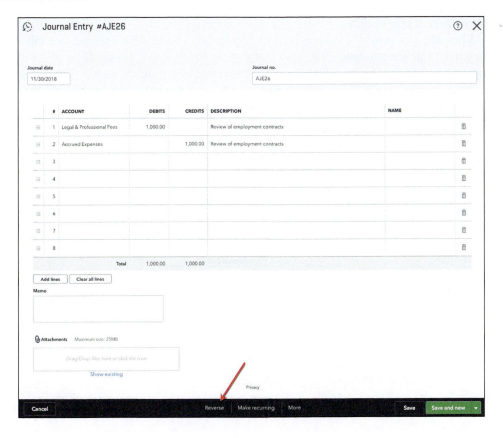

Clicking **Reverse** automatically creates a new entry.

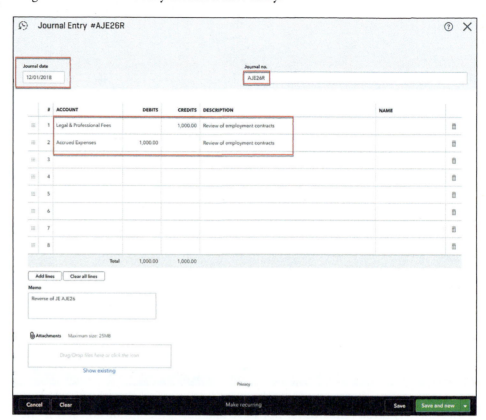

Reversing entries are always dated the first day of the subsequent month. The date can be changed later if appropriate.

When the attorney's bill is received in December, it would be entered as a **bill** using December 15 as the **bill date**. The debit to Legal & Professional Fees will be offset by the credit to Legal & Professional Fees from the reversing entry shown above. The expense is now properly reported in November's profit and loss statement and the **bill** will have the correct December 15 date.

The activity in the general ledger account would look like this:

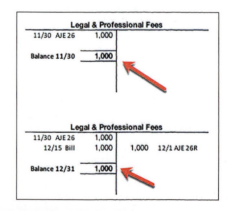

!   WARNING: Once created, reversing entries are not linked to the original entry. Deleting or modifying the original entry will not change the reversing entry. Changes to the reversing entry will not affect the original entry.

PRACTICE
EXERCISE

Prepare a reversing entry for Craig's Design and Landscaping.
(Craig's Design receives a $500 bill for legal services performed in the prior month.)

1. Click the icon on the icon bar.

2. Select **Journal Entry**.

3. Enter the current date in the **Journal Date** field.

4. In the first row, select **Lawyer** in the **ACCOUNT** field.

5. **Make a note** of the parent account for **Lawyer**.

6. Enter "500" in the **DEBITS** column.

7. In the second row select **Add new** in the **ACCOUNT** column.

8. Select **Other Current Liabilities** as the **account type**.

9. Select **Other Current Liabilities** as the **Detail Type**.

10. Enter "Accrued Expenses" in the **Name** field.

11. Click **Save and close**.

12. Enter "500" in the **CREDITS** field.

13. Click **Save**.

14. Click **Reverse**.

15. Click **Save and close**.

RECURRING TRANSACTIONS

Some companies have transactions that occur every month, in the same amount. For example, office cleaning service companies often bill customers a set fee for a particular monthly cleaning service. The entry for depreciation is another possible example.

QBO allows users to set up these recurring transactions so that they are easily recreated on a set schedule.

To set up a recurring transaction, click the **gear** icon on the icon bar.

Click **Recurring Transactions**.

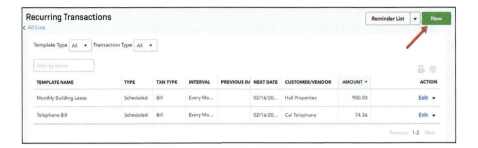

Click **New** to enter a new transaction.

The type of transaction to be entered is selected first.

The options available in the **recurring transaction** setup form would depend on the type of transaction selected. For example, if **Invoice** was selected, the form would look like this:

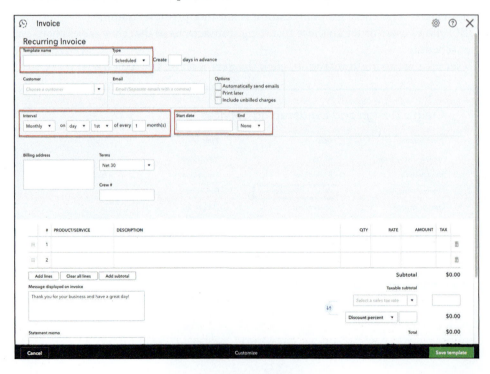

A name for the recurring entry must be entered in the **Template name** field. The name should clearly identify the purpose of the recurring entry. For example, "Weekly-Melton" would be a reasonable name for an entry to bill John Melton for weekly gardening services.

There are a number of options for recurring entries:

- In the **Type** field, transactions can be set as:
  - **Scheduled**
    - Transactions will be automatically created.
  - **Reminder**
    - Transactions will be added to a reminder list but will not be created until the user chooses to create them. (The user would then have the option of not recording the entry in a particular period.)
  - **Unscheduled**
    - Transaction is saved in the **Recurring Transactions** list but would not appear on the reminder list and would not be automatically created.
    - **Unscheduled** would normally be the **type** set when users don't have all the necessary information for the transaction yet.
    - The **type** could also be used to set up a template for a complex transaction that the user wants to have available when needed.

If **scheduled** or **reminder** transaction templates are created:

- The frequency of the transaction would be set in the **Interval** field.

- The date of the next entry would be identified in the **Start date** field.

- The user can specify how far into the future the transaction should be entered by entering a date or number of occurrences in the **End** field.

A **recurring invoice** for Craig's Design and Landscaping might be set up something like this:

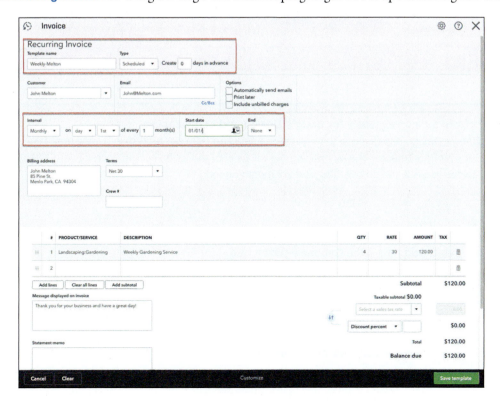

All **recurring** transactions can be accessed in the **Recurring Transactions** list (accessed by clicking the **gear** icon on the icon bar and selecting **recurring transactions**).

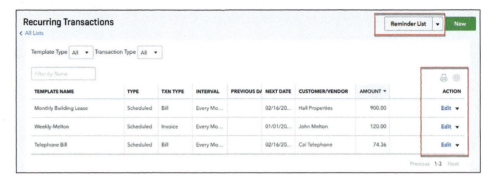

The options available in the **ACTION** column depend on the type of **recurring transaction**. For the **Weekly-Melton invoice** the options would be:

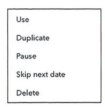

If **duplicate** is selected, an **invoice** would be created that includes the same terms, etc. This is a useful feature for a company that has a number of similar fixed monthly fee customers. Changes to customer name, etc. could be made on the duplicated form. A new **template name** would be entered to save the duplicated transaction.

The **recurring transaction** details are included on the **Reminder List**. The list is grouped by recurring transaction **type**.

> **!** **WARNING:** **Recurring transactions** can be very useful but they must be monitored, especially if they are set up as automatic entries.

PRACTICE
EXERCISE

Prepare a recurring entry for Craig's Design and Landscaping.
(Craig's Design has decided to try placing a small ad ($20 per month) in a local magazine, Trees for Sacramento. The advertising fee will be charged to the company credit card. Craig decides to place the ad over the next six-month period.)

1. Click the icon on the icon bar.

2. Select **Expense**.

3. Select **Add new** in the **Choose a payee** field.

4. Enter "Trees for Sacramento" as the **Name**.

5. Click **Save**.

6. Select **Visa** in the next field.

7. Enter the current date as the **Payment date**.

(continued)

8. Select **Visa** as the **Payment method**.

9. **Make a note** of the number of methods (other than **Add new**) appearing in the **Payment method** dropdown menu.

10. In the first row of the **Account details** section, select **Advertising** in the **ACCOUNT** field.

11. Enter "20" in the **Amount** column.

12. Click **Make recurring**.

13. Change the **Template name** to "Magazine ad."

14. Select **Scheduled** in the **Type** field.

15. Leave **Trees for Sacramento** as the **Payee** and **Visa** as the **Account**.

16. Select **Monthly**, **last** and **Friday** in the **Interval** fields.

17. Enter the current date as the **Start date**.

18. Select **After** in the **End** field.

19. Enter "6" in the **occurrences** field.

20. Click **Save template**.

SAVING CUSTOMIZED REPORTS

The reports most commonly used by companies are automatically included in QBO. In addition, QBO makes it relatively easy to customize reports to meet the specific needs of a company. Report modifications, however, take time.

For example, Craig's Design and Landscaping might create a **Journal** report in QBO that includes only **journal entry** transaction types.

The above report was customized from the standard **Journal** report as follows:

- The date range was changed at the top of the screen.

- In the **Customize** sidebar:
  - Transaction types were filtered to include only **journal entries**. (**Filter** section)
  - The **Name** column was removed. (**Rows/Columns** section)
  - The title of the report was changed. (**Header/Footer** section)

 HINT: Detailed instructions for customizing reports are included in the "Reporting" section of Chapter 1.

Once the customized report is created, the report is saved by clicking **Save Customization** on the toolbar at the top of the report to open a final dialog box.

In the dialog box, the user enters a name for the saved report. Users can also add it to a **report group**. In **Share with**, the creator of the report can select **All**, which allows all users to access the report, or **None**, which limits access exclusively to the creator.

 WARNING: A saved report retains the original report date(s) (i.e., the report will not automatically update to the current date(s) when the report is later accessed). The user would simply need to change the dates and click **run report** to update the data.

Saved reports can be accessed by clicking **Reports** on the navigation bar and opening the **Custom Reports** tab.

All reports in a **report group** can be scheduled for delivery by email on a scheduled basis. Clicking **Edit** in the **ACTION** column opens the following window:

Turn **Set email schedule** to **On**.

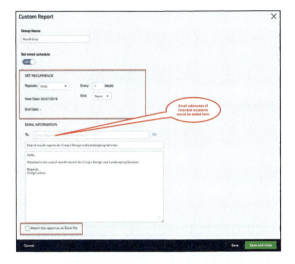

Users can set when reports are sent in the **SET RECURRENCE** section. Reports are sent as PDF files unless **Attach the report as an Excel file** is selected.

Customize and save a report for Craig's Design and Landscaping.
(Craig wants to review a monthly report of sales invoices.)

1. Click **Reports** in the navigation bar.

2. Click **Transaction List by Customer** in the **Sales and Customers** section.

3. Select **This Month-to-date** as the **Report period**.

   a. If no data appears in the report, go back and select **Last Month** as the **Report period** and click **Run report**.

4. Click **Customize**.

5. Click **Rows/Columns**.

6. Select **None** in the **Group by** dropdown menu.

7. Click **Change columns**.

8. Uncheck **Posting**.

9. Click the **keypad** icon next to **Num** and drag it to the top of the column.

10. Close the **Rows/Columns** section.

    a. **TIP:** Sections are closed by clicking the triangle to the left of the section name.

11. Click **Filter**.

12. Check the **Transaction type** box.

(continued)

PRACTICE
EXERCISE

13. Select **Invoice** in the dropdown menu.

14. Close the **Filter** section.

15. Click **Header/Footer**.

16. Enter "Current Month Invoices" in the **Report title** field.

17. Click **Run report**.

18. **Make a note** of the amount for Invoice #1037.

    a.   If #1037 doesn't appear on your report, change the report period to **Last Month**.

19. Click **Save Customization**.

20. Leave **Current Month Invoices** as the **Custom report name**.

21. Click **Add new group**.

22. Enter "Sales Reports" as the **new group name**.

23. Click **Add**.

24. Select **None** in the **Share with** dropdown menu.

25. Click **Save**.

CREATING MANAGEMENT REPORTS

There are certain reports that are most likely going to be shared with management every month. The financial statement group is one example. One method for sharing reports was described in the "Saving Customized Reports" section of this chapter.

QBO has also set up a number of more formal management report packets that can be edited to fit the needs of the company.

To access management reports, click **Reports** on the navigation bar and select **Management Reports**.

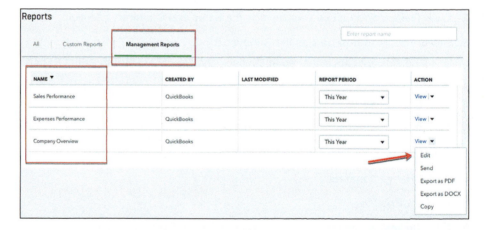

Each report setup by QBO includes a title page, table of contents, and default group of reports. The reports included and other features can be edited by clicking **Edit** in the **ACTION** column.

If the **Company Overview** management report was selected for edit, the initial screen would look something like this:

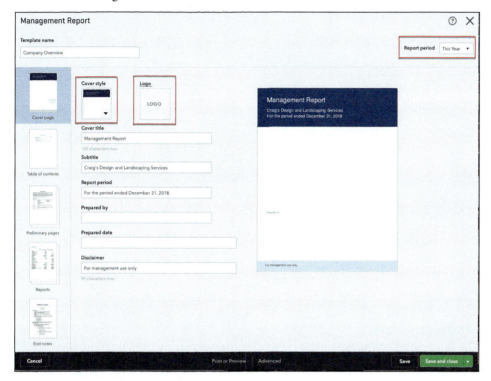

Changes to the **cover page** of the report are made on the first screen. (The **template name** can also be changed here.) The **Report period** is selected in this screen and users can select from a number of different **cover styles**. The company logo can also be added to the cover. (Logos are uploaded to the company file on the **Company** tab of **Account and Settings**.)

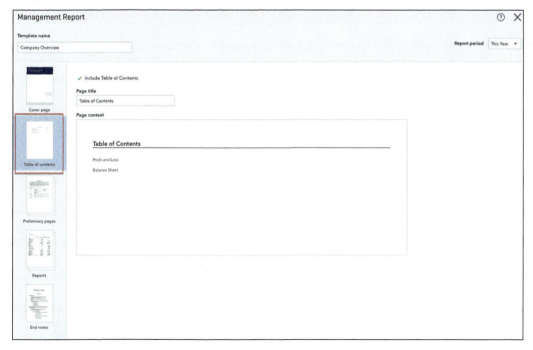

Click **Table of contents** to view the default table of contents. This page will change if the reports included are edited in the **Reports** section.

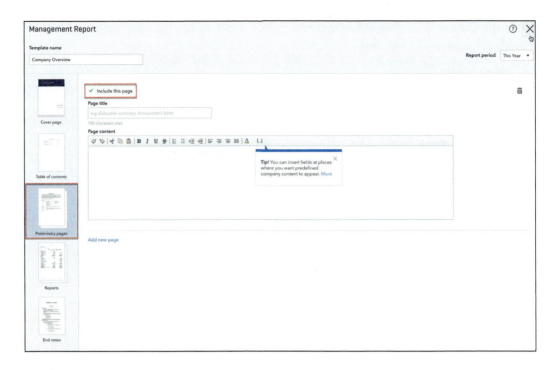

Click **Preliminary pages**.

The purpose of **preliminary pages** is to give users a place to add introductory or explanatory information. **Preliminary pages** do not need to be included in the management report.

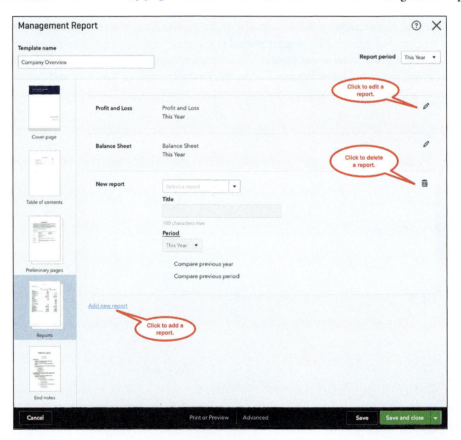

Financial reports to be included are identified on the **Reports** page. Reports can be added or deleted.

End notes, like **preliminary pages**, are optional. Final conclusions about financial operations or information about future plans could be included here.

If changes have been made to the defaults provided by QBO, a field for entering a new report name would appear after clicking **Save and close**.

Create a management report for Craig's Design and Landscaping.
(Craig wants a full sales management report.)

1. Click **Reports** in the navigation bar.

2. Click the **Management Reports** tab.

3. Select **Edit** in the **ACTION** column dropdown menu of the **Sales Performance** row.

4. Click **Cover Page**.

   a. Enter "Sales Report" as the **Cover title**.

   b. Enter your name in the **Prepared by** field.

   c. Enter the current date in the **Prepared date** field.

5. Click **Table of contents**.

   a. Make sure **Include Table of Contents** is checked.

6. Click **Preliminary pages**.

   a. Enter "Summary" as the **Page title**.

   b. Enter "A/R clerk will follow up, by phone, on all past due accounts by Monday."

7. Click **Reports**.

   a. Click the **pencil** icon in the **Profit and loss** section.

   b. Click the **trash** icon.

   c. Click **Add new report**.

(continued)

PRACTICE EXERCISE

(continued from previous page)

     d.   Select **Collections Report** in the **Select a report** dropdown menu.

     e.   Leave the **Title and Period** as is.

8. Click **End notes**.

     a.   Uncheck **Include this page**.

9. Select **This Month-to-date** as the **Report period**.

     a.   If no data appears in the report, go back and select **Last Month** as the **Report period** and click **Run report**.

10. Click **Save and close**.

11. Enter "Sales and Customer Accounts."

12. Click **Save**.

13. Click **Save and close**.

14. Your new report should now appear on the **Management Report** screen. If it doesn't, refresh your browser.

15. Select **This Month** in the **Report Period** in the **Sales and Customer Accounts** row.

16. Click **View** in the **Action** column.

     a.   **Make a note** of the amount owed by **Mark Cho** on Invoice #1035.

17. Click **Close**.

CREATING CUSTOM FIELDS

Although QBO provides many fields for tracking information, companies may need additional fields not currently built in to QBO.

For example, a sales representative field on sales forms would be very useful for companies that pay commissions to their sales staff. A purchasing agent field on purchase orders might be useful for companies that want to track purchases made by various employees. Neither of these fields is currently available in QBO.

QBO allows users to add up to three custom fields for use in sales transactions and up to three custom fields for use in purchase orders. Custom fields are currently not available for use in **bills**, **timesheets**, or other **transaction types**.

Custom fields are added in **Account and Settings** (accessed through the **gear** icon on the icon bar).

To add custom fields for sales transactions, click the **Sales** tab.

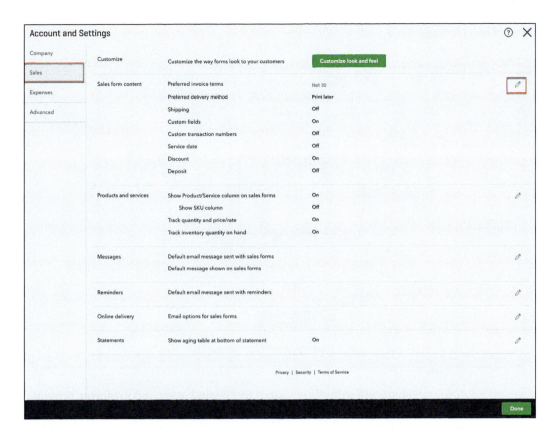

Click the **pencil** icon in the **Sales from content** section.

Labels for the custom fields are entered in the **Name** field. Users can elect to have the field visible only to those creating transactions (**Internal**) or to have the fields also visible on the forms provided to customers (**Public**).

Custom fields for purchase orders are set up on the **Expenses** tab of **Account and Settings**.

Custom fields for purchase orders will be visible to internal users and on forms provided to vendors.

Add some custom fields for Craig's Design and Landscaping.
(Craig wants to include the project manager initials as a custom field on invoices and the project manager and the purchasing agent initials as a custom field on purchase orders.)

1. Click the **gear** icon in the icon bar.

2. Click **Account and Settings**.

3. Click the **Sales** tab.

4. **Make a note** of the **Preferred delivery method** in the **Sales form content** section.

5. Click **Custom fields** in the **Sales form content** section.

6. Change **Crew #** to "Project Manager."

7. Click **Save**.

8. Click **Done**.

9. Click **Expenses** tab.

10. Click **Purchase orders**.

11. Change **Crew #** to "Project Manager."

12. Change **Sales Rep** to "Purchase Agent."

13. Click **Save**.

14. Click **Done**.

CUSTOMIZING FORMS

QBO has designed the basic forms needed in a business (**invoices**, **credit memos**, **sales receipts**, etc.). Most likely, however, a company will want to customize these forms by adding the company logo, changing descriptions, or by adding or deleting information included in the form. Companies can even have multiple customized forms of the same type. We're only limited by our imagination!

To customize a form, click the **gear** icon on the icon bar.

Click **Custom Form Styles**.

Click **New**.

Invoices, **Estimates**, or **Sales Receipts** can be customized. If **Invoice** is selected, the next screen looks something like this:

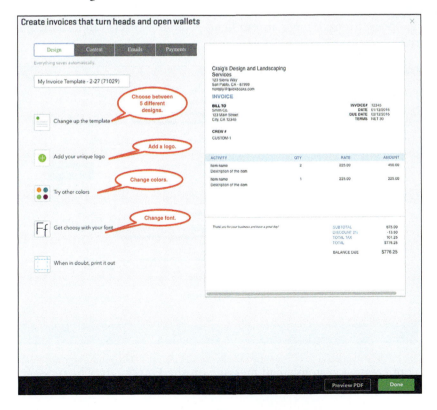

On the **Design** tab, the style of the form is set up. Clicking **Dive in with a template** displays five different invoice styles. The style differences include colors, font, and basic layout.

Users can further change colors and fonts on the selected style by clicking **Try other colors** and **Select a different font**. A company logo can also be added to the form.

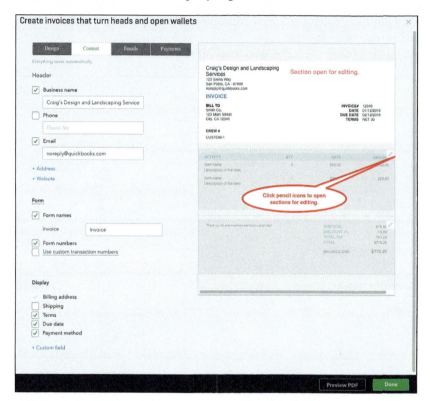

The **Content** tab includes options for adding or removing header information and options for including various columns in the body of the form. Clicking the **pencil** icon in a section of the form opens it for editing. Custom fields created by users can be added to the form if appropriate.

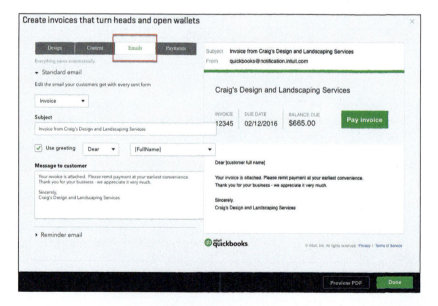

Users can create a custom email message on the **Emails** tab. The message would be included on every sent form.

Options for accepting online payment of **invoices** are included on the **Payment** tab. Online payment options will not be covered in this textbook.

Using Customized Forms

Customized form templates can be selected when a new transaction is entered. On an **invoice** form, the selection is made at the bottom of the screen.

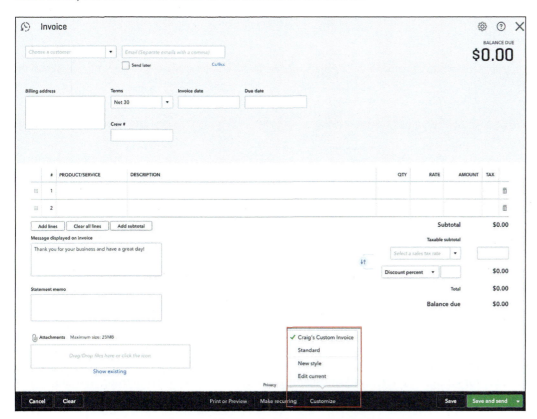

Users can also start a new custom form template by clicking **New style**.

There is no Practice Exercise for this section. You will be creating a custom form as part of the Chapter 12 assignment so use the directions above to help you.

EXPORTING REPORTS TO EXCEL

QBO reports can be exported to Excel. There are a number of reasons that a user might use this tool:

- The report format cannot be modified sufficiently in QBO to meet the needs of the users.

- A user might want to create a report that includes QBO data with data maintained elsewhere.

- A user might want to use Excel analysis tools on QBO data.

A report can be exported to new or existing Excel workbooks.

To export a report, the report window must be open.

On the dropdown menu next to the **send** icon, click **Export to Excel**. A balance sheet exported to Excel for Craig's Design and Landscaping Services would look something like this:

Formatting in Excel will be consistent with the formatting in QBO. Formulas for subtotals and total will be retained in Excel as can be seen below:

	A	B
	Craig's Design and Landscaping Services	
1		
2	**Balance Sheet**	
3	As of February 28, 2018	
4		
5		Total
6	ASSETS	
7	Current Assets	
8	Bank Accounts	
9	Checking	=1201
10	Savings	=800
11	Total Bank Accounts	=(B9)+(B10)
12	Accounts Receivable	
13	Accounts Receivable (A/R)	=5281.52
14	Total Accounts Receivable	=B13
15	Other Current Assets	
16	Inventory Asset	=596.25
17	Undeposited Funds	=2062.52
18	Total Other Current Assets	=(B16)+(B17)
19	Total Current Assets	=((B11)+(B14))+(B18)
20	Fixed Assets	
21	Truck	
22	Original Cost	=13495
23	Total Truck	=(B21)+(B22)
24	Total Fixed Assets	=B23
25	TOTAL ASSETS	=(B19)+(B24)

There is no Practice Exercise for this section. You may be exporting a report to Excel as part of the Chapter 12 assignment. If so, use the directions above to help you.

UPLOADING AND MANAGING ATTACHMENTS

Companies generally have a variety of documents specific to their customers and vendors. For example, a company might have:

- Contracts with customers or vendors
- Sales order from customers
- Lease agreements related to equipment or facilities
- Correspondence with customers or vendors

These documents can be uploaded to QBO and linked to customer or vendor records or to specific transactions. Having ready access to those documents and being able to attach them to customer/vendor records in QBO or to QBO forms can save a significant amount of time for users.

Documents can be uploaded in any file format (PDF, Word, Excel, JPG, etc.). At this time, there is no limit to the number of attachments that can be uploaded to a company file but there is a 25MB file size limit to a single attachment.

Adding Attachments to Customer or Vendor Records

Customer- or vendor-specific documents would generally be added to the appropriate vendor record. For example a completed 1099 Form for an independent contractor could be added to the contractor's vendor record.

Click **Expenses** on the navigation bar.

Click the **Vendors** tab and double-click the appropriate vendor name to open the vendor record.

On the **Vendor Details** tab, click the **paperclip** icon and locate and click the document to be added to the record or drag and drop the document into the **Attachments** box.

The vendor record after attaching a vendor's 1099 Form would look something like this:

 WARNING: Clicking the X next to the attachment will permanently delete it. Users should make sure another version of the document is retained outside of QBO.

Adding Attachments to Transactions

Documents can also be added to any QBO transaction form. For example, a picture of the finished project could be added to a customer **invoice**.

Click the ✚ icon on the icon bar and select **Invoice**.

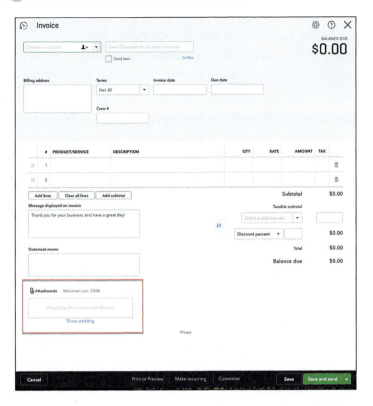

In the **Attachments** box, click the **paperclip** icon and locate and click the document to be added to the form or drag and drop the document into the box.

The **invoice** after attaching a jpg document would look something like this:

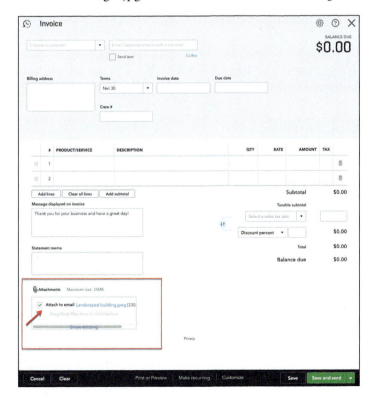

Note that you can opt to include **attachments** linked to forms in emails sent to the other party.

Adding Attachments Directly to the Attachment Lists

All attachments are maintained in the **Attachments** list in QBO.

The list can be accessed by clicking the **gear** icon on the icon bar.

Click **Attachments** in the **Lists** column.

The **Attachments** list looks something like this:

> **BEHIND THE SCENES** The attachments displayed in the screenshot above were added by the author.

Attachments can also be uploaded directly into the **Attachments** list by clicking the **paper-clip** icon and locating and clicking the document to be added to the list or by dragging and dropping the document into the **Attachments** box.

All documents in the list are available for attachment to customer or vendor records or to a transaction form.

For example, a company might upload a standard contract terms document to QBO. To add that document to a customer record, **Show existing** is clicked on the **Customer Details** tab.

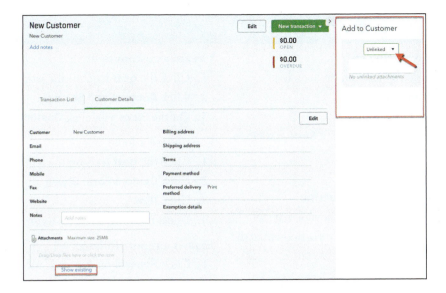

A sidebar opens that lists any currently unlinked **attachments**. To see all **attachments**, select **All** on the dropdown menu next to **Unlinked**.

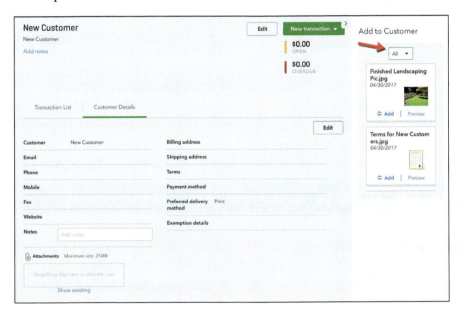

Any **attachment** can now be added to the record.

There is no Practice Exercise for this section.

CHAPTER SHORTCUTS

Create a reversing entry

1. Click the + icon on the icon bar
2. Click Journal Entry
3. Create initial entry
4. Click Save. Do not click Save and close or Save and new
5. Click Reverse

Create a recurring transaction

1. Click the + icon on the icon bar
2. Open the appropriate form and enter the details
3. Click Make recurring

Save a customized report

1. Click Reports on the navigation bar
2. Open the report to be customized
3. Customize the report
4. Click Save customization

Create a management report

1. Click Reports on the navigation bar
2. Click Management Reports
3. Click Edit on the Action dropdown menu for the report to be adjusted

Create a custom field

1. Click the gear icon on the icon bar
2. Click Account and Settings
3. On the Sales tab, click Custom Fields

Customize a form

1. Click the gear icon on the icon bar
2. Click Custom Form Styles
3. Click New
4. Select the form to be customized

Export a report to Excel

1. Click Reports on the navigation bar
2. Select report to be exported
3. Click Export to Excel on the dropdown menu next to the send icon

Upload attachments

1. Click the gear icon on the icon bar
2. Click Attachments
3. Drag and drop the document into the attachments box OR click the paperclip icon in the attachment box and locate and click the document to be uploaded

CHAPTER REVIEW (Answers available on the publisher's website.)

Matching

Match the term or phrase (as used in QuickBooks Online) to its definition.

1. recurring transaction
2. management report
3. reversing entry
4. scheduled transaction
5. form template
6. Custom reports
7. attachment
8. reminder transaction

_____   a specific form style for customization

_____   tab in the reports screen

_____   document that has been uploaded to QBO

_____   type of recurring transaction that sets up an automatic notification to user

_____   a transaction that can be duplicated on a set schedule

_____   an entry created by a user that is the exact opposite of an entry in a prior period

_____   a formal set of reports included in QBO

_____   type of recurring transaction that is automatically created by QBO on a set schedule

Multiple Choice

1. Which of the following forms can be customized? Select all that apply.
   - *a.* **Invoices**
   - *b.* **Bills**
   - *c.* **Sales receipts**
   - *d.* **Checks**

2. If a recurring transaction is set as **unscheduled** _____.
   - *a.* you will receive a reminder to record the transaction after two weeks
   - *b.* it will be entered once and only once
   - *c.* it will be available for posting but QBO will not automatically create the transaction
   - *d.* None of the above answers are correct. There is no such thing as an unscheduled recurring transaction.

3. Up to _____ **custom fields** can be created for use in sales transactions.
   - *a.* two
   - *b.* three
   - *c.* six
   - *d.* ten

4. On March 18, a user creates a journal entry and makes it a **reversing entry**. The date of the **reversing entry** will be _____.
   - *a.* March 19
   - *b.* the date selected by the user when the original entry was saved
   - *c.* April 1
   - *d.* January 1

5. The list of saved customized reports is found on the _____.
   - *a.* **Custom Reports** tab of the **Reports** screen
   - *b.* **All** tab of the **Reports** screen
   - *c.* **Management Reports** tab of the **Reports** screen
   - *d.* navigation bar

ASSIGNMENTS

Background information: Martin Smith, a college student and good friend of yours, had always wanted to be an entrepreneur. He is very good in math so, to test his entrepreneurship skills, he decided to set up a small math tutoring company serving local high school students who struggle in their math courses. He set up the company, Math Revealed!, as a corporation in 2018. Martin is the only owner. He has not taken any distributions from the company since it opened.

The business has been successful so far. In fact, it's been so successful he has decided to work in his business full time now that he's graduated from college with a degree in mathematics.

He has decided to start using QuickBooks Online to keep track of his business transactions. He likes the convenience of being able to access his information over the Internet. You have agreed to act as his accountant while you're finishing your own academic program.

He currently has a number of regular customers that he tutors in Pre-Algebra, Algebra, and Geometry. His customers pay his fees by cash or check after each tutoring session but he does give terms of Net 15 to some of his customers. He has developed the following fee schedule:

Assignment 12A

Math Revealed!

Assignments with the are available in myBusinessCourse.

Name	Description	Rate
Refresher	One-hour session	$40 per hour
Persistence program	Two one-hour sessions per week	$75 per week
Crisis program	Five one-hour sessions per week	$150 per week

The tutoring sessions usually take place at his students' homes but he recently signed a two-year lease on a small office above a local coffee shop. The rent is only $200 per month starting in January 2019. A security deposit of $400 was paid in December 2018.

The following equipment is owned by the company:

Description	Date placed in service	Cost	Life	Salvage Value
Computer	7/1/18	$3,000	36 months	$300
Printer	7/1/18	$ 240	24 months	$ 0
Graphing Calculators (2)	7/1/18	$ 294	36 months	$ 60

All equipment is depreciated using the straight-line method.

As of 12/31/18, he owed $2,000 to his parents who initially helped him get started. They are charging him interest at a 6% annual rate. He has been paying interest only on a monthly basis. His last payment was 12/31/18.

Over the next month or so, he plans to expand his business by selling a few products he believes will help his students. He has already purchased a few items:

Category	Description	Vendor	Quantity On Hand	Cost per unit	Sales Price
Books and Tools					
	Geometry in Sports	Books Galore	20	12	16
	Solving Puzzles: Fun with Algebra	Books Galore	20	14	18
	Getting Ready for Calculus	Books Galore	20	15	20
	Protractor/Compass Set	Math Shack	10	10	14
	Handheld Dry-Erase Boards	Math Shack	25	5	9
	Notebooks (pack of 3)	Paper Bag Depot	10	15	20

4/16/19

✓ You're meeting with Martin next week to go over the company's operating results. You decide to create a **Company Overview** management report for him.

✓ You customize (and save) the following reports to include in the package:
- Balance Sheet as of 3/31
  - negative numbers in parentheses
  - non-zero rows and columns only
- Profit and Loss 1/1–3/31
  - By month
  - negative numbers in parentheses
  - non-zero rows and columns only
- Budget vs Actual report 1/1–3/31
  - Total only (not by month)
  - Columns for dollar difference and percentage of budget column
  - negative numbers in parentheses
  - non-zero rows and columns only

✓ You create the Company Overview management report.

- You add an appropriate logo to the **cover page** and make one other style change.
  - ○ **TIP:** You'll first need to find or create a logo and upload it to the **Company** tab of **Account and Settings** first.
- On **Preliminary pages**, you include two comments about the first quarter operating results.
  - ○ **TIP:** You'll need to review the reports before you can add the comments. You can create the management report, view it, and then go back in and edit the report to add your comments. You can include comments about differences between months, trends, or overall results.
- Your do not include the **End notes** page.
- You save the report so you can use it again next quarter.

4/17/19

✓ After working with Martin these past 4 months, you realize that you really enjoy doing the accounting for small businesses and you decide to open your own bookkeeping business. You let Martin know that you'll be looking for other clients to work with but you'd like to continue doing his work as well. You both agree on a $500 monthly fee. You set up a scheduled recurring bill for the service with 5/31/19 as the first date and subsequent bills dated the last day of each month. Your terms are Net 15. You enter ACCT as the **Bill no.**

- **TIP:** You'll need to come up with a name for your company so that you can create a new vendor. Use your imagination.

✓ You also decide to set up recurring monthly journal entries for insurance and depreciation expense. You set them both up as automatic entries, with an **interval** of **monthly** on **last day** of every month, and a start date of 5/31/19:

- Insurance $40—This will end on 12/31/19.
- Office Equipment Depreciation—$157.25—No end date.

✓ Martin is considering hiring some additional tutors to do the same kind of work that Shaniya is doing at Sacramento Public Schools. He is also considering adding some new salespeople to sell the math games line. He wants to be able to identify the person responsible for the revenue on sales forms. You create a custom field for that purpose and call it "Representative." You want the name to show on the forms sent to customers.

✓ Martin asks if you can change the **invoice** form a bit. He'd like to see the following:

- The logo added to the form.
- The representative's name on the form.
- A different style.

✓ You use the new form on an invoice (#1048) for Alonso Luna for 3 **Persistence** sessions dated 5/2.

- Martin was Alonso's tutor.

✓ You're a little surprised at QBO's formatting of the balance sheet. You download the report as of 3/31 to Excel and change the formatting to better comply with what you learned in your financial accounting course.

Reports to create for Chapter 12:

All reports should be in portrait orientation.

- Management Report for the period 1/1-3/31 as described above.
  - ■ **TIP:** You may need to update the **REPORT PERIOD** on the **Management Reports** screen before you export the report. QBO sometimes defaults to a year-to-date report.

- Recurring Template List
  - **TIP:** You need to select **Run Report** on the **Reminder List** dropdown menu in the **Recurring Transactions List** window to access the list. The proper amount will show for the **Bill** but the journal entry amounts will show as **0** even though you entered the correct amounts in the recurring entry.
- Invoice for Alonso Luna dated 5/2 using customized form.
  - **TIP:** To save the form as a PDF, click **Print or Preview** at the bottom of the form. Click **Print or Preview** again. Hover your mouse over the form (midpoint of the bottom row) to see this toolbar.

  - Click the **download** icon (on the far right) and save the file.
- Balance Sheet as of 3/31 in Excel with formatting changes described above.

Assignment 12B

Salish Software Solutions

Background information: Sally Hanson, a good friend of yours, double majored in Computer Science and Accounting in college. She worked for several years for a software company in Silicon Valley but the long hours started to take a toll on her personal life.

Last year she decided to open up her own company, Salish Software Solutions (a corporation). Sally currently advises clients looking for new accounting software and assists them with software installation. She also provides training to client employees and occasionally troubleshoots software issues.

She has decided to start using QuickBooks Online to keep track of her business transactions. She likes the convenience of being able to access financial information over the Internet. You have agreed to act as her accountant while you're working on your accounting degree.

Sally has a number of clients that she is currently working with. She gives 15-day payment terms to her corporate clients but she asks for cash at time of service if she does work for individuals. She has developed the following fee schedule:

Name	Description	Rate
Select	Software Selections	$500 flat fee
Set Up	Software Installation	$ 50 per hour
Train	Software training	$ 40 per hour
Fix	File repair	$ 60 per hour

Sally rents office space from Alki Property Management for $800 per month.

The following furniture and equipment is owned by Salish:

Description	Date placed in service	Cost	Life	Salvage Value
Office Furniture............	6/1/18	$1,400	60 months	$200
Computer	7/1/18	$4,620	36 months	$300
Printer..................	5/1/18	$ 900	36 months	$ 0

All equipment is depreciated using the straight-line method.

As of 12/31/18, she owed $3,500 to Dell Finance. The monthly payment on that loan is $150 including interest at 5%. Sally's last payment to Dell was 12/31/18.

Over the next month or so, Sally plans to expand her business by selling some of her favorite accounting and personal software products directly to her clients. She has already purchased the following items.

Item Name	Description	Vendor	Quantity On Hand	Cost per unit	Sales Price
Easy1	Easy Does it	Abacus Shop	15	$100	$175
Retailer	Simply Retail	Simply Accounting	2	$400	$700
Contractor	Simply Construction	Simply Accounting	2	$500	$800
Organizer	Organizer	Personal Solutions	25	$ 25	$ 50
Tracker	Investment Tracker	Personal Solutions	25	$ 20	$ 40

4/16/19

✓ You and Sally agree to meet on Friday to go over the first quarter's results. You decide you want to put together a **Company Overview** management report for her.

✓ You customize (and save) the following reports to include in the package:

- Balance Sheet as of 3/31
  - ○ negative numbers in parentheses
  - ○ non-zero rows and columns only
- Profit and Loss 1/1-3/31
  - ○ By month
  - ○ negative numbers in parentheses
  - ○ non-zero rows and columns only
- Budget vs Actual report 1/1-3/31
  - ○ Total only (not by month)
  - ○ Columns for dollar difference and percentage of budget column
  - ○ negative numbers in parentheses
  - ○ non-zero rows and columns only

✓ You create the Company Overview management report.

- You add an appropriate logo to the **cover page** and make one other style change.
  - ○ **TIP:** You'll first need to find or create a logo and upload it to the **Company** tab of **Account and Settings** first.
- On **Preliminary pages**, you include two comments about the first quarter operating results.
  - ○ **TIP:** You'll need to review the reports before you can add the comments. You can create the management report, view it, and then go back in and edit the report to add your comments. You can include comments about differences between months, trends, or your overall results.
- You do not include the **End notes** page.
- You save the report so you can use it again next quarter.

4/19

✓ You review the management report with Sally. She thanks you for putting together a professional package and you discuss future plans for the company.

✓ You let her know that you have decided to open your own bookkeeping business. You let her know that you'll be looking for new clients but that you'd like to continue doing her work as well. She's happy to hear that and you agree on a $750 monthly fee. You set up a scheduled recurring **bill** for the service with 5/31/19 as the first date and subsequent bills dated the last day of each month. Your terms are Net 15. You enter ACCT as the **Bill no**.

- **TIP:** You'll need to come up with a name for your company so that you can create a new vendor. Use your imagination.

✓ You also decide to set up recurring monthly journal entries for insurance and depreciation expense. You set them both up as automatic entries, with an **interval** of **day**, **last** and a start date of 5/31/19:

  • Insurance $150—This will end on 12/31/19.

  • Office Equipment Depreciation $132.25—No end date.

✓ Sally is already in negotiation with several regional companies to offer setup and training services. She knows she's going to need to hire some help. She wants to be able to identify the person responsible for specific projects on sales forms. You create a custom field (called Agent). You want the name to show on the forms sent to customers.

✓ Sally asks if you can change the **invoice** form a bit. She'd like to see the following:

  • The logo you chose for the management report added to the form.

  • The representative's name on the form.

  • A different style.

✓ You use the new form on an invoice ((#1043) for mSquared Enterprises for 15 hours of **Train** time and 1 **Organizer** dated 5/2.

  • Sally was the agent.

✓ You're a little surprised at QBO's formatting of the balance sheet. You download the report as of 3/31 to Excel and change the formatting to better comply with what you learned in your financial accounting course.

Reports to create for Chapter 12:

- Management Report for the period 1/1–3/31.

  ▪ As described above

  ▪ TIP: You may need to update the **REPORT PERIOD** on the **Management Reports** screen before you export the report. QBO sometimes defaults to a year-to-date report.

- Recurring Template List

  ▪ **TIP:** You need to select **Run Report** on the **Reminder List** dropdown menu in the **Recurring Transactions** window to access the list. The proper amount will show for the **Bill** but the journal entry amounts will show as 0 even though you entered the correct amounts in the recurring entry.

- Invoice for mSquared Enterprises dated 5/2 using customized form.

  ▪ **TIP:** To save the form as a PDF, click **Print or Preview** at the bottom of the form. Click **Print or Preview** again. Hover your mouse over the form (midpoint of the bottom row) to see this toolbar.

  Click the download icon (on the far right) and save the file.

- Balance Sheet as of 3/31 in Excel

  ▪ With formatting changes described above

APPENDIX

A

Is Computerized Accounting Really the Same as Manual Accounting?

Accounting equation An expression of the equivalency of the economic resources and the claims upon those resources of a business, often stated as Assets = Liabilities + Stockholders' Equity.

Journal entries An entry of accounting information into a journal.

Debits An entry on the left side (or in the debit column) of an account.

Credits An entry on the right side (or in the credit column) of an account.

Before we compare the two, let's briefly review the basics of accounting. Accounting is an information system. The primary purposes of the system are:

- To identify and record accounting transactions
- To analyze, summarize, and report information about business activities

We identify accounting transactions by considering the impact, if any, of an economic event on the **accounting equation** (Assets = Liabilities + Equity). If any of the elements in the equation (assets, liabilities, or equity) change as the result of the event, it's an accounting transaction and must be recorded.

> **BEHIND THE SCENES** Assets are resources with future benefit that the entity owns or has a right to. Liabilities are obligations of the entity payable with money, product, or service. Equity represents owner claims on the assets of the entity. Equity includes owner investments in the company plus any undistributed earnings. The components of earnings are revenues and expenses.

We record accounting transactions using the double-entry bookkeeping system. Accounting transactions are expressed as **journal entries**. Each journal entry includes the date of the transaction, the names of the accounts to be debited and credited, and the amounts. Every journal entry must balance (the sum of the debit amounts must equal the sum of the credit amounts) so that the accounting equation stays in balance. **Debits** increase the left side of the equation; **credits** increase the right side of equation. Debits decrease the right side of the equation; credits decrease the left side of the equation.

The entries are then recorded in (posted to) the appropriate accounts. All the accounts and all the activity in the accounts are collectively known as the general ledger. Accounts are often depicted like this (referred to as T-accounts):

A-1

Account Name

Debit	Credit

Accrual basis of accounting
Accounting method whereby sales revenue is recorded when earned and realized and expenses are recorded in the period in which they help to generate the sales revenue.

Cash basis of accounting
Accounting method whereby sales revenue is recorded when cash is received from operating activities and expenses are recorded when cash payments related to operating activities are made.

To understand when and how journal entries are made, you need to know the method of accounting being used by the entity. The two primary methods are the **accrual basis of accounting** and the **cash basis of accounting**.

There are a few basic accounting principles that are fundamental to understanding when to record revenue and expenses under the accrual method of accounting. These are part of the body of generally accepted accounting principles (GAAP) that guide accountants.

- **Revenue recognition principle**—Revenue should be recognized when the earnings process is complete and collectibility of the revenue is reasonably certain.

- **Expense recognition (matching) principle**—Expenses should be recognized in the same period as the related revenue. In other words, expenses incurred to generate revenue should be recognized with the revenue generated.

Under the cash basis of accounting, revenue is recognized when collected and expenses are recognized when paid. The cash basis of accounting is not allowed under GAAP but cash-based reports can provide useful information to management so some companies prepare both accrual and cash-based reports.

The primary way we summarize and report information about business activities is through the preparation of four basic financial statements. These statements are issued at the end of an accounting period (generally a month, quarter, or year).

- The balance sheet presents the financial condition of the entity at a point in time.
  - All asset, liability, and equity accounts appear on the balance sheet.
  - The balance sheet is also known as the statement of financial position.

- The income statement presents the operating results of the entity for a period of time.
  - All revenue and expense accounts appear on the income statement.
  - The income statement is also known as the profit and loss statement or statement of operations.

- The statement of cash flows presents the cash inflows and outflows over a period of time.
  - The cash flows are grouped into three categories: operating activities, investing activities, and financing activities.

- The statement of stockholders' (or owner's) equity presents the changes in equity during a period of time.
  - The changes would include any additional investments from owners, any distributions to owners, and operating earnings (or losses) during the period.

ACCRUAL AND CASH BASIS ACCOUNTING IN QUICKBOOKS ONLINE

Most companies use the accrual basis of accounting.

You can choose, however, to use the cash basis for reporting transactions in QBO. This is done on the **Advanced** tab of **Account and Settings** (accessed by clicking the **gear** icon on the icon bar).

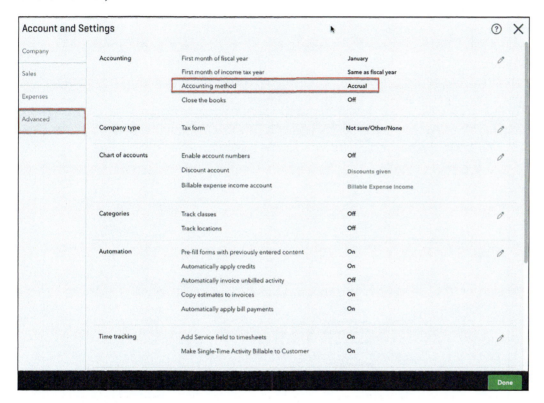

Click **Accounting method.**

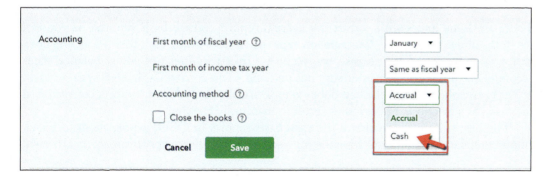

Select **Cash** in the dropdown menu next to **Accounting method.**

Click **Save** to complete the change of method.

Although most reports will now default to the cash basis, there are some reports that automatically default to the accrual method even when the user has selected cash as the preferred method. Taxable sales summary and detail reports are examples of reports that always default to the accrual method.

A condensed **Profit and Loss** report on the cash basis might look something like this:

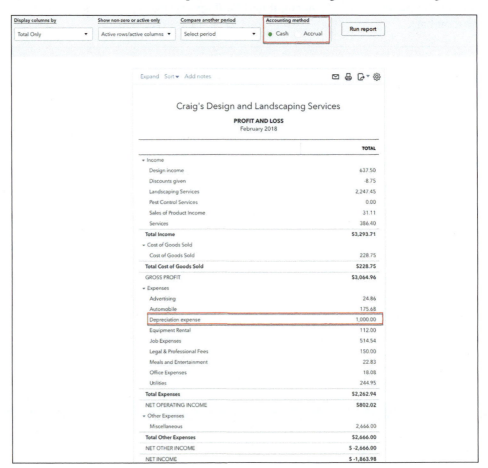

There are some issues with converting accrual reports to cash basis reports. As you can see in the above screenshot, **Depreciation expense** appears in the cash basis **Profit and Loss** although depreciation isn't a cash transaction. QBO also does not adjust balance sheet accounts like prepaid expenses or supplies on hand when converting from accrual to cash. Other non-cash accounts like bad debt expense are also included on reports converted to the cash basis in QBO. These issues result in inaccurate reports.

The best solution is to create the cash basis reports in QBO, export them to Excel, and then make any additional adjustments necessary to fully convert from accrual to cash.

COMPARISON OF COMPUTERIZED AND MANUAL ACCOUNTING SYSTEMS

As stated in Chapter 1, a computerized accounting system is **fundamentally** the same as a manual accounting system. If that's true, we should be able to find the same journal entries, journals, general ledger accounts (T-accounts), and trial balances in QBO that you would find in a manual system, right? They might look a little different but they should be there.

Journal Entries

As you've learned, QBO creates a journal entry for almost every *form* completed by the user. Let's take a look at the entry underlying Invoice #1036.

Click the magnifying glass on the icon bar.

Enter "1036" in the search field and click the magnifying glass.

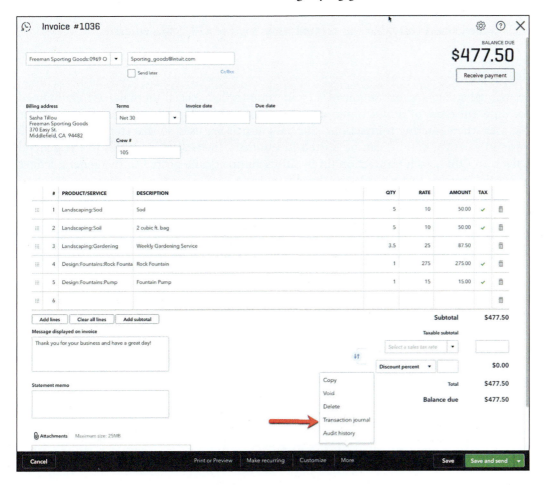

Click **More** and select **Transaction journal**.

Craig's Design and Landscaping Services

JOURNAL
All Dates

TRANSACTION TYPE	NUM	NAME	MEMO/DESCRIPTION	ACCOUNT	DEBIT	CREDIT
Invoice	1036	Freeman Sporting Goods:09...		Accounts Receivable (A/R)	$477.50	
			Sod	Landscaping Services:Job Ma...		$50.00
			2 cubic ft. bag	Landscaping Services:Job Ma...		$50.00
			Weekly Gardening Service	Landscaping Services		$87.50
			Rock Fountain	Cost of Goods Sold	$125.00	
			Rock Fountain	Inventory Asset		$125.00
			Rock Fountain	Sales of Product Income		$275.00
			Fountain Pump	Inventory Asset		$10.00
			Fountain Pump	Cost of Goods Sold	$10.00	
			Fountain Pump	Sales of Product Income		$15.00
					$612.50	$612.50
					$612.50	$612.50

This is the journal entry that was created when Invoice #1036 was entered.

Journals

In manual systems, separate journals (sometimes called special journals) are maintained for different types of transactions (sales, purchases, etc.). This simply makes it easier for the user when entering transactions. Special journals are used so that transactions for the period (usually a month) can be posted in summary (instead of in detail) to the general ledger. In QBO, each transaction (in detail) is automatically posted to the general ledger so special journals aren't needed to simplify posting.

As an example, the Sales Journal might look something like this in a manual system:

Date	Customer	Invoice #	A/R (DR)	Design income (CR)	Landscaping Services (CR)	Job Materials (CR)	Sales Tax Payable (CR)
	John Melton	1007	750.00	750.00			
	Amy's Bird Sanctuary	1021	459.00			425.00	34.00
	Jeff's Jalopies	1022	81.00		75.00		6.00
	TOTALS		1,290.00	750.00	75.00	425.00	40.00

Each transaction is recorded, in full, on a separate line instead of in journal entry form. In journal entry form, the first line (Invoice #1007) would be:

Accounts receivable		750.00	
Design Income			750.00

At the end of the period, the columns are totaled and all the sales transactions are recorded in one single journal entry as follows:

Accounts Receivable		1,290.00	
Design Income			750.00
Landscaping Services			75.00
Job Materials			425.00
Sales Tax Payable			34.00

Although QBO doesn't automatically create special journal reports, a user can create a similar report fairly easily. These reports can be saved so they can be easily accessed every month. (Saving customized reports is covered in Chapter 12.)

A **Transaction Detail By Account** report customized to show only **Invoice** transactions for a period of time and with Debit and Credit columns added would look something like this:

Craig's Design and Landscaping Services

SALES JOURNAL

TRANSACTION TYPE	NUM	NAME	DEBIT	CREDIT
▾ Accounts Receivable (A/R)				
Invoice	1001	Amy's Bird Sanctuary	$108.00	
Invoice	1032	Travis Waldron	$414.72	
Invoice	1009	Travis Waldron	$103.55	
Total for Accounts Receivable (A/R)			**$626.27**	
▾ Board of Equalization Payable				
Invoice	1032	Travis Waldron		$30.72
Invoice	1001	Amy's Bird Sanctuary		$8.00
Total for Board of Equalization Payable				**$38.72**
▾ Landscaping Services				
Invoice	1001	Amy's Bird Sanctuary		$100.00
Total for Landscaping Services				**$100.00**
▾ Job Materials				
▾ Fountains and Garden Lighting				
Invoice	1032	Travis Waldron		$84.00
Total for Fountains and Garden Lighting				**$84.00**
▾ Plants and Soil				
Invoice	1032	Travis Waldron		$300.00
Total for Plants and Soil				**$300.00**
Total for Job Materials				**$384.00**
Total for Landscaping Services with sub-accounts				**$484.00**
▾ Services				
Invoice	1009	Travis Waldron		$103.55
Total for Services				**$103.55**

The accounts are listed in rows instead of columns in the QBO Sales Journal but the basic information is the same.

General Ledger and T-Accounts

There is, of course, a general ledger in QBO. You can easily create a report to see the individual activity in a specific account in QBO. It doesn't look exactly like a T-account but it is close.

Click **Reports** on the navigation bar.

Click **General Ledger** in the **For my accountant** section. A report customized to show the Checking account and to include Debit and Credit columns (other columns removed) would look something like this:

Craig's Design and Landscaping Services

GENERAL LEDGER

TRANSACTION TYPE	NUM	NAME	DEBIT	CREDIT	BALANCE
▼ Checking					
Beginning Balance					3,752.61
Check	2	Mahoney Mugs		$18.08	3,734.53
Expense	13	Hicks Hardware		$215.66	3,518.87
Sales Receipt	1003	Dylan Sollfrank	$337.50		3,856.37
Cash Expense		Bob's Burger Joint		$3.86	3,852.51
Bill Payment (Check)	1	Brosnahan Insurance Agency		$2,000.00	1,852.51
Payment	2064	Travis Waldron	$103.55		1,956.06
Check	Debit	Squeaky Kleen Car Wash		$19.99	1,936.07
Payment		Freeman Sporting Goods:55 T...	$50.00		1,986.07
Deposit			$218.75		2,204.82
Bill Payment (Check)	3	Books by Bessie		$75.00	2,129.82
Refund	1020	Pye's Cakes		$87.50	2,042.32
Deposit			$408.00		2,450.32
Cash Expense		Chin's Gas and Oil		$63.15	2,387.17
Bill Payment (Check)	45	Tim Philip Masonry		$666.00	1,721.17
Bill Payment (Check)	6	PG&E		$114.09	1,607.08
Expense	108	Tania's Nursery		$46.98	1,560.10
Check	75	Hicks Hardware		$228.75	1,331.35
Deposit			$868.15		2,199.50
Expense	76	Pam Seitz		$75.00	2,124.50
Cash Expense		Tania's Nursery		$23.50	2,101.00
Total for Checking			$1,985.95	$3,637.56	

As you can see, the balances of the T-accounts are shown in a separate column in QBO instead of at the bottom of each T-account. It's a slightly different format than the T-accounts you're familiar with from your financial accounting courses but the information is the same.

Trial Balances

A trial balance is a report listing all the accounts and their balances at a point in time. In a manual system, trial balances are prepared for two primary reasons:

- To make sure the debits equal the credits in the general ledger.

- To use as a worksheet for preparing the financial statements.

In a computerized system like QBO, users don't need a trial balance for those reasons. Why? First, the program will not allow the user to create an unbalanced entry. (Unless, of course, the system malfunctions!) Second, QBO prepares the financial statements automatically.

Trial balance reports are available in QBO, however, and can be useful for other reasons.

Trial Balance reports are accessed in the **For my accountant** section of **Reports**. The report would look something like this:

Craig's Design and Landscaping Services

TRIAL BALANCE

	DEBIT	CREDIT
Checking	1,852.51	
Savings	600.00	
Accounts Receivable (A/R)	4,865.29	
Undeposited Funds	907.15	
Truck:Original Cost	13,495.00	
Accounts Payable (A/P)		1,417.17
Mastercard		448.54
Arizona Dept. of Revenue Payable		0.00
Board of Equalization Payable		270.64
Loan Payable		4,000.00
Notes Payable		25,000.00
Opening Balance Equity	9,905.00	
Retained Earnings		804.59
Design income		1,312.50
Discounts given	30.50	
Landscaping Services		600.00
Landscaping Services:Job Materials:Fountains ...		634.00
Landscaping Services:Job Materials:Plants and ...		2,120.72
Landscaping Services:Job Materials:Sprinklers ...		30.00

BEHIND THE SCENES It's really only the ending date that determines the amounts on a trial balance report. If you entered 12/31/18 to 12/31/18, you would get the same amounts as you got entering 6/30/18 to 12/31/18. Remember, a trial balance shows us the account balances at a point in time (not period of time). However, entering a specific period does give you the option of clicking on an amount and seeing the transactions that occurred during the identified period.

Account Types and Common Transaction Types used in QBO

Account Types				
Bank	Accounts payable	Equity	Income	Cost of goods sold
Accounts receivable	Credit card		Other income	Expense
Other current asset	Other current liability			Other expense
Fixed asset	Long term liability			
Other asset				

Common Transaction Types	Description
Bill	Bill received from vendor for purchase on account
Bill payment (check)	Payment on vendor balance by cash/check/credit card
Charge	Pending customer charge
Check	Direct payment (not including payroll checks, payments on vendor balances, payments of payroll or sales taxes)
Credit card credit	Credit from vendor on credit card purchase
Credit memo	Credit given to customer (cash or credit sales)
Deposit	Bank deposit
Estimate	Estimate of fees
Expense	Direct payment generally made using a credit card
Inventory qty adjust	Adjustment to inventory quantity
Invoice	Sale on account
Journal entry	General journal entry
Liability payment	Payment of payroll liability
Paycheck	Employee payroll check
Payment	Customer payment on account balance
Purchase order	Order to vendor
Refund	Refund to customer
Sales receipt	Cash sale
Sales tax payment	Remittance of state sales taxes
Statement	Direct charge to customer account balance
Transfer	Transfers between cash accounts
Vendor credit	Credit received from vendor

Note: There are a few other transaction types in QBO that are not listed here.

APPENDIX

Common Options Available on Various Forms

—Allows you to view recent transactions of the same type.

✖—Allows you to exit out of the form.

Audit history (on **More** dropdown menu)—Allows you to view the history of the transaction (date entered/modified, user name, etc.)

Cancel– Allows you to "erase" all the data entered on the form. This would only be used in the initial creation of the form.

Copy (on **More** dropdown menu)—Allows you to make a duplicate of the form

Delete (on **More** dropdown menu)—Allows you to delete the transaction

Make recurring—Allows you to memorize the form for later use

Print or Preview—Allows you to print or view the form

Revert—Allows you to return to the original saved form. This is only available when you open a saved form, make changes, and want to undo those changes. This would not be available if you had already saved the new version.

Save—Allows you to save the current form without exiting

Save and close—Allows you to save the current form and exit

Save and new—Allows you to save the current form and open a new form of the same type

Save and send—Allows you to save the current form and forward it to the customer or vendor via email

Transaction journal (on **More** dropdown menu)—Allows you to view the journal entry underlying the form

Void (on **More** dropdown menu)—Allows you to erase the amounts on the form but keep the remaining data.

C-1

Glossary

A

Account A record of the additions, deductions, and balances of individual assets, liabilities, stockholders' equity, dividends, revenues, and expenses.

Accounting equation An expression of the equivalency of the economic resources and the claims upon those resources of a business, often stated as Assets = Liabilities + Stockholders' Equity.

Accounting period The time period, usually one year or less, to which periodic accounting reports are related.

Accounting The process of measuring the economic activity of a business in money terms and communicating those financial results to interested parties. The purpose of accounting is to provide financial information that is useful in economic decision making.

Accounting transaction An economic event that requires accounting recognition; an event that affects any of the elements of the accounting equation—assets, liabilities, or stockholders' equity.

Accounts receivable A current asset that is created by a sale of merchandise or the provision of a service on a credit basis. It represents the amount owed the seller by a customer.

Accrual basis of accounting Accounting procedures whereby sales revenue is recorded when earned and realized and expenses are recorded in the period in which they help to generate the sales revenue.

Accruals Adjustments that reflect revenues earned but not received or recorded and expenses incurred but not paid or recorded.

Allowance for doubtful accounts A contra-asset account with a normal credit balance shown on the balance sheet as a deduction from accounts receivable to reflect the expected uncollectible amount of accounts receivable.

Allowance method An accounting procedure whereby the amount of bad debts expense is estimated and recorded in the period in which the related credit sales occur.

Assets The economic resources of a business that can be expressed in money terms.

B

Bad debt expense The expense stemming from the inability of a business to collect an amount previously recorded as receivable. It is normally classified as a selling or administrative expense.

Balance sheet A financial statement showing a business's assets, liabilities, and stockholders' equity as of a specific date.

G-1

C

Cash basis of accounting Accounting procedures whereby sales revenue is recorded when cash is received from operating activities and expenses are recorded when cash payments related to operating activities are made.

Classified balance sheet A balance sheet in which items are classified into subgroups to facilitate financial analysis and management decision making.

Closing process A step in the accounting cycle in which the balances of all temporary accounts are transferred to the Retained Earnings account, leaving the temporary accounts with zero balances.

Contra account An account with the opposite normal balance as other accounts of the same type.

Corporation A legal entity created under the laws of a state or the federal government. The owners of a corporation receive shares of stock as evidence of their ownership interest in the company.

Credit (entry) An entry on the right side (or in the credit column) of an account.

Credit memo A document prepared by a seller to inform the purchaser the seller has reduced the amount owed by the purchaser due to a return or an allowance.

D

Debit (entry) An entry on the left side (or in the debit column) of an account.

Direct write-off method An accounting procedure whereby the amount of bad debts expense is not recorded until specific uncollectible customer accounts are identified.

Double-entry accounting A method of accounting that results in the recording of equal amounts of debits and credits.

E

Equity The residual interest in the assets of a business after all liabilities have been paid off; it is equal to a firm's net assets, or total assets less total liabilities.

F

First-in, first-out (FIFO) method An inventory costing method that assumes that the oldest (earliest purchased) goods are sold first.

Fiscal year The annual accounting period used by a business.

Fraud Any act by the management or employees of a business involving an intentional deception for personal gain.

G

General ledger A grouping of all of a business's accounts that are used to prepare the basic financial statements.

Gross pay The amount an employee earns before any withholdings or deductions.

I

Income statement A financial statement reporting a business's sales revenue and expenses for a given period of time.

Internal controls The measures undertaken by a company to ensure the reliability of its accounting data, protect its assets from theft or unauthorized use, insure that employees follow the company's policies and procedures, and evaluate the performance of employees, departments, divisions, and the company as a whole.

J

Journal A tabular record in which business transactions are analyzed in debit and credit terms and recorded in chronological order.

Journal entry An entry of accounting information into a journal.

L

Last-in, first-out (LIFO) method An inventory costing method that assumes that the newest (most recently purchased) goods are sold first.

Liabilities The obligations or debts that a business must pay in money or services at some time in the future as a consequence of past transactions or events.

Lower of cost or market (LCM) A measurement method that, when applied to inventory, provides for ending inventory to be valued on the balance sheet at the lower of its acquisition cost or current replacement cost.

M

Materiality An accounting guideline that states that insignificant data that would not affect a financial statement user's decisions may be recorded in the most expedient manner.

Multi-step income statement An income statement in which one or more intermediate performance measures, such as gross profit on sales, are derived before the continuing income is reported.

N

Net pay The amount of an employee's paycheck, after subtracting withheld amounts.

Normal balance The side (debit or credit) on which increases to the account are recorded.

P

Partnership A voluntary association of two or more persons for the purpose of conducting a business.

Periodic inventory A system that records inventory purchase transactions; the Inventory account and the cost of goods sold account are not updated until the end of the period when a physical count of the inventory is taken.

Permanent account An account used to prepare the balance sheet—that is, an asset, liability, or stockholders' equity account, any balance in a permanent account at the end of an accounting period is carried forward to the following accounting period.

Perpetual inventory A system that records the cost of merchandise inventory in the Inventory account at the time of purchase and updates the Inventory account for subsequent purchases and sales of merchandise as they occur.

R

Reorder point The minimum level of inventory on hand that can safely meet demand until a new inventory order is received.

S

Sale on account A sale of merchandise or the provision of a service made on a credit basis.

Segment A subdivision of an entity for which supplemental financial information is disclosed.

Sole proprietorship A form of business organization in which one person owns the business.

Specific identification method An inventory costing method involving the physical identification of goods sold and goods remaining and costing these amounts at their actual costs.

Statement of cash flows A financial statement showing a firm's cash inflows and cash outflows for a specific period, classified into operating, investing, and financing activity categories.

Statement of stockholders' equity A financial statement presenting information regarding the events that cause a change in stockholders' equity during a period. The statement presents the beginning balance, additions to, deductions from, and the ending balance of stockholders' equity for the period.

Stock Inventory on hand.

Subsidiary ledger A ledger that provides detailed information about an account balance.

T

Trial balance A list of the account titles in the general ledger, their respective debit or credit balances, and the totals of the debit and credit balances.

W

Weighted average cost method An inventory costing method that calculates an average unit purchase cost, weighted by the number of units purchased at each price, and uses that weighted-average unit cost to determine the cost of goods sold for all sales.

Index

C

end-of-period activity, in merchandising companies *(continued)*

Q

S

© 2019 Cambridge Business Publishers

T

U

V

NOTES

NOTES